THE FOUNDATIONS OF THE BRITISH LABOUR PARTY

For Sid

The Hand That Rocks The Cradle Is Mine

The Foundations of the British Labour Party

Identities, Cultures and Perspectives, 1900–39

Edited by

MATTHEW WORLEY
University of Reading, UK

ASHGATE

Published by
Ashgate Publishing Limited
Wey Court East
Union Road
Farnham
Surrey, GU9 7PT
England

Ashgate Publishing Company
Suite 420
101 Cherry Street
Burlington
VT 05401-4405
USA

www.ashgate.com

British Library Cataloguing in Publication Data
The foundations of the British Labour Party: identities, cultures and perspectives, 1890–1939. – (Studies in labour history)
   1. Labour Party (Great Britain) – History 2. Labor movement Great Britain – History
   I. Worley, Matthew
   324.2'4107'09

Library of Congress Cataloging-in-Publication Data
Worley, Matthew.
The foundations of the British Labour Party: identities, cultures and perspectives, 1900–39 / Matthew Worley.
    p. cm. – (Studies in labour history)
   Includes bibliographical references and index.
   ISBN 978-0-7546-6731-5 (alk. paper)
   1. Labour Party (Great Britain) – History – 20th century. 2. Great Britain – Politics and government – 20th century. I. Title.
   JN1129.L32W5945 2009
   324.2410709'041–dc22

2008049702

ISBN 978-0-7546-6731-5

Mixed Sources
Product group from well-managed forests and other controlled sources
www.fsc.org Cert no. SA-COC-1565
© 1996 Forest Stewardship Council
FSC

Printed and bound in Great Britain by
MPG Books Ltd, Bodmin, Cornwall.

Contents

List of Figures

Studies in Labour History
General Editor's Preface

This series of books provides reassessments of broad themes in labour history, along with more detailed studies arising from the latest research in the field. Most books are single-authored but there are also volumes of essays, centred on key themes and issues, usually emerging from major conferences organized by the British Society for the Study of Labour History. Every author approaches their task with the needs of both specialist and non-specialist readerships in mind, for labour history is a fertile area of historical scholarship, stimulating wide-ranging interest, debate and further research, within both social and political history and beyond.

When this series was first launched (with Chris Wrigley as its general editor) in 1998, labour history was emerging, reinvigorated, from a period of considerable introspection and external criticism. The assumptions and ideologies underpinning much labour history had been challenged by postmodernist, anti-Marxist and, especially, feminist thinking. There was also a strong feeling that often it had emphasized institutional histories of organized labour, at the expense of histories of work generally, and of workers' social relations beyond their workplaces – especially gender and wider familial relationships. The Society for the Study of Labour History was concerned to consolidate and build upon this process of review and renewal through the publication of more substantial works than its journal Labour History Review could accommodate, and also to emphasize that though it was a British body, its focus and remit extended to international, transnational and comparative perspectives.

Arguably, the extent to which labour history was narrowly institutionalized has been exaggerated. This series therefore includes studies of labour organizations, including international ones, where there is a need for modern reassessment. However, it is also its objective to maintain the breadth of labour history's gaze beyond conventionally organized workers, sometimes to workplace experiences in general, sometimes to industrial relations, and naturally to workers' lives beyond the immediate realm of work.

Malcolm Chase
Society for the Study of Labour History
University of Leeds

Acknowledgements

My thanks must go to the contributors for participating in this project. Thanks, too, to my family and friends for their ongoing support, especially Amelia, Rosa, Sid, Pete and Chris. Finally, my thanks to David Howell, Karen Hunt, Kevin Morgan, Andrew Thorpe and Chris Wrigley for their encouragement and help over the years.

List of Contributors

Laura Beers is a junior research fellow at Newnham College, Cambridge. She has written articles on British politics, the mass media and public opinion. Her book, *Selling Socialism: Labour, Democracy and the mass media in interwar Britain*, is forthcoming from Harvard University Press.

Peter Catterall is Lecturer in History at Queen Mary, University of London. He is the founding editor of the journal *National Identities*, and the author of several books and articles examining the interface between ideology, politics and culture.

Gidon Cohen is Lecturer in Politics at the University of Durham. He is the author of *The Failure of a Dream: The Independent Labour Party from Disaffiliation to World War II* (2007) and the co-author, with Kevin Morgan and Andrew Flinn, of *Communists in British Society, 1920–91* (2007).

Gerald Crompton is Reader in Economic and Business History at the University of Kent. He has written widely on transport history, most recently publishing (with Robert Jupe) 'Network Rail – Forwards or Backwards?: "Not for Profit" in British Transport', *Business History*, 49/6 (2007).

June Hannam is Associate Dean for the School of Humanities, Languages and Social Sciences at the University of the West of England. She has written extensively on feminist and socialist history, co-authoring with Karen Hunt *Socialist Women In Britain, 1880s to 1920s* (2002). Her current research on such Labour MPs as Ellen Wilkinson and Margaret Bondfield examines the meaning of politics for women in interwar Britain.

Nicole Robertson is Lecturer in History at Northumbria University. She was the Economic History Society's R.H.Tawney fellow (2006-07) at the University of Nottingham. She has published on the co-operative movement and consumer protection, and member activity within co-operative societies. Her book examining the impact of the Co-operative movement on working-class communities in Britain will soon be published by Ashgate.

David Stack is Senior Lecturer in History at the University of Reading. His research examines themes of intellectual and cultural history in nineteenth and early twentieth-century Britain. His publications include *The First Darwinian Left: Socialism and Darwinism, 1859–1914* (2003) and *Queen Victoria's Skull: George Combe and the Mid-Victorian Mind* (2008).

Andrew Taylor is Professor in Politics and Modern History at the University of Sheffield. His publications include a two volume history of *The NUM and British Politics, 1944–95* (2003–5). Currently, he is researching South Eastern Europe and the growth of multi-level governance.

Robert Taylor is an associate member of Nuffield College, Oxford, and former labour editor of the *Observer* and *Financial Times*. The author of nine books, he is at present completing a history of the Parliamentary Labour Party. He is a regular contributor to the *New Statesman* and *Tribune*.

Jacqueline Turner is currently undertaking a PhD at the University of Reading. Her research is focused on the Labour Church and its influence on the growth of socialism and the emergence of the British Labour Party.

Matthew Worley is Reader in History at the University of Reading. He has written books on both the Labour Party and the Communist Party, and is currently completing research into Sir Oswald Mosley's New Party.

Chris Wrigley is Professor of History at the University of Nottingham. His many books include biographies of Winston Churchill, Arthur Henderson, David Lloyd George and A. J. P. Taylor, as well as several edited collections focusing on labour history in the twentieth century.

Chapter 1

Introduction

Matthew Worley

To describe the British Labour Party as a 'broad church' is to descend almost into cliché. Yet, like most clichés, it contains a kernel of truth. This, after all, was a party built on the back of a number of affiliated organizations: trade unions, socialist societies, trades councils, women's associations, professional groups and, from 1918, constituency parties and, on occasion, co-operative societies. Each of these brought with them a range of opinions, customs and expectations, uniting in different ways in different places to form an array of local Labour organizations boasting varied compositions, experiences and priorities. Labour's doctrine, meanwhile, non-determined to 1918 but recognizable as a form of socialism thereafter, combined a moral sense drawn from diverse religious and radical influences with a smart dose of working-class pragmatism instilled by those trade unions that formed the bedrock of the party.[1] During the Great War (1914–18), pacifists and internationalists continued to pay their dues into the same pot as committed pro-war patriots; throughout the party's history, the nature and extent of Labour's socialism has proven a matter of fierce political (and intellectual) debate.

Given this, Labour has sought from its formation in 1900, through its reconstitution in 1918, and onto the 'New' Labour Party of Tony Blair and Gordon Brown, to hold within its ranks an alliance of diverse 'labour', 'socialist' and 'progressive' outlooks. This has not always been easy. Throughout the twentieth and into the twenty-first century, Labour members have disagreed about policy, strategy and even the aims of their party; clashes between the political left and right have been a constant theme of Labour's history, occasionally leading to secession but more usually remaining a site of competing tradition and conception within the party's composite structure. Concurrently, of course, Labour has – from at least the early 1920s – proven more than capable of seeing off any challenge from either socialist or Liberal competitor, suggesting there remained a strong ideological, organizational, ethical and aspirational cement holding the party together. Across its diverse currents, Labour has successfully maintained its position as the principal alternative to Conservatism in Britain for nearly a hundred years.

Historiographically, Labour's general development and electoral progress (or lack of it) has received extensive attention, as has its record in and out of

---

[1]   M. Pugh, 'The Rise of Labour and the Political Culture of Conservatism, 1890–1945', *History*, 87/288 (2002).

government.[2] Arguably, however, beyond a sustained fascination with points of division inside the party, there has been somewhat less interest shown towards the more subtle intricacies of Labour's politics and organization.[3] The varied origins of the Labour Party have been neatly categorized, and institutional histories of its main affiliates have long been available.[4] But while political scientists search for a 'model' to understand Labour's place within the wider polity, and while historians argue over what exactly determined Labour's political trajectory, the ramifications of such diverse Labour experience – in terms of organization, geography and ideology – have perhaps been neglected.[5] Competing or distinct, rather than intertwining, narratives have become the norm, especially with regard to local studies.[6] And yet, it is only through recognition of Labour's variegated character that the party can really be understood. Labour's 'broad church' cannot simply be reduced to mean 'trade unionists' and 'socialists', 'men' and 'women'; nor

---

[2]   The historiography of the Labour Party is far too large to list here. For an excellent general overview of Labour's history, with an extensive bibliographical guide, see A. Thorpe, *A History of the British Labour Party* (Basingstoke: Palgrave, 2007 edition).

[3]   A few notable exceptions include L. Minkin, *The Labour Party Conference: A Study in the Politics of Intra-Party Democracy* (London: Allen Lane, 1978); *The Contentious Alliance: Trade Unions and the Labour Party* (Edinburgh: Edinburgh University Press, 1991); D. Howell, *MacDonald's Party: Labour Identities and Crisis, 1922–31* (Oxford: Oxford University Press, 2002); M. Worley, *Labour Inside the Gate: A History of the British Labour Party between the Wars* (London: I. B. Tauris, 2005); K. Morgan, *Labour Legends and Russian Gold* (London: Lawrence and Wishart, 2006).

[4]   H. Pelling, *The Origins of the Labour Party, 1880–1900* (Oxford: Oxford University Press, 1965); R. Dowse, *Left in the Centre: The Independent Labour Party, 1893–1940* (London: Longmans, 1966); G. Foote, *The Labour Party's Political Thought: A History* (Basingstoke: Macmillan, 1997 edition). For an overview of the trade unions, see H. A. Clegg, *A History of British Trade Unions since 1889*, 3 Vols (Oxford: Clarendon Press, 1964–94). Again, this is only the tip of a historiographical iceberg.

[5]   This should not suggest a dearth of brilliant studies. See, for a few examples, R. McKibbin, *The Evolution of the Labour Party, 1910–24* (Oxford: Oxford University Press, 1974); M. Savage, *The Dynamics of Working-Class Politics: The Labour Movement in Preston, 1880–1940* (Cambridge: Cambridge University Press, 1987); D. Tanner, *Political Change and the Labour Party, 1900–18* (Cambridge: Cambridge University Press, 1990); J. Lawrence, *Speaking for the People: Party, Language and Popular Politics in England, 1867–1914* (Cambridge: Cambridge University Press, 1998).

[6]   As well as Savage's study noted above, see – for some recent examples – C. Williams, *Democratic Rhondda: Politics and Society, 1885–1951* (Cardiff: University of Wales, 1996); S. Davies, *Liverpool Labour: Social and Political Influences on the Development of the Labour Party in Liverpool, 1900–39* (Keele: Keele University Press, 1996); C. Macdonald, *The Radical Thread: Political Change in Scotland: Paisley Politics, 1885–1924* (East Lothian: Tuckwell Press, 2000); M. Worley (ed.), *Labour's Grass Roots: Essays on the Activities of Local Labour Parties and Members, 1918–45* (Aldershot: Ashgate, 2005); D. McHugh, *Labour in the City: The Development of the Labour Party in Manchester, 1918–31* (Manchester: Manchester University Press, 2007).

can it always be divided neatly into a politics of left versus right. This, then, is a collection of essays designed to tease out certain strands within the Labour Party. It is in no way comprehensive. But by focusing on specific organizations, on certain ideological and cultural influences, and on particular identities within the party, it is hoped to give expression to the multiple character of Labour while also providing a means by which to recognize certain commonalities cutting across the party. As practically, it is intended to be of service to students confronted with the basic questions as to 'what was the Labour Party?', and 'what are the wider implications of its organizational, intellectual and political origins and development'?[7] First, however, let us sketch the essential details of Labour's history from 1900 to 1939, before positing certain questions that arise from such an approach.

The Labour Party: 1900–39

The Labour Party was founded as the Labour Representation Committee (LRC) in February 1900. The immediate impetus for this was a resolution passed at the 1899 Trades Union Congress (TUC); its objective, as stated in 1900, was to establish 'a distinct Labour group in parliament, who shall have their own whips, and agree upon their policy, which must embrace a readiness to co-operate with any party which may for the time being be engaged in promoting legislation in the direct interests of labour'.[8] More generally, a combination of legal and economic pressures, related social-political factors (including a socialist 'revival'), and grassroots Liberal equivocation towards 'labour' candidates ensured that by 1900 a growing body of opinion within the labour movement had come to recognize the need for independent political representation on the part of the working class. And although the early LRC received but minor support across a trade union movement that boasted some 2,022,000 members at the turn of century, it soon grew in response to the legal proceedings brought by the Taff Vale Railway Company against the Amalgamated Society of Railway Servants in 1901. A secret electoral pact with the Liberal Party was then secured in 1903, leading to the election of 29 LRC MPs at the 1906 general election and the formal establishment of the Labour Party. By December 1910, Labour registered 42 MPs, a steadily growing number of representatives on local government bodies, and an expanding party apparatus. Come the outbreak of the Great War, the party's official membership stood at 1,612,147, with support concentrated mainly in Britain's industrial and

---

[7]   It was as a result of teaching courses on labour history that the idea for the current volume came about. Recognizing the multifaceted basis and character of Labour is integral to an understanding of the party's history and development.

[8]   Labour Party, *Labour Party Foundation Conference and Annual Reports* (London: Labour Party, 1967 reprinted edition), pp. 1–2.

trade union heartlands.[9] Thus, Yorkshire, South Wales, Lancashire and the North East contained the principal bases of Labour support.

The importance of the Great War in Labour's history is difficult to underestimate. Although the conflict caused consternation among many socialists, not least Keir Hardie, the party rallied behind the war effort whilst simultaneously presenting itself as defender and representative of the British people's social-economic interests at home.[10] As well as gaining experience in office as part of a coalition government, Labour's ranks and coffers were swelled by the increase in trade union membership engendered by the war economy, and its political standing rose in contrast to a divided and demoralized Liberal Party. By 1918, the party's official membership numbered 3,013,129, peaking at 4,359,807 in 1920. In the process, Labour reconstituted itself in 1918, developing a more coherent national organization and, for the first time, presenting a comprehensive party programme (*Labour and the New Social Order*). From here on, Labour was officially committed to 'secure for the producers by hand and by brain the full fruits of their industry, and the most equitable distribution thereof that may be possible, upon the common ownership of the means of production and the best obtainable system of popular administration and control of each industry and service'. At the war's end, Labour was a party transformed politically and organizationally (see below, pp. 5–10).

The benefits of all this were not immediately apparent. Having withdrawn from the coalition and severed all ties with the Liberals, Labour stood a record number of candidates at the 1918 general election – 361 compared to 56 in December 1910 – but won just 57 seats. Nevertheless, the following year saw impressive gains at a local electoral level and, come the 1923 general election, Labour's progress was such that its 191 seats enabled it to form a minority government in January 1924. This lasted but nine months; in 1929 however, Labour returned to office, again as a minority government, but with 287 seats compared to the Conservatives' 260. Crucially, too, Labour's influence had spread nationwide. In addition to London, industrial Scotland and the heartlands noted above, 1929 saw the party break through in places previously resistant to Labour's appeal, not just in urban-industrial centres such as Liverpool and Birmingham, but in constituencies such as Loughborough, South West Norfolk and Enfield.

Neither Labour government proved particularly effective. The first demonstrated itself 'fit to govern' though its achievements were few; the second was quickly engulfed by a worldwide economic depression. Unemployment, which Labour

---

[9]   For a useful collection of essays on Labour's early development, see K. Brown (ed.), *The First Labour Party, 1906–14* (London: Croom Helm, 1985).

[10]   For Labour and the war, see J. M. Winter, *Socialism and the Challenge of War: Ideas and Politics in Britain, 1912–28* (London: Routledge, 1974); T. Adams, 'Labour and the First World War: Economy, Politics and the Erosion of Local Peculiarity?', *The Journal of Regional and Local Studies*, 10/1 (1990); J. Turner, *British Politics and the Great War: Coalition and Conflict, 1915–18* (New Haven: Yale University Press, 1992).

had pledged to alleviate, rose to over two million and the government drifted without apparent solution to the events unfolding around it. After just two years in office, and as economic crisis transformed into political crisis, the Labour prime minister – James Ramsay MacDonald – tendered his government's resignation only to depart Labour's ranks and head a National coalition dominated by the Conservative Party.

Not surprisingly, the debacle of 1931 led to Labour's being devastated at the polls in the ensuing general election. By the end of October 1931, the party boasted just 46 MPs. As importantly, the experience of 1929–31 led the party to reassess both its policy and its approach. Rather than relying on what Sidney Webb famously referred to as 'the inevitability of gradualness', by which socialism would evolve out of a prosperous capitalism, Labour reasserted its links with the TUC and committed itself to devising a detailed and applicable programme of nationalization and economic planning. The aspirational vagaries of the 1920s were replaced by the drier but more precise programme of *For Socialism and Peace* (1934); the charismatic leadership of MacDonald gave way – after brief sojourns by Arthur Henderson and George Lansbury – to the quiet determination of Clement Attlee.

Although the 1935 general election saw Labour remain some way behind the National coalition, the party at least boosted its parliamentary presence to 154 and continued to spread its vote more evenly around the country. The tumultuous events of the 1930s, including unemployed demonstrations at home and the rise of fascism abroad, created a heightened political climate in which Labour slowly but surely forged an effective opposition to the government. Internally, the party resisted calls to form a united front with the Communist Party of Great Britain (CPGB) whilst reconciling its propensity for peace with the realization that fascism could only be stopped by force. As the decade came to a close, therefore, Labour once more prepared to enter a war that would, in time, transform its fortunes. The party joined the wartime coalition in 1940; in 1945, the British people elected the first ever majority Labour government.

Labour Organization: 1900–39

As outlined above, Labour's progress looks relatively dynamic up to 1929, before the economic and political crises that engulfed the second minority Labour government led to a further period of rebuilding up to the outbreak of the Second World War. There was, however, far more to the party's development than a series of election results and spells in and out of office. Labour's emergence, growth and progress were forged not by fate or chance, but by the construction, articulation and presentation of a politics that both reflected and inspired the concerns, beliefs and hopes of a significant number of people. This happened at a local as well as a national level, and saw Labour's progress open to a series of alternate strategic, intellectual and political influences. Simultaneously, Labour's progress was determined by the construction of an efficient party apparatus, a political machine by which Labour could adapt itself to and help shape a constantly changing political and social-economic world. Into this, the various strands of Labour organization and the disparate features of Labour ideology were supposed to coalesce into effective electoral practice and language.

The Labour Party's apparatus was pieced together as a series of linked but distinct sections.[11] From 1900 through to the 1930s, the LRC and then the Labour Party mainly comprised affiliated trade unions and socialist societies, the aims and policies of which were devised through a system of delegates appointed to a national conference in relation to the size of their respective organization. Within such an arrangement, the trade unions were always dominant. The LRC had been instigated on a trade union initiative, their mass memberships dwarfed that of the Independent Labour Party (ILP) and other smaller party affiliates, and trade union values of loyalty and collective responsibility ensured that Labour was provided with a notable pool of support. Only in 1918 did the party constitution facilitate the formation of divisional parties at constituency level open to individual members, and these too affiliated to the national party and sent delegates to conference in accordance with their membership. Again, however, the number of individual members represented by the constituency parties could never compete with that of the trade unions.

From 1906, national Labour organization extended to the Parliamentary Labour Party (PLP), consisting of all Labour MPs inside the House of Commons. This elected its own executive committee and chairman (the position of party leader was not established until 1922), and retained a degree of autonomy from the bulk of the wider party. Such a premise had been established in 1907 by Keir Hardie, the first PLP chairman, and was reaffirmed in 1918. Labour MPs were initially sponsored mainly by a particular trade union or the ILP, before the reforms of 1918 led to an increasing number of Labour MPs being backed directly via their constituency organizations. In 1929–31, for the first and only time between the wars, the number of elected Labour MPs sponsored by their constituency party outnumbered those sponsored by the trade unions. Even so, the trade unions tended to have claimed Labour's safest seats and retained a dominant presence in the PLP over the 1930s. In 1935, when 395 of Labour's 552 candidates were financed by their constituency organization, 79 trade union MPs sat down next to 66 constituency party members and nine sponsored by the Co-op. The ILP's presence within the PLP was always significant in the early years of the Labour Party, but became increasingly marginalized in the lead up to its disaffiliation from the larger party in 1932. We should note, too, that Labour candidates and MPs often held multiple party affiliations.

Overseeing Labour affairs between conferences and acting as a link between the PLP and the affiliated organizations was the National Executive Committee (NEC). This was elected by conference, although its more 'hands on' role in the day-to-

---

[11]   For more on this, see Worley, *Labour Inside the Gate*, pp. 1–17 and 44–65.

day life of the party meant it soon developed what David Howell has described as a 'tutelary' relationship with the party, tabling resolutions at conference and co-ordinating the agenda.[12] Again, the trade unions appeared to ensure domination of the party executive. Thus, the early NEC comprised of 16 members, 11 of whom represented the trade unions, three the affiliated socialist societies, one the trades councils, women's and local organizations, and a treasurer. After some debate, the NEC was expanded to 23 in 1918 to include 13 representatives from the affiliated extra-party sections, five local party members, four women and the treasurer. Not surprisingly, the affiliated positions were occupied predominantly by trade unionists, although Fred Jowett regularly represented the ILP and Sidney Webb the Fabian Society for much of the 1920s. While the unions could have taken all 13 positions, due recognition was given to the role played by the socialist societies within the party; a piecemeal but significant concession that followed the abolition of separate socialist representation. Later, in 1929 and 1937, the NEC was further reformed to include an extra woman representative and two further constituency members.

At a local level, the Labour Party developed primarily around already established trades councils, although Labour organizations existed simultaneously in the form of Labour representation committees, local Labour parties and similar. These, like the national party, were initially federations of trade unions and socialist societies, and they functioned mainly as election committees prior to 1918. More often than not, the respective unions, socialist societies and trades councils retained their own organizational structures and carried out their own activities, co-operating only during municipal and parliamentary elections. Because of this, the ILP was able to cultivate its own distinctive place within the early Labour Party, propagating socialism and acting as a channel through which many prominent Labour leaders entered the party. This all changed somewhat from 1918, as the introduction of constituency organizations served to eclipse many of the functions of the trades councils and ILP, and to consolidate and extend Labour's presence throughout the country.[13] Indeed, Labour's new constitution was intended to establish the party as a national organization, more uniformly structured but with a broader electoral appeal. Its principal architect was Arthur Henderson, party secretary from 1912, and it was designed to open Labour up to those outside of the trade unions' ranks, to all members of the working class and beyond. Accordingly, provisions were made for individual members to join the party and for divisional parties to be founded in every parliamentary constituency. These, in turn, were to include women's sections formed in recognition of the extension of the franchise to most women over 30 and the wartime increase in female trade unionists. The divisional parties then established ward parties formed in accordance with municipal electoral districts, each with the same structure as the larger party organization.

---

[12] Howell, *MacDonald's Party*, p. 55.

[13] A. Clinton, *The Trade Union Rank and File: Trades Councils in Britain, 1900–40* (Manchester: Manchester University Press, 1976); Howell, *MacDonald's Party*, pp. 234–46.

Looming over all of this were the mass ranks of the TUC, or – at least – those unions affiliated to the Labour Party. As noted above, the party structure ensured that the large industrial unions dominant in the TUC similarly formed the majority of the Labour membership, a fact reinforced by the conference vote being commensurate with the size of the affiliated body. Based on the party membership registered for 1919, the unions cast 3,464,020 votes in comparison to the socialist societies', co-operative societies' and local parties' 47,270. By 1940, the equivalent figures stood at 2,226,575 and 344,588. This had obvious repercussions with regard to votes on policy and the composition of the NEC, both of which reflected the unions' financial and numerical support for the party. Throughout much of the period under review, the miners, textile workers and railwaymen comprised the largest Labour affiliates, though their standing and influence were challenged by the general unions over the interwar period, particularly Bevin's Transport and General Workers' Union (TGWU).

Yet, it would be wrong to thereby conclude that the trade unions completely dominated Labour, or that a trade unionist perspective helped form either a homogenous ideology or united 'block' within the party. As Charlie Dukes once lamented, 'the unions … never fought the employers half as tenaciously as they fought each other', and such inter-union 'rivalry' was evident in the Labour Party at both national and local level.[14] While the unions could and did shape much of Labour's culture, while they constituted the bedrock of the party's support, and while they could act as a restraint on the party leadership, the party constructed its own identity distinct from the trade unions. Indeed, the TUC – like many of its own affiliates – was wary that too close an association with the Labour Party could restrict its interests and room for manoeuvre in other spheres of activity. For Lewis Minkin, therefore, Labour and the trade unions formed a 'contentious alliance' sustained by an evolving system of custom and tradition, of mainly unwritten 'rules' that 'embodied an acceptance of the permanent differentiation of functions and spheres – the political and the industrial'.[15] Neither 'bossed' the other, but – in the words of Clement Attlee – each gave due 'recognition of their partnership in action on behalf of the workers, and of their freedom of action in their respective spheres'.[16]

Similarly, it is important to recognize that power and influence throughout and across the party could shift over time and, at a local level, could vary from place to place. To take an obvious example, if the miners' union dominated the Labour Party in a place such as County Durham, then a more diverse range of influences were apparent in the development of Labour in constituencies like East Grinstead, or in places such as Lewisham or Norwich where organized workers came from an assortment of occupations and did not necessarily constitute the

---

[14] Quoted in R. Shackleton, 'Trade Unions and the Slump', in B. Pimlott and C. Cook (eds), *Trade Unions in British Politics* (London: Longmans, 1982), p. 133.

[15] Minkin, *The Contentious Alliance*, pp. iii and 3–9.

[16] C. R. Attlee, *The Labour Party in Perspective* (London: Gollancz, 1937), p. 93.

dominant affiliated component of the local Labour membership. Likewise, the PLP's influence within the wider Labour Party was extensive by the end of the 1920s, as Labour's parliamentary pretensions extended to forming a government, but was far less significant in the immediate aftermath of 1931, when only one PLP member sat on the NEC and its presence in the Commons was negligible. Accordingly, the various components of Labour's organization and power structures – its foundations – were not fixed in terms of their immediate importance or relevance. They shifted over time and generation, as Labour's electoral fortunes fluctuated, as its founders were replaced by second and third generation members, and as Labour's organization stretched beyond its trade union base in Britain's old industrial heartlands. Throughout the Labour apparatus, moreover, party members brought with them a range of 'identities', as trade union and Co-op cardholders, as members of the ILP, Socialist League or Fabian Society, and/or as men, women, workers, housewives, professionals, Methodists, Anglicans, Catholics, Jews, atheists, mothers, fathers, sons, daughters, *ad infinitum*.

Institutionally, of course, the various affiliated organizations sought to exert their influence over Labour's development. Thus, the trade unions jostled to ensure that the party reflected their members' interests; the ILP to 1918 endeavoured to commit Labour to socialism and, thereafter, to influence the way by which the party reached such an objective – as did the Socialist League in the 1930s; the women's conference hoped to guarantee that the interests of Labour's female constituents received due attention. From this, two obvious conceptual questions arise. First, what were the principal intellectual and organizational foundations on which the Labour Party's history and development were built? Second, what did the various components of Labour's organization contribute to the party and how did they help shape Labour's politics, progress and character from 1900? Implicit in such questions are a range of related issues based on matters of class, gender, time and place. In what ways, for example, could large trade unions such as the Miners' Federation of Great Britain or the National Union of Railwaymen impact upon and inform Labour policy, perspective and practice? More ideologically, we may ask to what extent did the religious views of many Labour members shape the party's objectives, approach and socialism? Did Labour's variegated structure – its 'broad church' – help or hinder the party in constructing a tangible and effective political identity? How far did the class and gender composition of the party inform its policy, culture and approach to the electorate nationally and locally? What were the limits of Labour politics: why, for different reasons and from different starting points, did the Co-op and the CPGB have a rather equivocal relationship with Labour?

Just as any attempted definition of Labour's ideology remains contentious, so it is impossible to construct an indubitable argument – or model – to explain the party's growth, development and character. The factors which informed Labour's historical trajectory changed over time and were subject to multiple and overlapping influences and determinants. Essentially, the Labour Party could mean and embody different things to different people at different times; its purpose and priorities could vary depending on geographical context, on the level of its apparatus, and on the affiliated organizations represented. Hence, we return to our 'broad church', which stemmed from Labour's federated structure and the vagaries – or generalities – of its ideology.

Labour Foundations

Hopefully, the essays contained in *The Foundations of the British Labour Party* will go some way towards answering the questions outlined above. Very generally, the editor conceived Labour's 'foundations' to comprise three principal dimensions: affiliated organizations, people and ideology. These, in turn, provided the material that shaped the party's political identities, cultures and perspectives from its origin through to at least the late twentieth century. The objective was to unpick various strands within Labour's federated structure in order to assess the different ways in which they informed the party's character and development. Simultaneously, the overlapping nature of the book's themes should allow us to retain a sense of the collective kinship that lay at the heart of the Labour Party.

The organizational foundations of Labour are examined in half of the twelve chapters contained herein. Given the importance of the trade unions in defining, financing and advancing Labour's history, two chapters are dedicated to explaining the ways and means by which an affiliated union could inform Labour's political culture and programme. Specifically, Gerald Crompton and Andrew Taylor take the railwaymen and the miners as their point of departure, thereby allowing the reader to compare and contrast the extent to which two important unions exerted their influence on the Labour Party. As becomes clear, trade unions often had different priorities and cultivated different relationships with their political partner. These, in turn, could alter over time depending on the prevailing socio-economic context and the relative positions of the Labour Party and the individual trade union at any given moment.

Beyond the trade unions, Labour's membership came primarily from the socialists gathered in the ILP and, later, the members who subscribed to the constituency organizations developed by the party from 1918. Both wielded an influence on Labour's broader character and perspective that was contentious but significant nonetheless. As Gidon Cohen argues, the ILP continues to command an important place within Labour's early history, providing the party with a socialist heritage and several of its more prominent leaders. Given this, Cohen here examines the 'myths' that have grown up around the ILP, revealing the ways in which these have informed Labour's own political identity and that ascribed to it by subsequent historians. Matthew Worley, meanwhile, looks at Labour's constituency parties, arguing that their development from 1918 proved integral to the party's eventual rise to government. Not only did they help extend the Labour presence beyond Britain's industrial heartlands, but they provided the basis for a permanent party machinery dedicated to fighting elections and sustaining a physical core of active political support.

Inherent in Worley's understanding of Labour is the premise that the character and composition of the party could differ from place to place depending on the socio-economic and politico-cultural context in which the party formed and functioned. Subsequently, the foundations of some local Labour enclaves were open to influences beyond the obvious trade union, Lib-Lab and ILP ones. So, for instance, as Nicole Robertson demonstrates, the party's difficult relationship with the co-operative movement ensured that Labour could sometimes benefit (as well as suffer) from the presence of the Co-op in a particular locality or constituency. To this end, Robertson examines the permutations of Labour–Co-op interaction between the wars, outlining the various ways in which the two organizations influenced and informed each other.

Not dissimilarly, though focused on an earlier period of Labour history, Jacqueline Turner assesses the oft-neglected influence of the Labour Church on the party's rise to prominence. Formed by John Trevor in 1891, the Labour Church served to provide a social focus and platform for an emergent Labour socialism, the ramifications of which stretched beyond the Church's own relatively short history. Indeed, Turner's concentration on religious organization is complemented by at least one of the three chapters committed to explaining and contextualizing the ideological foundations of the Labour Party, as Peter Catterall makes explicit the extent to which Christianity and Britain's religious culture informed both Labour's socialism and the ways in which the party perceived its moral and political purpose. As such, Catterall argues that the contribution of religion and the chapel to Labour should not be reduced simply to that of personnel.

Of course, broader factors were also at play in determining Labour's evolving political perspective. The party's ideological position has forever been hard to define, and has continued to lend itself to varied interpretation. For David Stack, this may be due in part to the reciprocal suspicion that characterized Labour's relationship with Britain's intellectual milieu. Appropriately, therefore, Stack uses the ILP to provide an insightful exploration into the tensions that existed between Labour's collective instinct to unity and the intellectual desire to question and debate. Chris Wrigley, moreover, places Labour's thought and practice in a wider European context, assessing the ways in which Labour's politics and culture were informed by developments beyond British shores.

Finally, the notion of Labour identity is further explored though three very different chapters. First, Robert Taylor offers an overview of the life and thought of John Robert Clynes, a Labour leader, MP and trade unionist whose working-class background and moderate socialism appear to embody the early Labour Party. In truth, any search for a definitive Labour identity is akin to chasing shadows. Nevertheless, Clynes' attempt to embody the values of his class alongside a practical but morally appropriate socialism reveal much about the impulses that drove Labour's pioneer generation. They also bring to life the very real tensions that existed within the Labour Party as it sought to enact radical changes within the British polity via peaceable and inclusive means.

Second, June Hannam examines the complex relationship between Labour and its women members. In so doing, Hannam applies a refreshingly multi-layered approach to the subject, warning against lazy generalizations and calling for more in-depth studies of the ways in which individual Labour women negotiated their way through what was a generally male-dominated environment and culture. Third, Laura Beers considers the ways in which Labour's public identity was shaped by forces beyond the party, by its political opponents and the press. This is important. Politics may often prove to be just as much about perception as the nuts and bolts of policy and ideology. Given this, Beers helps us understand, first, the ways in which Labour stereotypes and preconceptions were constructed and applied by its opponents and, second, how Labour's response served to reinforce pre-existing tendencies within the party.

Taken as a whole, the essays collected here should prompt us to think about the pre-Second World War Labour Party in a more multifaceted and nuanced way; to recognize the varied and shifting contexts in which it struggled to establish itself as the people's party; and to understand both the extent and the limitations of its achievements. Just as the Labour Party was always more than an extension of the trade union movement, so its socialism was never easily defined. If Labour served, in part, to draw from a progressive and Liberal tradition, so it will never do to wholly excise the influence of Karl Marx from its general perspective. As this suggests, Labour's foundations were solid, in the form of the trade unions, but far from uniform. Labour was – and remains – a diverse organization held together by a series of shared values and a sense of purpose. The New Jerusalem, it seems, should be viewed only through a kaleidoscope.

Chapter 2

John Robert Clynes and the Making of Labour Socialism, 1890–1918[1]

Robert Taylor

Labour serves the British people because it is a movement of the people. We have faced the people's problems ourselves, in our own homes and in the humble homes of our parents. Many of us have found in political life not a splendid career but an expression of our religion. A position has not been viewed as a job but as a Cause.[2]

The socialist differs from the trade unionist in work and wage matters only in the fact that he would ask for the trade unionist more than the trade unionist asks for himself. These two bodies are not opposite sects; they are two branches of the same protest against leaving the workers to the mercy of capitalism.[3]

Powerful classes and vested interests have in the past determined much of the legislation of former parliaments. Labour comes in, not to begin class legislation, but to try and end it. Labour cannot govern on a class basis or seek merely the advance of one section, however big that section may be. There is a class, however, which is in need of first aid. That is the poorest and most downtrodden. Labour must act as the political Red Cross to that section of suffering humanity.[4]

John Robert Clynes has suffered from an undeserved neglect. In his long public life – between 1890 and his death in 1949 – he came to represent and reflect the British labour movement's dualistic character for much of the early twentieth century. Clynes played an important role in the transformation of the Parliamentary Labour Party (PLP) from a small, independent pressure group representing organized manual working-class interests and aspirations into a broader-based people's party that sought national political power. He was first elected as Labour MP for the working-class constituency of Manchester North East (later Manchester Platting)

---

[1]   The author would like to thank David Howell and Jim Cronin for their comments on this essay.

[2]   J. R. Clynes, *Memoirs, 1924–37* (London: Hutchinson, 1937), p. 294.

[3]   'Gasworkers and General Labourers Union Quarterly Report', March–June 1910.

[4]   *The General Workers' Journal*, November–December 1922, p. 4.

in the Liberal landslide of 1906; a seat he held – except for a brief interlude in 1931–5 – for the next 39 years.

During the Great War (1914–18), Clynes served as a junior minister in Lloyd George's coalition government, taking full responsibility for food distribution in June 1918. He resigned, albeit reluctantly, when the Labour conference instructed its members to leave the government and prepare to fight the forthcoming general election as an independent political force. He went on to serve as a senior cabinet minister in both interwar Labour minority governments; first as leader of the House of Commons and lord privy seal in 1924, and then as home secretary between May 1929 and August 1931.

For much of his political life, Clynes was also a prominent full-time official in the Gasworkers and General Labourers' union. This was later to become – after amalgamations – the second largest trade union in the country and renamed the General and Municipal Workers' Union (GMWU) in 1924. He was elected president of the union in 1912, a position he retained for 25 years. As such, Clynes was one of the creative builders of a wide range of collective and voluntary representative institutions established by the labour movement as a means to advance the progress of the unskilled and semi-skilled manual working classes. In his early life, Clynes also took an active part in the world of trades councils, and helped preside over efforts to form broad trade union federations in the period leading up to the Great War and in its immediate aftermath.

As an ethical rather than a scientific socialist, the young Clynes attended both the inaugural conference of the Independent Labour Party (ILP) in 1893 and, seven years later as a union delegate, the foundation conference of the Labour Representation Committee (LRC). Clynes sat on Labour's National Executive Committee (NEC) from 1904, first representing the trades councils and, four years later, its trade union section until the outbreak of the Second World War; from 1894, he attended the annual Trades Union Congress (TUC) as a delegate for his union.

Yet, despite Clynes' astonishing longevity in the higher reaches of the labour movement, he remains a relatively unknown figure.[5] He is, too often, overlooked as one of the nearly men of Labour politics; having served as chairman of the PLP in 1921–2, Clynes lost that position to James Ramsay MacDonald by just 61 votes to 56 following the 1922 general election. For some, including many of the newly elected left-wing MPs from Clydeside, Clynes was too cautious, respectable and

---

[5]   Beyond Clynes' *Memoirs* in two volumes (1937), there is only J. Middleton's short biography in the *Dictionary of National Biography* (Oxford: Oxford University Press, 2004); T. Lloyd's contribution to A. Haworth and D. Hayter (eds), *Men Who Made Labour* (London: Routledge, 2006); C. Wrigley's entry for Clynes in G. Rosen (ed.), *Dictionary of Labour Biography* (London: Politicos, 2001); and the entry in H. Tracey (ed.), *The British Labour Party, Vol. III* (London: Caxton, 1948). For his background as a Manchester MP, see D. McHugh, *Labour in the City: The Development of the Labour Party in Manchester, 1918–31* (Manchester: Manchester University Press, 2007).

conciliatory in his handling of parliamentary business and too focused on trade union matters. A further 30 MPs, many of whom were trade unionists, failed to vote. Even so, Clynes accepted his narrow defeat without any outward signs of bitterness; he never intrigued to challenge MacDonald's position over the next nine years, though his relations with the solitary and prickly Labour leader were never close. On two further occasions, in August 1931 and again in 1935, he might have become Labour Party leader, but he declined to accept the position. Hugh Dalton noted in his diary on 28 August 1931 that Clynes 'says that Uncle [Arthur Henderson] has strongly urged him to be the leader but he realises in view of all that has happened, that Uncle is the only possible choice'. 'For himself', Dalton continued, 'he has been so long in the Movement that he has no longer any undue personal ambition. But he has not lost the love of service.'[6]

Other contemporaries commented on Clynes' apparent magnanimity and self-effacement. In a Commons appreciation of him on his death in 1949, Labour prime minister Clement Attlee described Clynes as a 'man who never made an enemy'. 'His outstanding quality was his complete unselfishness and loyalty', added Attlee. 'He had a very clear mind, good judgement and without being eloquent had the gift of simple, lucid speech.'[7] For party secretary Jim Middleton, 'Clynes gained respect by the very reasonableness and gentleness of his approach', while Philip Snowden recalled Clynes – when a newly elected Labour MP in 1906 – as a 'diminutive figure … modestly retiring into some inconspicuous seat' on the Commons benches. Even so, the usually acidic Snowden also admitted that by the early 1920s Clynes had grown to be 'an exceptionally able speaker, a keen and incisive debater … [with] wide experience of industrial questions and a good knowledge of general political issues'.[8]

Although there are no Clynes papers, other sources help to provide the portrait of a man who came to represent the cause of unskilled manual workers in their workplaces and political life. In presidential addresses to his union's biennial conferences after 1912, in his shrewd quarterly reports written when regional secretary to its executive, in his annual reports to the Oldham Labour and Trades Council, in his carefully crafted contributions to parliamentary debates, and in innumerable articles written for a range of newspapers, there emerges evidence of the rationality, realism and calming influence that Clynes exercised on both political and industrial affairs.

---

[6]   H. Dalton, *Call Back Yesterday: Memoirs, 1887–1931* (London: Muller, 1953), p. 279.

[7]   Hansard, *Parliamentary Debates*, vol. 468, 25 October 1949, c1157.

[8]   Middleton, *Dictionary of National Biography*; P. Snowden, *An Autobiography*, 2 vols (London: Nicholson and Watson, 1934), p. 302 (vol. 1) and p. 531 (vol. 2).

Perspectives

Clynes was always more than a principled pragmatist. He combined fundamental socialist beliefs with a firm commitment to trade union principles based on worker solidarity and voluntary collective bargaining. In his history of the GMWU, Hugh Clegg wrote that, as its president, Clynes 'probably had a greater influence than anybody else on its policies', and that the union came to accept his philosophy of 'restraint and moderation'.[9] Indeed, Clynes' dual role as political leader and national trade union official suggests that he remains of enormous importance for our understanding of early twentieth-century Labour. Other trade union figures, most notably Jimmy Thomas, John Hodge, Will Thorne and George Barnes, pursued similar parallel careers in both parliamentary politics and industrial affairs. But it was Clynes who came to articulate most effectively a distinctive – though not easily definable – conception of working-class politics that may best be described as 'Labour socialism'.[10] An imprecise and sentimental ideology, it sought to mould together ethical values of community with a higher class-consciousness and an industrial and political purpose to pursue the creation of a commonwealth of labour. Such a perspective, at its height in the 1920s, co-existed uneasily and untidily alongside other strains of ethos and tradition that gradually eclipsed Lib-Labism, such as Fabianism, Labourism and Marxism. But it undoubtedly helped to shape the eclectic, peculiarly British and rather elusive nature of early Labour's broad creed.

In his lucid analysis of the cruel nature of capitalism and the subordinate role of labour within it, and in his firm belief in the crucial importance of creating collective and national institutions to represent working-class aspirations and demands in a counter-challenge to that economic system, Clynes gave eloquent testimony to the complexities of an early twentieth-century British labour movement that differentiated its ideology and organization from the socialist movements dominant in Europe. Although Clynes failed to produce a book-length exposition of his political ideas, his impressive corpus of speeches and articles provide a persuasive account of what he believed were the labour movement's core values and principles. They reflected the nuanced complexities of Labour socialism, which sought to reconcile and integrate a strong, visionary commitment to the creation of a new world of justice, freedom and peace that was to be achieved through means of persuasion, conversion and parliamentary action, with the formulation of a realistic reformist programme of practical proposals for social and political improvement to further the aspirations and interests not only of manual workers, but of all citizens in a democratic society.

Clynes believed the unjust economic system under which labour had to live had established formidable obstacles to the advance not just of the minority of

---

[9]   H. Clegg, *General Union* (Oxford: Basil Blackwell, 1953), p. 14.

[10]   S. Macintyre, *A Proletarian Science: Marxism in Britain, 1917–33* (Cambridge: Cambridge University Press, 1980).

manual workers organized in trade unions, but to the millions of other downtrodden people who remained outside the formal institutions of the labour movement. Even so, he never advocated the militant politics of class struggle through the exclusive use of industrial muscle. Although he did not oppose strikes, Clynes saw them as a last resort; he knew from bitter experience that unskilled workers were more likely as not to suffer genuine hardship as a result of industrial action. Nor did he believe Labour should be concerned only with the plight of manual workers. From an early age, he took a surprisingly inclusive view of the labour movement's political and industrial objectives. He argued that the movement needed always to widen its appeal to cover every citizen, whether they were trade union members or not.

Simultaneously, Clynes appealed, perhaps naively, to what he liked to believe was the better nature of employers. He believed that Labour needed to win converts across the divided social classes if it was to succeed. His socialism was not, however, based on class collaboration. Clynes argued that trade unions should be recognized and respected, but that they should not seek uncritical incorporation into the industrial system. He was a fierce critic of blackleg labour and an uncompromising believer in the closed shop. Clynes argued with hostile employers that it was in their interests to recognize and negotiate with their employees through trade unions. This meant upholding the autonomy and independence of industrial labour. He believed in public ownership of the means of production, distribution and exchange; but Clynes argued that the fundamental transformation of society would only come about when Labour had won the argument through education and reason. He did not take a sentimental view of the working classes and was well aware of their propensity to short-termism and ignorance born of an almost non-existent education. Unlike so many Labour leaders over the generations, he never mistook the organized workers and those active for Labour as being truly representative of the working classes as a whole. Clynes wanted Labour to become a mass party of a united democracy; but he accepted such an objective would take time to achieve.

Clynes was always a patriot but never a nationalist. He emphasized that the ideology and structures of the labour movement reflected the particular conditions and circumstances of a nation that had developed in different ways from other European countries. 'We must bear in mind the national temperament of our workers and remember we can expect them to carve out a model of unity based on methods suitable in countries otherwise situated', he once wrote. 'To set ourselves to organise the workers of Britain on a Marxist, Russian or French syndicalist plan would be setting ourselves a task inappropriate to our conditions and fatal for our purpose.'[11] The terrible experiences inflicted on British society during the Great War only strengthened his conviction on the need for a broad and generous Labour socialism rooted in a sense of national identity. Speaking

---

[11]   H. Tracey (ed.), *The Book of the Labour Party: Its History, Policy, Growth and Leaders* (London: Caxton, 1925), p. 6.

in August 1918, Clynes argued: 'We have not merely served our class but have pursued the national interest and through the peaceful agency of this organisation have averted disturbance.' He continued:

> I do not think Labour should be anxious to keep itself separated from the greater national interest which, to me, is the most supreme consideration of all. We are not in any sense subverting our distinctive Labour claim and we ought not to subvert it but we ought to ally ourselves as far as possible to the broad national interests and the claims of the community at large. Our interests are not distinctly selfish. Labour is the nation, not a mere section or small part of it.[12]

Clynes emphasized that it was through the advance of collective and voluntary institutions – such as the Federation of General Workers – that unskilled and semi-skilled manual workers could integrate their demands and aspirations in wartime with the rest of society, even with the country's capitalist class in partnership with an increasingly centralized and regulatory state. Through the machinery of industrial conciliation and the practice of sector or nationwide collective bargaining, the trade unions were raising the status and legitimacy of organized labour and becoming almost social partners in the management of the economy. This tentative development was seen by Clynes as crucial to the country's long overdue democratic advance towards the formation of a more representative system of government under which 'workmen have rights corresponding to those which the employers exercise, rights which will have to be not merely recognized in a grudging way but openly and wholeheartedly acknowledged by the employers of labour'.[13] In reality, most employers failed to abide by such high standards in practice.

Clynes regarded his political and trade union work as inseparable parts of an integrated whole. He argued that it made no sense to draw any rigid lines of demarcation between the activities of the different representative institutions that made up the early labour movement; labour's cause transcended the worlds of industry and politics in both theory and practice. As such, Clynes was able to move within the movement's complex federal structure of interlocking institutions without much strain or effort, managing the advance of trade union interests for unskilled and semi-skilled manual workers while simultaneously becoming a senior figure in the PLP.

It is wrong, therefore, to suggest that the labour movement functioned through two clearly defined and separated tendencies – one industrial, the other political. Of course, the tangled relationships between the two often proved difficult, fluid, unpredictable and contingent. However, men like Clynes sought successfully to reconcile whatever differences of opinion or emphasis might occur between labour's political and industrial worlds. While he acknowledged the existence of underlying tensions, Clynes emphasized the mutuality of common interests

---

[12]   Federation of General Workers, 'Conference Report', 15 August 1918.

[13]   Ibid.

that bound the movement's diverse cultures and traditions together. The often uneasy strategic alliance forged between the forces of ethical socialism and trade unionism during the early 1900s sought to create a new kind of progressive politics in Britain that would focus national attention on manual working-class interests and labour values. This was rooted in a principled commitment to the peaceful emancipation of the manual working classes (unskilled as much as skilled) from the social inequalities and poverty of capitalism, and was to be achieved through representative institutions such as the trade unions, the Labour Party, co-operative society, trades councils and the like.

In a characteristically shrewd address to the 1909 Labour conference, Clynes sought to explain the complementary nature of the balance of ideas and interests that constituted the early relationship between the party and the trade unions that created, funded and nurtured it:

> The only alliance we need is the one which the party itself possesses and which consists of the mutual association for immediate legislative gains of the trade unions and organised socialists in the country. No compact or understanding with other parties can be thought of. No restraint of any principle is placed upon those who form our alliance. The socialist is left entirely free to pursue his business in the politics of the country and is able to do his work to greater advantage by his contact with the organised workers who are in their trade unions in no way hampered but helped by the alliance in the industrial duties which called them into being. The trade unionist asks for but a share of the wealth he creates, the socialist tells him to claim the full product of his labour and calls upon all who are able to do so to give their share of service for their share of wealth.[14]

Clynes' view of parliamentary politics and industrial relations suggests we need to develop a more nuanced way of looking at the connections that existed between the political and the industrial in labour history. He was always a socialist as well as a social reformer. He believed in the need to create a commonwealth of labour through public ownership of the means of production, distribution and exchange, but he also pursued parliamentary strategies to improve working-class living standards through social legislation and the extension of political and trade union rights.

In Egon Wertheimer's perceptive *Portrait of the Labour Party* (1929), Clynes is bracketed with Henderson as one of the two key figures for understanding the British labour movement. 'No other proletariat in the world has brought forth men who – like these – combine the best qualities of the working man with such ease in the assumption of responsibility and so much aplomb in the bearing of its burdens', he wrote.

---

[14] Labour Party, *Report of the Annual Conference, 1909* (London, 1909), p. 37.

They are safe, homely men in whose hands the continuity of the party as a working-class organisation is assured. They have none of the vanity of the *homo politicus*. They serve the Movement and are always in harmony with its mood. They are not affected by fluctuations on the political exchange. They are gilt edged securities and lend the British Labour Movement that inner stability that is threatened beyond all doubt by the inrush of new men.[15]

Clynes' importance lies in his recognition that the labour movement needed to construct a multiplicity of inter-related institutions to advance commonly accepted values rooted in the social realities of class, but which needed also to transcend them. This entailed a subtle and complex interaction between a coherent and credible concept of Labour socialism and the working-class institutions that articulated the movement's purposes. In his own personal commitments and loyalties to the development of trades councils, trade union federations and the advance of the PLP, Clynes reflected an underlying tension that existed between thought and action in the early labour movement. In practical reality, its self-governing institutions were neither in conflict nor in competition with one another. Clynes believed they were bound together by a mutual acceptance of Labour's purpose to unify an ethical socialism with a practical public policy agenda designed to further common working-class interests beyond the limitations imposed by trade union based collective bargaining and organization. As such, he argued that unskilled and semi-skilled manual workers could achieve far more in co-operation with their skilled colleagues than in highlighting differences based on occupational status and concepts of manual skill. Clynes was consistent in his conviction that it was vital to promote unifying institutions for workers that overcame what was often a fragmented and divided labour interest rooted in parochial localism and particular workplace traditions. In short, Clynes urged the need to promote a national sense of identity of what Labour stood for both in parliamentary affairs and industrial politics in the years leading up to the outbreak of war in August 1914.

Without doubt, the impact of the Great War helped to deepen Clynes' conception of what Labour's role and purpose should be. In the immediate post-war years, he was to play an important part in ensuring that Labour socialism helped increase the party's growing, if uneven, appeal to the mass electorate. Nevertheless, his fundamental beliefs were developed much earlier in his life; his concept of Labour socialism had solidified through his personal experiences in the years before 1914.

The Making of a Labour Socialist

Clynes' Labour socialism emerged from the oppressive circumstances of his early life. He was born on 27 March 1869 in dire poverty, the eldest of two sons of

---

[15]   E. Wertheimer, *Portrait of the Labour Party* (London: Putnam, 1929), p. 183.

an illiterate Irish immigrant gravedigger – a survivor of the Great Famine – in a family of seven in the Lancashire textile town of Oldham. Clynes attended only elementary school and, at the age of 10, went to work part-time as a piecer in a local cotton mill. When he reached 12, he became a full-time piecer earning ten shillings a week.

Clynes educated himself during his teenage years through reading a wide range of literature in the Oldham co-operative society library, thereby becoming a life-long lover of the works of William Shakespeare, John Ruskin and Charles Dickens. William Cobbett's *Grammar* was of special importance to him in the development of his vocabulary and concise use of words. Curiously, Clynes' ideals and principles do not seem to have been influenced by any institutional form of Christianity. He may have been brought up as a Roman Catholic, but there is no mention of this in his autobiography. Clynes admitted in 1920 that after reading many times a book entitled *Is One Religion As Good As Another?* he came to the conclusion that: 'I thought less and less of ceremony or church service and became hardened in the view that it was not sectarian doctrine or creed but conduct which alone was worthy of the word "religion".' Nevertheless, Clynes was influenced by the teachings of Christ; Renan's *Life of Jesus* was one of his favourite books.[16]

In the 1880s, Clynes became something of a local phenomenon. He wrote a series of anonymous articles in the Oldham press under the pseudonym 'the piecer' that exposed the degrading cruelties and poverty inflicted on workers employed in the profitable cotton industry. He then demonstrated an early flair for organization in helping to form a separate trade union for the downtrodden piecers in a breakaway from the spinners' union which failed to represent them effectively. He was elected president of the Oldham Trades and Labour Council in 1890 at the age of only 21; he became its secretary in 1892, a position he held until 1912. In 1892, he accepted a full-time position as local secretary for the recently formed Gasworkers and General Labourers' Union. Four years later, Clynes became the union's Lancashire regional secretary and rapidly made the region one of the union's largest.

Oldham – like many south-east Lancashire industrial towns in the 1890s – found it difficult to establish any strong sense of organized labour unity through the activities of a trades council. Its organized working class suffered from political, ethnic and religious division, between Protestant Conservatives who were strong in the cotton spinning industry and Liberals associated with the engineering trades, Nonconformity, Catholicism and the Irish cause. It was not until 1910 that Labour established a presence on the town council. Clynes himself made three attempts to win election as a Labour councillor in the early 1900s without success.

The complexities of Oldham labour politics may have convinced Clynes of the need to establish a broad social base for working-class activism. During his formative years, Clynes developed a strong commitment to the concept of the trades council as a representative working-class institution that could unify trade unions

---

[16] *John O'London's Weekly*, 11 December 1920.

locally behind a wide labour interest. Certainly, Clynes did not hold the view of the council's erstwhile secretary Thomas Ashton that 'trades councils should not be made into political institutions for party purposes'. Rather, Clynes sought to argue – through his lucid annual reports to the trades council from 1894 – that a working-class unity of purpose should be expressed through the development of voluntary institutions (such as the trades council), and to persuade the doubters in Oldham's segmented working class that labour's cause could only succeed if it was organized around a shared view of what it stood for in the widest sense.

> The more our industrial system develops the more do our societies require a means of frequent mutual intercourse and cohesion such as a good trades council affords. This intercourse we believe should be more than sympathetic; it should be protective, educational, materially beneficial, defensive and where necessary ready for attack. Not that we desire workmen to prepare for an aggressive onslaught on employers. We desire that each should try and modify or altogether remove some plain and pernicious evils which are so harmful to both.[17]

As such, Clynes emphasized the common interests that were needed to hold manual labour together and, from the perspective of the 1890s, trades councils were the working-class bodies best able to address broad labour questions. In reality, they failed to develop in the way he envisaged, mainly because of worker rivalries and local parochialisms. Increasingly, Clynes came to recognize that labour needed to develop stronger and more effective national institutions if it was to challenge the existing political and economic order.

Such thinking was strengthened by the attitude of employers. Clynes believed that the forces of capital were organizing themselves collectively in the 1890s to challenge and crush independent trade unionism and labour-based politics. He pointed to 'a growing tendency to destroy or at least cripple the only power that workmen have, outside legislative enactment, of defending themselves in all matters relating to their own conditions of work and wages'. Similarly, Clynes criticized what he regarded as the essential class character of parliamentary politics in the 1890s. 'Governments move slowly in the direction of better legislation for the working classes though they have sometimes moved with great speed in giving favours to the wealthy classes or in keeping workmen [by acts of repression] in which is looked upon their proper place', he wrote in 1897.[18]

At the same time, Clynes' position as administrator and organizer of the Gasworkers and General Labourers led him to champion the cause of the unskilled and semi-skilled manual working class. In vivid language unfamiliar in such usually dry union records, Clynes argued eloquently about the condition of the general labourers and their families, of those who lacked either a recognized skill or negotiating power, and who were the lowest paid, the most exploited and the most

---

[17]   Oldham Trades and Labour Council [OTLC], 'Annual Report', 1894, pp. 4–7.
[18]   OTLC, 'Annual Report', 1897, p. 9.

difficult to organize among the working class. While other Labour autodidacts of his generation came mainly from the ranks of skilled workers, Clynes was exceptional because he championed men and women who were always, even in good times, living on the edge of the social abyss. 'In industrial centres like Lancashire', Clynes wrote, 'thousands of labourers are despised, driven and underpaid because they neglect the use of strength that can come from united numbers'. The mission of a union like the Gasworkers was to transform their 'ignorance' into 'wisdom'. 'Labourers', he argued, 'should imitate skilled tradesmen in their view of trade unionism and look upon it as an enduring condition attached to their life as wage earners and not as a temporary resort'.[19]

The success of the general labourers would come not from sporadic outbursts of industrial militancy that, at best, provided only transient moments of advance in wages and conditions, but in establishing permanent representative bodies that attracted workers as members for all their working lives through the ups and downs of the economic cycle. Clynes recognized that the unskilled were particularly vulnerable to the capricious behaviour of employers. He realized that the very nature of capitalism encouraged employers to drive down the wages of the unskilled and semi-skilled in the name of competition. Trade unions therefore needed to build up their collective powers on behalf of those vulnerable workers, but use them sensibly and sparingly in their relationships with companies. For a general union like the Gasworkers, this meant organizing unskilled and semi-skilled general labourers across a range of industries and services. Clynes succeeded during his years as Lancashire secretary in extending his union's membership into the ranks of general labourers in the brick, clay and iron industries of north-western England, as well as in construction, local government and the gas industry.

Again, however, Clynes realized that there was an urgent need to encourage a national movement to bring general labourers together across industries and regions in common cause. He claimed in 1899 that the concept of the trade union federation was moving out of the 'sphere of theory and into the sphere of actual fact', listing 14 trade unions that he described as emerging federations.[20] It was, therefore, through his work as trades council secretary and full-time regional trade union official that Clynes recognized that the industrial and political needs of the manual working classes were inextricably bound together.

The Parliamentary Road to Labour Socialism

Clynes believed from his early years that trade union work alone would never be enough to advance and defend the interests of the manual working classes, especially those employed in unskilled or semi-skilled jobs. Moreover, he was

---

[19]   OTLC, 'Annual Report', 1899, p. 5.
[20]   Ibid., p. 11.

committed from his early twenties to socialism: a grand vision of a commonwealth of labour to replace capitalist society.

Clynes was a founder member of the ILP, but unlike other leading figures in the Gasworkers and General Labourers – such as its founder Will Thorne – he was not active in the Social Democratic Federation (SDF), despite its being relatively strong in parts of Lancashire and more pragmatic than its Marxist rhetoric suggested. While Clynes recognized and deplored the class character of capitalism, he was never convinced that the road to socialism could be travelled through any dominant strategy of industrial militancy or class struggle for its own sake. He was always to be a staunch parliamentary democrat, as he explained later in his life in a critique of Soviet communism:

> In countries where no democratic weapon exists a class struggle for the enthronement of force by one class over other classes may be condoned, but in this country where the wage earners possess 90 per cent of the voting power of the country agitation to use not the power which is possessed but some risky class dictatorship is a futile and dangerous doctrine. Our work is therefore the work of conversion not coercion. We must advance by consent and gather force that will endure for the reason that people have signified their approval of our conceptions of national law, international relations and social needs.[21]

Even so, Clynes' uncompromising belief in the importance of parliamentary democracy in no way diluted his commitment to independent labour representation. In expressing his pleasure in 1903 at the increasing number of trade unions affiliating to the LRC following the Lords' Taff Vale judgement, Clynes commented that: 'We do not suppose there is in the world a political organisation equal in paying adherents to the Labour Representation Committee which has now over one million paying members'. 'Its object', Clynes maintained, was 'to elect to Parliament a party which shall act independently of any obligation to other parties and entirely for the good of those who labour for their living'. This, of course, stood in stark contrast to the 'vested interests, the profits of property, the claims of landlordism, the rights of wealth and capital' that were all 'well protected and monstrously over represented in both Houses of Parliament and on many local governing bodies'.[22]

Clynes later recalled the dramatic arrival of the Labour Party to the 1906 parliament. They brought to Westminster the social and industrial issues that preoccupied the working classes for the first time. 'When we asked – why a Labour Party? – we showed how little had even been attempted and how numerous and far-reaching were the weighty subjects never yet touched either by parties or Parliament.' The feelings of the political ruling class 'deepened into disgust when we revealed conditions concerning the houses of the people, their work, low wages, long hours, a travesty of education, workshop accidents and no

---

[21]   Tracey, *The Book of the Labour Party*, p. 148.
[22]   OTLC, 'Annual Report', 1903, p. 13.

compensation for the victims', he continued. For Clynes, Labour was more than just another conventional political party; it was one of the institutional expressions of labour's broader, moral cause:

> Our opponents told us we have nothing wherewith to move ahead. Nothing? They were thinking of influence, organisation, party power, a press and money. They soon saw we were not without substantial assets. We had abiding faith in a cause, a missionary zeal to preach it in the face of every sign of derision and best of all we have the facts on our side and when we uttered the facts the people knew that we merely spoke their own everyday experience. People then did more than listen, they were moved; they had lived enslaved and impoverished but did not know it, so accustomed were they to injustice and hardship.[23]

Clynes here seems unaware that his victory in 1906 stemmed from the Liberal–Labour electoral pact that gave LRC candidates an unopposed run in certain Conservative working-class seats. Nevertheless, Clynes and his colleagues gave eloquent voice to the labour movement's causes, influencing the social agenda of progressive politics alongside the radical wing of the Liberals and the emerging New Liberalism associated with Lloyd George and Winston Churchill.

Throughout his political life, Clynes was concerned with the scourge of mass unemployment. But he did not believe its eradication could be left merely to the free play of unregulated market forces. Political action through parliament was required to deal with it in a sensible way. Even so, his opinions on worklessness were unsentimental. In an echo of New Labour thinking nearly a century later, Clynes emphasized that while the state must recognize the right to work, it must fulfil such an obligation with a corresponding demand for responsibility by the jobless citizen. 'We see no need for the exhaustive and cumbersome enquiries', he argued.

> The only needful test on this question is the test of whether a man really wants work and can do it and no objection would be raised to any proper and reasonable provision to protect public money from being abused or wasted … Working men must conform to the obligations placed upon them by society and meet the conditions of citizenship or suffer various forms of punishment. Responsibilities should be accompanied by opportunities and if men are expected to lead a decent life and discharge their duties to society the meeting of these duties and expectations should not be left to chance.[24]

Clynes also argued fluently but unsuccessfully for Labour's Right to Work Bill in 1907. He welcomed the Liberal government's introduction of labour exchanges, the creation of wages boards to set minimum rates for some of the low paid, and a

---

[23] OTLC, 'Annual Report', 1906, p. 7.
[24] Ibid.

statutory limit on the length of the working week to eight hours a day for miners, though he wanted that right extended to all workers.

Clynes believed that the state should protect trade union freedoms from attack by the judiciary and capital. He took a leading role in Labour's campaign for a reversal of the Taff Vale judgement, and regarded the 1906 Trades Disputes Act as a measure to 'liberate the various trade unions from the restraints and fears imposed upon them during the past five years'. Clynes also welcomed the Workmen's Compensation Act passed in 1906 (though he called for higher compensation levels than half a worker's lost wages), and later emphasized Labour's influence on the Liberal government's decision to introduce old age pensions in 1908. However, the PLP's ability to exercise positive influence on the government's social and industrial agenda grew more limited after the two 1910 general elections. Indeed, Labour faced an uncertain political future after the Osborne judgement in 1909 threatened the freedom of affiliated trade unions to finance the Labour Party's organization and, in particular, its ability to field candidates in parliamentary elections. 'As usual', Clynes insisted, 'the pretence is maintained by rich parties of every step they take being in the interests of the poor working man', and he urged parliament to reverse Osborne 'in the interests of equity and democratic management'.[25]

Significantly, Clynes' opposition to the Osborne judgement reflected his belief that Labour's presence in parliament reinforced the growing importance of the labour movement in the wider society. 'Parliamentary action comes nearer the workshop and the workmen every day', he explained.

> Workmen must have their men in the House of Commons and if in the process of getting workers' representatives to parliament party prejudice is disturbed we can only regret it. Political opinions of workmen should be respected and these opinions will be fairly dealt with by the workmen's mates if scared politicians will allow the members of trade unions and the various branches of the Labour Party to settle their own business. The taunt that a small section of socialists want to use trade unions for unworthy ends is beneath notice though it proves that the real objection is not to trade unions acting politically but to their having freedom to join hands with a particular party. Socialist organisations are unaffected by the Osborne judgement and trade unions now crippled by it must assert their right with whom they choose.[26]

Although always an eloquent champion of Labour's lobbying role in parliament and a critic of those in the trade unions who wanted to subordinate political aims to industrial action, Clynes did not denounce the wave of general worker unrest that hit Britain between 1911 and 1914. He never sympathized with syndicalism as an alternative to representative parliamentary democracy, but Clynes recognized

---

[25]   OTLC, 'Annual Report', 1910, p. 7.

[26]   OTLC, 'Annual Report', 1910, p. 9.

the deteriorating social and economic conditions that lay behind the sudden upsurge of discontent. He also believed in the important role that Labour MPs – as representative intermediaries – needed to play in voicing those feelings in the House of Commons. 'While we regret the suffering and the losses endured during the severe and sometimes bitter conflicts between employers and their workers', Clynes reported in 1911, the experience proved 'that patient appeal and submission to existing conditions brings to the wage earner little or no prospect of improvement'. In the same year, he wrote perceptively of:

> the growing consciousness among wage earners of the sense of wrong and injustice under which many of them have worked and of the power which they can effectively exercise by the mere act of standing peacefully together for the common good and defence of all. Despite an abounding prosperity and a constant growth in the value and volume of national trade, the workers can obtain benefit only in so far as they are able to fight for it.[27]

But Clynes did not believe that the Labour Party should become the exclusive mouthpiece of trade union interests. At the 1907 party conference, he opposed a motion designed to restrict being a Labour MP, candidate or delegate to paid-up trade union members, insisting that he 'attached little or no importance to the mere fact of a man having a trade union card in his pocket'. Indeed, the 'cause of Labour had received from men and women who had no contribution card more worthy support, more brainy assistance, more self-sacrifice than it had received from some men who had contribution cards'. Certainly, Clynes did not believe that a man, because of his grandiloquence, could go to a constituency and win a nomination by saying – 'Here I am; you must adopt me'. In constituencies dominated by an ever-growing majority of trade union members, Clynes argued that 'the intelligence of the Movement was sufficient protection and there was no need whatever for the resolution'.[28]

Nor did Clynes believe that Labour should become an exclusively socialist party. At the 1908 party conference, he spoke out against a motion from Ben Tillett that wanted the PLP to agree Labour's 'ultimate object' as being to obtain for the workers 'the full results of their labour by the overthrow of the present competitive system of capitalism and the institution of a system of public ownership and control of all the means of life'. Clynes told delegates that while he believed in public ownership of the means of production, distribution and exchange, he also felt that 'in so far as we took part in politics we ought to be careful not to sharpen the weapons of the enemy'. Equally, if Labour forced such a declaration on the million trade union members represented in the party, the effect would be harmful. The party existed as an alliance; the conditions of the alliance ought to be respected, and the success of the alliance ought not to be ignored. Clynes argued that he

---

[27]   OTLC, 'Annual Report', 1911, p. 5.

[28]   Labour Party, *Report of the Annual Conference, 1907* (London, 1907), p. 55.

was more in favour of preaching to make converts to socialism than seeking to fasten the socialist label upon the large mass of organized workers who were not socialists at all. 'We were not out for ultimate objects', he insisted, but 'for old age pensions; for immediate industrial legislation; for some kind of effective and helpful legislation on the subject of unemployment'. Whilst simultaneously 'preaching ideals to the people', Labour should apply its 'immediate energies to existing political opportunities' in order to 'bring the best fruit and the most helpful matter for the working classes of the land'.[29]

This should not suggest that pre-war Labour socialism was thereby mild, moderate or accommodating. As Clynes explained to the voters in January 1910:

> I believe in seeking social welfare before private interests. The greatest profit a community can boast is the prosperity and joyful existence of the mass of its people. Poverty is costly in its waste of life and public money. People are impoverished by wretched wages and unemployment and millions are then spent in trying to cure the evils ... Those who give their service in useful labour, in trade or business should not be kept poor and my politics have always been to make war upon poverty. For this we are assailed as socialists. We have nothing to do with the travesty of socialism which so many invent merely to condemn. We are fighting for social justice and believe that the land and property required for our common needs should be owned by the people for the public and not for private gain.

Clynes argued in his manifesto that Labour remained a 'mutual alliance of trade unionists and socialists' united 'to secure from any quarter good legislation'. He – like other Labour candidates in January 1910 – explained that the 'right to work' should become the 'first and greatest subject' for the new parliament, and he aggressively attacked his Unionist opponent, the local industrialist Sir William Vaudrey. Where Clynes stood for 'democracy and a nation of free men living in a free world', Vaudrey stood 'for aristocracy, land monopoly, mining royalties and rents'.[30] In one election leaflet, Clynes came close to arguing for class war, referring to the 'constant struggle between two sections of the community' going on for more than a thousand years. On the one hand, there existed the 'mass of the people – the artisans, the peasants, the shopkeepers trying to live their lives in something like decency and comfort'; on the other hand, there were the 'idle, luxurious, selfish aristocracy and in later days men who live upon the toil of the producers and distributors, trying to keep the muscle and brain workers in political or economic serfdom or worse'. As such, Clynes urged workers to follow the example of the landlords and 'capture the legislative machine' for themselves. His arguments were similar to those of Liberals but from a manual worker perspective.

---

[29]   Labour Party, *Report of the Annual Conference, 1908* (London, 1908), p. 58

[30]   J. R. Clynes, 'General Election Address', 1910 (Labour Party Archives).

You workers of all grades, you are not a class, you are a nation. A small section lives upon your labour. Now is your time and opportunity. Hereditary aristocratic government with its selfish tyranny and injustice to the mass of workers has outlived its day. It should be relegated to the past. Workers! Sweep it once and for all into oblivion.[31]

By 1914, Clynes had reached a settled view of what he saw as Labour's purpose. The party was the result of a 'harmonious working alliance', which reserved 'to the trade unionist the liberty to go on with his industrial work, to preach combination, secure gains for the workshop and secure better laws in Parliament', and left the socialist 'free to spread his ideals, to teach his principles and to strengthen his organisation'. In this, 'freedom of opinion in no sense involving sacrifice of principle has been the foundation, has been the safety valve of this Labour Party'. While Labour 'did not bring party politics into the trade unions', it did bring the 'trades unions into parliamentary action'. This, in turn, did not diminish 'our pride in the trades unions', but it remained Labour's visionary commitment to the faith of Labour socialism that held the political and industrial together. 'Since I was a young man', Clynes recalled, 'I have been a Socialist. I have believed in the ideal of a social system in which not merely the land of the nations but the main means for making the material wealth shall be social property and used for social good'.[32]

Labour Socialism and the Challenge of War

With many reservations and anxieties, Clynes supported British participation in the Great War from its beginning to the end. He was one of only two sponsored ILP members in the PLP to do so. But unlike other trade union leaders, he was never a belligerent jingoist in his attitude to the conflict. Although he voted against Labour's decision to join the Asquith administration in May 1915, 18 months later Clynes backed Labour's participation in Lloyd George's coalition. He was appointed parliamentary secretary under Lord Rhondda, and later became food controller.

The impact of the Great War on the labour movement was complex and here is not the place to assess its overall significance. But Clynes recognized early on that the conflict provided opportunities for the trade unions and Labour to make themselves essential for the winning of the war and, more importantly, the peaceful reconstruction of Britain once it was over. In this, it was more than just the administrative experience gained by the labour movement during the war that convinced Clynes of labour's enhanced position in state and society. 'Every class has felt the nearness of the nation's struggle and the working classes, especially

---

[31]   Independent Labour Party Papers, 6/20/5.

[32]   American Federation of Labor, 'Annual Conference Report', 1908, p. 156. Clynes had attended the conference as a TUC fraternal delegate.

when the struggle is over, will feel the title they have established to own something in the land they have fought for', he wrote in 1915. 'The class that has had to make the greatest sacrifice during the war will be the class that after it is over can justly seek relief from an unfair share of the heavy burden that will have to be carried.'[33] It was to be a noble, but desperately optimistic hope.

During the early stages of the war, Clynes grew convinced that a voluntary partnership approach between employers and workers to boost production would not be enough to overcome deep-rooted divisions in industry. 'Co-partnership on the lines so far followed has diminished the freedom of workmen and their organisations', he complained. 'Mutual arrangements reached by means of free and fair discussion between accredited representatives of the various interests will ensure greater confidence from the working class side than the schemes of co-partnership so far tried.' The demands of the war effort necessitated 'collective action and the application of state authority acting in agreement with industrial organisations'. Clynes argued that wartime collaboration between capital and labour required active intervention by the state. As he explained: 'Co-partnership with freedom and a fuller share for the workers of the gains of their work would attract some support but capital would have to unlearn a lot before it could offer labour terms that labour could accept.'[34] This did not mean that manual workers could be bought off with 'higher coddling, flattery or mere better conditions in the workplace', Clynes argued towards the end of the conflict. Rather:

> What I mean is that if unity between classes in industrial and economic life is to be sought and secured it can be got only at a price paid in a twofold form – that of giving a greater yield of the wealth of the nation to those who mainly by their energies made that wealth and for placing the producing classes on a level where they will receive a higher measure of respect, of thanks and of regard that they have previously received from the nation as a whole.[35]

At the same time, the experience of war reinforced Clynes' belief that Labour's popular appeal must transcend the interests and aspirations of the manual working classes alone. 'Democracy is wider than the confines of the manual worker', he insisted. 'Democracy stands for the general progress of mankind and means the uplifting of men and the liberation and unifying of nations.' Indeed, Clynes predicted that there would be a transformation in British politics as a result of the war, and that this would be to Labour's advantage. 'The success of parties, in the old sense of the term, is a trivial thing to the success of the great ends to be secured', he asserted.

---

[33] *Christian Commonwealth*, 9 June 1915.

[34] *Manchester Dispatch*, 12 December 1915.

[35] General Workers' Union, 'Biennial Congress Report', 1916.

These ends will justify the use of any constitutional means for dethroning that form of power upon which privilege and the mere possession of wealth have rested. But democracy must not be duped by phrases nor be swayed by any influence which does not lead to a lasting advance for the nation as a whole. Nor should its leaders think that fundamental and enduring changes in our social system can be reached by any short cut to which the great mass of the people have not been converted. Progress will be faster in the future if impatience and folly do not retard it.

For Clynes, ever the practical visionary, it would not be enough for labour leaders 'merely to say that the future of the world must be decided not by diplomats or thrones or Kaisers but by the will of peoples'. Rather:

The will of peoples can find enduring and beneficial expression only when that will seeks social change by reasonable and calculated instalments and not by any violent act of revolution. Peaceful voters on their way to the ballot boxes and properly formulated principles will in the end go further than fire and sword in the internal affairs of a nation.

Given that the war had 'brought all classes together' in a 'common sacrifice, a common endeavour for a common cause', Clynes argued that it was surely now possible to maintain this common unity of purpose in peacetime as well.[36]

Yet, Clynes believed that it was only through the further development of manual working-class organization that any sense of national unity would be established and then deepened. The crucial work conducted by the War Emergency Workers' National Committee revealed the competence and practicality of the movement's response to the crisis. As president of the General Workers' Union in 1916, Clynes pointed to the enormous growth in trade unionism brought about by the war. 'By means of legitimate agitation, conference, discussion of men's claims and by placing before courts of arbitration the merits of demands which we have made, our members have continued to reap the fruits of trade union power', he told delegates to his union's conference.

There has been an immense gain to the wage earning classes from the fact that general labourers have in the past quarter of a century been lifted to a place of influence and of importance in the trades and industries of the land. The lesser skilled and unskilled men and women were regarded formerly as an inferior race in the community. They were subject to all the evil influences not only of unrestrained competition amongst employers but of foolish competition amongst themselves. These evils are not yet abolished but they have been considerably diminished and now in most cases small groups or large armies of unskilled workers can stand up for their rights ... A sense of greater freedom and of

---

[36]   Ibid.

independence has been implanted in the mind of the labourer. He has been made
to feel that he is a man as well as a toiler and that he is entitled not only to fair
wages for useful work but to a due share of the people's respect in exchange for
the value given to his country by his daily labour.

Clynes pointed to the enormous sacrifices the manual working classes were
making in the war, and while he acknowledged that 'several rich men … [had] set
a fine patriotic example', it was the 'poor' who were 'first to go in large numbers',
proving the 'faithful defenders of their country's fate' in a way that entitled them
to 'look for a higher and more secure place in the future history of their country'.
Clynes estimated that as many as 40,000 of his union's members were participating
in the war. 'If they are good enough now to fight for their native land they should
be good enough to own and enjoy more of it when they have conquered its enemies
and maintained its freedom', he continued. This, Clynes acknowledged, would
not be achieved easily. The unions had agreed to an industrial truce and severe
curbs had been imposed on voluntary wage bargaining; but, despite this, many
employers were less willing to make sacrifices for the common good. 'Now that
human life must by law respond to the call for military duty, property, land and
capital should be made to yield equal sacrifice and service so far as that can be
done', he insisted to loud applause.[37]

Clynes highlighted three obstacles that blocked the way to the 'higher national
life and progress' that Labour sought. First, there were 'political interests and
the squabbles of parties in local and national politics'; second, 'the quarrels of
sects and denominations in the realm of religion'; and last, there were 'the class
distinctions and privileges based on the power which the ownership of property
bestowed'. It was Labour's task to challenge these forces in government. In his
defence of Labour's decision to join Lloyd George's coalition in December 1916,
Clynes explained:

> Labour wants greater authority to direct the affairs of the state and become in
> fact the maker and administrator of laws instead of an appellant for gifts for the
> thousands of the poor who are in search of what they think is their due on matters
> like pensions, army treatment, personal freedom and improvements in civil and
> industrial life. Labour cannot have power in these respects unless Labour takes
> office. Taking office is stigmatised by some as merely taking a job with a title
> and a salary and satisfying only some unworthy motive. Such a line of criticism
> has after all, whenever it has been treated by great representative conferences,
> been discarded by big majorities of Labour delegates.

But, although Clynes admitted that the PLP had been split over what to do and
that it had found itself in 'a position of embarrassment', he believed Labour's
direct participation in government provided the party and the trade unions with an

---

[37]   Ibid.

opportunity to exercise a practical power and influence over the state and ensure the coalition was not dominated by capital. 'If the war does not change fundamentally the relations between Capital and Labour, it will at least tend greatly to modify in favour of Labour the basis of these relations', he believed in 1918.

> Before the war Labour was in a very subordinate position and Capital was regarded as conferring a favour on workmen in providing them with employment. The war has shown to workmen that it is work which matters most … It makes wealth in times of peace and in war it makes munitions, maintains soldiers, and it provides for a nation in the hour of its greatest need the services to enable the nation to continue the struggle for success.[38]

In other words, Clynes believed Labour socialism would emerge in a more powerful position when the war was won because the working class on the battlefields and in the workplaces had shown their love of their country through sacrifice and effort.

Simultaneously, Clynes argued that Britain's war experience pointed to the emergence of a more enlightened system of industrial relations that recognized the social justice sought by the trade unions. He contrasted the pre-war industrial system – where any question of 'welfare for workers under conditions of organised action and treatment was viewed as either stupid interference with other people's business or at best as the well meant attention of persons who in regard to trade affairs were at the level of grandmothers' – with a peacetime in which there would be 'the emergence of a more cooperative system of joint consultation and collective negotiation, where voluntary arbitration would be preferred to the use of the strike weapon in advancing the workers' cause'. 'Prosperity', Clynes argued, 'cannot be said to exist … if masses of producers are miserable in their periods of service'. As such, he favoured 'the establishment of better relations for their own sake', meaning 'uninterrupted work, greater efficiency and … better output'. To achieve this, there must be a 'higher status for workmen in their places of toil. Better relations could not be established without a fuller sense of partnership in the businesses in which the men are engaged'. Clynes did not favour workers' control, but he did believe that workers should be given a 'share in the responsibility of maintaining discipline and for improving the general internal conditions of workshop life'. Improved conditions must be accompanied by higher real wages for workers. Clynes therefore favoured the use of arbitration and a new system of industrial courts at local level to resolve disciplinary and demarcation problems, as well as the settlement of new processes and changes in machinery. This enlightened approach would run in parallel with voluntary collective bargaining on wages, hours and working conditions. But, Clynes emphasized:

> Improved relations are impossible without organisation. No friendly relationship is possible unless the workmen's organisation is fully recognised and treated as

---

[38]　Labour Party, *Report of the Annual Conference, 1918* (London, 1918).

the agency for advancing the men's interests and settling their affairs. Private or group interests there will continue to be and the more these interests are expressed in the terms of mutual gain from the business and the partnership in many phases of workshop management, the better that it will be for all. Fundamentally the question of industrial systems and ownership can be left untouched. Other principles and methods can in due course deal with these larger issues. We need not wait for a social or industrial revolution to affect great reforms which mean so much with respect to making workshop life less of a burden than it has been up until now. [39]

Conclusions

In the immediate post-war years, Clynes' hopes were quickly dashed by the onset of depression and the arrival of mass unemployment. There was a hankering to restore pre-war economic conditions through cuts in public spending, free trade and balanced budgets. While Labour had become the second largest political party in the House of Commons, the trade unions – after a dramatic growth – fell into sharp decline by 1922. Moreover, the Labour socialism of Clynes and his colleagues was found to be wanting in the resulting economic and social crisis of capitalism. After 1931, the labour movement sought renewal through a fundamental revision of what it meant by socialism with a new focus on the need for economic planning and the public ownership of financial institutions such as clearing banks and insurance companies, as well as the Bank of England.

Nevertheless, Clynes' own commitment to the ideology of Labour socialism, shaped by his experiences of nearly half a century earlier, seemed just as relevant to him in 1934 when he moved a resolution at the TUC on the 'failure of capitalism'. Clynes suggested that such were the evils of the economic system that parliament had to frequently intervene to restrain its excesses, supplemented by trade unions who sought to 'minimise its distresses and to humanise if possible the general conditions of capitalist methods'. He added that parliament had 'frequently misused its powers', as it had done over the recent introduction of the means test for unemployment benefit and the 1927 Trade Disputes and Trade Unions Act. He also saw capitalism as the cause of war. But, true as ever to his belief in parliamentary democracy and voluntarist industrial relations, Clynes argued that if the answer to capitalism was socialism, then this could come about only through the genuine conversion of a free people. 'I do not believe that socialism can come from any artificial devices or through the force merely of a parliamentary decision that may not be backed by the popular will', Clynes insisted. 'Socialism must be submitted in a manner to be so acceptable to the mind and conscience of the people that they

---

[39]   J. R. Clynes, 'The Future of the Workers', *The Globe*, 31 May 1917.

will not only agree to have it but to make it successful when they have got it … It cannot be said that socialism has failed because it never has been tried.'[40]

Clynes remained convinced that Labour socialism's advance would come only through patience, restraint and slow growth as exemplified in the evolution of the movement's self-governing institutions in both political and industrial life. 'The democracy towards which we are irresistibly moving, whatever be the setbacks or diversions, represents in human history a new principle', he wrote. 'Our long established parliamentary institutions responding to a widely enfranchised electorate are the medium through which British labour will modify or revolutionise those conditions of social and industrial life which Labour fervently believes to be wrong.'[41]

In pursuit of this, Clynes remained flexible as to how labour's organizations should develop, seeking to reconcile institutional means to an ideological end. He recognized the crucial importance of autonomous, representative and collective institutions in ensuring labour's advance. His conception of Labour socialism was never the soulless expression of a paternalistic, intrusive state. It involved the pursuit of a delicate balance between political and industrial, parliament and trade unions, producer and citizen, class and nation. But it was also a socialism strongly rooted in the thoughts and actions of his generation of labour pioneers. Above all, what Clynes provided was a very British response to the organizational complexities of the movement. Clynes – perhaps more than any of his contemporaries – came to represent and articulate both in word and action Labour's diversity and breadth during its formative years.

---

[40]   TUC, *Annual Report of the TUC, 1934* (London, 1934), p. 368.
[41]   Tracey, *The Book of the Labour Party*, p. 6.

Chapter 3

Lines of Division:
Railway Unions and Labour, 1900–39

Gerald Crompton

The railway trade unions had a large and early impact on the Labour Party. The Amalgamated Society of Railway Servants (ASRS) moved the resolution at the 1899 Trades Union Congress (TUC) to set up the Labour Representation Committee (LRC), of which it was accordingly a founder affiliate with 60,000 members. The Associated Society of Locomotive Engineers and Firemen (ASLEF) joined the LRC in 1902, with 10,000 members and, like the ASRS, entered the Labour Party on its foundation in 1906. The Railway Clerks' Association (RCA) was slower off the mark, affiliating in 1910 with 9,000 members, but this was precocious for a white-collar organization. Subsequently, the rail unions remained an important element in the party's union base. The ASRS alone was the fourth largest union in 1900, and the third largest in 1920 and 1933, having merged in 1913 into the National Union of Railwaymen (NUR). The NUR affiliated to Labour on the basis of 317,000 members in 1926 and 341,000 in 1931 (out of a total of 387,000 and 295,000 respectively). The RCA signed up for 60,000 and 47,000 in the same years. ASLEF had 60,000 members in 1925 and 53,000 in 1937. The collective influence of the rail unions probably declined slightly after 1920, as their employment base had peaked and the party had a wider spread of affiliations. But Labour constituency parties and local trades councils benefited continuously from the dispersed nature of railway employment. By 1945, the NUR had more than 1,600 branches, ASLEF over 450, and the RCA nearly that number. For this reason, it has often been observed that railway trade unionists 'play[ed] a large part in the general work of the labour movement, especially in the more backward areas'.[1]

Significantly, in the case of both ASLEF and the RCA, the decision to affiliate to Labour was driven by the Taff Vale and Osborne cases respectively, two defining moments in Labour's early history. These both ended relatively happily for the unions, but they were rooted in adversity and exposed considerable internal division along the way. The decision of the Law Lords in 1901 in favour of the Taff Vale Railway Company and against the ASRS cost the union £42,000 and

---

[1] F. W. Dalley, 'Trade Unionism on the Railways', in G. D. H. Cole (ed.), *British Trade Unionism Today* (London: Gollancz, 1939); D. Howell, *MacDonald's Party: Labour Identities and Crisis, 1922–31* (Oxford: Oxford University Press, 2002), p. 419; N. Barou, *British Trade Unions* (London: Gollancz, 1947), p. 244.

threatened to undermine the legal position of unions in future strikes. The conduct of the strike had exacerbated existing differences between ASRS general secretary Richard Bell and another organizer, James Holmes, who had given much more active encouragement to the strikers. The subsequent campaign for obtaining legislative redress for the legal setback – in which rail unions were naturally prominent – underlined the political divisions between Bell and other ASRS leaders, though it greatly raised the profile of the LRC in the process. Whilst Bell remained committed to a 'Lib-Lab' approach that he pursued on some occasions in defiance of his union's policies, others – though often as cautious in outlook as Bell – clearly favoured independent labour politics.

The 1909 Osborne judgement ruled against unions undertaking political expenditure in the interests of their members. Osborne was a Great Eastern porter active in the Walthamstow branch of the ASRS. His own political views were of the Lib-Lab variety, and his original aim had been to stop union funds being spent in promoting 'socialism', i.e. the LRC and then the Labour Party. In this, he undoubtedly had substantial minority support in the union, winning 20 per cent of the vote in one internal ballot, and gaining financial support from branches of other unions.[2] Nevertheless, the effect of the court's ruling was that all political expenditure by unions was *ultra vires*.

In both instances, the reversal of such legal restriction owed much to pressure from the LRC, Labour Party and the unions, ensuring that 'the early years of the Labour Party were inextricably entwined with the politics of railway trade unionism'.[3] Indeed, the mover of the 1899 resolution that formed the LRC, James Holmes, was still speaking at meetings in the 1920s. In so doing, he served 'as a living link with this official tradition'.[4] Yet the railway unions' association with Labour was neither straightforward nor uniform; lines of division were always present and thereby helped shape one of the key relationships within the British labour movement.

Railway Employment and Organization

The most distinctive features of railway employment were the size and the unusual character of its principal institution, the railway companies. Several of the pre-1914 companies were already extremely large in relation to their counterparts in manufacturing. The 'big four' arising from the Railways Act of 1921 were not matched in scale in other sectors of the economy. Before 1914, these companies still enjoyed considerable economic dominance and financial strength. They were

---

[2]   A. J. Reid, 'Labour and the Trade Unions', in D. Tanner. P. Thane and N. Tiratsoo (eds), *Labour's First Century* (Cambridge: Cambridge University Press, 2000), p. 225.

[3]   D. Howell, *Respectable Radicals: Studies in the Politics of Railway Trade Unionism* (Aldershot: Ashgate, 1999), p. 254.

[4]   Ibid.

disciplined by regulation and price control, which increased their intolerance of avoidable costs, such as higher wages. Managerial requirements in terms of discipline and loyalty were little diminished from the early days of the industry. These companies were too strong for the nascent trade unionism of the period and could emerge unscathed from even such a challenge as the national strike of 1911.

After the war, much had changed. The giant groups of post-1923 had to face constantly expanding road competition and major economic problems which first affected their best customers in the heavy industries and, later, encompassed the whole economy. Regulation was burdensome and profits lower than anticipated. The bargaining status of the unions was securely entrenched, and the 1919 strike had conclusively demonstrated their ability to bring the railways to a halt. Management was well aware of its implicit public utility role and of its dependence on the goodwill of government and public opinion for any amelioration of the regulatory position. Shareholder power was weaker than in any other privately-owned sector and the unions did in fact achieve a marked shift in the balance of distribution of the net product of the industry from about 50–50 in 1913 to roughly 75–25 in favour of labour by the early 1930s.[5]

Railway employment provided a powerful focus for the working lives of very large numbers of people – some 643,000, or 4.5 per cent of the labour force, in 1913. The service, as it was usually known, of such large and distinctive companies imposed in itself a strong sense of common identity, but the jobs created by the railways were enormously diverse in their nature, status and associated rewards. This reality underlay the divisions among various grades of worker and the emergence of multiple trade unionism. It is possible to observe here not merely diversity, but competition between different concepts of trade unionism: craft, industrial and white collar. The latter, in the form of the RCA, established in 1897, was atypically strong on the railways in this period and owed something to the co-existence of large numbers of organized manual workers. Tension between the rival pulls of solidarity and sectionalism was not always aligned with boundaries between organizations, but was often a significant element in railway trade unionism.

The NUR, like its largest predecessor, the ASRS, aimed to promote industrial unionism, with a goal of including all railway workers in a single organization. It frequently presented its programmes on an all-grades basis. In this perspective, it was unfortunate that the strongest and most cohesive group of railway employees, the locomen, had been organized since 1880 in ASLEF, a union constituted on sectional lines. The weakest areas of union organization were those closest to the poles of pay and status, the lower grades of manual worker and the higher grades of white-collar staff. The locomen offered a field for competitive recruitment by NUR and ASLEF, with the latter increasingly successful. A statement to the National Wages Board (NWB) in the early 1930s conveyed ASLEF's powerful self-image of 'a good class of men who had worked very earnestly to fit themselves for

---

[5]   *Railway Gazette*, 30 July 1937.

their jobs'.[6] Although ASLEF had in its earlier days presented itself as prudent and moderate, its leaders often took up the argument that the NUR both marginalized the claims of the locomotive grades and was weak. Comments to this effect provided the basis for a successful NUR libel action in 1917. Although, in formal terms, the NUR was oriented towards a wide-ranging solidarity and ASLEF committed to craft exclusiveness, the behaviour of the two unions often escaped from these categories. There were times when positive co-operation was achieved without undue difficulty; other occasions when the NUR could be accused of sectionalism as easily as ASLEF; and also circumstances in which the strength and self-confidence of ASLEF won advances which could be generalized to the advantage of others.

Solidarity emerged most easily in periods of heightened consciousness and trade union activity, as in the three major strikes of 1911, 1919 and 1926, when both union executives and ordinary members mostly worked well together. In quieter times, too, when it was felt that something unusually important to everyone was involved, similar feelings might prevail. ASLEF contributed to the legal expenses of the ASRS in both the Taff Vale case and the Osborne judgement.[7]

It was initiatives by ASLEF in the final stages of the war in 1918, and a credible strike threat in February 1919, which clinched the eight-hour day and guaranteed week, along with other major gains of that year. The effective national strike of September 1919 was to ensure that the government extended to all other grades the principle of standardization upwards, which had already been conceded to the locomen. Unsurprisingly, 1920 was a high water mark of inter-union harmony, with each general secretary making a welcome appearance at the conference of the other union. A low point was reached only four years later in consequence of the locomen's strike, when ASLEF – encouraged by a very favourable membership ballot – took action alone in opposition to the reduction of the mileage allowance. The NUR expressed outrage that ASLEF had rejected a National Wages Board (NWB) report, which had been signed by its own representatives. A circular asked members to work normally and described the ASLEF action as 'a blow at the very principle of collective bargaining'. Predictably, ASLEF then failed to join the unsuccessful all-grades claim made by the other two railway unions and, further, encouraged dissident signalmen within the NUR to break away and form a separate union.[8]

Relations between the RCA and its two fellow organizations were in a lower key than those between the manual unions. It built goodwill among NUR and ASLEF ranks through benevolent neutrality and opposition to blacklegging during their strikes. The RCA did not call a strike itself until 1919, when it took this momentous step (which it proved unnecessary to implement) in order to gain

---

[6]   *Railway Gazette*, 16 December 1932.

[7]   R. Griffiths, *Driven by Ideals: A History of ASLEF* (London: ASLEF, 2005), pp. 32 and 45.

[8]   G. Crompton, '"Squeezing the Pulpless Orange": Labour and Capital on the Railways in the Interwar Years', *Business History*, 21/2 (1989), 66–83.

recognition, which had always been denied by the pre-war companies who were sensitive about the loyalty of their 'confidential' clerical and supervisory staff. The success of the strike call marked a major gain in status and esteem for a union which, in its earlier years, had sported a banner with the slogan 'Defence not Defiance'.

Lack of recognition had by no means nullified the RCA before 1919. Exploitation of its links and affiliations was always a favoured strategy. In 1909, parliamentary obstruction of a North Eastern Railway bill persuaded the company to end its ban on trade unionism for its clerks. Similarly, the Midland in 1913 was prevented from intimidating union members. For such good reasons, the RCA continued to rely more heavily than the other rail unions on platform and press publicity, parliamentary lobbying and obstruction, thereby helping to explain the high importance attached by the union to its Labour and TUC connections. The first sponsored MP was elected in 1923 and, by the following year, the RCA had four MPs, as against three for the NUR and one for ASLEF. By the late 1930s, the RCA had seven MPs to the NUR's four. By the same date, over four-fifths of RCA members had 'contracted in' to pay the political levy to the Labour Party, whereas the corresponding figure for the NUR was nearly two-thirds and, for ASLEF, less than a quarter. By the mid 1920s, it was clear that the railway industry was unique in that a majority of the clerical employees were enrolled in a TUC and Labour-affiliated union which could be credibly called on to join a general strike. It was also clear that the figures for formal political activity did not correlate with levels of industrial militancy or class consciousness.[9]

Leaders and Members

Contrast has often been drawn between the two long-serving general secretaries of the NUR and ASLEF: J. H. Thomas (1916–31) and John Bromley (1914–36). Both were accomplished bargainers, proficient speakers and generally dominant in their own organizations. Both were Labour MPs as well as trade unionists. Thomas could serve as a model of the conservative union leader, alert to the interests of the employers, anxious to avoid conflict, fearful of its consequences, proud of the achievements of his union and of the bargaining machinery it had established. In politics, always a populist nationalist, he moved so far to the right that he deserted Labour in 1931 to join the National government. Bromley was a respectable but often combative craft unionist, assertive about the traditions and rules of his organization. He was obviously influenced by a wider political radicalism than Thomas' business unionist outlook. His political statements were inconsistent, and often on subjects outside his union activities, but at times he appeared to hold revolutionary perspectives, as at the Leeds Convention of 1917. He was for some time friendly towards, and well regarded by, many communist activists.

---

[9]   Dalley, 'Trade Unionism', p. 306.

More recently, however, it has been argued by David Howell that the differences between Thomas and Bromley were less than is commonly assumed, beyond the somewhat erratic rhetoric of the latter. Both were experienced operators in a rule-based bargaining system, within which their room for manoeuvre was restricted by the mood swings of their membership and the deteriorating economic circumstances from the late 1920s. Significant similarities can be seen in several respects, particularly in their hostile attitude towards the miners during the 1926 General Strike.[10]

In Thomas' case, his well-known preference for calling off the strike as soon as possible was not surprising. For Bromley, however, 1926 has been described as 'a Rubicon'.[11] He joined Thomas and other members of the TUC general council in supporting the ending of the strike without obtaining guarantees against victimization, and without any improved terms acceptable to the miners. Indeed, Bromley proceeded to polemicize against the miners whilst they were still locked out, releasing TUC documents to his own union journal in order to justify the actions of the general council. He persuaded the 1926 ASLEF conference to back the decision to terminate the strike, partly by making sneering and condescending attacks on the miners (reminiscent of remarks by Thomas on the same subject). In early 1927, however, the ASLEF executive rejected the TUC general council's report on the strike and, at the TUC special inquest conference soon afterwards, the union was one of a minority which sided with the miners against the general council. It was Bromley's conduct at this time which primarily explains his characterization as 'a flawed colossus' by the union's most recent historian.[12]

But such controversies raise a wider issue. Another important, if usually latent, line of division among railway workers was that between leaders and rank-and-file, and sometimes between leaders and lay activists. This is apparent both in differences in material conditions and prestige, as well as in occasional revealing expressions of contempt by leaders for followers. One response to the events of 1926 came from Thomas' fellow NUR leader, Charlie Cramp, who explained that whilst he did not blame the general council for calling the strike off, 'I do blame our people who for years had made it impossible for the General Council to resist the general strike'.[13] Bromley committed to paper his view of his own executive in 1922: '[The] majority of them are illiterate, extremely ignorant of the trade union and labour movement, and barren of ideals'.[14]

Within the RCA, A. G. Walkden – general secretary between 1906 and 1936 – had probably as many admirers and fewer enemies than either Thomas or Bromley in their respective organizations. The union's historian, while appreciative of his contribution, concludes that 'he had been something of a dictator'; that 'it was

---

[10]   Howell, *Respectable Radicals*, chapter 7.

[11]   Ibid., p. 278.

[12]   Griffiths, *Driven by Ideals*, p. 138.

[13]   Howell, *Respectable Radicals*, p. 322.

[14]   Griffiths, *Driven by Ideals*, p. 96.

not unknown for Walkden to act first, and then tell the [executive committee] later what he had done'. His successor 'played down the personality cult which had developed in Walkden's time', as he felt uneasy at the frequent references to 'Our General', 'Our Leader' and the 'Captain of the RCA Ship'. The union's headquarters were later named 'Walkden House'. A contributor to the debate over his successor's salary (which was lower than Walkden's) asserted that 'trade unions spoiled their leaders'.[15] Thomas had, of course, been spoiled more than most. After the 1919 strike, NUR members gave him more than £2,500, raised by collection, to buy and furnish a house in Dulwich.[16]

Attempts were made to organize independent rank-and-file opposition to both management and, if need be, to official union policy. In the late 1920s, the lead was taken by the Railwaymen's Minority Movement (RMM), a section of the communist-led National Minority Movement (NMM). This contained some able and energetic activists – including its principal leader, W. C. Loeber, a London carriage cleaner – and produced some lively local bulletins. More regular publications from the same stable – such as *Labour Monthly* – also provided a focus for railway militants. The RMM and the communist-influenced Labour Research Department (LRD) produced several vigorous and well-informed pamphlets relating downward pressure on railway wages to wider issues of capitalist crisis and rationalization.[17] One comment on the NUR's voluntary acceptance of pay cuts in 1928 suggested that Thomas' achievement should be commemorated by an illuminated address depicting a kneeling railway director in each corner, a top hat rampant in the top centre, and a coffin containing the all-grades programme in the bottom centre.[18] The RMM, however, suffered increasingly from the constraints imposed by the Communist Party of Great Britain's (CPGB) sectarian 'class against class' policy (1928–34), which discouraged participation in official union bodies, and by TUC proscriptions of CPGB and NMM members. More effective was the reconstituted Railwaymen's Vigilance Movement and its regular publication, the *Railway Vigilant*, from 1933 onwards. This followed a strategy of working through the official machinery, and had an impact outside its own ranks in strengthening demand for restoration of pay cuts and resistance to attacks on conditions. Several future executive members and full-time officials, including one general secretary, came through its ranks.

---

[15]   M. Wallace, *Single or Return? The History of the Transport Salaried Staffs Association* (London: TSSA, 1996), chapter 19.

[16]   P. S. Bagwell, *The Railwaymen: History of the National Union of Railwaymen* (London: Allen & Unwin, 1963), p. 399.

[17]   RMM, *November 13th – What it means to Railway Workers* (London: RMM, 1930); RMM, *Railway Nationalization – The Argument in a Nutshell* (London: RMM, 1931); LRD, *Wages and Profits on the Railways* (London: LRD, 1932).

[18]   Bagwell, *The Railwaymen*, pp. 521–3; Crompton, '"Squeezing the Pulpless Orange"', pp. 73–5; G. Crompton, '"Good Business for the Nation": The Railway Nationalization Issue, 1921–47', *Journal of Transport History*, 20/2 (1999), 148.

The demands of work did not by any means prevent railway workers from filling their off-duty hours actively and variously. Education was probably taken most seriously by the three unions; the NUR and RCA were closely – and sometimes controversially – involved with Ruskin College and the National Council of Labour Colleges. But there was much else of a less demanding nature. Within the RCA, 'whist drives, annual dinners and dances were held, rambling and Esperanto groups flourished, and the London divisional councils jointly held an annual concert'. The annual conference was also the 'pinnacle' of the union's social life, with dinners, dances and concerts complementing fringe meetings.[19] Glasgow branches formed a male voice choir, which toured the UK both to entertain and promote the RCA and the trade union movement. Several branches were particularly enterprising. In Dublin, an RCA club was set up with a library and many facilities. Sport was an activity specially favoured within this union, which had run football and cricket teams from its very early days. A divisional council in Scotland founded a golf club in 1925, two years after the launch of an RCA Inter-Railways London Nightworkers' Football League. A cricket section followed the next year. Some members, notably Thomas Groom and Maurice Bunyan, became sports organizers in a wider trade union framework, exchanging tours with comparable sporting organizations on the continent. This activity was conducted initially through the British Workers' Sports Federation. After rifts with communist-affiliated elements, Bunyan was later prominent in the TUC-approved British Workers' Sports Association, encouraging RCA participation. At least a marginal motive in the development of trade union sport was to respond to the building of expensive sports clubs by the railway companies. This was resented both because the cost was perceived as equivalent to a deduction from wages, and because of the implicit rivalry for workers' participation.[20]

What is certain is that the railway companies offered an alternative framework within which much sport and leisure was organized. The most paternalist of the interwar 'big four', the Great Western Railway (GWR), was especially prominent in this respect. In 1923, the GWR inaugurated a Social and Educational Union (SEU), which replaced the long-standing GWR Temperance Union. A major reason for this change was that 'intemperance had become practically non-existent among Great Western employees', and that a new body with a different name might have more success in promoting similar aims, namely 'to encourage sports and pastimes, to form choirs and orchestras, to arrange concerts and similar functions'.[21] The SEU and its successor, the GWR Staff Association, catered for virtually all mainstream sports, often at the company's many own sports grounds. Football, rugby union, hockey, tennis, swimming, rifle shooting, athletics and bowling were all mentioned in the company magazine. Other organized spare time activities included debating, chess, music in many forms, opera, dancing, drama (from farce

---

[19]   Wallace, *Single or Return?*, chapter 18.

[20]   Ibid.

[21]   *Great Western Railway Magazine*, January 1923.

to Shakespeare), fur and feather, scouting, arts and crafts, and horticultural and floral exhibitions. Directors and senior staff, from the chairman downwards, took part regularly in meetings, functions, carnivals and prize-givings. The larger social occasions would often be attended by a director who lived in the region, while such activities were supported by the many halls, institutes, clubs and reading rooms provided by the company. The GWR's paternalist stance was completed by a number of schemes for material assistance to staff or their dependents in various kinds of need. There were convalescent homes, a medical fund which ran a substantial hospital at Swindon, a 'helping hand' fund for distressed – mainly sick – employees, assistance with housing and, via the GWR's membership of the Railway Benevolent Institution, annuities for widows and care for orphans. It was this range of social and cultural facilities and fringe benefits which underlay the management's frequent invocation of the 'family' or 'big happy family' of employees. The company made consistent efforts to construct and maintain its caring image, making a strong continuing bid for the primary loyalty of its staff.[22]

One hard line of division among railway workers was that between male and female employees. The companies, like most employers before 1945, operated a marriage bar, according to which women were required to resign when they married. Company magazines contain frequent references to female employees 'resigning on marriage', or 'leaving the service to be married'. This practice does not appear to have been challenged, although other radical notions for the time, such as equal pay, were certainly raised within the unions. The main operating grades did not normally recruit women, and so female employees experienced both vertical and horizontal segregation, being heavily concentrated in a number of distinct sections and much less likely than male colleagues to be promoted to higher grades. The earliest employment of women was probably in refreshment rooms, and then – on the London, Midland and Scottish Railway (LMS) – in the carriage and wagon works at Derby. Eventually, clerical work became predominant, with a major niche in railway hotels. New specialisms in company telephone exchanges, of which the LMS had more than 300, emerged in the interwar years. Certainly, gender stereotyping was alive and well in this period. A female welfare assistant, writing on 'why do we work?' in the *LMS Magazine* in 1939, noted that women 'are eminently fitted for certain types of work; that in the offices we can be neat, accurate and quick in setting out letters and figures; in the workshops our fingers are nimble and the jobs go through; in our contacts with the public, on the telephone, at stations and on steamers, we can be courteous, helpful and sympathetic – all of which adds to the efficiency of the service'.[23] This issue of the magazine was enthusiastic about 'the important and integral part they play in our great organization'. It did not merely pay tribute to traditional female virtues, but also made a link with modernity, pointing out that the mechanization of office work in the interwar period had promoted the employment of women. The GWR

---

[22]   See *Great Western Railway Magazine*, 1923–39.

[23]   *LMS Magazine*, April 1939.

acknowledged in 1938 that, since the war, women had become 'a permanent part of our organization'. Although few had by then reached retirement age, it was decided that the time had come to establish a pension fund for female clerks. In a few cases, female employment was of much longer standing. In 1935, the manageress of the refreshment rooms at Bristol Temple Meads retired after having worked there since 1886. Occasionally, women were appointed to more senior positions, such as the 'representative' in the superintendent of the line's office. She was confidently said by the GWR to be 'the first saleswoman to act for a British railway company', with a brief to keep in touch with all kinds of women's organizations to promote outings and excursions.[24]

The Great War (1914–18) had, of course, boosted the recruitment of women. Whereas just over 4,500 were employed in 1914, the figure reached almost 56,000 by the end of the war, including porters, cleaners, ticket collectors and signal workers. This was considerably smaller than the number of male employees who had left for the armed forces. Nevertheless, the increase was sufficiently compelling to persuade the NUR in 1915 to reverse a decision of only two years earlier and admit women to membership. It had originally been a major concern of the union that the companies 'would make the cheaper labour of women a permanent substitute for that of the men who had enlisted'. A guarantee was obtained in 1915 that returning employees would be re-engaged in positions as senior as those previously occupied. It remained the policy of the union, however, that temporary workers should be paid at the minimum rate for the relevant grade and the NUR was not yet prepared to accept the permanence of female employment.

The attitude of management was less favourable to women. Some companies were not willing to pay the minimum, and the union gained satisfaction on this principle only after threatening to end the wartime industrial truce – the only such threat during the war. The employers also insisted that the war bonus, which became an increasingly important part of total remuneration, should be smaller for women than for men (20 shillings and 6d instead of 33 shillings by the end of the war). This stance was justified with the implausibly precise claim that women's labour was only three-fifths as productive as men's. Many NUR members were much more supportive of the female staff than the union leadership, with several district councils passing resolutions in favour of equal pay.[25] Although some women were taken on by the railways as cleaners of engines rather than the more usual floors, ASLEF did not see this as particularly alarming. The union did employ three female clerks in place of men who had gone to the war. In 1924 it set up an internally separate 'women's society', claimed as 'the first ... ever to be attached to a trade union in Britain, and headed by the wife of the general secretary'.[26]

24   *Great Western Railway Magazine*, October 1936.

25   Bagwell, *The Railwaymen*, pp. 357–9.

26   Griffiths, *Driven by Ideals*, pp. 70–72; N. McKillop, *The Lighted Flame: A History of ASLEF* (London: Nelson, 1950), p. 162.

Employment of women in clerical grades expanded rapidly during the war, and then went into steep decline before growth was resumed from a much lower base some 10 years later. The RCA had responded quickly to the new opportunities and signed up more than 13,600 women members by 1918, out of about 25,000. This success faded and a low point of 2,600 was recorded in 1927. A steady rise then ensued, to a figure of 6,350 in 1938, just over half of the total. The RCA was, not surprisingly, the railway union in which female members were most prominent. It had decided as early as 1907 to recruit women, although none actually joined until 1910. A policy of equal pay was adopted in 1914, shortly before the outbreak of war. The first woman delegate attended the annual conference in 1915. In 1930, a woman was elected to the national executive. The annual conference of 1935 passed a resolution for the immediate application of equal pay, against strong opposition from the leadership which urged that the economic situation made it unfeasible to change the women clerks' agreement with the companies. After the executive ignored this decision, a repeat debate the following year ended in another vote in favour of priority for equal pay, though only after the general secretary had described his leading female critic as 'a dangerous woman'. A long-standing demand that the RCA should appoint a national women's organizer met with apparent success in 1938, but few members applied and the post was not filled. This drew complaints at the 1939 conference that the salary offered was lower than the pay of head office male clerical staff.[27]

Collective Bargaining

Some lines of division during this period were chronological rather than sectional. Between 1900 and 1914, an impressive growth in union membership was not reflected in any substantial improvement in pay. Despite the first widespread strike in 1911, the companies succeeded in denying even full recognition to the unions, which had to rely on the unsatisfactory conciliation machinery. The Great War proved to be a turning point and, subsequently, the 1920s and 1930s were decades of strikingly different character. Important advances had been made during the period of government control between 1914 and 1921, including recognition of, first, the manual unions and then the RCA. The guaranteed eight-hour day and the guaranteed week had been obtained in 1919, and a week's paid holiday in 1920. The new negotiating machinery, given statutory approval in 1921, entrenched union recognition. The 1919 strike had already emphasized the ability of the unions to organize an effective national stoppage. In 1920, the principle had been accepted of a limited sliding scale for wages, subject to a base rate for each grade. This was briefly unpopular, but when prices fell from late 1920 pay declined by less than the cost of living. It was also beneficial that a general pay increase had been obtained in mid-1920, close to the peak of the post-war inflation, and on comparative rather

---

[27]   Wallace, *Single or Return?*, chapters 8 and 17.

than cost-of-living grounds. New standard rates of pay were adopted in early 1920 on the basis of percentages (at least 100) above the pre-war figure.

This new bargaining machinery was a clear example of Britain's 'first industrial relations system', which had emerged between the 1890s and the end of the war. Often dubbed 'collective laissez-faire', it was based on industry-wide regulation of industrial relations, and was believed to provide the best way to contain economic and social instability, especially in conditions of extensive growth, competition and fragmented ownership. The state was now supportive of such institutions, through both legislation and a range of departmental initiatives, having abandoned the hostile judge-driven strategies of the 1900s. Employers' motives for the adoption of the new system were more deeply rooted in export industries such as coal and cotton than in the circumstances of the railways, where domestic competition was much more restricted. However, the unforeseen threat to railway prosperity from both road competition and economic depression were factors which would have caused much greater instability in the interwar years in the absence of the new arrangements. The increased emphasis on bargaining at industry level shifted power upwards in the unions and enhanced the authority of national officials.[28]

Railway workers were conscious throughout the 1920s of enjoying greatly improved living standards and working conditions, especially by comparison with the very unsatisfactory situation before 1914. They were aware of having retained more of their war-related gains than their counterparts in other trades, having avoided any major defeat in the early 1920s. Indeed, they became – allegedly – a good example of the category of workers in 'sheltered' or 'protected' industries, which were often contrasted with the hard-hit export sectors. But the plight of these industries was itself a source of pressure for the reduction of transport costs and, therefore, of railway wages. Nevertheless, the unions managed through the NWB to resist demands from the employers for cuts in pay and conditions in 1923 and 1925. The main setbacks were the institution of 'spread-over' to nine or 10 hours instead of the strict eight-hour day in 1922, the reduction of mileage payments for locomen in 1924 (delayed by the ASLEF strike), and the withdrawal of the war bonus for new entrants in 1926. A blip occurred in 1928, when the unions were sufficiently alarmed by the deterioration in freight receipts to concede a voluntary 2.5 per cent wage cut for all employees, including managers and directors. This was done partly to avoid a more radical package of economy measures initially demanded by management. Thomas of the NUR described the agreement as 'the best ever made', and won the endorsement of a delegate conference by a margin of 77–2. This was not simply a reflection of Thomas' personal influence and persuasiveness, but a broader vote of confidence in the long-term success of NUR policies. The finances of the railways then improved

---

[28]   C. Howell, *Trade Unions and the State* (Princeton: Princeton University Press, 2005), chapter 3.

definitely though briefly, reaching a peak for net revenue in 1929. The 1928 cut was restored in May 1930.[29]

The major change in climate came when the impact of world depression was felt from late 1930 onwards. A reduction of around 4.75 per cent was conceded amid difficult circumstances in mid-1931. By 1932–3, the companies were back with a serious bid to replace this with a cut of 10 per cent. Firm resistance set in at that point. The chairman of the NWB reported in favour of a smaller reduction than the companies were seeking, but his authority was rejected by all the union executives, and the employers declined to enforce his decision unilaterally. The NWB, which had been badly split, was eventually reconstituted as the Railway Staff National Tribunal. It was a tribute to the defensive strength of the unions that, for those railway workers who kept their jobs, the drop in earnings between 1931 and 1934 was no more than 2 or 3 per cent. But the 1930s proved to be a different world from the 1920s. It was obvious that the railways failed to share in the generally quite strong economic recovery of 1933 to 1937. During this period, average earnings rose by about 4.7 per cent, while the cost of living rose by 12 per cent. It took six years for the unions to achieve the restoration of the 1931 pay cuts. Railway pay lagged behind the average after money wages and prices resumed their general upward movement from 1934. The renewed depression of 1937–8 hit the railway sector harder than most, and it became the first major industry to threaten absolute cuts in pay since recovery had begun in 1933.[30]

The labour force also had to experience an unpleasant deterioration in conditions, amid widespread complaints about the 'economania' and relentless rationalization practiced by management. There were redundancies, an extension of partial payment by results systems (bonus elements in earnings in relation to miles travelled or tonnage handled), increased employment of young workers, partly at the expense of those in adult grades, greater use of seasonal and casual workers, 'de-grading' of jobs (tasks carried out by employees in a lower grade than previously), and the blocking of promotion opportunities through the device of 'putting-back' (effectively, temporary demotion for an unspecified period) from higher to lower paid work. Footplate staff worked long hours of overtime, even when 'put-back' drivers and firemen were firing and cleaning respectively. From a management angle, all this was a necessary response to crisis. It was for them an achievement to have reduced the labour force by some 200,000 between 1921 and the low point in 1933, to have cut costs almost in line with falling receipts through the late 1920s and early 1930s, and then to have contained the increase below the general level of inflation.

---

[29]   Crompton, '"Squeezing the Pulpless Orange"', pp. 66–70.

[30]   G. Crompton, '"Efficient and Economical Working"?: The Performance of the Railway Companies, 1923–33', *Business History*, 27/2 (1985), 231–5; Crompton, '"Squeezing the Pulpless Orange"', pp. 71–80.

Nationalization

A continuing concern of the railway unions throughout the whole period was the issue of public ownership, especially of their own industry. There was no shortage of reasons why railway workers should favour nationalization. The industry was unique in the extent to which it had been progressively subjected to state regulation. Before 1900, governments had intervened to specify the running of cheap trains, the publication of rates and fares, the standardization of accounting systems, maximum hours of work (even for adult males), signalling and braking technologies and, most crucially, from 1894, maximum fares. These measures had mostly been taken in order to prevent corruption and preserve competition, or by concern for the welfare of passengers rather than employees.[31] But regulation was obviously capable of being taken further, and given a different orientation. Furthermore, government worries about monopolistic tendencies almost invited the response that the only safe owner of a monopoly was the state.

Advocacy of nationalization did not originate with the unions or the Labour Party. Rather, it built on an existing tradition of belief that public ownership of the railways 'would benefit the national community and not just railway employees'. Some of the characteristic metaphors used in this 'national interest' discourse were that railways should be regarded as 'beasts of burthen to the nation', as a 'national means', not a business, or as circulatory 'life blood' for the community. To this 'national interest' approach was added a 'left' perspective by socialists and trade unionists, who believed that state ownership was appropriate for all major sectors of the economy and/or that it would serve the interests of railway employees.[32]

The ASRS had first adopted a policy of nationalization of the industry in 1894.[33] The TUC called for railway nationalization in 1896; the Labour Party, despite its original distaste for programmes and a vague, rhetorical resolution in 1908, was by 1914 more specifically in favour of nationalizing railways, mines and canals.[34] ASLEF adopted a policy of nationalization of the railways in 1909.[35] The RCA first committed itself to railway nationalization in 1910, also on the basis that this would be in the interests of the whole community. In its first appearance at a Labour Party conference in 1911, the union won approval for a motion that the

---

[31]   T. R. Gourvish, 'The Regulation of Britain's Railways: Past, Present and Future', in L. Andersson-Skog and O. Krantz (eds), *Institutions in the Transport and Communications Industries* (Canton: Science History Publications, 1999), pp. 117–32.

[32]   D. C. H. Watts, 'On the Causes of British Railway Nationalization: A Re-examination of the Railway Question between 1866 and 1921', *Contemporary British History*, 16/2 (2002), 6–15.

[33]   Bagwell, *The Railwaymen*, p. 238.

[34]   D. Howell, *British Social Democracy: A Study in Development and Decay* (London: Croom Helm, 1976), p. 29.

[35]   Griffiths, *Driven by Ideals*, pp. 46–7.

state should have the right at any future date to acquire the railway companies for 25 years' purchase of annual earnings.[36]

The RCA continued to press the issue, with Walkden serving as secretary of the Railway Nationalization Society (RNS). In February 1914, he personally lobbied the prime minister and was told that a royal commission was imminent. Walkden's next initiative came at the 1916 TUC, repeating the nationalization demand and adding a call for trade unionists to share in management.[37] By 1917, the ASLEF leader John Bromley was also sitting on the executive of the RNS and, later that year, his union sent two motions to the Labour conference. The first called for 'complete control of the railways for the people' through state purchase. The second proposed that a committee representing the Labour executive, the three rail unions and the RNS should draft a scheme for nationalization. Also in 1917, at a special conference of the NUR on 'After War Matters', Thomas claimed it would be 'nothing short of madness to talk of railway nationalization alone', as it was 'not a mere "railway" problem, but a "transport" problem affecting the nation as a whole'. Neither he nor the conference, however, made any further proposals on these lines. Despite his union's adoption of the principle of equal representation of workers in management, Thomas made it clear that he 'did not want the railways to be run by railwaymen'. This was one of the first indications of the potential of this subject for intra-union disagreement and confusion.[38]

The RCA had by now developed its own policy for a co-ordinated 'united national public service of communications and transport', 'with a steadily increasing participation of the organised workers in the management', winning agreement on this at both the Labour and TUC conferences in 1918.[39] In an increasingly promising political atmosphere, the RCA next prepared – 'as a propaganda exercise' – a National Transport Services Bill, covering nationalization, co-ordination and workers' participation. A minister of transport and communications would be the key policy figure, but six commissioners would manage the network on his behalf, three of whom would be appointed by the government from nominees of the railway unions. The RNS accepted the superiority of the RCA document to its own, but cautioned that the workers' representatives should remain responsible to their constituency.

It now seemed that both nationalization and workers' participation were serious political possibilities. When Geddes introduced a bill in early 1919 giving the government powers to nationalize transport, he conceded the crucial point that 'in the past private interest made for development, but today I think I may say that it makes for colossal waste'. Even so, the government – under pressure from both the Railway Companies Association and the Federation of British Industries – changed its mind on nationalization. The RCA response was to revise its earlier

---

[36]   Wallace, *Single or Return?*, pp. 3–14.

[37]   Ibid., pp. 6–7.

[38]   Bagwell, *The Railwaymen*, p. 370.

[39]   Wallace, *Single or Return?*, pp. 7–11.

scheme and, in association with ASLEF, to put forward a parliamentary bill for nationalization based on the issue of 60-year bonds as compensation for railway shares. The number of commissioners was now to be seven, with three nominated by the unions. The bill was eventually presented – unsuccessfully – in the House of Commons by Thomas in 1921. By then the government had devised a new method of returning the railways to private ownership, based on a limited number of giant companies formed by compulsory merger. However, a White Paper of June 1920 confirmed the government's intention to provide places for elected representatives of the workforce on the boards of the new companies. It looked as if the loss of the public ownership objective would be compensated with success on the other main union goal. Yet, not only did the railway companies oppose such a measure with predictable vigour, but doubt set in on the union side too. After the principle had been accepted on more than one occasion by all three railway unions, the retreat was led by the NUR. By May 1921, the unions reached agreement with the companies over new bargaining machinery for the industry to be included in the forthcoming Railways Act. The idea of worker-directors was dropped. For Thomas, the main value of the principle had probably been as a bargaining counter, to help obtain improvements in the pay determination system. Others, especially in ASLEF and the RCA, questioned the value of minority representation on boards which would still be accountable to railway shareholders.

The legislation of 1921 could be interpreted either as a halfway house to nationalization, or as the most effective alternative to it. A resolution at the 1924 conference of the NUR took the optimistic line, welcoming the grouping as a step towards state ownership and control. This, however, attracted an amendment which 'condemned such a gradualist perspective as naïve', viewing the amalgamations not as a positive move towards nationalization, but rather as a measure of capitalist rationalization in post-war circumstances. The executive was asked to produce a bill for both public ownership and 'democratic control', but the ambiguities in this concept were not resolved.[40]

The Railways Act was 'an apparently authoritative settlement' and certainly removed nationalization from the political agenda for at least a few years. Within a decade, however, the rail unions found that opportunity had recurred, and that the case for public ownership could now command wider sympathy. The unexpectedly poor financial performance of the 'big four' companies was a trigger to declining confidence in the regulatory system. But this reflected other critical developments, such as the rise of road competition and the depressed condition of the staple industries. Both the Balfour Committee on Trade and Industry, reporting in 1929, and the Boscawen Commission on Transport (1931) provided highly respectable support for the unification of the transport system. The latter had a wide brief and Walkden of the RCA took confident advantage of its request for evidence, submitting a 60-paragraph plan for nationalization. Under a controlling and co-ordinating ministry, a Railway Board (covering canals and ferries also) and a Road

[40]   Howell, *Respectable Radicals*, pp. 259–60.

Board would each be run by a chairman and six commissioners (three experts and three worker representatives, who would be nominated by their unions but would then resign from membership). Consumers would not be represented at this level, but would have voice through advisory boards. Walkden also proposed the building of a Channel tunnel as a joint venture with French railways, the standardization of railway equipment, and the commercial development of railway land and station premises. In contrast, the NUR's proposals, occupying 16 lines of a single printed page, were 'perfunctory' and the performance of its joint general secretary, Cramp, showed 'a lack of thought about either national control or national ownership'.[41] There was some irony here, as Cramp had frequently sought to present the NUR's attitude to politics and collective bargaining as based on reason (or science) and mastery of detail, thereby differing from that of other unions, especially ASLEF.[42]

The RCA evidence both 'foreshadowed much of the legislation passed between 1930–47' and influenced the main report of the commission.[43] This was positive in its attitude to both co-ordination and unification of the transport system, though it flinched from 'raising political differences of a party character' – i.e. from calling for nationalization. Rather, co-ordination was expected to develop gradually by natural processes. However, a minority addendum, signed by three members who had been appointed to the commission by the 1929–31 Labour government, explicitly advocated public ownership under a National Transport Trust, which would operate 'for service rather than profit' under the leadership of directors and managers chosen solely on grounds of individual ability.[44] This went further than the majority, but indicated that the three had similarly bought into the new concept of a public corporation as the appropriate vehicle for public ownership. The main elements of post-1945 Morrisonian nationalization were clearly present in their addendum. The three rail unions had, somewhat characteristically, failed to consult together over their evidence to the commission. A special joint committee from the three executives, however, called for nationalization under a National Transport Authority, and sent a deputation to the prime minister in the spring of 1931. This followed the significant pay cuts announced by the NWB in March of that year. The union representatives on the NWB had issued a memorandum underlining the necessity of public ownership and control of transport. [45]

From this time onwards, a commitment to the nationalization of the whole transport sector, and to some kind of representation of workers at high level, became the common currency of the rail unions. Planning, nationalization and

---

[41] Ibid., p. 251.

[42] *Railway Review*, 8 February 1924; Howell, *MacDonald's Party*, p. 59.

[43] Bagwell, *The Railwaymen*, p. 529.

[44] G. Crompton, 'The Railway Companies and the Nationalization Issue', in R. Millward and J. Singleton (eds), *The Political Economy of Nationalization in Britain, 1920–50* (Cambridge: Cambridge University Press, 1995), p. 121.

[45] Bagwell, *The Railwaymen*, p. 530.

socialism were embraced by virtually the whole spectrum of union opinion 'as alternatives to the uncertainties, inefficiencies and moral reprehensibilities of capitalism'.[46] The importance of the issue was continually reinforced by economic depression and by the cold climate for pay bargaining. Labour was politically weak after 1931, but the basic argument for comprehensive public ownership appeared to have been won within the party and the unions. The policy statement of 1932, *The National Planning of Transport*, established this point securely. Subsequently, major party documents such as *For Socialism and Peace* (1934) and *Labour's Immediate Programme* (1937) contained references, if not precise short-term commitments, to transport nationalization. Implementation was not, of course, feasible until the Transport Act of 1947, within two years of the parliamentary majority of 1945. From 1932, the distinctive emphasis of Labour's approach, strongly led by Herbert Morrison, was on public ownership as 'good business for the nation' and on the superiority of national to private ownership in terms of efficiency. 'Independent and disinterested management' was the key to success, with non-political and non-representative institutions in charge, owing only a loose responsibility to parliament.[47]

This position prevailed, and determined the form of nationalization adopted in 1947. It had to survive a number of challenges in the course of the 1930s. Some came from railway trade unionists who continued to believe that industrial democracy required direct representation of workers on any proposed transport board. Divisions were evident, however, and union leaders such as Walkden and Cramp successfully supported Morrison in debates on this issue at both the 1932 TUC and Labour conferences. The RCA was plunged into internal controversy between 1933 and 1935 in attempts to define its own line, which eventually favoured a compromise in the form of worker membership of the board, but on a strictly non-delegate, non-representative basis.[48] Despite occasional reverses, the Morrisonian view remained dominant. Discontent with the new line was, however, never completely eradicated within the rail unions; perhaps not surprisingly, given that the NUR had from 1914 favoured 'substantial representation of the workers on the board of management'. The first conference after the 1945 election passed a resolution asserting that workers' participation in management was essential for the success of nationalization. The union's historian has pointed to the lack among the members at this time of 'any strong sense that the railways were *their concern* in whose future they had an important voice'. These worries were responsible for a flurry of interest in the subject of 'workers' control' in the union journal in the years from 1946 to 1948.[49] ASLEF also registered rapid disillusionment with the governance structure of the new nationalized railways, with a popular speech at the

---

[46]   M. Worley, *Labour Inside the Gate: A History of the British Labour Party between the Wars* (London: I. B. Tauris, 2004), p. 159.

[47]   Crompton, 'Good Business for the Nation', 144–51.

[48]   Wallace, *Single or Return?* chapter 17.

[49]   Bagwell, *The Railwaymen*, p. 623.

1948 conference lamenting that 'workers' control of industry seems as far away as ever'. Resolutions were passed calling for operating grades to be represented on management boards and for the removal of any administrators found to be working against the interests of the industry.[50] The TUC in the same year demanded greater workers' participation in the control of the railways and other industries. For all the genuine enthusiasm for nationalization shown by the rail unions over the years, it finally arrived in the form of a public corporation with marked similarities to large private companies, with conventional management hierarchies and industrial relations, and with a lack of significance for central economic planning. The interwar debates had failed to achieve clarity or to anticipate all the issues which would be relevant in the post-war world.[51]

Conclusion

The rail unions contributed heavily both to the emergence of the Labour Party and its development into a national political force, and to the regulation of the relations between party and unions during the fluctuations and uncertainties of the 1920s. The first phase included the foundation of the party and the response to Taff Vale and the Osborne judgement, through to the end of the Great War. The second period covered such episodes as the national rail strike of 1919, the 1924 strike and the first Labour government, the General Strike of 1926, and the collapse of the second Labour government in 1931.[52] The 1919 strike not only consolidated the new strength of the unions in terms of pay and bargaining structures, but because of its obvious significance for both the national economy and national politics, induced wide recognition of the need for greater unity and co-ordination between labour's political and trade union institutions. The principal long-term survivors from a range of initiatives were the TUC general council, the National Joint Council (with Labour and TUC representatives), and various local mergers of Labour parties and trades councils.[53] The 1924 ASLEF strike, along with industrial action by the transport workers, helped to confirm notions of separate spheres for Labour governments and unions. ASLEF, in the teeth of strong NUR disapproval, showed its willingness to practice industrial business as usual, despite the recent arrival of Labour in government. The new government demonstrated its readiness to threaten its trade union allies with the Emergency Powers Act. The events of 1926 further confirmed the separateness of the spheres: principally for the negative reason that the unions were seriously weakened by the outcome and suffered a reduction in both appetite and ability to take large-scale strike action in opposition

---

[50] Griffiths, *Driven by Ideals*, pp. 162–3.

[51] Crompton, 'Good Business for the Nation', 149–57.

[52] L. Minkin, *The Contentious Alliance: Trade Unions and the Labour Party* (Edinburgh: Edinburgh University Press, 1991), chapters 1 and 2.

[53] Ibid., pp. 18–20.

to government policy. The Labour Party, despite its extreme ineffectiveness in supporting the unions in 1926, subsequently experienced a renewed surge of union support, as the ballot box appeared to offer better prospects than strike action and because – as after 1901 and 1909 – both the party and the unions wished to remove the punitive legislation of 1927, which harmed them both financially and organizationally. As we have seen, the rail unions were inevitably split in reaction to the ending of the strike, with Thomas, Bromley and others prominent in defending the surrender. In 1931, when Labour suffered the defection of several leading ministers to the Conservative-dominated National government, there was again a split. This time Thomas was almost isolated among rail unionists, though he succeeded in retaining his parliamentary seat at Derby with the support of some of his former members. Almost all sections of the unions could agree about the necessity for government–union consultation in future crises. After 1931, despite increased turbulence in industrial relations in their own industry, the influence of the rail unions was less pronounced, and Labour was politically more stable, though scarcely successful. The main exception was the major issue of nationalization, where the rail unions helped to consolidate the party's evolution towards a new programmatic version of socialism and national planning.

Chapter 4
Deadweight or Bedrock?
The Mineworkers and Labour

Andrew Taylor

The Mineworkers' Federation of Great Britain's (MFGB) formal relationship with the Labour Party begins with the MFGB's affiliation to Labour in 1908. For 10 years, this was a contested relationship. The mineworkers and Labour became synonymous because of the 1914–18 war, the franchise extension in 1918, Arthur Henderson's reorganization of the party, and Labour's 1918 constitution that put nationalization at the centre of Labour's project.

This chapter examines the development between 1918 and 1939 of a reciprocal relationship between the MFGB and the Labour Party, a reciprocity anchored in a commitment to the parliamentary road to socialism. The first part considers the legacy of conflict in mining and the resulting ethical code that influenced the mineworkers' industrial and electoral politics. Characterized by a tension between unity and fragmentation, MFGB politics emphasized the creation of an intra-organizational consensus based on the ideology of Labourism. The second part deals with strategy. By 1922, the debate between syndicalism and parliamentarianism was resolved in the latter's favour and was reinforced by the MFGB's defeat in 1926. The minority 1924 Labour government, 1926 and economic depression reinforced the strategic primacy of a majority Labour government for the mineworkers. Labour's coalfield electoral hegemony and mines nationalization, discussed in the third section, cemented the mineworkers' identification with the Labour Party. This identification was reinforced by the disaster of 1931. The final section examines the MFGB's 'maximum gain at minimum cost' strategy in the context of the post-1931 party–union relationship. The MFGB would not engage in industrial action except in the most favourable circumstances, or assert itself inside the party; it would defer to the party leadership's electoral strategy and defend the leadership. In return, the party and a future Labour government would have special regard for the union's needs in so far as these were compatible with the party's strategy. The evolution of the nationalization doctrine reflected the contours of this relationship, a relationship that was fundamental to social democracy.

History and Ethos

The mineworkers perceived themselves to be, and wished to be recognized as, the most ruthlessly exploited section of society.[1] This perception was central to the relationship with Labour and the articulation of the mineworkers' past, current and future relationship with society, economy and polity. Exploitation was the progenitor of the mineworkers' industrial solidarity and political consciousness, whose vehicles were their unions and the Labour Party.

'No other industry', Will Lawther wrote, 'has such a record of hardship, poverty, endurance, terrorism, disaster, unemployment, and the constant menace of death'. This was 'the history that is known today in every miner's home' and any improvement 'had to be fought for and won … the owners have never willingly given a single concession'. Lawther attacked the hypocrisy of a society that in turn ignored and reviled mineworkers, but then subscribed to disaster relief funds to assuage its guilt. Not surprisingly, mineworkers 'were the first to send their representatives to Parliament, the best financial supporters of the Labour Party and Trades Union Congress [and] the most class conscious and politically advanced of any section of the British working class'. The industry's crisis was so severe that 'a point had been reached where the miners are determined that an end shall be made for all time to the root cause of all their troubles and difficulties – namely, the private ownership of the mining industry'.[2] Lawther defines and articulates the situation addressed by the MFGB and the Labour Party, to which the 1945 Labour government responded by nationalizing the mines.

Mineworkers had powerful symbolic and material connections with Labour.[3] The MFGB affiliated large numbers to the party, its lodges were often surrogate party organizations, and ex-mineworkers were a substantial element in the PLP. The mineworkers' believed they had a special call on the movement, which sometimes led to incomprehension, resentment and frustration.[4] Ramsay MacDonald certainly thought the mineworkers and coal owners were on a par when it came to bone-headedness. In 1926, Herbert Smith – the MFGB president – lamented: 'We are fighting everybody. We are not simply fighting the owners and the Government, we are fighting everybody. We are fighting even the Trade Unions.' High levels of

---

[1]   The classic representations are G. Orwell, *The Road to Wigan Pier* (London: Penguin, 1962, first published 1937), and B. L. Coombes, *These Poor Hands* (London: Gollancz, 1939). A. J. Cronin's bestselling novel *The Stars Look Down* (1935), which culminates in a pit disaster, was made into popular film in 1939.

[2]   M. Heinemann, *Britain's Coal: A Study of the Mining Crisis* (London: Gollancz, 1944), pp. 5–10.

[3]   This chapter has benefited greatly from D. Howell, *MacDonald's Party: Labour Identities and Crisis, 1922–31* (Oxford: Oxford University Press, 2002).

[4]   D. Gilbert, 'Imagined Communities and Mining Communities', *Labour History Review*, 60/2 (1995), pp. 47–8.

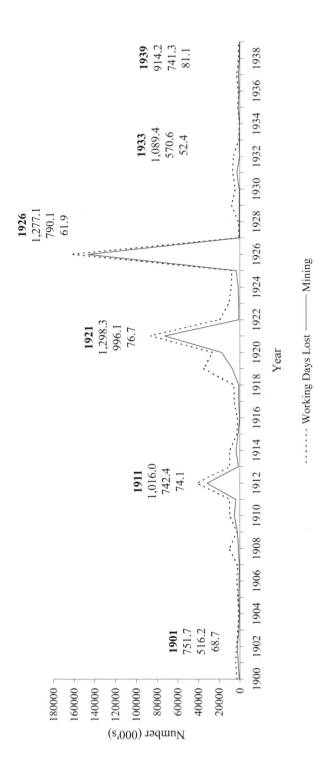

Figure 4.1   Aggregate Working Days Lost (Stoppages in Progress in Year). All Industries and Mining (000s)

union membership and frequent experience of conflict are often presented as the source of the mineworkers' political and industrial solidarity. Figure 4.1 shows the scale of the four great disputes – the 1912 minimum wage strike, the 1920 Datum Line Strike, the 1921 lockout, and the General Strike and lockout.[5] The period of state control (1917–21) coincides with the mineworkers' growing intimacy with the Labour Party and so is of great importance in the evolving relationship.

Despite the scale of these disputes, 85 per cent of all strikes in mining were small (involving fewer than 200), and on average 94 per cent (1912–40) affected a single colliery. These disputes often lasted only one day and by the end of the 1930s were concentrated in Scotland and South Wales.[6] This structure pointed as much to fragmentation as solidarity, and to a particular type of consciousness: conflict consciousness.

Soon after nationalization, a close observer of the mineworkers wrote:

> Whenever you start a conversation with the miner on the pits, he invariably begins by telling you about the Coal Strike in 1926. The Coal Strike is vividly impressed on their minds, like an event which only happened yesterday. To any troublesome problem you may bring up, the first statement you will hear will be; 'You know that we had a General Strike in 1926, and all the worst troubles in coalmining started then.'[7]

Mineworkers explained the difference between the 1920s and the 1950s in terms of a temporary power shift ('We've got the whip-hand and we've got to make it bloody well crack'). A mineworker (aged 55 in 1953) insisted vehemently that gains 'had to be fought for, and with the existence of a Conservative government these conditions might again be attacked'. This 'came from a man with no special interest in political matters, and far from being an isolated example, it represents the general trend of discussion whenever political questions arise in conversation'.[8] Mining had a history of conflict and mineworkers were well aware of that history but the lesson they drew was one of defeat or contingent victory. Class-consciousness had various elements. First, mineworkers saw themselves as part of 'a separate class of men, who earn their living by working with their hands, and whose interests are served by the unions'. Second, the working class 'must always be on its guard to get a fair deal – which he is not likely to get by arguments

---

[5]   *British Labour Statistics: Historical Abstract, 1868–1968* (London: HMSO, 1971), p. 396 and G. S. Bain and R. Price, *Profiles of Union Growth* (Oxford: Blackwell, 1980), p. 45. The data in the figure gives date, potential union membership (000s), MFGB membership (000s) and density (per cent).

[6]   R. Church and Q. Outram, *Strikes and Solidarity: Coalfield Conflict in Britain 1889–1906* (Cambridge: Cambridge University Press, 1998).

[7]   F. Zweig, *Men in the Pits* (London: Gollancz, 1948), p. 10.

[8]   N. Dennis, F. Henriques and C. Slaughter, *Coal Is Our Life: An Analysis of a Yorkshire Mining Community* (London: Tavistock, 1969, first published 1956), p. 59.

... but only by the strength of the whole body of the working class, by its physical and organized power'. Common to the working class, these attributes were at their most developed amongst the mineworkers and produced an attraction to collectivism that had little to do with socialist ideology. Mineworker consciousness and behaviour was a complex mixture of the sectional and collective (reflected in the, sometimes substantial, voluntary deductions from his pay packet).[9]

The resulting code – struggle, unity, solidarity – led to a deep loyalty to, and identification with Labour and socialism (a majority Labour government plus nationalization) amongst mineworkers. Yet: 'Nowhere can we find a greater range of variation than in the work and life of the coalminer. From coalfield to coalfield, from country to country, from colliery to colliery, from village to village, you find astonishing and perplexing differences.'[10] Mining historiography has recently stressed the sources of disunity and fragmentation over the sources of unity and solidarity. This literature has identified the multiple competing identities, from pit, through coalfield, to national union and class that composed the mineworker's view of the world. Multiple identities, from class to individual, hardly seem a secure foundation for any organization or relationship. 'Mineworker' conjures an image of solidarity that disguises and simplifies a highly complex and structured reality. As the debates in the MFGB in 1926 demonstrate, division was equally authentic.[11]

Centrifugality in the MFGB encouraged a political process pulling in the opposite direction. In its ideal presentation, this process of aggregation began at the pit and culminated in the Labour Party conference, and was a process whereby the fine grain of individual interest was squeezed into a conception of the collective good and a strategy for collective action. The aggregation and reconciliation of diverse interests was an imperfect and antagonistic process governed by rules (majority decisions), norms (solidarity) and policy (socialism). Each generated an antithesis: the problem of minorities, oligarchical manipulation and doctrinal debate so generating ample space for vitriolic conflict within the MFGB and between the MFGB and the Labour Party. This was regulated by doctrine and ethos which were 'an expression of the dominant group in the party. It incorporates sets of values which spring from the experience of the working class'. Union dominance meant the Labour Party was a response to the working class's experience of exploitation. This distinctive background produced an ethic based on loyalty, solidarity and unity, the importance of rules and procedures and their 'creative' interpretation. This was sustained by a strong sense of the past that vindicated a resilient belief in 'labour's forward march' and the inevitability

---

[9]   Zweig, *Men in the Pits*, p. 39.

[10]   Ibid., pp. 14–16.

[11]   A. Campbell, N. Fishman and D. Howell, 'Introduction', in Campbell, Fishman and Howell (eds), *Miners, Unions and Politics, 1910–47* (Aldershot: Scolar Press, 1996), pp. 1–7; A. J. Taylor, 'So Many Cases but So Little Comparison: Problems of Comparing Mineworkers', in S. Berger, A. Croll and N. LaPorte (eds), *Towards a Comparative History of Coalfield Societies* (Aldershot: Ashgate, 2005), pp. 12–15.

of victory. Intra- and inter-organizational politics were concerned with forging a consensus to embrace disparate and conflicting elements. The tension between centrifugal and centripetal forces resulted in negotiation and renegotiation.

In 1918, the MFGB took three decisions that shaped its relationship with the Labour Party.[12] The first was that Labour should withdraw from the wartime coalition government and fight the election independently; Labour could, and should, seek to form a government. Second, reaffirming decade-old decisions it decided that MPs receiving MFGB support should be Labour MPs. Moreover, full-time MFGB officials could no longer be MPs. Finally, nationalization became the core of the MFGB's platform. These decisions signalled the MFGB's recognition of two distinct spheres, the industrial and political, and that Labour was the mineworkers' political instrument.

The interwar party–union relationship was managed 'by unwritten rules and protocol derived mainly from trade union values and priorities. These "rules" embodied an acceptance of the permanent differentiation of function and spheres – the political and industrial'.[13] Differentiation created borders but these borders were permeable and policed by membership of a movement with a common culture. This was particularly important in the MFGB's case. The MFGB's diversity meant it was well accustomed to the sort of politics required to forge a consensus and had an instinctive sympathy for, and identification with, party leaders trying to do the same. Co-operation was encouraged by doctrinal and ideological overlap. This produced a complicated reciprocity based on four attitudes. The first was freedom. This meant the absence of party interference in internal union affairs and that the unions would not use industrial power against a Labour government or assert their organizational resources in the party. Second: democracy. Internally this was a blend of delegatory and majoritarian democracy, and externally embraced parliamentary democracy. Third: unity. This was fundamental but it required the unions accept a secondary role in electoral politics, deferring to the party leadership's definition of strategy. Finally: solidarity. This required the sacrifice of the immediate sectional interest to the long-term collective; again, this redounded to the benefit of the party leadership.

In political–industrial strategy, these attitudes were articulated as Labourism.[14] Labourism was not a deformed reflection of 'true' class-consciousness imposed on the working class by union bureaucrats and party careerists. Labourism was a robust political tradition that recognized the hostility of the movement's environment. Chapter 29 of Robert Smillie's autobiography, 'Progress Slow but Sure', expresses the strategy. It is reflected in Smillie's analysis of the 1924 government, 'the

---

[12]   See *MFGB Special Conference Reports*, 20–22 August, and 8 November 1918.

[13]   L. Minkin, *The Contentious Alliance: Trade Unions and the Labour Party* (Edinburgh: Edinburgh University Press, 1991), p. xiii.

[14]   J. Saville, 'The Ideology of Labourism', in R. Benewick et al. (eds), *Knowledge and Belief in Politics* (London: Allen & Unwin, 1973), pp. 215–16, and Saville's, *The Labour Movement in Britain* (London: Faber & Faber, 1988), pp. 14–22.

difficulties … the limitations imposed by the fact that Labour is in office and not yet in power' would be understood by working people who would work all the harder for 'real power'.[15] The key to political and industrial emancipation, and Labourism's core, was the parliamentary majority. Parliament was a machine 'worked hitherto by one section of the community, but capable of being worked by other sections. Labour has voted, but it has not run the machine'.[16] In reviving the party and responding to MacDonald's 1931 'betrayal', the unions' Labourism was critical. Joe Hall, told the Yorkshire miners, for example,

> If Socialism is to be achieved, if we are to get back to where we were in 1929 and 1930 with a Labour Government in office, then the greatest asset of the Labour Party, that is the Trade Union movement, must have the support of every man working in the mine or in any other industry. So it is for us to tame the chaos, to scatter the seeds of Socialism.[17]

The contours of Labourism varied and, in some coalfields, it was strongly opposed by communists, but it was dominant in the MFGB. Its physical embodiment was, perhaps, Herbert Smith, the president of both the Yorkshire miners and the MFGB in the 1920s, who as long ago as the 1890s had supported minimum wage legislation, a compulsory eight-hour day, the abolition of coal royalties and the nationalization of the mines.[18]

Strategy and Doctrine

A strike of 200,000 South Wales miners in 1915 led on 29 November to the coalfield being placed under government control, the rest of the industry following on 5 December 1916.[19] By February 1917, a Coal Controller was responsible for supervising output and also wages and conditions on a national basis. For the first time, coal was managed as a single entity. The mineworkers' experience of war was mixed. On the one hand, the centrality of British coal to the Allies' war effort increased their sense of indispensability and status; but, on the other, the intensity

---

[15]   R. Smillie, *My Life for Labour* (London: Mills and Boon, 1924), pp. 306–7.

[16]   J. Ramsay MacDonald, 'Parliament and Revolution' (1919) in B. Barker (ed.), *Ramsay MacDonald's Political Writings* (London: Allen Lane, 1972), p. 221.

[17]   Yorkshire Mine Workers' Association, *Annual Demonstration: Report of Proceedings*, 19 June 1933, p. 22.

[18]   E. Hobsbawm, *Worlds of Labour: Further Studies in the History of Labour* (London: Weidenfeld & Nicolson, 1984), pp. 211–13.

[19]   There is no modern full-length study of the mineworkers in the war. The best is G. D. H. Cole, *Labour in the Coal-Mining Industry, 1914–21* (Oxford: Clarendon Press, 1923). The definitive history of the industry in this period is B. Supple, *The History of the British Coal Industry: Volume 4, 1913–46* (Oxford: Clarendon Press, 1987).

of work increased. Mineworkers generally remained loyal to the war effort but resented accusations of a lack of patriotism, which, they believed, reflected a failure to grasp the state of the industry. They also deeply resented profiteering by the coal owners.

Convinced their problems could not be resolved within the status quo, the MFGB drew closer to Labour and Arthur Henderson's reforms were designed in part to achieve this.[20] Wartime control reinforced trends in Labour Party thinking that culminated in the 1918 Constitution, the socialist objective, and *Labour and the New Social Order*. For many, coal nationalization was the first and most obvious step for a Labour government. Nevertheless, growing industrial unrest and the syndicalist tradition in the MFGB ran counter to this. An MFGB Special Conference (14 January 1919) approved a programme that sought a 50 per cent increase in wages, a six-hour day and nationalization. A pit head ballot supported industrial action to achieve this by 615,164 to 105,082 if the government refused.

With coal exports booming (from which government received substantial receipts), with unrest on the railways and in the docks, with the engineers and textile workers restive, and with no effective strikebreaking organization, the Lloyd George coalition prevaricated. Lloyd George offered a Committee of Inquiry, the Sankey Commission, to examine hours, wages and ownership, and the MFGB (narrowly) agreed to participate. Four members were appointed by the MFGB (two by agreement between the union and government), the government appointed three, and the owners three. Sankey promised an interim report by 20 March and, in response, the MFGB postponed the strike until 22 March.

The interim report approved the principle of nationalization ('the present system of ownership and working in the coal industry stands condemned'), but the MFGB had not foreseen the possibility that the commission might split. The Majority Report signed by Sankey, the MFGB's members and the two MFGB/ government appointees found in favour of an immediate wage increase, a reduction in the working day to seven hours and nationalization. On 20 May the government reluctantly accepted 'the spirit and letter' of the Majority Report and Sankey began work on the final report that would include a nationalization scheme. Playing for time and exploiting divisions in the commission, the government delayed its response for eight weeks. Lloyd George eventually rejected nationalization and the MFGB appealed for support to force legislation. In early 1919, the Triple Alliance was revived. Composed of the MFGB, National Union of Railwaymen (NUR) and Transport and General Workers' Union (TGWU), this had emerged before by 1914 but was not formally ratified until June 1917. The threatened use of industrial power for political ends represented a threat to both the state and Henderson's Labour Party. Tempted to reactivate industrial action, the MFGB – faced by hostility from the unions – accepted a special TUC's decision to launch instead a propaganda

---

[20]   F. M. Leventhal, *Arthur Henderson* (Manchester: Manchester University Press, 1989), chapter 4; R. McKibbin, *The Evolution of the Labour Party, 1910–24* (Oxford: Clarendon Press, 1974), chapter 5.

campaign. 'The Mines for the Nation' failed dismally. Nevertheless, by endorsing publicly the MFGB's condemnation of private ownership, the Majority Report set the terms of the interwar debate on coal policy.

A short-lived surge in coal prices allowed the MFGB to seek a wage increase; an unsatisfactory offer led to notices being tendered for 25 September 1920. Reluctant to face a major dispute, the government reopened negotiations but its offer was rejected. The result was the Datum Line Strike (16 October–3 November) that was called off after a second ballot showed a marked decline in support. This strike is sometimes portrayed as a serious strategic error by the MFGB as it dissipated the Federation's resources and, moreover, the state was now better prepared. In October, the Emergency Powers Act (1920) became operative, giving the state a well organized and reliable strikebreaking capability.[21] This and the collapse of the Datum Line Strike encouraged the government to decontrol the mines, which was announced on 31 March.

Decontrol meant a return to district negotiation and wage cuts and, on 1 April, a lockout began; the MFGB called for the support of the Triple Alliance, which on 15 April (Black Friday) was refused. The reason was a suggestion by Frank Hodges, the MFGB secretary, at a private meeting at the House of Commons that the MFGB might be prepared to compromise. On 17 June, the mineworkers voted 434,614 to 180,724 to reject the owners' terms. Faced by government and owner intransigence, the MFGB reopened negotiations on 27 June and, on 1 July, the mineworkers were ordered to return to work. During the dispute, the government declared a state of emergency under the 1920 Act and troops were deployed in the coalfields. As a result, in South Wales for example, wages fell by 40–49 per cent. Despite a temporary revival in trade consequent on the French occupation of the Ruhr, the industry's basic dynamic was unchanged. The Baldwin government's decision to return to the gold standard at 1914 parity triggered the process that was to culminate in 1926.

Deeply hostile to industrial strength being used for political gain, MacDonald argued that parliament's failures should not lead to abandoning electoral politics in favour of syndicalism. Political strikes jeopardized Labour's electoral growth, so postponing mines nationalization, and the unions, on which Labour relied, would be severely damaged in a confrontation with the state. Unions should leave

---

[21] See for example, R. Geary, *Policing Industrial Disputes: 1893–1985* (London: Methuen, 1985), pp. 53–66; S. Peak, *Troops in Strikes: Military Intervention in Industrial Disputes* (London: Cobden Trust, 1984), pp. 32–48; C. Townsend, *Making the Peace: Public Order and Public Security in Modern Britain* (Oxford: Oxford University Press, 1993), chapter 5; K. Jeffery and P. Hennessy, *States of Emergency: British Governments and Strikebreaking since 1919* (London: Routledge, 1983), chapters 1–5; C. Wrigley, *Lloyd George and the Challenge of Labour: The Post War Coalition, 1918–22* (Brighton: Harvester Wheatsheaf, 1993), chapters 7 and 8.

politics to the party.[22] The MFGB's resources were intended for sectional gain not 'general human regeneration'. 'It is', he wrote, 'a mining organization formed for industrial purposes; its membership is confined to mine workers, its immediate objects are concerned with the pits', so using industrial resources for political gain was anti-social behaviour.[23] The MFGB's geographical concentration and organizational and financial resources could lead to the MFGB ignoring the movement's wider destiny. This potential for anti-social behaviour meant the miners could not be trusted to be good socialists. Disillusion was not parliament's fault, 'but of Labour outside'.

> I doubt if the Labour Party has yet discovered the best way of selecting candidates. Until selection conferences are wise enough to search for certain qualities rather than accept men of a certain status is local bodies or in organizations whose method of work and training are not those of the House of Commons, the governing machinery will not be captured from the inside.

'A parliamentary election', MacDonald believed, 'will give us all the power Lenin had to get by a revolution'.[24]

The years 1919–21 were crucial to the MFGB–Labour Party relationship. 'The Mines for the Nation' expressed the MFGB's developing conceptualization of nationalization. It was not, significantly, 'The Mines for the Miners'. This conceptualization meshed with the state-centred rationalization strategies that embraced both wartime control (quasi-nationalization) and clause four, which tried to reconcile the interests of consumers and producers. The MFGB's attempts to secure nationalization by agreement – through negotiation with Lloyd George or a majority Labour government – was designed to combine in a persuasive appeal, legitimacy, morality and efficiency, attributes the MFGB argued that private ownership could not deliver. Labour and the MFGB were united in pursuing a supra-class national integrative strategy intended to appeal beyond the organized working class. The industrial working class was too narrow a political base for a Labour government. Nationalization and Labour had to be acceptable to an electoral majority. Many voters feared union militancy and were suspicious of a seemingly union dominated party. Nationalization needed a majority Labour government; sceptical voters had to be convinced that a Labour government was in the national, and their personal, interest.

---

[22]　J. Ramsay MacDonald, *Socialism: Critical and Constructive* (London: Cassell, 1929, first published 1921), pp. 206–7.

[23]　MacDonald, 'Parliament and Revolution', p. 230.

[24]　Ibid., p. 224 and p. 232.

Convergence

In the polity, Labourism's most obvious manifestation was Labour's coalfield hegemony; in industry, it was the union's drive for unity and solidarity. Both overlapped and were reinforcing.

Structural factors (a single industry, socially homogenous communities, the integration of work and non-work life, the transmission of workplace solidarity into politics) are commonly used to account for Labour's coalfield electoral hegemony.[25] This hegemony was, however, sometimes halting and always conditioned by local factors. In 1923 and 1929, one in six mineworkers voted Liberal (one in six voted Conservative in 1923) and, in 1918 and 1931, Labour lost mining seats.

Variation between coalfields meant local strategies were critical.[26] Nevertheless, contemporaries believed that the connection between community (men and women), voters and union organization in mining constituencies betokened a new configuration of class politics:

> Political action today is conceived of in quite a different spirit from that of a generation ago. Not only is the working class alive to the need for political action in the wider sense, but its elected officials and representatives are taking an active part in the local life of the community, and throughout South Wales Labour plays a very prominent part in Local Government. Today, the activities

---

[25]   The foundational studies are C. Kerr and A. Siegel, 'The Interindustry Propensity to Strike: An International Comparison', in A. Kornhauser, R. Durbin and A. M. Ross (eds), *Industrial Conflict* (New York: McGraw-Hill, 1954), pp. 189–212, G. Rimlinger, 'International Differences in the Strike Propensity of Coal Miners' Experience in Four Countries', *Industrial and Labor Relations Review*, 12/3 (1959), 389–405; M. Bulmer, 'Sociological Models of the Mining Communities', *Sociological Review*, 23/1 (1975), 61–92. D. Rossiter, 'The Miners' Sphere of Influence: An Attempt to Quantify Electoral Behaviour in Mining Areas between the Wars' (unpublished PhD dissertation, University of Sheffield, 1980) remains the authoritative study of the mining electorate in this period.

[26]   For variations in the political development of mining constituencies see, for example, Lord Williams of Barnburgh, *Digging for Britain* (London: Hutchinson, 1965), chapter 4 (Don Valley); Lord (Bernard) Taylor of Mansfield, *Up The Hill All the Way: A Miner's Struggle* (London: Sidgwick and Jackson, 1972), chapter 9 (Mansfield); J. Griffiths, *Pages From Memory* (London: Dent, 1969), chapter 4 (Llanelli). These memoirs, often disparaged or ignored as part of the discredited 'forward march' labour historiography, provide an insight into the activists' perception of their world. Academic studies are R. J. Waller, *The Dukeries Transformed: The Social and Political Development of a Twentieth-Century Coalfield* (Oxford: Clarendon Press, 1983), chapter 6 (Nottinghamshire); H. Beynon and T. Austrin, *Masters and Servants: Class and Patronage in the Making of a Labour Organisation: The Durham Miners and the English Political Tradition* (London: Rivers Oram, 1994), chapter 11; A. Campbell, *The Scottish Miners, 1874–1939, Volume Two: Trade Union and Politics* (Aldershot: Ashgate, 2000), chapter 8; C. Williams, *Democratic Rhondda: Politics and Society, 1885–1951* (Cardiff: University of Wales Press, 1996).

of the Labour Member of Parliament are of a wider and more general scope than
the mere safeguarding of the special interests of an industry.[27]

Labour's capture of local government and its determination to use it to deliver
material gains – health, education and welfare – to working-class communities
emerged before 1914, but the extension of the franchise in 1918 and Labour's
emergence extended it to national politics.

Despite the MFGB's affiliation to the Labour Party, many MPs and local union
branches remained loyal to Liberalism.[28] By 1914, change was underway; as new
mining areas developed so did new political loyalties, but the 1914–18 war was
critical. Between 1918 and 1924, Labour's dominance of the coalfields grew; but
this and the mining unions' dominance were untypical. In the interwar period
in constituencies where the percentage of miners in the electorate fell below
33 per cent, Labour could not be guaranteed working-class support. Similarly,
religious loyalties, or where coal companies remained active in the community
rather than confining themselves to the workplace, Labour's task was made harder.
Psephological analysis of the 1918 election shows Labour's dependence on the
coalfield constituencies.[29] This dependence deepened in the 1920s and became
more pronounced after 1931 when Labour's support in non-mining constituencies
fell by more than 20 per cent compared to mining seats. The mineworkers'
electoral identification with Labour was grounded on the process 'by which
social structures and political approaches interacted to turn a community's self-
identification and interests into increasingly firm political allegiances'.[30] The
mining vote was critical at two points: it underpinned Labour's electoral take-off
in 1918 and its survival in 1931. If the coalfield vote had been comparable to
the vote in neighbouring working-class constituencies, Labour would have been a
very different party. Labour's dominance in the coalfields was a significant factor
in the structuring of modern British politics based as it was on class politics and a
'two-party' duopoly.

---

[27]   Commission of Enquiry into Industrial Unrest, No. 7 Division, *Report of the
Commissioners for Wales, including Monmouthshire* Cd. 8668 (1917), pp. 17–18.

[28]   R. Gregory, *The Miners and British Politics, 1906–14* (Oxford: Clarendon Press,
1968), sets out a typology of relationships with the Labour Party: 'The Front Runners'
(Durham, Northumberland, Lancashire, Cumberland and Scotland), 'The Slow Starters'
(Yorkshire and South Wales), and 'The Laggards' (Derbyshire, Nottinghamshire,
Staffordshire and Warwickshire).

[29]   J. Turner, *British Politics and the Great War: Coalition and Conflict, 1915–1918*
(New Haven: Yale University Press, 1992); K. D. Wald, *Crosses on the Ballot: Patterns
of Voter Alignment since 1885* (Princeton: Princeton University Press, 1983) emphasizes
that 1918–24 marks the emergence of class voting. Coalfield constituencies were at the
forefront of this shift.

[30]   D. Tanner, 'The Labour Party and Electoral Politics in the Coalfields', in Campbell
et al., *Miners, Unions and Politics*, p. 60.

The 1929 general election was critical for the MFGB and the Labour Party. It demonstrated Labour could win seats outside the heartlands and that its programme had (potentially) great appeal, but neither had yet reached the point where Labour could win a majority. These factors enabled Labour to ride-out the 1931 crisis and encouraged the evolution of the party–union relationship. The party accepted the organized working class had a special call on the party, but the union leadership recognized the party's primacy in electoral strategy. The mining constituencies were one of major foundations of a social contract that reached its apogee in 1945. By the 1935 general election, there was absolutely no doubt that mining communities would vote Labour, but mining constituency parties were poorly organized with low levels of individual membership.[31] This dependency, suggestive of union control, concerned the party leadership and inspired the Hastings Agreement (1933) regulating union financing of party organization. Mining constituency Labour parties, nevertheless had some party organization and individual membership (non-miners and women) grew during the war, developing an existence separate from the mineworkers and their union.

The events of 1926 demonstrated the MFGB's potential for both solidarity and fragmentation.[32] George Spencer and Arthur Cook were equally authentic products of the mining community, and the tension between these tendencies constituted the motor of the MFGB's politics. 1926 confirmed the danger of confronting the state; nationalization and improved living standards needed a Labour government. At the end of the dispute, Herbert Smith mused: 'I think we have to take a stronger position in regard to political action.'[33] Defeat was in a sense essential for Labour's growth because it confirmed the catastrophic consequences of 'unconstitutional' action. Thus, 'If the actions of the present government had not taught every miner and every worker in Great Britain the necessity for a Labour Government, nothing would', and 'There had been a diabolical attack to defeat the miners ... Why were they up against it? Simply because they had failed to obtain political power'.[34]

Joseph Jones, general secretary of the Yorkshire miners, drew three lessons from 1926. First, 'the most reactionary government in modern times' had defeated the mineworkers, a government put in office by working-class votes. The MFGB and the unions generally must therefore devote every effort to securing a Labour victory. Second, 1926 'proved conclusively that sufficient care and thought have not been given to the strike as an industrial weapon'. Strikes should be the last resort, used only after careful preparation and with no hint of political motivation. Third, only nationalization could secure the immediate and long-term interests of the mineworkers and the country. Nationalization would only come from a

---

[31] 'The Problem in Mining Divisions', *Labour Organiser*, 18 (1938), 135.

[32] J. McIlroy, A. Campbell and K. Gildart (eds), *Industrial Politics and the 1926 Lockout: A Struggle for Dignity* (Cardiff: University of Wales Press, 2004).

[33] *MFGB Special Conference Report*, 10–13 November 1926, p. 13.

[34] 'The Mining Crisis', *Report of the Labour Party Conference, 1926* (London, 1926), pp. 162 and 196.

majority Labour government. Realizing these objectives required having 'the manpower within the industry well organized and well disciplined', unity and solidarity with the MFGB and the movement was therefore imperative.[35] Jones was a member of the MFGB executive (1924–31), vice-president (1932–3) and president (1933–8), and this analysis became MFGB orthodoxy in the 1930s. In 1935, when the MFGB was contemplating industrial action, 1926 loomed over the debates. For example, 'We want to avoid a repetition of 1926'; 'Our people hope we may be able to avoid a clash or a struggle like we had in 1926'; 'We have got to sit down and think it out. Don't let us lead our men wrongly. None of us want another 1926 if it can be avoided'.[36] The MFGB observed, 'those who deride the present fashionable demand for political action and call for some speedier means of redress, are blinding themselves, consciously or unconsciously, to the plain, though important fact, that no speedier way exists at the present moment'. However, 'If a Labour Government is returned the nationalization becomes a not too distant prospect'.[37]

The remaking of the Labour Party after 1931 was based on the unions and party drawing together; 1931 created the betrayal myth that proved so important for convergence. Will Lawther, for example, regarded MacDonald as a criminal: 'There's no crime worse in my opinion than social crimes. Individual crimes the individual pays the price [*sic*]. Social crimes, like betraying movements … that has to be paid by countless thousands … he betrayed them.'[38] One of 1931's effects was closer union tutelage of the party. This led not to union dominance, but to convergence for mutual support. Ernest Bevin, one of the key figures in this convergence, argued:

> I just want to say that the foundation of the Labour Party and the Socialist Movement in this country is the Trade Unionist Movement. That is its strength. If you want to maintain a powerful political organization you must first of all maintain a powerful Trade Unionist movement.[39]

By 1931, Labourism had five elements. First, it stressed the supremacy of the MFGB as the authentic and accurate expression of the mineworkers' interests in

---

[35]   YMWA, *Annual Reports*, 1926–27, pp. 2–5 and p. 9.

[36]   *MFGB Special Conference*, 17 October 1935, pp. 7–8 and p. 18. One delegate complained about 'a sort of psychology that because we were defeated in 1926 we cannot possibly win today. What is the logic of that policy? Are you suggesting that once you are defeated you must never fight again?' (p. 51).

[37]   *The Miner*, 15 October 1927.

[38]   J. F. Clark, 'An Interview with Will Lawther', *Bulletin of the Society for the Study of Labour History*, 9 (1969), 17. For 'betrayalism's' longevity see D. Howell, 'Where's Ramsay MacKinnock?', in H. Beynon (ed.), *Digging Deeper: Issues in the Miners' Strike* (London: Verso, 1985), pp. 181–97.

[39]   YMWA, *Annual Demonstration: Report of Proceedings*, 19 June 1933, p. 14.

the industrial and political spheres. Second, the MFGB's industrial and political purposes were to secure the best possible deal for their members at the lowest cost. Third, in a complex organization sectionalism and competing interpretations of the public good were inevitable but had to be managed to avoid the erosion of the all-important solidarity and unity. This depended on rules and procedures, but in the final analysis, on majority rule. Fourth, fundamentally flawed and irredeemably antithetical to the mineworkers' good, private ownership had to be replaced by nationalization. For the MFGB this was a political, moral and economic imperative. Finally, the MFGB's political objectives could only be achieved via the Labour Party and that a majority Labour government was the mineworkers' salvation. Labourism was not a recipe for monolithic unity but it provided the framework for a relatively stable dialogue within 'the rules'. Industrial and political Labourism was the language in which the relationship was articulated. It was the language of solidarity and unity.

Accommodation

MFGB politics in the 1930s overlay considerable complexity derived from different political cultures, institutions, economic fortunes and the strength of communism in the districts. The common denominator in MFGB politics was, however, loyalty to Labour. MFGB complexity could, because of the mineworkers' presence in the party, lead to serious embarrassment. Fissiparousness was mitigated by the rules governing their relationship and the growing MFGB loyalty reflex. Tom Williams, for example, saw loyalty as a given in need of no analysis:

> I claim no special credit for being loyal to my Party and its leader. I was educated in politics as a trade unionist and that is a training which instils loyalty and discipline. Too often during the course of my political life I have seen the future of the Labour Party placed in real jeopardy by the irresponsible, self-seeking actions of those who lacked this training.[40]

This loyalty was present in electoral politics and the accommodation of the MFGB's platform to Labour's, reflected in the development of the movement's policy on nationalization.[41] Despite a strong attraction to workers' control for the management of a nationalized coal industry, the MFGB acquiesced in what became known as the Morrisonian public corporation. This retained both the dominance of professional technocratic managers and a separation of union and management as the only practicable model. The MFGB accepted this for two reasons: first, acutely conscious of the industry's problems, many leaders were uncomfortable with the

---

[40]   Williams, *Digging for Britain*, p. 188.

[41]   A. J. Taylor, 'The Miners and Nationalisation', in *International Review of Social History*, 38/2 (1983), 176–99.

notion of the mineworkers (in effect the union) taking managerial responsibility. Second, for electoral and ideological reasons, neither the Labour Party nor the TUC would accept any model of nationalization that hinted at workers' control. If the mineworkers wanted nationalization, they had no option other than to accept Labour's model.

As the Labour Party edged closer to government, the MFGB's role as a lobby had to be reconciled with Labour governing in 'the national interest'. The minority governments of 1924 and 1929 attracted and repelled the MFGB: Labour was in government but lacked the power to achieve much. Labour's preservation of Lloyd George's strikebreaking machinery and its refusal to provide government time for a private member's bill to reduce working hours sponsored by the MFGB showed Labour would not respond automatically to union wishes. The MFGB's response was ruthlessly pragmatic: accepting the logic of the parliamentary situation and Labour's governing strategy that was intended to appeal beyond the organized industrial working class to create a parliamentary majority. The circumstances surrounding the government's fall confirmed the duplicity of the ruling class and that the labour movement must maintain its solidarity and work for a majority. The events of 1926 strengthened this and its logic dominated relations with the 1929 Labour government.

The controversy over the MFGB's attempts to secure an act enforcing a reduction in working hours encapsulated the complexity of the relationship. The Labour government saw its role as being to encourage the unions and employers to find a mutually acceptable solution. The MFGB believed the Labour government to be committed to passing an act to reduce working hours by an hour. The government believed a 30-minute reduction was politically feasible. The lack of a parliamentary majority, the legacy of 1926 and deteriorating economic conditions ruled out industrial action. The ever-present centrifugal forces in the MFGB emerged (Yorkshire's delegation refused to accept any change in the 'agreed' policy and walked out of the conference called to discuss the issue), as they did between the MFGB and a Labour government. This pattern was to be repeated throughout the MFGB's and NUM's history.[42]

Being thrown back onto coalfield bargaining where success varied according to market, employer attitudes and density of membership gave the Labour Party considerable room for manoeuvre. Before the 1929 election, Labour's NEC made it clear to the MFGB that if elected the Labour government would determine its legislative priorities.[43] Labour devoted considerable time and political capital to the passage of the Coal Mines Act (1930). Despite the act's weaknesses, the MFGB executive narrowly endorsed it, provoking further conflict within the

---

[42]   *MFGB Special Conference Report*, 26 March 1924 and *MFGB Special Conference Report*, 7 November 1929 set out the contours of the debates over the MFGB's relationship with a Labour government.

[43]   'Joint Meeting with the Labour Party National Executive', MFGB Executive Committee, 9 April 1929.

MFGB and between the MFGB and Labour. In part, the crisis was the result of the MFGB pressing ministers to pursue policies the latter regarded as politically and electorally dangerous.

For some mineworkers 1924 and 1929–31 confirmed the futility of parliamentary politics but, in the main, the effect was to reinforce the commitment to the parliamentary road to socialism. Jack Lawson, elected for Chester-le-Street in a by-election in 1919, testified to the grip of the House of Commons on the union's political imagination,

> All the bare days of childhood, the sweaty wrestle in the pit, the years of battle for a definite place for the toiler in the social and political life of the nation – all the dream and work of the years was crowded into that movement. I sat down and looked around the assembled company. This was the House of Commons!

Lawson viewed the Commons 'through the long, low dark underground tunnel of a telescope' and he drew a distinction between the institution of parliament and those who currently sat in it:

> The sum of my feelings as I daily watched the assembly, and took part in its life, was that more than ever I was convinced that the workers were right in shaping their course to capture this citadel, for it is a place of great strength and power, just as capable of great things for the humblest in the land as it has been for the wealthy in the past.[44]

Labour in government was more powerful as a symbol than for its achievements. That a man who had started work in the pit at 12 could become a minister of the crown was, in this perspective, proof of the basic responsiveness of political institutions. Others were less sanguine. Lawther (elected in 1929 but who lost his seat in 1931) commented: 'It was one of the best jobs I ever had – a good thing going from the pit to the House. It was when we came back and lost our seats, when MacDonald did the double-crossing that indicated the price you'd got to pay.'[45]

The illness and death of A. J. Cook in 1931 removed someone identified by many, rightly or wrongly, as emblematic of the failed strategy of 1926. His successor as general secretary, Ebby Edwards, argued forcefully for a new strategy,

> We know that within the forms of the contradictions of Capitalism we have to settle by negotiation to get the best wages and conditions for our men. We have to agree that as Capitalism exists we have to seek the maximum for our men with the minimum of sacrifice.[46]

---

[44]   J. Lawson, *A Man's Life* (London: Hodder & Stoughton, 1944), p. 162 and p. 164.

[45]   Clark, 'An Interview with Will Lawther', p. 17.

[46]   *MFGB Special Conference Report*, 14 February 1935, p. 44.

Economic conditions ruled out industrial action; 1931 relegated a majority Labour government to a distant future. Edwards constructed a strategy that sought to hold the owners – not the government or international economy, and certainly not the mineworkers – responsible for the industry's plight. This was rejecting 'the policy of continual conflict'. For Edwards, the MFGB – afflicted by a fatal mismatch between its history and capabilities – was damaged by the absence of a unifying 'immediate programme'. Edwards argued this programme should be national recognition coupled with a general wage increase. These could be used as wedge issues to rebuild and mobilize the mineworkers and which, once conceded, could provide a basis for further advances. This strategy required conceding greater power to the national executive over the districts, enabling it to focus the MFGB on realizable gains. This resulted in the successful 1935–6 campaign that secured national recognition and a national wage increase.[47]

The 1935–6 wages campaign, the Harworth dispute and the merger of the Nottinghamshire Miners' Industrial Union with the NMU, and a revival in trade made the integration of the MFGB the next logical step. As Britain re-armed, the national dimension was becoming increasingly important. In this environment, Joseph Jones declared, the MFGB could not continue much longer, warning the delegates that: 'If you expect a national organization to function nationally in these circumstances I say frankly it will not work.'[48] 1926 demonstrated the threat to unity and solidarity posed by sectional interests. The strength of regionalism is reflected in the failure of the Horner–Watson proposals. The MFGB's stability and coherence depended on recognizing district autonomy and, at its crudest, reform had to bring Nottinghamshire back into the MFGB and keep it there. The 1935–6 campaign showed that the MFGB as constituted could mobilize solidarity in the right circumstances and organize an effective national campaign. The 1935 general election campaign confirmed the resilience of the party–union link and the mining constituencies as Labour's bedrock. By 1938, the party–union relationship was stabilized and institutionalized.

The MFGB was a collection of district unions whose complex internal politics could collapse with the assertion of district autonomy. It took nearly ten years and a world war for the MFGB and Labour to align. Even then, hangovers from the old regime persisted and new, highly critical elements (for example, advocates of direct action, the Communist Party, the Minority Movement, non-political unionism) complicated the MFGB's politics. Nonetheless, the MFGB's politics

---

[47]   A. J. Taylor, '"Maximum Benefit for Minimum Sacrifice": The Miners' Wage Campaign of 1935–36', *Historical Studies in Industrial Relations*, 2 (1996), 65–92.

[48]   *MFGB Annual Conference Report 1937*, p. 311. The 1937 conference led to the appointment of a reorganization committee to propose a structure for a single union. Horner–Watson recommended a union of eight areas. Endorsed by the national executive, the Communist Party and several areas, the 1938 conference pushed the report back to the districts for further consideration. The Special Conference called to discuss reorganisation in January 1939 was cancelled.

stabilized into a Communist/Labour-left minority and orthodox Labour majority. This had a geographical dimension with some coalfields being identified as 'left' and others as 'right', but both tendencies were, to a greater or lesser degree, present in every coalfield. The outcome was a stable, even predictable, pattern of internal and party–union politics that dominated until the end of the 1960s.[49]

Lawther recalled, 'one of the consequences [of 1926] was that we learned … we got more by arbitration than we ever got by all the strikes we ever had. I was once asked in '36 when I was advocating the acceptance of certain terms … "was this the Will Lawther of '26?" – I said – yes – ten years older and twenty years wiser'.[50] Men who began on the left, for example Arthur Horner, Will Lawther and Ebby Edwards, recognized that the political balance in the union, as well as the wider political and economic environment, dictated a long-term strategy of consensus building endorsed by the members. Those from opposite political traditions such as Joseph Jones and Sam Watson recognized that the left must be harnessed to the MFGB's goals.

Clement Attlee enjoyed a very close relationship with the miners' MPs and MFGB. Though he supported the MFGB in 1926, he had private doubts and the outcome confirmed Attlee's belief in the primacy of political action. His judgement was typically laconic: 'A good thing to get it out of the way. The Labour movement got back on the political track.'[51] In 1935, Walter Citrine, the TUC general secretary and, with Bevin, a key figure in forming the post-1931 movement, told the MFGB:

> If Labour is successful at the next General Election there is no shadow of doubt that the policy of the Federation will be put into operation. The hesitation which characterized the last Labour Governments will not be revealed if Labour is elected to power … I can give you this assurance from the Labour Movement.[52]

This commitment was sustained by the network of rules, norms and policy that developed after 1918 and established a reciprocity that 'was to be a fundamental stabilising element in the relationship'; these 'enmeshed both sides in mutual expectations, and obligation' in a flexible and adaptive structure.[53]

---

[49] A. J. Taylor, *The NUM and British Politics: Volume 1, 1944–1968* (Aldershot: Ashgate, 2004), pp. 3–11.

[50] Clark, 'An Interview with Will Lawther', p. 14.

[51] Quoted in K. Harris, *Attlee* (London: Weidenfeld & Nicolson, 1982), p. 74. When Lansbury resigned, two miners' MPs, David Grenfell and Tom Williams, proposed Attlee as leader. 'They [the miners' MPs] were for Attlee to a man, and Attlee never forgot it' (p. 121).

[52] *MFGB Annual Conference Report 1935*, p. 123.

[53] Minkin, *Contentious Alliance*, p. 47.

Irrespective of its union origins, Labour was 'not a mere political expression of Trade Unionism. The Trade Unions are the backbone of the movement, but the Party represents something more than the needs of organized Labour. It is a national party with a Socialist objective'. Whilst Labour was 'ready to support the demands of organized Labour, [it must] have due regard to the interests of all sections of the workers and the nation as a whole'. In an important observation distilling the experience of the 1924 and 1929–31, Attlee cautioned that a Labour government 'may come to the conclusion that certain immediate demands of a Trade Union are in conflict with Socialist policy'.[54] Despite the inevitability of 'misunderstandings', this was a partnership for mutual gain and central to Labour's short programme was nationalization of the mines:

> [We] allow this great business to be shamefully mismanaged and we are content
> as a nation to sweat the men on whose dangerous and heavy toil we depend ...
> The Labour Party will take over the whole coal industry and reorganize it on the
> basis of giving adequate wages and good conditions to the miner.[55]

By 1937, relatively few mineworkers dissented from Attlee's description of the party–union relationship.

---

[54]   C. R. Attlee, *The Labour Party in Perspective* (London: Gollancz, 1937), p. 66.

[55]   Ibid., pp. 184–5.

Chapter 5

The European Context:
Aspects of British Labour and Continental Socialism Before 1920

Chris Wrigley

While the distinctiveness of the British Labour Party is rightly a norm of writing about European labour movements, it is easy to overstate its 'otherness' and isolation from continental European socialism. The intellectual and physical links with European socialism have received some attention from historians of the British labour movement and socialism.[1] Nevertheless, it is an aspect of the Labour Party's development which is often understated. This chapter offers a fresh consideration of several aspects of the European connections which influenced the identity and some features of the Labour Party's broad culture during the period of its foundation and its early development.

The Labour Party, like its radical predecessors and the socialist societies of the 1880s and 1890s, was influenced by European and, indeed, world developments. British labour was not cocooned. There were substantial external influences. There was a diffusion of ideas and ideology from continental Europe to Britain, just as British ideas (ranging from those of capitalist entrepreneurs to Owenites) went the

---

[1]   Examples include: G. D. H. Cole, *A History of Socialist Thought: The Second International 1889–1914* (London: Macmillan, 1956); E. P. Thompson, *William Morris: Romantic to Revolutionary* (London: Lawrence & Wishart, 1955); H. Pelling, *The Origins of the Labour Party* (London: Macmillan, 1965); S. Pierson, *Marxism and the Origins of British Socialism* (Ithaca: Cornell University Press, 1973); R. McKibbin, *The Evolution of the Labour Party, 1910–24* (Oxford: Oxford University Press, 1974); D. Howell, *British Workers and the Independent Labour Party, 1888–1906* (Manchester: Manchester University Press, 1983); A. J. A. Morris, 'Labour and Foreign Affairs: A Search for Identity and Policy', in K. D. Brown (ed.), *The First Labour Party 1906–14* (London: Croom Helm, 1985); D. J. Newton, *British Labour, European Socialism and the Struggle for Peace, 1889–1914* (Oxford: Oxford University Press, 1985); S. Berger, *The British Labour Party and the German Social* Democrats (Oxford: Clarendon, 1994), L. Barrow and I. Bullock, *Democratic Ideas and the British Labour Movement, 1880–1914* (Cambridge: Cambridge University Press, 1996); D. Sassoon, *One Hundred Years of European Socialism* (London: I. B. Tauris, 1996); M. Bevir, 'Marxism and British Socialism', *European Legacy*, 1 (1996), 545–9, and 'William Morris: The Modern Self, Art and Politics', *History of European Ideas*, 24 (1998), 175–94.

other way. In the 1880s, a notable example of this was the impact of *Das Kapital* on early Social Democratic Federation (SDF) luminaries such as H. M. Hyndman, William Morris and Belfort Bax (who needed linguistic skills to read it before it was translated into English). Similarly, it was reading 'some German Social Democratic and Working Women's papers' which made Margaret Gladstone (soon to marry James Ramsay MacDonald) consider how she could 'best work to help in the socialist and labour movement'.[2] Marcel van der Linden has written of transnational labour history: 'Dramatic developments in one country may cause turbulence in other countries; strike waves often have a transnational character; new forms of campaigning are imitated elsewhere; national labour movements communicate with each other, learn from each other and create international organizations.'[3] British labour generally, including the Labour Party, was influenced by people and ideas from outside of the country, and while the European connection was most prominent, there were wider international influences as well.

The Labour Representation Committee (LRC) arose from the wishes of the 1899 Trades Union Congress (TUC) to set up 'a distinct Labour Group in Parliament' made up of 'men sympathetic with the aims and demands of the Labour movement'. The original notion had been for it to represent the co-operative societies as well as the trade unions and socialist societies, with an executive committee made up of 12 trade unionists, 10 co-operators and six socialists (two each from the Fabians, Independent Labour Party (ILP) and SDF), each elected by their own body.[4] With the co-operators not participating, the resulting body was trade union dominated; but with trade unionists who believed that political action, not just collective bargaining, was necessary to remedy working people's grievances. This belief had won widening support from the late 1880s, on the issue of the eight-hour day in particular. The Taff Vale judgement reinforced such convictions and brought many more trade union affiliations to the LRC. As such, the LRC and the early Labour Party were heavily dominated by male trade unionists. The quarterly circulars of the LRC and early Labour Party make very clear the value-for-money consciousness of the organization, which needed to demonstrate that independent representation and the careful fostering of trade union issues were paramount.

And yet, there was a little more. The LRC sent David Shackleton MP and Ramsay MacDonald as its representatives to the Amsterdam meeting of the Second International in 1904. MacDonald informed affiliated organizations: 'An International Parliamentary group has been formed to promote labour legislation and international peace, and our Members of Parliament are qualified to sit upon

[2]   Margaret Gladstone to James Ramsay MacDonald, 9 July 1896, in J. Cox (ed.), *A Singular Marriage: A Labour Love Story in Letters and Diaries* (London: Harrap, 1988), p. 81.

[3]   M. van der Linden, 'Introduction', *Transnational Labour History: Explorations* (Aldershot: Ashgate, 2003), p. 3.

[4]   *Report of the Conference on Labour Representation, 27 February 1900* (London, 1900), p. 8.

it.'[5] As the promotion of labour legislation was the initial major concern of the LRC, this phraseology was the wisest way to lessen opposition to participation, especially given the Amsterdam congress's strong Marxist tone. Nevertheless, when the British National Committee (BNC) was formed to facilitate British links with the Second International, the TUC's parliamentary committee on 28 July 1905 resolved to take no part in it even though four of the BNC's seven members were designated for trade unionists. Despite this, Arthur Henderson, John Hodge, Will Thorne and Ben Tillett filled the places, doing so by invitation, not as delegates. By 1907, the Labour Party's executive included in its annual report a section entitled 'Internationalism'. In 1908, when reporting on the Second International's congress at Stuttgart, the impeccably moderate trade unionists David Shackleton and Walter Hudson concluded with the opinion: 'The Conferences are an excellent means of securing better understanding between the workers of all countries, and in our view, are fast becoming the greatest security for peace the world possesses.'[6]

While LRC and Labour MPs devoted most of their parliamentary efforts to domestic concerns, there were also a number of overseas issues which they took up. Not surprisingly, many of these related to labour conditions. As well as matters within the Empire such as the flogging of labour at Lagos and a Nigerian railway strike in 1907, their concern extended to Congo labour (1906), German striking miners (1906) and striking dockers in Hamburg (1907) and Buenos Ayres (1912). A long-running foreign policy issue which did gain notable trade union backing was the cause of striking workers in St Petersburg and the widows and orphans left after the tsarist massacre there on 'bloody Sunday', 22 January 1905. The trade unions donated £749/4s/8d, which included £300 from a special levy of members by the Amalgamated Society of Engineers, out of a total of £915/19s raised.

The issue of Russia was also prominent at a conference representative of Socialist and Labour parties from Germany, France, the Netherlands, Belgium, Austria and Russia on 17–19 July 1906. Held in Essex Hall, London, and chaired by Keir Hardie, it was addressed by Duma member M. Anikine. On 18 July, a demonstration in support of the Russian people's struggle for freedom was held in Hyde Park, whereat trade unionists joined others in the labour movement, as well as radical Liberals, in opposing the tsarist regime. It was, however, the socialists in the LRC who had most enthusiasm for internationalism, and who sometimes participated in the ideological debates so much a part of German, French, Russian and other countries' socialist movements. Moreover, they eagerly discussed politics with the many distinguished European exiles then in London.

---

[5]   Labour Representation Committee, *Quarterly Circular*, 9 September 1904, p. 3; Labour Party, *Report of the Annual Conference of the Labour Party, 1908* (London, 1908), pp. 10–11.

[6]   Newton, *British Labour*, pp. 46–7.

Echoes of the Past

The socialist movement of the 1880s and 1890s had drawn on, and was stimulated by, echoes of a British and wider European radical and socialist past. The English Revolution, Peterloo (1819), Owenism and the People's Charter (1838) resonated alongside the fall of the Bastille (1789), the 1848 revolutions and the Paris Commune (1871). Just as earlier events and causes (1789, 1830, 1848 and 1871; national liberty in Greece, Hungary, Italy, Poland) had stimulated British radicals and socialists and interlinked them with progressives on the continent, so there were cross-currents of support and ideas in the late nineteenth century between British and other European socialists. Thus, the First International (1864–76) provided continuity between the era of the Chartists and the 'new unionists'. One reason for British organized labour supporting the founding of such an international body was, as van der Linden has argued, that some British employers in the 1850s and 1860s imported German and French strikebreakers. Another issue with a strong international dimension was the eight-hour day, a key issue in the late 1880s and the 1890s, which had been raised by the First International in 1866.[7]

The British left, not least in London, was very aware of continental European developments. As Henry Pelling has observed of 1880, 'what interest there was in socialism sprang largely from the success of the German Social Democratic Party [SPD], which in 1877 had polled nearly half-a-million votes, and had won thirteen seats in the Reichstag'. Such interest was shared by old Chartists and the substantial political émigré population centred on London. Pelling refers to John Sketchley, an old Chartist of Birmingham, whose 1879 pamphlet *The Principles of Social Democracy* was published from a club in Rose Street, Soho, of German socialist exiles and others. This Social Democratic Club, set up in 1877, became a centre for assisting Germans suffering under the Anti-Socialist Laws of 1878. Harry Lee, when looking back to the socialism of the early 1880s in London, referred to the 'Manifesto to the World' issued in July 1883. His account brings out the cosmopolitan nature of the socialists then, whom he described as 'mostly foreign groups with a sprinkling of English'. He wrote: 'The bodies signing the manifesto were the International Club, Poland Street; the German Club (the old Rose Street Club), Stephens Mews, Rathbone Place; the German Club, Featherstone Street, City Road; certain French Communards; the Labour Emancipation League; the Manhood Suffrage League; the Chelsea Labour Association; the Homerton

---

[7]		Among much literature on the subject, see H. Collins and C. Abramsky, *Karl Marx and the British Labour Movement: Years of the First International* (London: Macmillan, 1965), pp. 301–3; M. van der Linden, 'The First International', *Transnational Labour History*, p. 16. More generally, see E. Hobsbawm, *Echoes of the Marseillaise: Two Centuries Look Back on the French Revolution* (New Jersey: Rutgers University Press, 1990), pp. 41–5.

Socialist Club; the Democratic Federation; and two Radical Clubs, the Stratford and the Patriotic.'[8]

The politically active émigré community held a range of leftist views, including communist, social democrat and anarchist. While there was often fierce ideological debate, there was nevertheless much overlap in practice and sometimes mutual tolerance. Walter Crane later recalled that he first met George Bernard Shaw, the Fabian, at William Morris' house. He commented: 'There was indeed a general interchange of lecturers and speakers between the various socialist groups'.[9] This overlapping was also displayed at the Second International's 1896 congress in London, when Keir Hardie and Tom Mann both went against their ILP mandate and urged that anarchist delegates be allowed to participate. When they went on to speak at an 'Anarchist–Communist' meeting at Holborn Town Hall, they defended themselves by claiming that 'they were interpreting the spirit of the ILP in welcoming such distinguished workers for the cause as Prince Peter Kropotkin, Domela Nieuwenhuis, Louise Michel, [Errico] Malatesta, [Christiaan] Cornelissen, [Elisée] Reclus and others'. John Bruce Glasier was even closer to the anarchists, taking the chair for them at a Trafalgar Square demonstration calling for the release of imprisoned Walsall anarchists.[10] Similarly, in the late nineteenth century, there were strong links with some major Irish Nationalist figures such as Michael Davitt. Davitt spoke frequently throughout the British Isles, emphasizing the community of interest between Irish and British working people. He became a familiar figure at labour movement occasions. For instance, he chaired a major protest meeting on 20 February 1888 to welcome the release from prison of Robert Cunninghame Graham and John Burns, and to protest at police obstruction of free speech in Trafalgar Square.[11]

Earlier, in 1889, Keir Hardie attended on behalf of the Scottish Labour Party the Marxist conference in Paris, which marked the centenary of the French Revolution. After being elected to the House of Commons, he went to parliament

---

[8]   Pelling, *Origins*, pp. 13–14. Sketchley also wrote for *The Commonweal*. Rose Street, now Manette Street, is close to Gresse Street and Tottenham Court Road tube station. J. Quail, *The Slow Burning Fuse: The Lost History of the British Anarchists* (London: Paladin, 1978), p. 8; H. W. Lee and E. Archbold, *Social Democracy in Britain: Fifty Years of the Socialist Movement* (London: SDF, 1935), p. 53.

[9]   W. Crane, *An Artist's Reminiscences* (London: Methuen, 1907), p. 257.

[10]   C. Wrigley, 'The ILP and the Second International: The Early Years, 1893–1905', in D. James, T. Jowitt and K. Laybourn (eds), *The Centennial History of the Independent Labour Party* (Keele: Keele University Press, 1992), pp. 300–301.

[11]   Crane, *An Artist's Reminiscences*, pp. 272 and 329; T. W. Moody, 'Michael Davitt and the British Labour Movement, 1882–1906', *Transactions of the Royal Historical Society*, 5/3 (1952), 53–76; and his *Davitt and Irish Revolution, 1846–82* (Oxford: Clarendon Press, 1981), pp. 548–9.

in a two-horse brake, with a cornet player performing the 'Marseillaise'.[12] This was an expression of Hardie's republicanism and internationalism as well as being still the most obvious radical choice of tune for the occasion. Indeed, the 'Marseillaise' was performed by the bands that performed in the great processions of London dockworkers during the 1889 strike.[13]

Celebrating earlier heroic European working-class deeds was a common feature of the left, especially in London. Frank Kitz, secretary of the Manhood Suffrage League in 1875–7 and later a leading anarchist, recalled his associates' enthusiasm for remembering the Paris Commune. He deemed 'a most enthusiastic demonstration' held at the Cleveland Hall 'to celebrate the Commune' as marking 'the beginning of the revival' of socialism in Britain. He also observed that 'the socialist movement in England owes its origins largely to the propagandist zeal of foreign workmen', though this was truer of London than 'England'.[14] Certainly, the Commune was much taken up by William Morris and the Socialist League. In April 1885, *The Commonweal* published as a main front-page feature 'Vive La Commune' by Edouard Valliant and, inside, Morris' verse 'The Pilgrims of Hope'. Also, in April 1886, the League published a substantial pamphlet on the subject. The anniversary of the outbreak was commemorated across Europe and in London at the South Place Institute, where Kitz, Mann, Eleanor Marx-Aveling, Kropotkin and others spoke, with some speeches in German, French and Italian. The meeting concluded with the 'Marseillaise'.[15] Enthusiasm for the Paris Commune was also expressed later by the ILP. In London in late 1895, it agreed to approach 'all the socialist bodies of London with a view to a united meeting and demonstration on the anniversary of the Commune, March 18th'.[16]

May Day: Labour's Internationalism at the Grassroots

The celebration of 1 May built on old traditions in Britain and other countries, marking the rebirths and renewals of spring. For the labour movements of Britain, Europe and the rest of the world, the May Days initiated by the Second International

---

[12]   W. Stewart, *J. Keir Hardie* (London: ILP, 1921), pp. 61–5; K. O. Morgan, *Keir Hardie: Radical and Socialist* (London: Weidenfeld & Nicolson, 1975 edition), p. 54.

[13]   Commemorating the French Revolution was taken as an affront by British Conservatives, as displayed in 1889 by Lord Salisbury when he forbade the British ambassador to France from participating in celebrating the centenary and, a century later, by Margaret Thatcher taking a comparable stance.

[14]   Quail, *Slow Burning Fuse*, pp. 6–7. For contemporary responses (1871 mostly), see R. Harrison (ed.), *The English Defence of the Commune* (London: Merlin, 1971).

[15]   *The Commonweal*, 1/3, April 1885; 2/3, April 1886. W. Morris, E. Belfort Bax and V. Dave, *A Short Account of the Commune of Paris* (London: Socialist Platform, 1886).

[16]   General Council of the London Federation of the ILP minutes, 6 December 1895, quoted in Wrigley, 'The ILP and the Second International', p. 304.

from 1890 offered a focal point for workers to demonstrate in support of their causes. As Eric Hobsbawm has observed, labour was inventing a tradition, thereby investing their movement with a degree of authority and benefiting from a range of existing symbols and social traditions.[17]

The early May Days of the 1890s in London brought together the trade unionist many and the socialist few. In so doing, they were something of a dress rehearsal for the LRC and early Labour Party. The great bulk of the 250–300,000 demonstrators in Hyde Park in 1890, 1891 and 1892 were trade unionists, and the scale of their presence was due to the upturn in the trade cycle and the accompanying successes of 'new unionism' among unskilled workers as well as the enlarged skilled trade unions. May Day demonstrations also provided a space for women and children to participate, sometimes within an almost holiday or even carnival atmosphere.

Both the holding of May Day meetings and their content represented British labour's international concerns, at least to the extent of participating in a general call for the eight-hour working day. May Day meetings were most successful when held on the nearest Sunday to the first of the month (if not itself a Sunday), rather than on the first itself if a weekday, and when the events of the day had the local trades councils' or major trade unions' support. The May Days of the early 1890s were almost celebrations of the new-found strength and victories of new unionism. Tom Mann later recalled the attitude of the older trade union leaders to the new unionists: 'It was accounted a fault that they made use of demonstrations, of bands and banners, thereby making needless public display.'[18] At the time, in 1891 in Hull, Mann commented: 'It is culture we are striving for; it is culture we are yearning for; it is culture we must have … There is a dignity in labour.' This enthusiasm carried over into the early May Days and into political organization, initially in London in the London County Council (LCC) elections. By courtesy of Walter Crane, too, the LCC had its link with French revolutionary imagery in the design of the Common Seal. John Burns, who had proposed Crane to design it, wrote with satisfaction: 'The cap of Freedom and the labourer is good propaganda.'[19]

While the mass trade union demonstration in 1890 was on Sunday 4 May, the Socialist League and some others demonstrated on 1 May. Their banners were notably internationalist, with one at the head which began with 'Workers Of The World Unite' in English, French and German, followed by others which read 'Workers Of The World We Hail You As Brothers', 'Those Who Do Not Celebrate This Day Are Slaves', 'No Master, High Or Low' and 'Away With

---

[17]   E. Hobsbawm, 'Mass-Producing Traditions, Europe 1870–1914', in E. Hobsbawm and T. Ranger (eds), *The Invention of Tradition* (Cambridge: Cambridge University Press, 1983), pp. 263–307; and 'Birth of a Holiday: The First of May', in C. Wrigley and J. Shepherd (eds), *On the Move: Essays on Labour and Transport History Presented to Philip Bagwell* (London: Hambledon Press, 1991), pp. 104–22; C. Wrigley, 'May Day and After', *History Today* (June 1990).

[18]   T. Mann, *Tom Mann's Memoirs* (London: Labour Publishing, 1923), p. 71.

[19]   Crane, *An Artist's Reminiscences*, pp. 332–3.

Authority And Monopoly! Free Access To The Means Of Life'. There were also trade union banners, including a topical one declaring 'Metropolitan Railwaymen Boycotted For Joining A Federation'. The account in *The Commonweal* reported 'the "Marseillaise" ringing out defiantly' and that 'over all floated the red flag, the emblem of revolted labour in every land'. *The Times* in its report also emphasized the French revolutionary tradition, noting groups 'with a flag party bearing red flags mounted with caps of liberty' and also a 'band in uniform with red French caps'. When the procession began, it commented on 'the bands making a fearful clamour in an endeavour to play, in separate places at once, the "Marseillaise"'.

At the huge demonstration on 4 May, there were many trade union banners (including the railwaymen again), as well as Lib-Lab banners and slogans, such as 'We Kill Ourselves To Feed Ourselves' on one side of a drum on a pole, with a picture of William Gladstone on the other side. The largest number of banners were those of the new unions, with the *Star* noting that the Gas Workers' Union had 'no less than thirteen new banners, most of which have been unfurled in the last week or so'. At a May Day rally in Sittingbourne in 1891, 'the handsome silken banner of the Gas Workers' was dominant, being on the wagon used as a platform for the speakers.[20]

The great majority present at the early mass London May Day demonstrations were there through the efforts of the London Trades Council, but the audience's choice of speakers went beyond trade unionists. While several of the most popular speakers on the many platforms in Hyde Park were heroes of new unionism (Burns, Mann, Tillett, Thorne), there was also a broad range of distinguished European political figures associated with the SDF or Eleanor Marx's circle (which was the main instigator of the first London mass May Day demonstration). A feature of the revival of socialism and the development of independent labour politics in the late nineteenth century was the relative lack of an older generation of major British celebrities, with Morris and Hyndman the main exceptions, and a willingness to welcome distinguished continental figures almost regardless of their ideologies. At the London May Day rallies of the early 1890s, as at other meetings, 'star' speakers included refugees from the Commune (Michel, Leo Melliet), anarchists (Malatesta, Nieuwenhuis, Kropotkin), nihilists (Sergei Stepniak), and European socialists such as Marcel Sombat (France), Felix Volkhovsky (Russia), Stanislas Mendelssohn (Poland), and the Germans Friedrich Lessner (who had participated in the 1848–9 revolution in Germany and the First International), Eduard Bernstein and, notably, Friedrich Liebknecht, the German social democrat leader. Consequently, as a result of such a galaxy of European exiles, the main London May Day had a sharper ideological edge than some of the European demonstrations.

In 1890 there were also demonstrations in Northampton, where – according to *The Times* – 'nearly 10,000 working men assembled on the market square,

---

[20]   *Star*, 2 May 1890; *The Times*, 2 May 1890; *Leicester Daily Mercury*, 5 May 1890; *The Commonweal*, 10 May 1890; *East Kent Gazette*, 2 and 9 May 1891.

representing almost every branch of labour in the town and district, including about 2,000 agricultural labourers from adjacent villages'; Plymouth, where some 2,000 paraded; Birmingham, where brass bands played in a parade of some 500; and Edinburgh, where Keir Hardie spoke to a crowd estimated to be between 400 and 600. In 1891, there were more reports of demonstrations around the country. These included Norwich, where 2,000 paraded and 5,000 were present for the speeches; Chatham, where the parade had some 20 bands and 8,000 were present for the speeches; Liverpool, where some 7,000 took part; Leeds with between 3,000 and 5,000; Dublin, Newcastle upon Tyne and Jarrow.[21]

Another marked feature of the May Days was that they encouraged the Labour movement to reach out beyond male trade unionists. In Germany and some other European countries, it became something of a family occasion, with picnics held during the nearest weekend (as well as political meetings on the evening of May Day). In Britain, women were often prominent among the speakers and appear to have been reasonably well represented among the marchers and the audiences. Those speaking at one or more of the huge London May Day demonstrations of 1890–5 included – as well as Eleanor Marx – Annie Taylor (1890 and 1891), Mrs Hutchinson (1891 and 1894), Mrs Ellis (1891), Mrs Addis (1894), Miss Marland (1894), who was active on behalf of the Women Workers' Union, Miss Mears (1894) and Miss Trew (1894). In 1895, and in at least some earlier years, one of the nine platforms in Hyde Park was allocated to the Women's Trade Union League (or to women trade unionists generally). One report of the 1892 rally noted that 'curiously enough the women speakers had an audience composed almost entirely of men'.[22] At the smaller London demonstrations held on May Day itself (not the nearest Sunday), speakers included Charlotte Despard, Edith Lupton, a notable organizer for new unionism, and Mrs Gray. Outside of London, such leading ILP figures as Enid Stacy and Katharine St John Conway were notable speakers, as well as Eleanor Marx who spoke at Northampton in 1890.

Reports of the early May Days also noted the presence of many women in the demonstrations. At the 1 May 1890 London demonstration, women envelope

---

[21] *The Times*, 5 May 1890 and 4 May 1891; *Star*, 5 May 1890; *Glasgow Evening News*, 5 May 1890 and 4 May 1891; *Edinburgh Evening News*, 5 May 1890 and 4 May 1891; *Manchester Guardian*, 4 May 1891; *Manchester Examiner and Times*, 4 May 1891; *Newcastle Daily Leader*, 4 May 1891; *Leeds Mercury*, 4 May 1891; *Leicester Daily Mercury*, 4 May 1891; *The Argus* [Norwich], 5 May 1891. On the international figures see, for example, Cole, *Second International*; Quail, *Slow Burning Fuse*; H. Oliver, *The International Anarchist Movement in Late Victorian London* (London: Croom Helm, 1983). For the greater ideological aspect of the early London demonstrations compared to those in Belgium, France and Germany, see G. Deneckere, M-L. Georgen, I. Marssolek, D. Tartakowsky and C. Wrigley, 'May Days', in J.-L. Robert, A. Prost and C. Wrigley (eds), *The Emergence of European Trade Unionism* (Aldershot: Ashgate, 2004), pp. 141–65. More generally, see A. Panaccione (ed.), *The Memory of May Day* (Venice: Marsilio Editori, 1989).

[22] *Leicester Daily Mercury*, 2 May 1892.

workers, who were then on strike, were prominent. In Norwich in 1891, there were 'several young women' among the Norfolk and Norwich Labour Union contingent and, two years later, there was 'a considerable number of women' in the 5,000-strong procession. Similarly, the substantial presence of women among the 20,000 people attending the 1894 May Day rally in Nottingham was commented on.[23]

After the turn of the century, May Day demonstrations were often smaller but women remained prominent. As with the SPD in Germany, many women present may have been trade unionists or the wives of trade unionists. Of the 1904 London demonstration, it was noted in one press report that women were more numerous than before and were well dressed, reflecting the prosperity of the artisan class. In Huddersfield at a St George's Square demonstration in 1906, the press commented that women 'formed a considerable proportion of the audience' and many wore red rosettes.[24]

The Huddersfield May Day of 1906 was just one of many where the presence of children, most probably of socialists, was also noted. At Huddersfield that year, 'the children of the Socialist Sunday schools wore red sashes'. At the London May Days of 1905 and 1906 there was a platform in Hyde Park for the children, at which (according to a 1906 report) the Socialist Sunday School organizers spoke of 'the advantages of the training given in the schools' and the 'children from time to time sang socialist songs'. The children had arrived on wagonettes, accompanied by tailoresses and furriers from the East End of London. During both the 1905 and 1906 processions, it was noted that the children sang and the bands played the 'Marseillaise', and similar displays were evident elsewhere in Britain, including in the West Riding of Yorkshire and Glasgow.

By 1900, May Day demonstrations were a norm in the calendar of the labour movement locally as well as nationally, albeit usually attracting less people than the early 1890s. For instance, in 1901 in Bradford, a 'good attendance' heard Philip Snowden and Ben Tillett. In Halifax 3,000 paraded behind a brass band to Shibden Park. In Leicester, over 1,000 listened to W. C. Steadman and Pete Curran, both soon to be Labour MPs, and also to J. H. Yoxall, Liberal MP for Nottingham West, secretary of the National Union of Teachers and a vice president of the Transport Salaried Staff Association. In Glasgow, there were smaller crowds than usual due to misunderstandings between the trades council and the SDF, but the ILP was present. The speakers included James Connolly, W. Dingwell, George Neil and J. Johnstone. There was also a demonstration at Kilmarnock.

In the following years, the May Days continued to be successful where there was strong trade union support. The major speakers referred to continental socialists but distinguished émigrés were rare. In Norwich in 1904, there were loud cheers at talk of electing Labour candidates to parliament. W. R. Smith,

---

[23]   *Leicester Daily Mercury*, 1 May 1890; *The Times*, 2 May 1890, 8 May 1893 and 7 May 1894; *The Commonweal*, 10 May 1890; *The Argus* [Norwich], 5 May 1891.

[24]   *Eastern Daily Press*, 2 May 1904; *The Leeds and West Yorkshire Mercury*, 7 May 1906.

president of the trades council, denounced imperial wars in Africa and employers' failure to employ those aged over 35. In Leith, the Labour Party and ILP focused on a resolution greeting workers worldwide. In Leicester, in 1905, the 'star' speakers were notably moderate: the MPs Richard Bell and Henry Broadhurst, both in practice Lib-Labs. Similarly, at Loughborough in 1906, John Burns spoke on the need for old-age pensions, though in the evening the May Day supporters sang Labour hymns. Generally, the non-London May Days rarely had continental socialist speakers and relied more on Labour MPs or trade union leaders if having 'star' outside speakers. Otherwise, the main speaker usually reflected the local labour movement or, sometimes, sympathetic local pressure groups.

May Day 1906 followed Labour's first notable electoral breakthrough. In strong Labour areas, the red colours were present while the speakers were often Labour MPs. In Halifax, James Parker spoke to 3,000 people. In Leeds Keir Hardie predicted, '[in] 30 years hence Labour will rule this country'. In London, meanwhile, the 1906 May Day continued to reflect the impact of European émigrés on the capital's labour movement. Bands played the 'Marseillaise' at the head of groups in the procession to Hyde Park. *The Times'* account reported many Russian and Polish Jewish émigrés, carrying banners inscribed in Yiddish; a band of French workers were led by a woman wearing a red cap of liberty and carrying a red banner. These were followed by 'the London group of the Russian Social Democratic Labour Party'. Other émigrés carried anarchist banners. At the park, there were 12 platforms, one given over to the organizers of Socialist Sunday Schools, at which speeches were interspersed with children singing socialist songs.[25]

Labour's Internationalism

While the May Days provided occasions for mass meetings and the expression of international sentiments, some of the Labour Party's leaders were genuinely interested in fostering European and wider links. For them, British labour was very much a part of a wider movement. This was true of such a moderate trade unionist as Arthur Henderson as well as such an upwardly mobile and cosmopolitan figure as James Ramsay MacDonald.

Henderson's approach to internationalism owed much to his Cobdenite views and to his Methodism. He was twice president of the Brotherhood Movement, and was one of six of the 1906 elected Labour MPs who preached at Brotherhood meetings. Henderson spoke warmly of Gladstone's recourse to arbitration over the *Alabama* in 1871 when speaking at the International Arbitration League's dinner in March 1909. Then, when praising a large delegation of Labour MPs going to Germany, he observed: 'If they could demonstrate the good will between the working classes it would be difficult for officials … to embroil them' in war.

[25] *The Leeds and West Yorkshire Mercury*, 7 May 1906; *Eastern Daily Press*, 2 May 1904; *The Times*, 2 May 1905 and 3 May 1906; *Glasgow Daily Record*, 2 May 1898.

Another example of the continuity of nineteenth-century radical belief in the culture of fraternity and peace among moderate trade unionists was Ben Turner. Turner, an able writer of poetry in dialect, wrote verse in mainstream English to celebrate internationalism at the 1911 International Textile Workers' Congress held in Amsterdam. The second verse read:

> Once the workers were but cattle,
> Ordered out to wicked battle,
> Heroes then, mid cannons' rattle,
> Fighting without hope or aim.
> Changed the tune, and changed the story,
> War's mad visions, wild and hoary,
> Flee before proud peace's glory,
> And no more we prize war's shame.[26]

Henderson himself went twice to Germany before the Great War (1914–18). In late 1908, he and George Barnes travelled to Düsseldorf, Cologne, Berlin, Frankfurt and Strasbourg to enquire about labour exchanges and the early experimental unemployment insurance second. Eduard Bernstein helped them accomplish their research. On the second visit, in September 1912, he travelled with Ramsay MacDonald, Ben Turner, Pete Curran and others to Munich, Stuttgart and elsewhere on 'a crusade for peace'. However, like his German trade union counterparts, he was not willing for the trade union rank-and-file's livelihoods to be put at risk by socialist idealism in the form of calling workers to strike against the outbreak of a European war, a policy for which Keir Hardie secured major support at the Second International.[27] Henderson, along with the other trade unionists in the Parliamentary Labour Party supported the national war effort from 1914, just as the trade union part of the SPD did in Germany.

Before the Great War, Keir Hardie, MacDonald and Henderson established a moderate British Labour presence in the Second International. Their policies were a long way from the policies advocated by the Russian or German Marxists. They were closer to Eduard Bernstein and the 'revisionist' wing of the SPD. Indeed, Henderson, with his considerable past as a Liberal activist, only became a member of a socialist society on becoming secretary of the Labour Party in 1912 and thereby the British secretary of the British section of the International Socialist Bureau (i.e. the British arm of the Second International). He chose the most moderate of the socialist bodies, the Fabian Society.

---

[26]   G. N. Barnes and A. Henderson, *Report to the Members of The Parliamentary Labour Party* (1911).

[27]   K. D. Brown, 'Nonconformity and the British Labour Movement: A Case Study', *Journal of Social History*, 8/2 (1975), 113–20; C. Wrigley, *Arthur Henderson* (Cardiff: GPC Books, 1990), pp. 41–2 and 73–6.

Keir Hardie's international connections also stemmed, at least partly, from trade unionism. He attended and spoke at the November 1888 International Trades Union Congress where, according to *The Commonweal*, 'the reactionary trade unionism of the ordinary English workingmen and the Socialism more or less of their Continental brethren' met. David Nicoll, the Librarian and Propaganda Secretary of the Socialist League in 1887–8, although scathing of the old trade union leadership, felt that the congress 'has been in many ways a complete success, and has done much to establish a feeling of solidarity among a strong section of English workers and their Continental comrades'.[28] With his internationalism reinforced, Keir Hardie went to the July 1889 Marxist congress in Paris and the May 1890 International Miners' Congress in Jolinánt, Belgium. Later, at the Second International's congress in 1904, he was mightily moved by the Russian and Japanese representatives embracing each other in spite of the war between their countries. According to Bruce Glasier, Hardie exclaimed: 'That's worth having lived to see!' He then elaborated:

I am not speaking simply of the fact of two Socialists whose countries are at war showing they are not enemies but comrades, but of the fact that one is of the white and the other of the yellow race, and that this has been done before the eyes of the workers of the world. It is worth all our International resolutions put together.[29]

Like Richard Cobden earlier, he was 'the international man'.

Keir Hardie's international concerns and activities were many and various. Prominent among these was his admiration for the German social democrats before the outbreak of war in 1914. 'English Labour', he told the SPD's annual conference in 1910, 'stood to German Socialism as a son to a father. All the great names of Socialism were German'.[30] On his return to Britain, he proclaimed that all the Germans he had spoken to saw Anglo-German naval spending as 'monstrous folly'. Before the 1912 Reichstag elections Keir Hardie wrote in *Vorwärts* (the SPD's paper) that it was 'universally admitted' in Britain that the SPD was 'whole heartedly on the side of peace. If, therefore, the Social Democrats make substantial gains at the polls everyone ... – anti-German and pro-German alike will accept that as indisputable proof that the German people desire peace'.[31] For him the

---

[28]   *The Commonweal*, 17 November 1888, 24 November 1888. See also F. Reid, *Keir Hardie: The Making of a Socialist* (London: Croom Helm, 1978), pp. 122–5.

[29]   J. Bruce Glasier, *James Keir Hardie: A Memorial* (Manchester and London: National Labour Press, undated), pp. 24–5.

[30]   For Hardie's international activities, see Morgan, *Keir Hardie*, pp. 39–41 and 178–200. For Hardie's speech, see *The Times*, 20 September 1910.

[31]   Speech at Radstock, Somerset, 22 October 1910, *The Times*, 24 October 1910; Merthyr Tydfil *Pioneer* translation of *Vorwärts* article, *The Times*, 30 December 1911.

SPD's vote for war credits at the outbreak of war in summer 1914 (along with socialists elsewhere) savagely undermined his international faith.

Hardie's enthusiasm for the SPD was tempered by his dislike of Marxist orthodoxy and a strong preference for the revisionism of Eduard Bernstein. His views on German revisionism were shared by MacDonald, Glasier and other ILP and Labour Party leaders.[32] MacDonald had known Bernstein since at least the mid 1890s. In his biography of MacDonald, David Marquand wrote: 'Eduard Bernstein, the leading theorist of German revisionism, was a frequent correspondent as well as a philosophical mentor.' After the 1911 Agadir crisis, at Bernstein's request, MacDonald sought information for the SPD to use in a major Reichstag debate.[33] MacDonald's belief in the SPD's good will and good faith towards Britain contrasted with his distrust of Sir Edward Grey, Lloyd George and the other makers of British foreign policy, and contributed to his political stance during the war.

Another aspect of MacDonald's wider outlook was his extensive travelling, something possible because of his wife's income. This, combined with his Second International connections, contributed to the self-assurance he displayed in 1924 in taking on the post of foreign secretary as well as that of prime minister. The MacDonalds were far from unique in broadening their experience generally and engaging in ideological debates in particular through political tourism. As Karen Hunt has shown, such travel was undertaken by wealthy socialists such as Dora Montefiore (whose ideas were fostered by time in Scandinavia and at the 1912 Second International Congress in Basle, as well as in Australia and South Africa), and also by the occasional working-class male socialist who worked his way to an international congress. In the case of Keir Hardie, his travel beyond Europe – his world tour of July 1907 to April 1908 – was funded by the Salvation Army and Joseph Fels, the American philanthropist.[34] Bruce Glasier, in his tribute to Keir Hardie, put the emphasis on what Hardie gave others through his travels. He wrote that 'his influence was much greater than is commonly recognised' in the 'wider spheres of International and Imperial politics', and went on to comment:

> How valuable has been his influence on the Socialist movement on the Continent is testified by the warm messages of appreciation evoked by his death from the Socialists of France, Germany, Russia, Belgium, Holland, Italy and other European countries.[35]

---

[32]   Newton, *British Labour*, pp. 197–8.

[33]   D. Marquand, *Ramsay MacDonald* (London: Jonathan Cape, 1977), pp. 164–5.

[34]   K. Hunt, 'Dora Montefiore: A Different Communist', in J. McIlroy, K. Morgan and A. Campbell (eds), *Party People, Communist Lives* (London: Lawrence & Wishart, 2001), pp. 29–50; Morgan, *Keir Hardie*, pp. 188–9.

[35]   Bruce Glasier, *Hardie*, pp. 21–2.

While there was truth in this, it needs to be emphasized more that it was very much a two-way process. For Hardie, as well as the other travellers, the European and wider international connections also strengthened their beliefs, both in terms of ideology and in being part of a growing movement more radical and of greater scale than that of Britain alone. Like the early May Days, the pre-1914 travel provided not only intellectual stimulation but much succour in being part of a rising international movement. The downside of this was that it also reinforced awareness of the apparently inherent ideological divisions abroad as at home. Such divisions became deeper with the Great War.

Labour and Russia after February 1917

The issue of Russia, within the context of the Great War, was crucial in removing Arthur Henderson from participation in Lloyd George's wartime coalition government and so enabling him to focus on reconstructing the Labour Party's constitution, its programme for the post-war world, and its organization.[36] In addition, with Henderson pro-war yet out of office and eager to conciliate, not alienate, Ramsay MacDonald and others outside of the pale of the war effort, Russia was an issue which helped to ensure that the Labour Party did not split in the manner of the German socialists and other continental socialist parties. There were only a few ultra-patriots who broke away to the right, and there were not that many who could meet the ideological requirements of the Moscow-based Third International.

After the overthrow of the tsar in the February revolution of 1917, Henderson and the Labour Party leadership came to admire Kerensky. When he was overthrown by Lenin and the Bolsheviks, Henderson continued to support him. At the Labour Party conference in June 1918, Henderson arranged for Kerensky to speak as 'a distinguished visitor' (after speeches from fraternal delegates M. Renaudel, Jean Longuet, Albert Thomas, Emile Vandervelde and Hjalmar Branting), and restated his support for Kerensky in the House of Commons in November 1919, speaking warmly of him and other moderate socialists and the Kadets. In so doing, he commented:

> I am prepared to admit that in the ranks of international Labour and socialism, and even in the ranks of the Labour movement at home there have been strong differences of view with regard both to theory and the practice of Soviet Russia. I do not think I need state, as I have done publicly on more than one occasion,

---

[36]   These and other themes have been discussed often. See in particular J. M. Winter, *Socialism and the Challenge of War: Ideas and Politics in Britain 1912–18* (London: Routledge, 1974), pp. 184–286.

that I personally am strongly opposed to a Proletarian Minority Dictatorship just as I am opposed to a dictatorship either of a Czar or a Kaiser.[37]

For Henderson the Russian revolution was February 1917, and he expected Russia to return to its short-lived prelude to democracy:

> We can rest assured that one tyranny has bred another. The crimes of Czarism have been followed by the ruthless dictatorship of the Soviet system. But the spirit of Russia is free and the tremendous constructive forces released by the revolution will speedily create a regenerated Russia fit to be a partner in the free commonwealth of nations.[38]

Henderson, who had played his part at pre-war Second International meetings, was familiar with socialist divisions internationally, as he was as a politician and trade union official of long standing. Other leading Labour politicians were as hostile, or more so, to communism. J. R. Clynes, for instance, observed of Russia in the House of Commons in March 1919: 'I believe that, bad as the old regime was, it is infinitely worse today, and I have never hesitated outside the House as well as inside to denounce any such system or constitution.'[39] Similarly, J. H. Thomas commented in April 1919 that the reports he had read by Sir George Bucharan (the British ambassador) and Robert Bruce Lockhart (British agent) had convinced him that 'bad as the German government may have been, it was certainly preferable to the atrocities that are committed in the name of the Soviet Government'. Jack Jones was emphatic that he could not support negotiating 'with the men whose hands are red with the blood of innocent men, women and children', or recognize 'those who have killed their fellow socialists'.[40] Nevertheless, Jones as well as the more prominent figures all condemned the Whites and rejected intervention as 'a violation of one of the most important of the Fourteen Points [of President Wilson], namely the principle of self-determination' and also as counterproductive in prolonging civil war in Russia.[41]

Before 1914, denouncing tsarist absolutism had been a unifying issue for the British left, not least at the time of the 1905 revolution or the tsar's visit to Britain in August 1909. After 1917, attitudes towards Russia divided the British labour movement at all levels, with the acceptance of the certainties of Moscow becoming increasingly a matter of faith-over-evidence as other socialists and, in

---

[37]   *Report of Annual Conference of the Labour Party, 1918* (London, 1918), pp. 35–9 and 54–61.

[38]   Adjournment debate on Russia, 17 November 1919, 121 H.C. Deb. 5s, cc. 698–701.

[39]   Debate on the Army Estimates, 3 March 1919, 113 H.C. Deb. 5s, c. 153.

[40]   H.C. Deb. 5s, cc. 2167 and 2179–80.

[41]   As stated by Henderson on 17 November 1919, but a policy clearly stated earlier also by W. Adamson, J. R. Clynes, J. H. Thomas and others, 121 H.C. Deb. 5s, c. 698.

due course, old Bolsheviks were slaughtered. May Days remained an international occasion with some degree of unity, at least sometimes at local level, but the levels of support achieved depended much on the enthusiasm generated by other issues of the day, such as the Spanish Civil War and, later, the Campaign for Nuclear Disarmament and the Vietnam war.

Conclusion

Continental European influences were always present in the British Labour Party and were far more than a ghost in the wings. British radicalism owed much to French traditions and, during the Second International, British socialists looked to Germany and the SPD for a pattern of development to emulate. Yet, Labour did not have the deep confessional divisions of parts of Europe (though they were strong in Lancashire and parts of Scotland) and its ideological disagreements were less severe given much of the British working class's attachment to the politics of the Liberals, Conservatives, Irish Nationalists or democratic Labour. British exceptionalism, such as it was, lay in its relative unity and in the vast majority's moderation.

Chapter 6

Myth, History and the Independent Labour Party

Gidon Cohen

The New Labour project has often been portrayed as a straightforward rejection of Labour's past, a disavowal of all that went before.[1] However, as the battle between New Labour's two key protagonists developed into a public spectacle, their alternative visions of Labour's identity were evident. The Independent Labour Party (ILP) had a small but instructive part in these euphemistically played out debates. In 2002, as speculation was mounting about the leadership of the Labour Party, Gordon Brown re-released his biography of James Maxton, the leader of the ILP as it moved to the left in the late 1920s. Brown himself remained quiet about his motivations for doing so, but it was widely commented by those sympathetic to his cause that this indicated his greater understanding of and loyalty to Labour's past and values.[2] Tony Blair took a rather different approach. Along with rejecting 'Old Labour', he sought to situate himself with the 'core values' of carefully selected Labour predecessors, particularly Clement Attlee and Keir Hardie, ethical socialist and founder of the ILP.[3] Both positions may be taken in important respects to be historically misleading. Numerous commentators have pointed out the apparent oddity of Blair claiming moral sympathy with the pacifist Hardie. Similarly, although rather less referred to, the relevance to loyalty to Labour Party institutions of Jimmy Maxton who, frustrated with Labour's failure to promote socialism, led the ILP out of the Labour Party, is perhaps unclear except in a negative direction. It is, of course, important to note these tensions. However, to finish an argument by exposing the reliance of both accounts on myth rather than history would seem to miss most of the point, which might be taken to be that historical accuracy is but a small component in understanding the power of images of the past in political debate.

If the ILP has had a minor role to play within debates about New Labour's relationship with the past, it has similarly – but perhaps more surprisingly – been

[1]   I am grateful to David Howell, Lewis Mates and Sarah Cohen for comments on earlier drafts of this chapter and to Matthew Worley for his patience.

[2]   See for example Robert Taylor, 'Gordon the Red', *New Statesman*, 9 December 2002.

[3]   R. Toye, '"The Smallest Party in History"? New Labour in Historical Perspective', *Labour History Review*, 69/1 (2004), 371–91.

given but a walk-on part in many recent histories of the origins of the Labour Party. In stark contrast, Henry Pelling in the 1950s argued that the 'very birth of the ILP, the creation of this institutional form, was an event of primary importance not only in labour history but also in the general political and constitutional evolution of the country'.[4] This chapter outlines how the ILP might be understood by looking at these changes. It begins by looking at Pelling's broad adherence to a 'forward march' version of Labour's history and his main focus on the ILP's central institutions, arguing not just that we need a more differentiated understanding of these structures than he provided, but also that institutional accounts are insufficient in themselves. The chapter then looks at two other important but rather less developed aspects of Pelling's account, individual activity and ideology. In terms of individual activity, the chapter argues that earlier uncritical accounts of leadership have been effectively challenged not just by better biography, but also by revised understandings of the nature of leadership based in the local variation which underpinned the ILP's early years. Similarly, looking at ideas and ideology, it not only suggests that we need a more critical appreciation of the ILP's socialism, but also that taking such a focus leads to a revised understanding of the nature of the party. One central aim of this overall discussion is to indicate the limitations of the 'forward march' view as a means of illuminating the history of the ILP, and to indicate the lines on which a revised understanding has been developed in the intervening period. However, the purpose, as in the disputes between Blair and Brown, is not simply to expose the myths embodied in this now widely rejected teleology, but also to suggest the importance of these myths for understanding the identities bound up in the relationship between the ILP and the Labour Party.

From Myths to Institutions

Initial consideration of both the Labour Party and the ILP emerged within the narrative of a 'forward march of labour'. This view, rarely far from the party's self-image, came to dominate writing about Labour in the wake of the 1945 general election. A simple story was told by party members and, perhaps, most notably by Harold Wilson's press secretary Francis Williams in his book *Fifty Years' March* (1949). In this, from its origins in the formation of the ILP in 1893, socialists and trade unionists had joined together to form the Labour Party between 1900 and 1906. Struggling onwards through the difficulties and challenges of the Great War (1914–18), they became a 'Socialist Party at Last' with the party's new constitution in 1918, which saw the ILP's socialism accepted by the larger organization. With this new sense of purpose, they strode onwards to 1924 and the first Labour government, a 'gamble … [which] did not quite come off', and then a second in 1929, this time as the single largest party. All this was achieved against

---

[4]   H. Pelling, *The Origins of the Labour Party, 1880–1900* (Macmillan: London, 1954), p. 131.

opposition and adversity. As well as Conservative trickery, there was MacDonald and Snowden's great betrayal in 1931. But whilst the 'long march was halted … it could not be stayed'. There followed the 'Road to Power' and a landslide Labour government in 1945. Of course, to Williams, 'the march [was] not over [but] only just beginning. These fifty years and the years that went before them [were] but the prelude to the greater story'. Such a story contained within it a conventional picture of the ILP and its significance, in which the smaller party contributed three main things to the growth of Labour. First, it was fundamental because it marked the formation of the first body that was recognizably a Labour Party independent of the Liberals. The ILP was seen as a 'stage on the way', with 1893 as a key date in a series of Labour milestones: 1900, 1906, 1918, 1924 and 1945. Prior to 1900, the story of the ILP, its hopes, expectations and, to a lesser extent, its frustrations, form a legitimate part of Labour's story. Amongst the relevant hopes were those which followed the election of the Hardie and Burns in 1892, which provided context for the party's formation and, given their different trajectories, shaped its early identity. The frustrations included those stemming from failure in the 1895 general election.

Second, in the *Fifty Years' March* account of this heroic period, the separation between the party and its leaders is less than clear; the particular importance of the 'prophet' Keir Hardie, 'whose true life's work came to an end when the Labour Party was born', is a central aspect of his story. The ILP's greatest significance is thereby attributed in the period before the Labour Party was formed, and stress is placed on it as 'the only effective way' in which an alliance could be reached between socialists and trade unionists.

Finally, the ILP's retains a crucial role in Labour's history in the period up to 1918, when the socialist aspect of the alliance was fully embedded in the party constitution. In 1918, with the ILP's historic mission accomplished, and with no obvious function left to play, the smaller party ceases to be of interest.[5]

As this officially endorsed version of the Labour Party's history was being set out, a new generation of professional historians, perhaps most notably Henry Pelling, were working on a version which, whilst retaining many aspects of the forward march narrative, was set to challenge it. In particular, they sought to replace 'mythology and vague memory by painstakingly-researched and documented historical analysis'.[6] What this involved, according to Pelling, was primarily studying the 'development of new political structures'. Tracing the origins of the Labour Party backwards, Pelling argues that the socialists' contribution was central because they 'were the one active political group interested in bringing the party

---

[5]   F. Williams. *Fifty Years' March: The Rise of the Labour Party* (Odhams: London, 1949), quotes from pages 342, 85, 104. The account mentions the post-1918 ILP just four times.

[6]   Jay Winter cited in A. Reid, 'Class and Politics in the Work of Henry Pelling', in J. Callaghan, S. Fielding and S. Ludlam (eds), *Interpreting the Labour Party: Approaches to Labour Politics and History* (Manchester University Press: Manchester, 2003), p. 101.

into being'. Thus, what became the standard account of the origins of the Labour Party was written 'almost entirely from the standpoint of the socialists', particularly the ILP, because their whole strategy was based on the conception of collaboration with the trade unionists.[7] His assessment of the ILP rests on its identification of the 'path to political success'. 'Success it unquestionably was: for their alliance with the trade unions was decisive for the future of the British party system.'[8]

Contrast can be drawn in the *Origins of the Labour Party* (1954) with the treatment of other organizations which sought to promote working-class representation. Earlier bodies, such as the Labour Representation League (1869), were primarily concerned with the registration of working-class voters and became absorbed into the Liberal Party. Subsequently, many trade unions also became concerned with issues of representation. From the 1870s, a series of working-class candidates financially supported by trade unions were accepted and supported by the Liberal Party, often via the work of the Labour Representation League. The Trades Union Congress (TUC) formed a Labour Electoral Committee in 1886, changing its name to the Labour Electoral Association in 1887. To some, these Lib-Lab MPs appeared to offer the best prospect of increasing working-class representation in parliament; the Fabian Society, for example, adopted a policy of gradual permeation of the Liberals within two years of its foundation in 1884. In contrast to the ILP and other socialists, such bodies only just merit a mention in Pelling's account. Indeed, Pelling spoke directly to the ILP's first generation of leaders and arguably accepted much of their interpretation of their own achievement and of others, including for example the characterization of the Social Democratic Federation (SDF) as 'foreign'.[9]

In certain respects, then, Pelling's detailed – even meticulous – research offered a challenge to the mythology of the forward march. However, central features were left in place, with the same expectations about the 'normal' course of development. As even those sympathetic to Pelling's work have been forced to concede, in important ways it was teleological.[10] In respect to the ILP, this meant that whilst we had greater documentation of the central institutions of the party, both the periodization and its significance were understood in much the same terms as before. So whilst the ILP is seen of being of 'primary importance', this significance is understood in terms of providing an institutional base, ideas of socialism, and seeking to bring together socialists and trade unionists. Hence, it is largely restricted to the period before 1906.

Understandings of political history so firmly rooted in institutional accounts have been challenged from a number of important directions. Even in terms of the institutions themselves, however, Pelling's account has been subverted in significant

---

[7]   *Pelling, Origins*, pp. v and 229.

[8]   F. Bealey and H. Pelling, *Labour and Politics, 1900–1906* (Macmillan: London, 1958), p. 282.

[9]   Pelling, *Origins*, p. 122, fn. 3.

[10]   Reid, 'Class and Politics', p. 107.

ways. Subsequent research has questioned the extent to which institutions such as political parties can be viewed as the unified structures implied by Pelling. In terms of the ILP, this view has perhaps been most notably challenged by David Howell. Rather than conceiving the ILP as a unified political actor, Howell addresses the complexities of party structure. In so doing, crucial questions emerge in relation to the differing local power bases of the newly formed party, suggesting that there was extensive negotiation about questions of party structure and organization. In particular, Howell points to the initially limited role provided for the National *Administrative* Council (NAC) as the ILP's central organizing body, especially when set alongside the National Conference. He then documents the ways in which the NAC accumulated further powers for itself, moving from 'servant to oligarch'.[11] Others, taking this further, have documented how institutions including not just the formal party machine but also those surrounding the party, such as socialist newspapers, the organization for public speaking and new unionism, were crucial in structuring opportunities for activists and developing networks upon which the power of the leadership depended.[12] The picture which emerges serves, in part, to reinforce the view that institutions matter, but suggests also that we need a much more nuanced account of the way in which they matter.

From Hagiography to Agency

Even in Pelling's work it was evident that institutions could not account for the high regard in which the ILP was held by Labour's early historians. Indeed, despite his focus on the constitutional significance of institutional developments, individuals played a fundamental role; the big four, James Keir Hardie, Ramsay MacDonald, Philip Snowden and Bruce Glasier, in particular.

Hardie appeared to tower over the others as a symbol of the party. He was born the illegitimate son of farm servant, Mary Keir, in 1856 in Lanarkshire. Aged about five, his mother, his sporadically employed, secularist, republican stepfather and their rapidly growing family moved from the countryside to Glasgow. He was sent to work at eight and then, back in a rural environment, to the mine at the legal minimum age of 10. A self educated and insatiable reader, Hardie was introduced to the romantic idealist philosophy of Thomas Carlyle at 16. He was drawn into the Evangelical Union as lay preacher and temperance advocate, and to mining trade unionism as an organizer, from where he was offered a position as a journalist supported by Radical Liberals. In the wake of failed 1887 Lanarkshire coal strike and consequent crisis of miners' trade unionism in Scotland, and impressed by the arguments of socialists, Hardie broke with Liberalism. No

---

[11]   D. Howell, *British Workers and the Independent Labour Party, 1888–1906* (Manchester University Press: Manchester, 1983).

[12]   C. Levy, 'Education and Self-education: Staffing the Early ILP', in Levy (ed.) *Socialism and the Intelligentsia, 1880–1914* (Routledge: London, 1987), pp. 135–218.

longer was he prepared to think of the miners occupying a place in the queue of 'faddists' within the Gladstonian Liberal Party. The following year, he was heavily defeated as a 'National Labour Party' candidate in the Mid-Lanark by-election, before working to establish and act as first secretary of the Scottish Labour Party formed to develop a broad coalition of trade unions, radical societies, land reformers and socialists. In his work with the Scottish Labour Party and through journalism, Hardie built up contacts with the working-class movement nationally and internationally, as a result of which he was invited to fight the parliamentary seat of West Ham South as an independent Labour candidate in 1892, which he won with support from the Liberals. As an MP, he presented a provocative image to parliament, not just with his outspoken defence of the poor in general and the unemployed in particular, but also with his dress, including his famous deerstalker cap which the press, both sympathetic and hostile, saw as a definite challenge to established norms. When the ILP was formed the following year, Hardie chaired the foundation meeting and subsequently accepted the invitation to become president of the new organization. Defeated in the 1895 general election, he was elected as MP for Merthyr Tydfil in 1900 and, as it emerged in 1903, took on the role of first chairman of the Parliamentary Labour Party (PLP). He may not have been a great success at reconciling conflict within the PLP, but even before his death in 1915, Hardie's life had taken on an iconic status that, with time, came to be of huge significance. His early years, as he himself told of them, appeared to sum up the brutality of childhood of the time; his political career presented him as a lonely and incorruptible warrior for labour. With such credentials, his life was sanctified by the party, as Emrys Hughes, his son-in-law, biographer and himself a Labour MP, wrote in 1956:

> Religious organizations have a habit of making the prophets who had been stoned in their lifetime into saints. Then they put them into stained glass windows and forgot their message and inspiration. Let us hope that the Labour Party of to-day will not do that with Keir Hardie.[13]

No less important for the Labour Party's self image was the figure of James Ramsay MacDonald. Ten years younger than Hardie, MacDonald was also an illegitimate Scot with an early influence from Liberalism. Introduced to socialism on his travels searching for a career, he sought to combine his vision of the new life with Radical Liberal politics. However, he became frustrated trying to work within the Liberal Party, particularly by his failure to be treated fairly in their selection procedure for the second of two Southampton seats in 1894. This led to a break, but of an expressly non-sectarian kind, and a move to join the ILP in the year after its formation. MacDonald shared with many early socialists a mastery of platform oratory, but he also had valuable organizational and interpersonal skills. Combined with his desire to make the Labour alliance as broad as possible, he

---

[13]　　E. Hughes, *Keir Hardie* (Allen & Unwin: London, 1956), p. 10.

campaigned forcibly to ensure that the 1900 accord with the trade unions worked in practice. It was he, too, who was responsible for negotiating the secret deal with the Liberals for an electoral understanding which was crucial to Labour's electoral breakthrough in 1906, not least securing his own election as MP for Leicester. Elected chairman of the ILP in 1906 and of the PLP in 1911, MacDonald was a crucial figure in managing the emerging tensions between the two organizations. Although he became more distant from the ILP over the pre-war period, his identification with it was both strengthened and reinvigorated by his opposition to the Great War, a position shared by the ILP if not by many others in the wider party. After the war, he lost his seat in the 1918 khaki election but rapidly regained both his place in the Commons (as MP for Aberavon) and his reputation in the party, becoming its first official leader in 1922 and serving as prime minister in the Labour governments of 1924 and 1929–31. In 1922, his close friend and supporter Clifford Allen was elected chairman of the ILP, with the smaller party in turn providing much of the support which MacDonald needed to secure his position within the larger organization. In this period, MacDonald came to be seen as Labour's hero, standing head and shoulders above other Labour politicians. However, with his defection from the Labour Party to lead the coalition National government in 1931, the hero was turned overnight into villain. The great betrayal became a standard explanation for the interruption to Labour's forward march, the roots of which could be traced to failings in MacDonald's character evident long before 1931, and his role in the ILP and Labour Party were whitewashed from the party accounts of their own histories.

The other two of the big four served as the ILP's chairmen in between Hardie and MacDonald, Glasier in 1900 and Snowden in 1903. Snowden was born in 1864 just outside the West Riding woollen village of Cowling, with an upbringing steeped in Methodism, temperance and Gladstonian Radicalism. His pursuit of self improvement led him from board school to the beginnings of a career in the civil service, only for it to be cut short in 1891 by a debilitating illness which left him unable to walk without the aid of two sticks. In his autobiography, Snowden recounts his conversion to socialism whilst debating the then newly formed ILP on behalf of the Liberals in Cowling. As an ILP propagandist, he obtained a reputation as a fierce critic of the establishment with an evangelical style. He was elected onto the ILP's NAC in 1898 and became MP for Blackburn in 1906. In crucial respects, his politics were closely allied to those of MacDonald, particularly in terms of their playing down the importance of continual electoral opposition to the Liberal Party. Nevertheless, Snowden frequently sought to stress their differences, harbouring his own leadership ambitions. With other ILPers, he opposed the Great War, losing his seat in 1918 but re-entering parliament in 1922 as the representative for Colne Valley. Unable to see the relevance of the ILP in the post-1918 period, he called for it to be wound up, finally resigning his membership in 1927. He served as Labour chancellor in both 1924 and 1929–31, developing a reputation for extreme fiscal orthodoxy. With MacDonald, he chose to leave the Labour Party in 1931 to join the National government. His subsequent legacy and writing about his role in the early Labour Party was, despite their differences before and after 1931, bound up with MacDonald's sullied reputation.

Glasier, like MacDonald and Hardie, was an illegitimate Scot born in 1859 in Glasgow, though his birth was never registered. Both his parents had Radical tendencies and his early politics were heavily influenced by the Glaswegian land reform movement and Radical association. However, perhaps more of an influence came from his poetic aspirations, with the attraction of William Morris' politics leading him into the SDF and the Socialist League. Glasier was particularly notable for his romantic style, which proved integral to the appeal of ethical socialism. He joined the ILP in late 1893 and was elected to the NAC in 1897; he succeeded Hardie as chairman in 1900 and took over the editorship of the *Labour Leader* when Hardie sold it to the party in 1905. This period signalled a moderation in his approach as a loyal supporter of the pragmatic and electorally focused direction of the party leadership, whilst his emotional style gave an important appearance of continuity with older traditions. Although he stood unsuccessfully in the 1906 general election, Glasier never became an MP, preferring instead to stand in support of his heroes Hardie and, latterly to some extent, MacDonald. This eschewal ensured a legacy which was less prominent but, in crucial ways, no less romantic.

Of course, Pelling recognized that there were more figures in the ILP than just the big four. The ILP at various points contained not just the first generation of Labour's political leadership, but also provided a training ground for subsequent generations of Labour politicians. The ILP accommodated many trade unionists. For some of these, like Bob Smillie of the Miners' Federation of Great Britain, the connection was a proud one. For others, like J. R. Clynes, a foundation member and the moderate president of the Gasworkers' and the General and Municipal Workers', the link was scarcely publicized, though he remained an ILP-sponsored MP until the war. Further, as Pelling commented, 'the "new woman" was almost as important an element in the leadership as the new unionist'; in particular, he drew attention to four ILP women who acted as extremely effective propagandists for the party.[14] Katherine St John Conway, who became a socialist whilst teaching in Bristol in 1890, and was elected onto the ILP's first NAC in 1893, marrying John Bruce Glasier in the same year. She edited the *Labour Leader* during and after the Great War, remaining in the ILP until disaffiliation in 1932. Caroline Martyn, whose Christian Socialist belief in equality led her to reject distinct campaigning for women's rights, came from a Conservative Anglican background. She was elected onto the NAC in 1896, but died unexpectedly later that year aged just 29. Margaret McMillan established a reputation as a speaker and for her approach to 'making socialists' through education and childcare, believing in the regenerative power of healthy, clean children. She moved to Bradford after the foundation of the ILP, being elected as an ILP candidate onto the School Board in 1894. Enid Stacy, a schoolteacher who lost her job due to agitating for increased trade union organization amongst Bristol's women workers, came from a Christian Socialist

---

[14]   Pelling, *Origins*, p. 164.

family. She was a foundation member of the ILP, serving for three years on the NAC and leading the campaign for women's suffrage within the party.

Early writing about the origins of the Labour Party therefore depended to a large degree on representations of these leadership lives. Bound up with a view of politics and history advanced by Carlyle, the story was one of great men, of heroes, and of course their counterpoint villains. The big four played the main parts with the rest as supporting cast. Hardie, for a time MacDonald, and to a lesser extent Glasier played the key roles as heroes. The events of 1931 dramatically transformed the content of this narrative, with MacDonald and, behind him, Snowden cast in the role of villains. The marks of this mode of thinking about Labour's leaders can clearly be seen in the post-1945 writing and, indeed, form a key component of Pelling's account. One task, then, has been for historians to rewrite the biographies of these Labour leaders, in particular to challenge the mythological views of Hardie as saint and MacDonald as villain.[15]

More fundamentally, some have argued that this picture, with a focus on national institutions and national leaders, misunderstands the ILP. The case was put most forcefully by E. P. Thompson in his essay 'Homage to Tom Maguire'. Writing about the early ILP, he questioned whether 'the techniques of the political or constitutional [historian were] adequate to deal with the tensions and lines of growth in movements', calling for much greater understanding of local activists and the specific social and industrial situations in which they operated. In looking at the origins of the ILP in Yorkshire, he questioned the validity of earlier accounts which simply pointed to the Manningham Mills strike, and which did not explain 'why a strike at one firm could have become the focus for discontent of a whole Riding'.[16] The picture which he built up depended on the particularities of the West Riding woollen district, with its distinctive patterns of association and migration. Above all, stressing the contribution of Tom Maguire, 'a semi-employed Leeds-Irish photographer in his late twenties', Thompson sought to stress the importance of local activists. Maguire's propaganda activity amongst local labourers, his involvement in and organization of labour struggles, and his role in developing a strategy which enabled the ILP to develop – these were all contributions of the highest order. What Thompson achieved was to show that the 'theory of the spontaneous combustion of the Yorkshire ILP' should be discarded; it is impossible to understand the emergence and trajectory of the ILP without understanding the role of local level activists.

Thompson's suggested emphasis was taken on, developed and refined by other authors. In particular, it provides the defining theme for David Howell's *British Workers and the Independent Labour Party* (1983), which took in not just one region or industry, but looked at the complex mosaic of ILP politics.

---

[15]   See for example F. Reid, *Keir Hardie* (Croom Helm: London, 1978); D. Marquand, *Ramsay MacDonald* (Jonathan Cape: London, 1977).

[16]   E. P. Thompson, 'Homage to Tom Maguire', in A. Briggs and J. Saville (eds), *Essays in Labour History* (Macmillan: London, 1960), pp. 277–8.

Howell began by examining trade union bases of ILP support in the larger unions (Mining, Cotton, Railways), in two smaller craft unions (Engineering, the Boot and Shoe Operatives), and in the new unions, as well in the national TUC. He also examined the fortunes of the party region by region, including those areas in which the ILP was successful and, as in many places, where the party remained weak. The thrust of the argument is to stress the importance of individual agency, the importance of membership and activism over the view that political actions are 'the product of impersonal economic forces'. The picture which, perhaps inevitably, emerges from such an argument is one which stresses complexity and a diversity of outcomes. However, it also advances new theoretical claims. In terms of union activity, Howell argues for looking at the differing opportunities available to, and challenges facing, activists in particular industrial situations, whilst recognizing that very different situations pertained in different industries. For example, the specific pressures emerging from technical change and management decisions enabled ILPers and socialists within the National Union of Boot and Shoe Operatives to construct a situation where a union commitment to socialist objectives could appear as a practical response to common problems. Howell's conclusions surrounding the spatial variations in support for the ILP are in many ways dependent upon the opportunities for industrial activity. Crucially, however, he argues that other factors play a major part in this understanding. Indeed, the emergence of ILP politics, and their character, are understood as developing out of activity within particular political spaces. Factors such as the size of community played a major role, with the ILP's most secure bases located in areas 'large enough to avoid control [by dominant employers], yet not so vast as to produce the transitoriness and atomization of many city areas'.[17] Perhaps even more important was the nature of other political parties, particularly the strength and quality of local Liberalism. What emerges is a far more sophisticated view of the ILP, which analyses structures, including the relationship with other institutions, but particularly emphasizes the importance of political actors.

Much, perhaps most, subsequent work on the ILP has followed in this tradition, stressing the importance of the local and specific in their attempt to understand the party.[18] This more recent work continues to provide crucial clarification of the nature of the ILP, and to develop our understanding of its activity. Some of this has significantly enhanced our comprehension of the interdependence between the party and trade unions in areas of obvious strength, such as those parts of

---

[17]   Howell, *British Workers*, pp. viii, 94–108 and 278.

[18]   For example, well over half of the substantive chapters in D. James, T. Jowitt and K. Laybourn (eds), *The Centennial History of the Independent Labour Party* (Ryburn Academic Publishing: Halifax, 1992) are focused on local and regional studies, whilst some of the remaining chapters develop more thematic understandings through the use of local case studies.

Yorkshire associated with the formation of the party.[19] Some provides significant insights into areas which had remained largely neglected in earlier studies. Others still have used local studies to highlight the impact on the ILP from the viewpoint of political actors outside the party.[20] However, the local approach does more than raise questions about the adequacy of earlier accounts of the origins of the Labour Party. It also points to a greater range of significances for the ILP. In some regions, perhaps most notably in Scotland, the relationship between the ILP and the Labour Party looked very different. In many parts of Scotland, the ILP effectively was the Labour Party on the ground right through the 1920s, and its attitudes and approach to politics, particularly on Clydeside, were distinctive.[21] The emphasis on locality and agency has thus done much to change the prevailing view of the ILP, providing a compelling critique of the traditional institutional accounts of the party, stressing the importance of understanding local political cultures and activity prior to – and then in a two-way dialogue with – national institutional forms. They also indicate alternative ways in which the ILP was significant and the different time periods in which such significance may be found.

Ideas and Ideology

At the ILP's foundation conference, the answers to central questions were designed to accommodate alternative interpretations and emphases. Most particularly, the questions as to whether the primary purpose of the party was the extension of working-class representation or the promotion of socialism, and with regard to how it should relate to the political priorities of other existing parties, were treated in this way. Although deciding on a *labour* rather than *socialist* name, the conference overwhelmingly accepted that the object of the party should be 'to secure the collective and communal ownership of the means of production, distribution and exchange'. This socialist goal was complemented with calls for a range of reforms, which although congruent with the political reforms standard in Radical organizations had far more stress on the social – an eight-hour working day, provision for sick, disabled, aged, widows and orphans, and free 'unsectarian' education 'right up to the universities'.[22]

In Pelling's narrative, the ideological contribution of the ILP is both central and multifaceted. First, the ILP brought a conception of working-class electoral success based on a combination of political and industrial elements. Second, it

---

[19]   K. Laybourn and J. Reynolds, *Liberalism and the Rise of Labour, 1890–1918* (Croom Helm: London, 1984).

[20]   J. Moore, 'Progressive Pioneers: Manchester Liberalism, The Independent Labour Party and Local Politics in the 1890s', *Historical Journal*, 44/4 (2001), 989–1013.

[21]   A. McKinlay and R. J. Morris (eds), *The ILP on Clydeside 1893–1932: From Foundation to Disintegration* (Manchester University Press: Manchester, 1991).

[22]   Howell, *British Workers*, pp. 293–8.

contributed the idea of socialism, which provided a unity to the project of working-class representation. Indeed, Pelling suggests that 'the political independence of the Labour Party always seemed to be in doubt until in 1918 it accepted a Socialist Constitution'. As important was the way in which the party interpreted its ideas; Pelling particularly stresses the importance of the ideological restrictions of the desire for unity with the non-socialist trade unions which led, in contrast to the SDF, to the ILP not behaving as a 'narrow creed'.[23] Its socialism, then, might be seen as one more symbol of independence alongside, but sometimes in tension with, working-class self-reliance. The implication for Pelling, and for many subsequent writers, appears to have been that the pragmatism of the party makes the detailed study of its ideological pronouncements of relatively minor significance. Yet, the assumptions underpinning this simple narrative of the ILP's socialism adopted by the Labour Party in 1918 are deeply problematic. There remained in 1918 sharp divisions with the patriotic trade unions over the war and the general structure of Labour's constitution. The deliberate vagueness of wording indicated that it was designed to appeal particularly to a general collectivist view amongst trade unionists and to the middle classes rather than the ILP. Indeed, the lack of commitment to particular courses of action left many within the smaller party frustrated to the point of there being a considerable movement for disaffiliation at the ILP's 1918 conference.[24]

Even if the ILP was not the sole, or even the main, source of Labour's constitutional commitment to socialism, it can still be argued that other Labour policies have their origins in the ILP. Perhaps most notable in this respect have been ideas of women's suffrage, where many subsequent authors have followed the ILP's self-description as the most sympathetic of all political groups to the 'woman question'.[25] Certainly, the party was committed to ideas of equality between the sexes, with some of its leaders being amongst those arguing most vocally for limited suffrage and equal rights. Yet, here too, ILP attitudes were more problematic and equivocal than the conventional picture allows. There was, for example, considerable conflict between the ILP and the women's suffrage movement – particularly after 1907, when it adopted an adult suffrage position – and the party's attitudes towards economic equality were ambiguous in practice.[26] From the perspectives of institutions and policies, the ILP had an importance as a location where debate and discussion could take place and where ideas could be clarified. However, the complexity, equivocation and lack of overall continuity undermines those who point in a straightforward way to the importance of the

[23]   Pelling, *Origins*, pp. 229–31.

[24]   R. McKibbin, *The Evolution of the Labour Party, 1910–24* (Clarendon Press: Oxford, 1974), pp. 91–106.

[25]   K. Laybourn, *The Rise of Socialism in Britain* (Sutton Publishing: Stroud, 1997) p. 35; J. Hannam, 'Women and the ILP, 1890–1914', in James et al., *Centennial History*, pp. 205–6.

[26]   Hannam, 'Women and the ILP', pp. 205–24.

party's ideas for subsequent political debates. Further, this is to approach matters from the perspective of institutional and policy development. Instead, taking the ideas and ideology of the ILP seriously in their own terms yields a rather different view of the party and its significance.

One approach to the study of the ILP's ideology has been to consider the origins of its conception of socialism. In tracing the ideological roots of British socialism it was common even before W. T. Stead's 1906 survey of Labour MPs to locate the origins of ILP thought much more firmly with Carlyle and the Bible than with Marx, supposedly marking the exceptional British labour movement apart from continental European variants. Indeed, it is clear that many ILPers were substantially influenced by Carlyle, not least Hardie himself, who frequently used direct quotes from Carlyle in his own writings, attributed or unattributed. The central elements taken by Hardie and other ILPers from Carlyle include his moral interpretation of society, a cyclical view of social change, a rejection of class in favour of community consciousness, a call for a new order based on greater distributive justice and, to a certain extent, the view that history is directed by divine power dictated to heroes.[27] Yet, on closer inspection, it is not clear that such a characterization holds up. In the first place, according to Mark Bevir, those – including Eric Hobsbawm – who have sought to diminish the importance of Fabianism have argued that early ILP socialism owed much to 'Labour Marxists' such as Henry Hyde Champion.[28] Despite the common view to contrary, ILP leaders were familiar with debates within Marxism, particularly with revisionist positions, making use of the thinking in these debates to inform their own intellectual developments.[29] Indeed, it has been argued that some of the ILP's major breaking points with Carlylian thought, its emphasis on egalitarianism, support for collective and communal ownership, and the presentation of 'the working class as hero' point to Marx as well as Carlyle as inspiration.[30]

Debates about the sources of ILP ideas can help clarify the general nature of the commitments held. But, as Duncan Tanner suggests, such an approach quickly becomes misleading. Viewing the development of British socialism in terms of the absorption of views from one or other political tradition fails to recognize the dynamic way in which the ideas and strategy of the party leaders developed in response to ongoing practical challenges. Thus, Tanner traces the arguments of ILP leaders for the democratization of the state which came in response to Liberal and Tory economic policies, were expressed in their views on collectivism and mass politics, and particularly in MacDonald's commitment to democracy based on

---

[27]   J. Mendilow, 'Carlyle, Marx and the ILP: Alternative Routes to Socialism', *Polity*, 17/2 (1984), 225–47.

[28]   M. Bevir, 'Fabianism, Permeation and Independent Labour', *Historical Journal*, 29 (1996), 179–96.

[29]   D. Tanner, 'The Development of British Socialism, 1900–18', *Parliamentary History*, 16/1 (1997), 48–66.

[30]   Mendilow, 'Carlyle, Marx and the ILP', pp. 241–7.

active citizenship.[31] Crucially, then, tracing the political ideas of the ILP leadership shows that far from being uninterested in ideology, the party was engaged in a sophisticated and ongoing relationship with ideas in the British political arena and in the emerging socialist parties across Europe. Further, because the parties were responding to each other, in more or less informed ways, reconstructing the ideas of the leadership of the ILP is crucial if we want to understand the structure of ideological debates across the parties of this period.

Of course, thinking about politics was not the preserve of the leadership alone. To understand the nature of the ILP as a whole it is necessary also to consider the ideas and ideology of the party's members and activists. Even so, the thoughts of the rank-and-file are notoriously difficult to pin down and, in part, require the use of new forms of evidence and the inventive use of a wider range of sources than those conventionally used by political historians. Some have approached these issues by tracing changing attitudes to particular concepts. This is, perhaps, most notably done by Logie Barrow and Ian Bullock in their study of democratic ideas in the British labour movement, which traces alternative conceptions of democracy: a 'strong' view, which took ideas of self-government literally, and a 'weak' view based more on passive consent. Advocates of both could be found in all parties. Within the ILP, however, advocates of the weak view, following Hardie, won out over alternatives put forward by, most notably, Fred Jowett in his scepticism towards British parliamentary democracy in general and the cabinet system in particular.[32]

Others, with different questions, have adopted a biographical approach, reconstructing the changing views and thoughts of particular individuals as they confronted various issues and difficulties. For example, June Hannam and Karen Hunt trace the evolving political imaginations – alongside the activities – of women in the ILP and the SDF who aimed to construct a 'woman-centred socialism', discussing primarily those who were not amongst the leadership ranks of the two parties. Approached in this way, we see the many different meanings of 'woman-centred socialism' and the alternative ways in which such a commitment could be expressed; for example, in adult as well as limited suffrage positions, and in consumption as well as production.[33]

These alternative approaches bring different things to the understanding of the ideas of the party rank-and-file, raising questions as to the meaning of the party itself. When looking at democratic ideas, there is considerable fluidity between parties, and indeed other groups. In terms of their ideas of democracy, more may be shared between some ILPers and Radical Liberals than with the leadership of their own party. Looking at the biography of particular individuals indicates the

---

[31]   Tanner, 'Development of British Socialism', pp. 48–66.

[32]   L. Barrow and I. Bullock, *Democratic Ideas and the British Labour Movement, 1880–1914* (Cambridge University Press: Cambridge, 1996), pp. 75–88 and 196–217.

[33]   J. Hannam and K. Hunt, *Socialist Women: Britain 1880s to 1920s* (Routledge: London, 2002).

ways in which some individuals shifted their loyalties over time, sometimes not at all, sometimes gradually, sometimes rapidly. The question of just what it was that people identified with, and considered themselves loyal to, is central. For some, the overriding commitment was to the party, to a large extent regardless of what the party did or said, but because of what the party *was*. This proved the case with most, but of course not all, party leaders, at least in the period of their leadership but also beyond. For others, this was cut across by loyalty to concepts whereby the party was recognized as a means by which to see an idea implemented or promoted. For others still, loyalty was to specific individuals, whether leaders or rank-and-file members. Certainly, in most cases, a variety of different commitments can be found, and their relative significance changed over time. In such a context, it is particularly important to consider the ways in which ideas were held as well as their content.

Such questions are directly addressed by Stephen Yeo, who argues that the popular 'religion of socialism' movement of the 1880s and 1890s was not just a way of talking about socialism, but both a mode of understanding and experience which was often genuinely religious and a way of thinking about the socialism of the period which provides new insights into individual activity and the movement as a whole. This meant that involvement in the socialist 'crusade' was preceded by an intensely experienced conversion, often in the context of considerable personal upheaval, and resulted in a wholesale change in way of life. The language of socialist activity was couched in religious terms, with frequent references to such things as 'confessions of faith', 'evangelists' and 'apostles'. This mentality was not restricted to any one political party, or to a particular viewpoint; it could accompany revolutionary Marxism as well as gradualist approaches to politics. There are, inevitably, considerable complexities in this way of thinking, shown for example in the often antagonistic relationship with the established church and the differing attitudes, including hostility, towards God. The ideas and values embedded in the religion of socialism were not fully worked out, but Yeo argues the 'religion of socialism did not just degenerate ... it was also destroyed', destroyed not least by the changing emphasis of the ILP as it moved towards more conventional concerns such as electoral politics and the associated financial and business modes of operation necessary to sustain such organization. Of course, it did not disappear completely from the ILP's discourse, but the history of the ILP looks very different when viewed through the 'religion of socialism' than it does in the account put forward by Pelling. The period of greatest flourishing is before institutionalization takes places, when institutions appear not as the creators of a great tradition but as the destroyers of ways of thinking. If Yeo is accepted, then the religion of socialism should be seen as no 'mere tributary feeding into the mainstream – "the origins of the Labour Party"', it was more significant than that: 'the tributary soon looked larger than the river'.[34] As with the study of local agency, the study of the ideas of

---

[34]   S. Yeo, 'A New Life: The Religion of Socialism in Britain, 1883–96', *History Workshop Journal*, 4/1 (1977), quotes pp. 31 and 7.

the ILP not only adds nuance and detail to the institutional picture, it suggests new forms of significance and requires an alternative periodization.

From Myth to History and Back Again

In important ways, the search for identity was central to the Labour Party's formation and its subsequent activity. This involved constructing both what the party was and what it was not. Of course, these matters were not settled at the time of Labour's inauguration. In crucial respects, the alliance between different components of the Labour Party depended precisely on not resolving such questions, or even subjecting them to close scrutiny. In the post-1945 accounts of both Williams and Pelling, the tensions between the socialist idealists and the pragmatic trade unionists are left in place in the early Labour Party but resolved in the 1918 constitution. In forming this view, the ILP has a complex but important legitimating role to play as the guardian of one important part of Labour's identity: the bearers of a tradition of socialist idealism that is at once pragmatic and heroically visionary. As we have seen, this account of what the Labour Party was at its origins depends on a partial and distorted view of the ILP.

In his more recent account of the Labour Party in the 1920s, David Howell argues that the ongoing process of searching for identity involved a series of exclusions.[35] The process of exclusion, whether formally in the sense of expulsion or, less formally, in curtailing types of discussion or delegitimizing particular ideas and activities, was central to the developing sense of Labour's identity and particularly to defining what the party was *not*. Such exclusions, voluntary or enforced, included the communists, the taboo on alliances with Liberals and others, and the contested position of women. However, perhaps most illuminating was the increasingly precarious position of the ILP after 1918, which saw the smaller party trying to come to terms with the revised structure of the larger organization with its socialist objective and individual membership. The ILP reinvented itself as a socialist think-tank, but struggled when its proposals were not adopted. After 1926, with the election of the iconoclastic Glasgow MP James Maxton as party chair, the ILP moved to the left and eventually to disaffiliation from the Labour Party in July 1932.

The exclusion of the ILP is instructive in terms of Labour's identity because it introduces directly questions about what it was to be part of the Labour coalition, where ideological questions, institutional loyalties and organizational structures and functions were all raised and explicitly considered by the leadership and membership of both parties. These reflections and their eventual practical resolutions indicate the extent to which the construction of Labour's identity in this period depended very heavily on loyalty to particular and contingent institutional forms

---

[35]   D. Howell, *MacDonald's Party: Labour Identities and Crisis, 1922–31* (Oxford University Press: Oxford, 2002), pp. 234–308.

much more than attachment to ideology. Moving past older myths and obtaining a deeper and more nuanced understanding of the longer term trajectory of the ILP can therefore be seen as having a crucial role to play in the deeper appreciation of the nature of the Labour Party.

At the same time as recognizing the importance of developing this historical understanding, the study of the relationship between the ILP and the identity of the Labour Party is bound up in the stories told by Labour members as to how they came to the party. The extent of the tensions between the two organizations and the ways in which they were experienced and contested is telling. In part, this emerges from alternative narratives of the past, but perhaps to a greater degree it stemmed from a shared conception of what the ILP had been, the vision which came to be articulated most explicitly in the post-war histories of Labour's origins. To challenge these myths is one central task of the historian, but once they have been exposed it is all the more illuminating to return to them. The heroic vision of the early ILP meant that when the smaller party's legitimacy within the larger organization was questioned it brought into sharper focus the nature of Labour's identity as alternative claims to the same history cut across institutional divides.

There has, over time, been considerable change in the understanding of the ILP, which leads in turn to a reconsideration of the party's place in the early history of Labour. Its early mythology was based on a general and undifferentiated picture of a forward march in which the heroic activity of the ILP established the basic institutions of the early Labour Party, gave it a self-sacrificing and dedicated leadership, and provided socialism as an ideological purpose so evident it was taken to scarcely need further examination. Each element of this post-war account has now given way to a more historically balanced picture. The institutional legacy has been more carefully differentiated, the biographies of ILP leaders have been established on a more historical footing, the general significance of agency has been explored, the importance of the local context and its relationship to the national has been outlined, and the ideas and motivations of ILP members developed. Taken as a whole, this marks a considerable challenge to the early view of the ILP's significance. Thus, Andrew Thorpe concludes that the ILP and other socialists 'were not mere sects, but they were small and sometimes struggling … [t]heir involvement in the formation of the LRC was not decisive, although it helped'.[36] Although the general thrust of this comment is understandable, it is perhaps a little overstated. The broad set of significances set out in the early accounts still hold some water. The ILP established institutions and settlements which influenced the structure of and, in important respects, provided a partial model for the formation of the Labour Party. The early leaders of the ILP did provide an important component of the Labour Party leadership, and not just in its first generation. Other ILP activists, including trade unionists, went on to be important figures in the larger organization, with the smaller party being often a critical training ground and, in

---

[36]   A. Thorpe, *A History of the British Labour Party* (Palgrave: London, 2001, second edition), p. 5.

some cases, a power base. The ideas and attitudes which developed within the ILP, or were held by its members, can be seen as an important background to the wider ideological trajectory of the Labour Party. Even if the 1918 constitution should not be seen as a vindication of the ILP's socialism, the decisions cannot be properly understood without reference to it. Thus the history of the ILP retains a central role in understanding the rise of the Labour.

However, the research discussed in this chapter suggests other significances. Local studies indicate alternative ways in which the ILP could be important and suggest different periods in which the ILP's political relevance may be found. An emphasis on activism shows not only the different ways in which the party was understood, but also to the move away from institutions as the sole, or even the main, focus of historical interest. Instead, parties like the ILP can appear as important in so far as they provide spaces or arenas in which individuals can express themselves and develop ideas and identities. The study of ideology points to considerable diversity and the relative sophistication of at least some early socialist thought, and again to a move away from institutional developments as a way of understanding the party. Such emphases may be considered in the light of more general shift away from an exclusive focus on structures found in the history of the Labour Party. More specific to the ILP is its connection to the myths of Labour's early history.

Myths about the ILP and its leaders have been a consistent theme in arguments within the Labour Party, even with regard to recent conflicts inside New Labour. To return briefly to what we might take from Blair and Brown's claims in these latter debates, the alternative continuity stories of Blair and Brown may be measured by asking how central a serious engagement with history is to their presentations. For Blair, the engagement is undoubtedly more superficial; images developed by others and congruent with his message, for example Hardie as the first Labour modernizer, are utilized without being interrogated. For Brown, the engagement with the past is more serious, we have not just a soundbite but a biography which began as his undergraduate dissertation and which can be favourably compared with the work of academic historians. Where there is such sustained thought, the relationship between the usage of the past by politicians and the work of historians repays careful scrutiny. One theme of this chapter has been the close relationship between the framework of writing about the ILP and its usage by the post-war Labour Party. In such a context, the task of showing these views as oversimplifications and considering their usage is not easily separable. Careful examination of these arguments is crucial not only to understanding how they framed subsequent writing about the ILP, but also to understanding the power of the relationship between the ILP and the Labour Party. The early histories of Labour should not simply be dismissed as myth; they continue to reward serious study.

Chapter 7

Labour and the Intellectuals

David Stack

> Between the myopic attitude of the purely 'practical man' and that of the
> 'intellectual', who sees society merely in terms of ideas, lies a fertile terrain ready
> to be cultivated by all who are prepared to recognise that political intentions are
> secular, always limited, but nevertheless frequently dynamic.[1]
>
> Aneurin Bevan (1952)

Labour's 'inherent suspicion of left-wing intellectuals' has frequently been
matched the intellectuals' condescending incomprehension of the Labour Party.[2]
Both the party and the category were products of the late nineteenth century. It
was in 1884, as the 'socialist revival' that culminated in the foundation of Labour
Representation Committee began, that the *OED* recorded the first modern use of
the word 'intellectual' as a noun to denote a particular kind of person. The change
in usage from terms such as 'men of letters' to intellectuals was, according to
Thomas Heyck, 'no trivial change in linguistic style; rather, it marked a profound
transformation of the economic, social, and conceptual relations in which the
writers and thinkers stood'.[3] The simultaneous birth of the intellectual and of Labour
politics, that is, was more than a coincidence of timing: both were products of social
change. Unfortunately for future relations their trajectories were divergent. The
category of the 'intellectual' was the product of a process of professionalization and
specialization to which socialist thought, rooted in civic humanism, was generally
opposed.[4] Of more immediate relevance, the newly professional and specialist

---

[1]   A. Bevan, *In Place of Fear* (London: Quartet, 1978 edition), p. 33.

[2]   B. Pimlott, 'The Socialist League: Intellectuals and the Labour Left in the 1930s',
Journal of Contemporary History, 6/3 (1971), 12–38.

[3]   T. W. Heyck, 'From Men of Letters to Intellectuals: The Transformation of
Intellectual Life in Nineteenth Century England', *The Journal of British Studies*, 20/1
(1980), 158–83. See also P. Allen, 'The Meaning of "an Intellectual": Nineteenth and
Twentieth Century Usage', *University of Toronto Quarterly*, 55 (1986), 34–58.

[4]   S. Collini, *Public Moralists: Political Thought and Intellectual Life in Britain,
1850–1930* (Oxford: Clarendon Press, 1991), pp. 18–19, 27. On socialism and 'civic
humanism', see J. G. A. Pocock, *The Machiavellian Moment: Florentine Political Thought
and the Atlantic Republican Tradition* (Princeton: Princeton University Press, 1975);
G. Claeys, *Citizens and Saints: Politics and Anti-Politics in Early British Socialism*
(Cambridge: Cambridge University Press, 1989).

intellectual was defined in opposition to the 'useful knowledge' movement, of mechanics' institutes and adult education out of which the early Labour Party emerged.[5] From the very start, as the above quote from Aneurin Bevan indicates, Labour occupied a different terrain to that of the intellectual.

The grandiloquent Bevan, of course, was not averse to ideas. He delighted in telling readers of *In Place of Fear* (1952) how, as an impressionable adolescent, he had eagerly scoured the polemics of Eugene V. Debs and Daniel de Leon, the novels of Jack London and, later, the writings of Marx, Engels, and even Lenin, in Tredegar Workmen's Library. The effect of this study on his mind, he asserted, had been 'profound'. And in this experience, he maintained, he was representative of 'thousands of young men and women of the working class' in Britain and beyond.[6] What separated these autodidacts from the mere intellectual – as Bevan saw it – was not an aversion to ideas, but a demand that ideas possess a 'practical' aspect. The self-educated, Bevan explained, seized on that knowledge that was 'useful', in the sense of making their existence intelligible. This did not make them exclusively utilitarian, but it limited their interest in abstract ideas to that which their 'own experience provides a reference'. Self-educated men like Bevan had no time for the gadfly games of the intellectuals. They clung to what they learnt 'with more tenacity than the university product', and had no instinctive empathy with Cardinal Newman's assertion that 'knowledge is capable of being its own end'.[7]

Anti-intellectualism would be too strong a term in which to encapsulate the attitude of Bevan and the Labour Party more generally: 'unintellectualism' has been preferred by at least one commentator.[8] But, in its utilitarian prejudices, it is fair to say that Labour has never shaken off its roots in the same Victorian philistinism that Matthew Arnold had railed against in *Culture and Anarchy* (1869). The party has rarely displayed any real enthusiasm for the questioning, ideas and debate that characterize intellectual life. Rather, it has harboured the Victorian suspicion of any form of knowledge that could not demonstrate its 'usefulness'.[9] This has been reinforced by a persistent suspicion of intellectuals themselves as fickle, rootless and impractical. In part, this can be explained in class terms, as an instinctive wariness of middle-class 'outsiders' attempting to insinuate themselves

---

[5]   J. F. C. Harrison, *Learning and Living, 1790–1960: A Study in the History of English Adult Education* (London: Routledge, 1961); M. D. Stephens and G. W. Roderick, 'Science, the Working Classes and Mechanics Institutes', *Annals of Science*, 29 (1972), 349–60; J. Laurent, 'Science, Society and Politics in Late Nineteenth Century England: A Further Look at Mechanics' Institutes', *Social Studies in Science*, 14 (1984), 585–619.

[6]   Bevan, *In Place of Fear*, pp. 38–9.

[7]   Ibid.

[8]   R. Desai, *Intellectuals and Socialism: 'Social Democrats' and the Labour Party* (London: Lawrence & Wishart, 1994), p. 34.

[9]   More kindly, perhaps, we might argue that Labour was rooted in the 'common sense' tradition of the Scottish Enlightenment with its inherent distrust of all that was imaginative and speculative.

into a working-class organization. In a movement that above all else valued the virtues of integration, discipline and loyalty, intellectuals, by their nature, seemed detached, ill-disciplined and prone to ask awkward questions. It was also rooted, however, in a cultural aversion to the notion of Priesthood. Labour's dissenting roots in radical Protestantism imbued the party with an enduring 'democratic epistemology' that rendered it unwilling to abdicate the tasks of 'thinking' and doctrinal interpretation to any separate group.[10]

In any case, there was no perceived need. Even before the birth of Labour, the British left had never displayed an appetite for intellectualism. Its successes had always been built around emotional bonds more than intellectual ties. From Feargus O'Connor's celebration of 'unshorn chins and blistered hands' and the Chartist churches, through to Keir Hardie's 'ethical socialism' and the Labour Church movement, labour politics in Britain has always been *felt* more than *thought*.[11] It was this that was to make Bevan's celebrated denunciation of Hugh Gaitskell as 'a desiccated calculating machine' so resonant.[12] The unadulterated intellectual has always fared badly. Chartism was notable for its lack of a theorist of distinction and the ignominious end of James Bronterre O'Brien well illustrated the fate of the intellectual in an activist movement.[13] In the early Labour Party, it was men – most obviously Keir Hardie, but others too – who embodied the ethos and ambition of Labour in their person and their personal struggles, rather than their theory and intellectual analysis, that were lauded.[14] 'Intellective elements' could always be found in radical and labour politics, but these existed within a complex web, in which the emotional warp was more fundamental than the intellectual weft.[15] At various points, intellectual ideas were woven into the fabric of the Labour Party, but their success depended upon roots in the kind of emotional commitment that could only be derived from the lived experience to which Bevan averred.

This makes it dangerous to accept, too uncritically, the conventional view that the Fabians 'acted as the brains of the Labour Party', while Keir Hardie and the

---

[10] On the 'democratic epistemology' of the British left, see L. Barrow and I. Bullock, *Democratic Ideas and the British Labour Movement, 1880–1914* (Cambridge: Cambridge University Press, 2006). On the elitism of turn of the century intellectuals, see John Carey's venomous *The Intellectuals and the Masses: Pride and Prejudice among the Literary Intelligentsia, 1880–1939* (London: Faber & Faber, 1992).

[11] P. Pickering, 'Class without Words? Symbolic Communication in the Chartist Movement', *Past and Present*, 112 (1986), 144–62.

[12] For more on this, see D. Howell, *The Rise and Fall of Bevanism* (London: Independent Labour Publications, 1978).

[13] A. Plummer, *Bronterre: A Political Biography of Bronterre O'Brien, 1804–64* (London: Allen & Unwin, 1971).

[14] In recent years, a similar indulgence has pardoned the existence of John Prescott.

[15] See G. Stedman Jones, 'The Determinist Fix: Some Obstacles to the Further Development of the Linguistic Approach to History in the 1990s', *History Workshop Journal*, 42 (1996), 19–35.

ILP provided the heart.[16] Even Sidney Webb's undoubted intellectual ascendancy in 1918 – when his *Labour and the New Social Order* policy statement quickly followed his draft of the party's constitution – depended upon expressing prevailing Labour sentiment, rather than imposing an extraneous ideology upon the party.[17] The Fabians have deserved much of the attention they have received as the most prominent and enduring 'intellectual' group within the Labour Party. But this has contributed to the relative neglect of the ideological input of other groups.[18] On this occasion, therefore, it seems legitimate to put the Fabians to one side and to probe a different aspect of the relationship between Labour and the intellectuals. Instead of another trawl through the misdemeanours of the Fabians, this chapter will explore the terrain between the 'practical man' and the mere intellectual that Bevan thought the natural home of Labour. We will do this by studying the political education activities of the Independent Labour Party (ILP) in the period up until the 1926 General Strike. In particular, we will focus on two book series issued by the ILP either side of Bevan's forays in Tredegar Workmen's Library, which provide an insight into the role of ideas in ILP activity.

Ideology, Education and the ILP to 1914

At first sight, the political education activities of the ILP do not seem a very promising subject. Historians of the party have given scant attention to the role of ideas and ideology in shaping the ILP. Ever since E. P. Thompson's 'Homage to Tom Maguire', it has been de rigueur to claim that the ILP is best studied at a local level.[19] But however useful such studies have been, they have tended to obscure the national political education initiatives and encouraged an unthinking assumption

---

[16]   A. J. Davies, *To Build a New Jerusalem: The British Labour Party from Keir Hardie to Tony Blair* (London: Abacus, 1996), p. 49.

[17]   John Maynard Keynes was correct in his judgement, 'I do not believe the intellectual elements in the Labour Party will ever exercise adequate control,' if by 'adequate' he meant full or even predominant. Quoted in P. Clarke, *Liberals and Social Democrats* (Cambridge: Cambridge University Press, 1978), p. 238.

[18]   This was noted even by as unsympathetic an observer as David Marquand. See D. Marquand, *The Progressive Dilemma: From Lloyd George to Kinnock* (London: Heinemann, 1992), p. 50.

[19]   E. P. Thompson, 'Homage to Tom Maguire', in A. Briggs and J. Saville (eds), *Essays in Labour History, 1886–1923* (London: Macmillan, 1960), pp. 276–316; J. A. Jowitt and R. H. S. Taylor (eds), *Bradford, 1890–1914: The Cradle of the Independent Labour Party* (Leeds: University of Leeds, 1980); D. Clark, *Colne Valley: Radicalism to Socialism* (London: Longman, 1981); K. Laybourn and D. James (eds), *The Rising Sun of Socialism: The ILP in the Textile Districts of the West Riding of Yorkshire between 1880 and 1914* (Leeds: WYAS, 1991); A. McKinlay and R. J. Morris (eds), *The ILP on Clydeside, 1893–1932, from Foundation to Disintegration* (Manchester: Manchester University Press, 1991).

that the ILP's politics can be summed up as an ill-defined 'ethical socialism'.[20] With ethical socialism by definition quintessentially 'British', the circle has closed with the ILP left an apparently insular organization, cut off from more general trends in European thought.[21] Indeed, so strong is the attraction of portraying the ILP as ideologically adrift from the continent, that even those inclined to narrate the history of the British left within the context of West European socialism, argue that it was only with the 1918 adoption of the Fabian-inspired clause four that 'the British labour movement entered the mainstream of European socialism'.[22] That the ILP had a similar form of words in its constitution from its foundation in 1893 has proven no bar to portraying 'British socialism' as pragmatic, undogmatic, theoretically eclectic and detached from the European intellectual mainstream.[23]

This is as true of David Howell, who presented the ILP as a lost opportunity for achieving 'socialist unity' with the Social Democratic Federation (SDF), as it is of the 'currents of radicalism' approach associated with Eugenio Biagini and Alastair Reid, which viewed 'labour politics' as an unnecessary divergence from a radical-progressive liberalism.[24] From their differing perspectives, both emphasize how little that was specifically socialist or innovative went into formulating the ideology of the ILP, and how much that was peculiarly British and ethical. For Howell, especially, this found its inevitable denouement in the abandonment of Robert Blatchford's evangelical mission to 'make socialists' in favour of the pursuit of a narrow electoralism.[25] Thus, whereas once Henry Pelling saw the birth of the ILP as 'an event of primary importance ... in the general political and constitutional evolution of the country', the historical research agendas of the

---

[20]   The seminal article on ethical socialism is S. Yeo, 'A New Life: The Religion of Socialism in Britain, 1883–1896', *History Workshop Journal*, 4 (1977), 5–56.

[21]   D. Howell, *British Workers and the Independent Labour Party, 1888–1906* (Manchester: Manchester University Press, 1984); C. Wrigley, 'The ILP and the Second International: The Early Years, 1893–1905', in D. James, T. Jowitt and K. Laybourn (eds), *The Centennial History of the Independent Labour Party* (Halifax: Ryburn, 1992), pp. 299–310.

[22]   D. Sassoon, *One Hundred Years of Socialism: The West European Left in the Twentieth Century* (London: I. B. Tauris, 1996), p. 16.

[23]   Howell, *British Workers*, pp. 5 and 362.

[24]   E. F. Biagini and A. J. Reid (eds), *Currents of Radicalism: Popular Radicalism, Organised Labour and Party Politics in Britain, 1850–1914* (Cambridge: Cambridge University Press, 1991); J. Lawrence, 'Popular Radicalism and the Socialist Revival in Britain', *Journal of British Studies*, 31/2 (1992), 163–86.

[25]   Howell, *British Workers*, pp. 5 and 10; B. Winter, *The ILP: Past and Present* (Leeds: Independent Labour Publications, 1993), p. 11; M. Crick, '"A Call to Arms": The Struggle for Socialist Unity in Britain, 1883–1914', in James et al., *Centennial History*, pp. 181–204.

past 30 years have rendered the ILP ideologically uninteresting and uninnovative: ethical, insular and electoralist.[26]

Something of Pelling's wonder at encountering the ILP might be recaptured, however, if we focus in on its political education activities. For the largely self-educated membership of the ILP, lacking either the rigid dogmatism of the SDF rivals or the urbane insouciance of the Fabian Society, political education was an important activity. The electoralism which Howell lamented, and contrasted with the 'making of socialists',[27] did not prevent the ILP from attempting to 'make' a generation of socialists through positive propaganda work. That this has not been recognized is, in part, due to a failure to give detailed consideration to the pre-1914 party.[28] In the period before the Great War (1914–18), there was a genuine attempt to connect with European socialism and, more particularly, to use political education to 'make socialists'. This may have fallen some way short of the missionary activity envisaged in Robert Blatchford's *Clarion* but there was no simple antithesis between making socialists and garnering votes, and there was a determined effort to educate the rank-and-file, which has not received due recognition.

These efforts began early in the party's existence. In 1897, its fourth annual conference established a publications committee and adopted a policy of publishing in support of its aims. Initially it limited itself to a monthly report for members, which became *ILP News* in 1898, and to the production of a few small pamphlets and single-page leaflets. The take-off in the ILP's publishing activities came only in 1901, with the resolution of the National Administrative Council (NAC) that:

> [The] time has now come when the ILP must take upon itself the task not only of greatly extending the socialist agitation in the country, but of promoting the active reform propaganda which the Liberal and Radical parties have relinquished.[29]

The resultant propaganda drive was designed to build upon the prevailing anti-Boer War and social reform feeling. It dealt predominately with practical problems, such as pensions, unemployment, housing and intemperance, and largely eschewed any consideration of socialist theory. These campaigns met with such success that the following year the ILP launched a weekly propaganda leaflet, entitled *The*

---

[26] H. Pelling, *Origins of the Labour Party, 1880–1900* (Oxford: Clarendon Press, 1965 edition), p. 131.

[27] Howell, *British Workers*, p. 392.

[28] R. E. Dowse, *Left in the Centre: The Independent Labour Party, 1893–1940* (London: Longmans, 1966), dispenses with the pre-Great War period in 20 pages. Howell's *British Workers* is better, but obscures the overall ideological picture in a mass of local detail. See also D. Tanner, *Political Change and the Labour Party, 1900–18* (Cambridge: Cambridge University Press, 1990).

[29] G. B. Woolven, *Publications of the Independent Labour Party, 1893–1932* (Warwick: SSLH, 1977), p. vii.

Platform.[30] By 1904, following the purchase of a majority shareholding in the *Labour Leader* newspaper the previous year, the party's Literature and Publications Department was showing its first annual profit – of £73 – and the NAC was claiming that '[experience] has shown that it should be possible to dispose of a first edition of at least 50,000 copies of every pamphlet we publish'.[31] Indeed, the print run for Philip Snowden's four-page pamphlet, *The Aims and Policy of the I.L.P.*, exceeded 100,000.[32] Flushed with this success, the NAC entertained hopes that its publications might consistently contribute to the financial, as well as the propaganda, success of the ILP, as profits soared to over £100. It was at this point that the Socialist Library was launched.

The Socialist Library

The Socialist Library was a series of 12 books published between 1905 and 1919, and edited by James Ramsay MacDonald. The Library was specifically conceived to increase the attractiveness of the party to the intellectual class and introduce intellectual discussion to ILP members. In the Library's *Prospectus* MacDonald complained of the 'deplorable lack' of socialist literature produced in Britain, and of the necessarily 'ephemeral nature' of those newspapers and pamphlets that were in circulation. This was one reason, according to MacDonald, that British socialists had failed to make the advances of their continental comrades. In other countries, vigorous socialist movements had an equally vigorous socialist literature, 'and owing to it Socialism has taken a firmer hold upon the intellectual classes and amongst Socialists themselves'. To meet this dual demand – of converting the intelligentsia and making better socialists of existing ILP members – the Library proposed to publish book-length studies dealing with both socialist theory and specific social problems. Some of these works were to be specially commissioned, and others were to be 'translations of the best works of foreign Socialists': 'for it is to be regretted that Socialists in this country have been cut off so long from the foreign literature of the movement'.[33] Their reintegration, MacDonald hoped, would prove doubly salutary: breaking the British socialist's 'happy-go-lucky disregard for theory' and countering the presentation of continental theory, 'through reddened spectacles', as the 'cause of revolution'.[34]

---

[30]   Ibid.

[31]   ILP, *Report of the Annual Conference, April 1904* (London, 1904), p. 18.

[32]   ILP, *Report of the Annual Conference, April 1905* (London, 1905), pp. 18–19.

[33]   'The Socialist Library Prospectus', reprinted in E. Ferri, *Socialism and Positive Science (Darwin-Spencer-Marx)* (London: ILP, 1905), pp. 175–8.

[34]   J. R. MacDonald, 'Preface' to J. Jaurès, *Studies in Socialism* (London: ILP, 1906), p. xiv; J. R. MacDonald, *Socialism and Society* (London: ILP, 1905, second edition), pp. xi–xii.

The Library marked an important moment in ILP activity. It was the only series of full-length books that the ILP published before 1914 and, prior to the launch of the largely unread *Socialist Review* in 1908, the Library was the party's only major outlet for discussions of socialist theory. Consistent with his pledge in the *Prospectus*, MacDonald ensured that the Library's publications were equally divided between 'theoretical' and 'practical' works, although there was inevitably some blurring of the boundaries. Enrico Ferri's *Socialism and Positive Science* (1905), MacDonald's own *Socialism and Society* (1905) and Edward Bernstein's *Evolutionary Socialism* (1908) were primarily theoretical texts, whilst Margaret McMillan's *The Child and the State* (1910) and Philip Snowden's *Socialism and the Drink Question* (1908) concentrated on specific social problems. Other volumes, particularly those by Jean Jaurès, Emile Vandervelde, Sydney Olivier, and MacDonald's *Socialism and Government* (1909), offered a mixture of ideology and policy.

MacDonald was crucial in determining the character of the Library. Not only did he write three of the 12 volumes himself; he personally commissioned texts from other ILP members; and chose which continental authors to translate. Friendship played some part in his choice. MacDonald favoured Second International stalwarts whom he had met on many occasions,[35] and was close enough to Vandervelde and Bernstein to consult them about which texts to include in the Library.[36] In total, five of the 12 works in the Library were translations: two by Germans, one by an Italian, one by a Frenchman and one by a Belgian.[37] What united them – with the exception of Jaurès – and what intrigued MacDonald, was that they had each received a formal scientific training and attempted to make Darwinism the basis of their socialist theory. This was precisely what the self-educated MacDonald himself attempted in his *Socialism and Society*. The claim in the *Prospectus* that the texts chosen for inclusion in the Library would 'not be selected because they advocate any particular school of thought, but because they are believed to be worthy expositions of the school to which they belong', was disingenuous. They were chosen to reinforce what he saw as the most essential characteristic of ILP propaganda: 'We believe in evolution. We have made "the Social Revolution" a hackneyed shibboleth on our platforms.'[38]

The Library was a twofold success. First, it went a considerable way to popularizing the works of some of the leading European socialist intellectuals among a British lay-audience. For example, the Library's second volume, *Socialism and Positive Science*, had not previously appeared in Britain, despite

---

[35]   At the 1904 Congress of Amsterdam, MacDonald, along with Jaurès, Vandervelde, Kautsky and Ferri, had formed part of the committee that spent three days together drafting a resolution on socialist tactics and methods. H. Goldberg, *The Life of Jean Jaurès* (Wisconsin: University of Wisconsin Press, 1962), p. 325.

[36]   Vandervelde to Ramsay MacDonald, 9 April 1904 (PRO 30/69, 1148, ff. 32–3); Bernstein to Ramsay MacDonald, 17 April 1908 (PRO 30/69, 1152, ff. 44–9).

[37]   In addition, a Latvian wrote the Special Volume.

[38]   ILP, *Report of the Annual Conference, April 1907* (London, 1907), p. 33.

having been translated into French, German and Spanish, and published in the US in 1901. Its author, Enrico Ferri, a Professor of Penal Law in Rome and a sometime collaborator of the criminal anthropologist Cesare Lombroso, was unlikely to have seen his book pass through five editions in four years without its inclusion in MacDonald's Library.[39] Vandervelde's *Collectivism and Industrial Evolution* (1907) proved even more popular, and the success of these books was testimony to the thirst for intellectual literature among ordinary ILP members.[40] According to the NAC report to the 1907 ILP conference, 'a considerable market for Socialist and Socialistic literature' existed in Britain and 'at least two series have been projected similar to our own Library'. To an extent, therefore, the hope of the NAC 'that as many … members as possible – especially the younger members and the speakers … study these volumes, so that they may gain a firm grip on the principles and work of the Socialist movement at home and abroad' was fulfilled.[41] The very existence of the Library is evidence of a more vibrant, outward looking and active intellectual culture than the ILP – at national level at least – is usually given credit for.

Second, the Library was crucial in integrating British socialists into the European debate on the relationship between socialism and Darwinism. MacDonald's choice of the title *Evolutionary Socialism* for Bernstein's *Die Voraussetzungen des Sozialismus und die Aufgaben der Soziakdemokratie* (1898), encapsulated the Library's intellectual ethos.[42] His description of Ferri's aim, in his introduction to the first volume in the series – 'to show that Darwinism is not only not in opposition to Socialism, but is its scientific foundation' – could have stood as the Library's motto.[43] A variety of British-based writers, such as Alfred Russel Wallace, the co-founder of the theory of evolution by natural selection; the Fabian David Ritchie; and the naturalist and Marxist, Edward Aveling, had all written on the relationship of Darwinism and socialism. But prior to the Library's translation

---

[39]   MacDonald, 'Preface', p. v.

[40]   Bruce Glasier to Ramsay MacDonald, 12 March 1908 (PRO, MDP, 30/69, 1152, fo. 117).

[41]   ILP, *Report of the Annual Conference, April 1907*, p. 12.

[42]   This ethos was not strictly Revisionist. Bernstein's 'revisions' of Marx had little resonance in Britain and were ostensibly opposed by Kautsky, Vandervelde and even, to an extent, Jaurès. But Revisionism, as MacDonald noted, was also a positive programme for integrating an organic and evolutionary language into socialist thought, with the aim, as Bernstein put it, of encouraging socialism 'to emancipate itself from a phraseology which is actually outworn' – the revolutionary language of Blanquism – and to replace it with a more accurate language and imagery of 'organic evolutionism'. In this project, even Kautsky was a participant. And MacDonald – who had long admired Kautsky and sought to procure his services for the *Socialist Review* – not only published his *Dictatorship of the Proletariat* in 1919, but plagiarised its arguments for his own book, and the final volume in the Socialist Library, *Parliament and Revolution* (1919).

[43]   MacDonald, 'Preface', p. v.

of Ferri, no book-length treatment of the issue existed in Britain. And, prior to MacDonald's *Socialism and Society*, the second volume in the Library, no British socialist had given the issue a sustained treatment. Whatever we might think of MacDonald's intellectual pretensions – and it is common for historians to scoff – the success of *Socialism and Society*, which reached its sixth edition in just three years, suggests that his arguments were well-received within the ILP.[44]

The successes of the Socialist Library, however, were always fairly limited. To an extent it rode the upturn of the party's more general publishing ventures and was pulled down by their subsequent failure. Its greatest triumphs came in the first two years of its existence, a period when the ILP's Literature and Publications Department experienced a swift burgeoning in its profits. By 1913, when the NAC reported that 'sales of literature are so small that the publication of any pamphlet is unsafe', the Library had been in abeyance for two years.[45] The first hint of trouble had come with the publication of an 'Extra Volume', intended to raise funds for socialists in the Baltics. Perhaps predictably, the volume failed to cover its costs and ate into some of the profits generated by the earlier volumes. This coincided with MacDonald according the Library less priority following his success at Leicester in the 1906 general election and his subsequent elevation to the Labour Party chair in 1909. In addition, the launch of the ILP's theoretical journal, *The Socialist Review*, in 1908, not only provided an additional distraction for MacDonald, who was its editor, and a competitor for the Library, but also proved a loss-making drain upon ILP coffers. By 1909, the publication department was operating at a loss, and the situation was exacerbated by the ILP's misguided decision to emulate the *Vorwarts* printing press in Berlin by establishing the National Labour Press in Manchester. The relocation from London disrupted the printing and delivery of publications, as well as breeding resentment within the party, at precisely the moment when sales of socialist literature were beginning to dip.[46]

Following the appearance of volume nine, Margaret McMillan's *The Child and the State*, in 1911 the Library ceased publication. This meant that a number of projected volumes, including the Reverend A. L. Lilley's *Socialism and Religion*, H. N. Brailsford's *Socialism and Foreign Affairs*, Sydney Ball's *Progress of Socialism in England*, and unassigned studies of *Socialism and the Rural Population* and *Socialism and the Position of Women*, never appeared. In 1919, however, the Library was briefly revived with a 'twelfth' volume, MacDonald's *Parliament and Revolution* (1919). The appearance of this 'twelfth' volume forms a curious coda to the Library. Not because of its content: an evolutionary argument against Bolshevism was consistent with the other volumes in the series. But because it raises the question of what happened to volumes 10 and 11. Two books, Kautsky's *The Dictatorship of the Proletariat* and Hayward and Langdon-

---

[44]   A point that seems to be confirmed by the success with which MacDonald regularly deployed evolutionary arguments to beat off challenges from the ILP left.

[45]   ILP, *Report of Annual Conference, April 1913* (London, 1913), p. 11.

[46]   ILP, *Report of the Annual Conference, April 1910* (London, 1910), pp. 13, 42–3.

Davies' *Democracy and the Press*, had appeared in a new series entitled 'The I.L.P. Library' in early 1919, but this does not seem to have been intended as a renaming of the Socialist Library; the two series had different publication arrangements, and the ILP Library was presented as an ongoing venture.[47] Nonetheless, given that the ILP Library came to an abrupt halt after these two volumes and the Socialist Library re-emerged with a twelfth number it seems reasonable to treat them as the two missing volumes. Whatever the case, the Library's revival was as short-lived as it was unexpected. The post-war period demanded a different approach.

From Library to Study, 1918–26

The Bolshevik success in Russia provided a double stimulus to the ILP's political education activities. A new generation of socialists, Walton Newbold warned MacDonald in August 1919, were 'clamouring for classes' and 'keenly enthusiastic [for] devouring literature'.[48] It was a situation that MacDonald, and the ILP leadership, could not necessarily view with equanimity. Calls such as that by the Liverpool delegate to the ILP's 1919 conference for the party to produce literature of an 'increasingly Marxian' character 'in order to create Socialists, [as] class-conscious rebels', suggested a membership worryingly sympathetic to the communist cause.[49] To meet this demand and to counter a political threat, therefore, the 1919 ILP conference established an Information Committee charged with providing political education through a 'great propaganda by leaflets, pamphlets and books'.[50] In theory, the committee had an arm's length relationship with the party, having been established 'on the understanding that it would be an independent organization entirely responsible for raising its own finances'.[51] In reality, with the chair of the party – MacDonald – ex officio chair of the Information Committee, and a substantial subsidy from the NAC, the committee was fully integrated into the ILP's work.

The functional objective of the committee was evident in its title. It was not conceived to stimulate open-ended intellectual debate but to spread partisan information. It was conceived to disseminate precisely that type of useful knowledge that Bevan thought self-educated men hungered for. According to the NAC report to the 1921 conference, the party needed to pay 'greater attention' to 'the "education" of the membership to make it more effective for propaganda along the lines of the promised new Programme, and thus help to quickly influence

---

[47]   See ILP, *Report of the Annual Conference, April 1920* (London, 1920), p. 21.

[48]   Walton Newbold to Ramsay MacDonald, 13 August 1919 (PRO 30/69, 1163).

[49]   ILP, *Report of the Annual Conference, April 1919* (London, 1919), p. 21.

[50]   Ibid., p. 54.

[51]   ILP, *Report of the NAC to the Twenty-Ninth Annual Conference, Easter 1921* (London, 1921), p. 15.

public opinion'.[52] The Information Committee's contribution to just this task was celebrated four years later when the NAC commended its 'enormous service' to the party in providing 'unfailing sources of facts and figures for our speakers, members of Parliament, study circles, Policy Commissions, and literature'. Opponents, it continued, were 'often envious of the knowledge possessed not only by our better-known speakers, but by the rank-and-file propagandists of the Party'.[53] This information was supplied in special leaflets, 'Weekly Notes', which by 1925 were received by 2,000 members, and 'Monthly Notes', which was sent to 675 members. Perhaps most important of all, however, in terms of the ILP's political education, was the 'Study Course Series' of books the committee published and the complementary branch study circles that were formed around them.

In comparison with 'past periods', the party's 1921 annual report noted, it was an auspicious moment to launch a new book series.[54] Most of the financial travails of the National Labour Press had finally been resolved; the publications department was reporting 'considerable' sales of pamphlets and leaflets; and the previous year had seen 'a substantial increase in the sale of all kinds of books'.[55] A small success was gained with the 'Social Studies Series', the direct successor to the Socialist Library, which had opened with MacDonald's *Parliament and Democracy* (1921) – the companion volume to the Library's last number, *Parliament and Revolution*. On the whole, however, the activities of the Information Committee were far less 'intellectual'. The ILP Study Course Series launched in 1921, and which ran for four years and 11 volumes, was far more typical of the Committee's work. The volumes in the Study Course Series were not conventional monographs, but study syllabuses designed to facilitate group discussions of aspects of ILP policy. It was intended, that is, that each book – or 'syllabus' – would form the basis for a study circle to explore a chosen topic. Thus, each volume provided notes for lecturers and class leaders, explaining how they should structure discussions around different aspects of socialist theory and ILP policy, with accompanying notes of further reading.

From volume six onwards, each book also contained a ten-point guide on 'How to Conduct a Study Circle'. Just how seriously members were expected to take this activity can be seen in the almost Soviet-sounding injunction in point two: 'Socialist study must be efficiently organised – casualness and anything-will-do-ism kills any class.' The guidelines suggested calling a special branch meeting to discuss 'Socialist education', inviting 'all the people who are keen on working-class education, especially those who have some experience of tutorial classes and the like', with the intention of establishing a study circle 'outside the ordinary

---

[52]   Ibid., p. 11.

[53]   ILP, *Report of the NAC to the Thirty-Third Annual Conference, April 1925* (London, 1925), p. 24.

[54]   ILP, *Report of the NAC to the Twenty-Ninth Annual Conference, Easter 1921* (London, 1921), p. 17.

[55]   Ibid.

Branch machinery'. The study circle was expected to have its own dedicated class leader. Although 'co-operation' was supposed to 'be the keynote of the class' in almost every respect, it was a decidedly top-down affair. The class leader was advised to provide a syllabus, keep a register and 'do everything to encourage punctuality and regularity'. The 'students' meanwhile, were to be exhorted to fulfil their 'duty' by following up the chosen subject by reading throughout the week and writing essays on 'provocative subjects'. All of which rather militated against the injunction that '[students] should be encouraged to heckle the leader and to thrash things out to the bitter end'.[56]

The key difference between the Study Course Series and the Socialist Library was evident in their titles. Whereas a 'library' implied a store of knowledge from which readers were free to sample at their own discretion, a 'study course' implied a more utilitarian agenda, with a prescribed end. An intellectual might visit a library – and the Library, remember, was partly founded to attract intellectuals to socialism – an intellectual was much less likely to participate in a study course, unless he (or less frequently she) was teaching that course. A brief scan over the authors of the two series immediately highlights another difference between them. Whereas almost half of the authors in the Socialist Library had been drawn from continental Europe, in the Study Course Series all the authors were British. This was consistent with both a hardening insularity in the ILP, and a leadership keener than ever to disassociate from the taint of 'foreign' Marxism, and a shift towards a more pragmatic, policy-driven politics. Thus, the Library's emphasis on developing socialist theory gave way to a consideration of practical problems, such as railway nationalization and industrial policy; such concerns reflected the growing political maturity of the ILP, as it began to seriously engage with issues of governance.

MacDonald's initial editorship of the Study Course Series ensured that the early volumes in the series continued in the same ideological vein as the Socialist Library. Thus, MacDonald's *History of the ILP*, Mary Agnes Hamilton's *The Principles of Socialism*, and Ernest Hunter's *Socialism at Work*, were each underlain by strong evolutionary assumptions. MacDonald urged class leaders to emphasize the 'steady evolution' of the socialist idea; Hamilton encouraged them to assert that 'Socialism carries out the teachings of science', and to make Peter Kropotkin's *Mutual Aid* the basis of a class discussion; and even the more practically-minded Hunter argued that that the ILP's 'chief work' lay in 'speeding up the evolutionary processes which tend in the direction of Socialism'.[57]

---

[56]   E. Hughes, *Socialism and the Mining Industry: Ten Outline Lectures for Study Circles, With Notes and Bibliography for Class Leaders and Students* (London: ILP, 1923), pp. 2–3.

[57]   J. R. MacDonald, *The History of the I.L.P.* (London: ILP, 1922); M. A. Hamilton, *The Principles of Socialism* (London: ILP, 1922); E. E. Hunter, *Socialism at Work* (London: ILP, 1922). See also F. W. Pethick-Lawrence, *Socialism and Finance* (London: ILP, 1924).

Volume four in the series, Clement Attlee's *Economic History*, was something of an oddity. The first three volumes had all followed the same format of a 10-part syllabus consisting of a short introduction, notes for class leaders, questions to discuss and recommended reading. Attlee, by contrast, included little in the way of notes and further reading, and framed a series of stultifying and inappropriate questions, such as 'Discuss the effect of geographical discoveries on history and economic development'; 'Estimate the influence of the new ideas of the Renaissance and the Reformation on economic thought and social action'; 'Work out in detail the position of the principal industries before the industrial revolution'; 'Discuss the motives of the promoters of the repeal of the Corn Laws and the Factory Acts'; and 'Account for the rise of economic nationalism'. It was not an 'intellectual' work, in the sense of opening up grounds for discussion and exploration – it was made clear how each of the questions were to be answered – yet neither was it a 'practical' pamphlet.[58]

Volumes five through to 11 were all better conceived and executed than Attlee's effort. They were also more directly addressed to the practical policy matters that faced the ILP, through its role in the Labour Party, as a potential party of government. This did not mean an abandonment of ideological thought and ideas, but it did help to concentrate the mind. As G. D. H. Cole put it in volume 11, 'a great deal more Socialist thinking is needed as a preparation for the use of power'.[59] But it did mean that there was even less space for esoteric 'intellectual' debates. This perhaps, in part at least, explains why many of the volumes paid scant regard to their proclaimed aim of presenting a genuine study syllabus. Volume five was especially remiss in failing to even provide notes for lecturers or class leaders. More often the volumes, as Cole conceded of his own *Industrial Policy for Socialists*, were 'too dogmatically stated' to act as the basis for genuine discussion.[60] Volume seven on *Socialism and Finance*, for example, made almost no effort at promoting discussion and simply presented a straightforward argument about 'the direction in which Socialist finance must proceed and the first steps which can and must be taken by a Socialist Government'.[61] Sam Smith's study of *Unemployment and Capitalism* made a far more serious effort at acting as a syllabus, by providing short reading lists and one or two essay style questions for discussion. But Emrys Hughes' *Socialism and the Mining Industry* and F. E. Lawley's *Socialism and Railways*, by contrast, were more like agit-prop primers for contemporary disputes and the case for nationalization. That said, both were serious, erudite works of considerable substance. What they were not was an open invitation to intellectual discussion. Only one answer, for example, was expected to Lawley's question 'Should any form of competition be retained in the Socialist State?'.[62]

---

[58]   C. R. Attlee, *Economic History* (London: ILP, 1923).

[59]   G. D. H. Cole, *Industrial Policy for Socialists* (London: ILP, 1926), p. 2.

[60]   Ibid.

[61]   Pethick-Lawrence, *Socialism and Finance*, p. 20.

[62]   F. E. Lawley, *Socialism and Railways* (London: ILP, 1925).

One might have expected a more open-ended discussion to emerge from Minnie Pallister's *Socialism and Women*, but even here it was a case of schooling the ILP membership rather than inviting their views. The pamphlet offered abrupt history lessons followed by questions that provided their own answers on topics such as the shortening of working hours and the advantages of communal living. It ended with a two-page list of 'Points for Discussion', which was nothing of the sort. It was a rallying cry to rectify the position of women in society and a plea to women themselves to take an interest in politics, read political literature and work with men in bringing about social change.[63] The underlying message was the need to link the 'women's movement' to the movement for socialism. It was conceded that the specific 'grievances' of women had their roots beyond the general injustice wrought by capitalism, but it would only be possible to remedy their suffering through a general change. The so-called 'sex-war', Pallister argued, was a product of 'an unorganised system of industry', and male resentment at female competition for work was a natural reaction to any perceived competitor. This problem, however, would be overcome in a socialist future where well-paid and interesting work would be plentiful.[64]

Pallister's retreat into the hazy image of a rational, aesthetic, rural and artistic socialist future as an answer to all possible objections, brought to mind the 'glorious indefiniteness' of MacDonald's theoretical writings.[65] Such 'Turner landscapes', however, were not characteristic of the later volumes in the series, which tended to be plain, sober affairs. The lifespan of the Study Course Series coincided with, and reflected, an important change in ILP ideology. Between 1921 and 1926, the party increasingly freed itself from what the *New Leader* newspaper disparaged as 'the deadening idea that Socialism can only be established by slow gradualism over generations of time', and what MacDonald had promoted as 'evolutionary socialism'.[66] In its place, the ILP committed itself to a more actively interventionist economic policy, a shift which culminated in the 1926 'Socialism in Our Time' statement. Concurrently, the series became less and less preoccupied with MacDonald's favourite theme of evolutionary socialism and more and more interested in questions of workers' control, nationalization and under-consumptionist economics. The increasing influence of Keynes is evident in a number of volumes and most obvious in Sam Smith's *Unemployment and Capitalism*.[67] In one sense, we might see this as a retreat from 'theoretical' – and thereby intellectual – socialism towards a more practical politics, but it was less clear-cut than that. The volumes on mining and railway nationalization were, for

---

63   M. Pallister, *Socialism for Women* (London: ILP, 1924), pp. 31–2.

64   Ibid., pp. 4 and 10.

65   L. MacNeil Weir, *The Tragedy of Ramsay MacDonald: A Political Biography* (London: Secker & Warburg, 1938) p. xi.

66   Dowse, *Left in the Centre*, pp. 122–3.

67   S. Smith, *Unemployment and Capitalism* (London: ILP, 1925); G. Foote, *The Labour Party's Political Thought: A History* (London: Routledge, 1985), pp. 126–48.

example, arguably more erudite and than anything offered by MacDonald and the concluding volume 11 was written by the series' only bona fide intellectual, in the form of Cole.

The recruitment of Cole to the series is an indication of how quickly ILP thought was changing. When the Study Course Series was launched it was, in part, intended to rival a similar series published by the Labour Research Department (LRD). The LRD's 'Syllabus Series', launched in 1920, was edited by Cole and anticipated the template of the ILP's Study Course Series by including class materials, guides to reading, and advice on running study circles. Indeed the ILP series not only copied the format of the Syllabus Series but, on occasion, copied its chosen topics too. Attlee's volume on *Economic History* and Sam Smith's study of *Unemployment and Capitalism*, in particular, seem to have been inspired by volumes four and eight in the LRD series, which were both written by Cole.[68] The difference between the two series was that the LRD's volumes, written by Cole, Raymond Postgate, Maurice Dobb, Robin Page Arnot and the like, and carrying adverts for the Communist Bookshop in Convent Garden, evinced more sympathy for the Russian cause than was ever to be found in its ILP counterpart, where sympathy for the Soviets was presented as a misapprehension from which ILP members needed to be disabused.[69] Indeed, in the Study Course Series the Russian experience provided a consistent counterpoint against which ILP socialism was defined.

This was most obvious in the early volumes, where MacDonald and Hamilton especially, used every opportunity to contrast the ILP experience and ILP ideology with that of the Bolsheviks.[70] But the same theme, less boldly stated, ran through the later volumes too and was evident even in Attlee's guide to economic history.[71] The motivation for this – at time when elements within the ILP were pushing for affiliation to the Third International and political opponents were seeking to smear the party as treacherous communists – was obvious. The consequence was to reinforce British socialism's growing insularity. In the series, a strict contrast was drawn between the British tradition, traceable to 'early Christian times' and advanced 'by the currents coming from Carlyle, Ruskin and, above all, William Morris', and the Marxist tradition of continental Europe.[72] Thus, whereas the Socialist Library had placed great importance upon connecting the party to continental socialist thought, the Study Courses Series emphasized that ILP socialism was an indigenous tradition.[73] Again, as with the shift towards

---

[68]   G. D. H. Cole, *English Economic History. A Syllabus for Classes and Study Circles* (London, 1922); G. D. H. Cole, *Unemployment* (London, 1923).

[69]   See especially R. Page Arnot, *The Russian Revolution. A Narrative and a Guide for Reading* (London, 1923).

[70]   MacDonald, *History of the I.L.P.*, pp. 2–3, 10–11, 14–16; Hamilton, *Principles*, pp. 1, 6–7, 21–5.

[71]   Attlee, *Economic History*, p. 1.

[72]   Hamilton, *Principles*, p. 1.

[73]   MacDonald, *History of the I.L.P.*, pp. 7–9.

a more 'practical' politics, one must be careful not overstate the change. Even before 1914, many in the Labour Party as a whole, including ILP members, would have emphasized the indigenous (and idiosyncratically English) socialist tradition. Nonetheless, the ILP appeared to be a more insular party after the Great War than before.

Conclusions

The conclusions one can legitimately draw from this brief comparison of two series of political education tracts are, inevitably, limited. The chief one is that the image of the ILP as an ethical, insular and electoralist organization is a generalization that, while broadly correct, telescopes important changes of emphasis in ideology and activity in the period before 1926. To the extent that this image rests upon the New Left nostrum of 'labourism', our study would seem to bear out Raphael Samuel and Gareth Stedman Jones' complaint that too much 'left-wing' history has failed to pay sufficient attention to nuances and context.[74] This is a criticism, too, that can easily be made of the (limited) consideration usually given to the relationship between Labour and intellectuals. More often than not, this has been told from the perspective of the intellectuals' incomprehension of a primordial political beast. We have sought to show two less well understood aspects of the relationship. First, what ought to be an obvious fact that the place of intellectual ideas in Labour Party history differed in different periods. In particular, we have shown how the ILP became less and less open to intellectual debate as the political challenge from the left, in the form of Bolshevism, strengthened, and as Labour increasingly came to see itself as a pragmatic party of governance. Second, we have demonstrated the important, though declining, role of ideas in the political education initiatives of the ILP. Although always a distinct body, much of what we have had to say about the ILP, we would argue, was also true of the Labour Party more generally.

Most importantly, we have attempted to illustrate Bevan's argument that Labour has always tended towards a distinctive terrain – between the purely practical man and the mere intellectual. This, more efficaciously than any other factor, helps explain the often-troubled relationship of Labour and the intellectuals. The Socialist League, which largely consisted of ILP intellectuals who remained loyal to Labour following the party's disaffiliation in 1932, failed according to Ben Pimlott because of its fatal inability to understand either Labour's culture or power structure. The social background of its leaders was one problem, but just as debilitating was the League's determination to work through the party's 'democratic structures' and to promote open debate. This clashed with Labour's instinctual desire for unity, and its distrust of dissension, even before questions of

---

[74]   R. Samuel and G. Stedman Jones, 'The Labour Party and Social Democracy', in their *Culture, Ideology and Politics: Essays for Eric Hobsbawm* (London: Routledge, 1982), p. 325.

policy were broached. It also, of course, clashed with the power politics of trade union leaderships keen to keep the party in line. A similar culture clash occurred in the late 1970s and early 1980s with the rise of the so-called Bennite left. The struggle for intra-party democracy provided a forum for open discussion in which ideas and the contribution of intellectuals was welcome. This brief flourishing of ideas and debates, however, coincided with electoral disaster; since 1983, the party's instinct for self-preservation and dismay with dissension has been elevated into an overriding political principle.

An 'intellectual approach' of openness, questioning and debate has never gained more than a fleeting acceptance in the Labour Party.[75] The paradox is that intellectuals have only flourished in the Labour Party when they have jettisoned their most attractive trait and most democratic instinct – restless inquiry and open questioning. This, perhaps, helps explain why it was the Fabians who were the intellectual group who achieved most success within the party. Their top-down, 'mechanical', brand of reformism was – in its aversion to open, democratic debate – suitably 'unintellectual' and utilitarian for the needs of Labour. And was able to triumph at moments when the party most desperately felt the need for public unity – in 1918 and again after 1931. The Fabians provided ideas, but without any of the dangers of open intellectualism. In recent times, a loose conglomeration of think-tanks and 'gurus' has achieved a similar ascendancy. The triumph of the 'new times' agenda, spawned by *Marxism Today*, which eventually transmogrified into 'New Labour' ideology, via the medium of Geoff Mulgan and his fellow policy wonks, was made possible by the systematic shutting down of avenues of discussion and dissent within the party – a process begun by Kinnock and completed by Blair.[76] 'Intellectuals', that is, now exercise a much greater influence over party policy than the ordinary party membership, but the Labour Party itself has never been less intellectual. 'New Labour' represents a new philistinism, both in terms of internal democracy and public policy, and, to an extent, that means it continues a Labour tradition.[77]

---

[75] Pimlott, 'The Socialist League'; P. Seyd, *The Rise and Fall of the Labour Left* (London: Macmillan, 1987).

[76] R. C. Blank, *From Thatcher to the Third Way: Think-tanks, Intellectuals and the Blair Project* (Stuttgart: Ibidem-Verlag, 2003).

[77] For an engaging critique of 'New Labour' and the intellectuals, see F. Furedi, *Where Have All the Intellectuals Gone? Confronting 21st century Philistinism* (London: Continuum, 2004).

Chapter 8

The Distinctiveness of British Socialism? Religion and the Rise of Labour, *c.*1900–39

Peter Catterall

In 1964, the then leader of the Labour Party, Harold Wilson, introduced his remarks about the distinctiveness of British socialism with some observations on the role of religion:

> It was the late Secretary of the Labour Party, Mr Morgan Phillips, who said that Socialism in Britain owed far more to Methodism than to Marx. If he has forgotten his alliteration and said 'Nonconformity', he would have been very near the truth, though that would have been to underrate the great contributions to nineteenth-century socialist thinking of such Anglicans as Charles Kingsley and Charles Gore.[1]

Kingsley and his fellow Christian socialists in the mid-nineteenth century were concerned, in the aftermath of Chartism, both with the links between political radicalism and atheism, and to demonstrate that Christianity spoke to the material as well as the spiritual needs of the poor. In the ensuing decades, the churches – albeit rarely as radically as those who went on to lead the nascent labour movement in the late nineteenth and early twentieth centuries might have liked – tried to move away from a narrow evangelicalism of individual salvation to a broader engagement with contemporary social conditions.[2]

Quite what contribution Wilson thought Kingsley or his successors made to the development of the Labour Party, however, remains unclear. Whatever he thought

---

[1] H. Wilson, *The Relevance of British Socialism* (London: Weidenfeld and Nicolson, 1964), p. 1.

[2] See K. S. Inglis, *Churches and the Working Class in Victorian England* (London: Routledge and Kegan Paul, 1963); P. d'A. Jones, *The Christian Socialist Revival, 1877–1914: Religion, Class and Social Conscience in Late Victorian England* (London: Longman, 1985); K. Heasman, *Evangelicals in Action: An Appraisal of their Social Work in the Victorian Era* (London: Geoffrey Bles, 1962); S. Mayor, *The Churches and the Labour Movement* (London: Independent Press, 1967); W. W. Knox, 'Religion and the Scottish Labour Movement, c1900–39', *Journal of Contemporary History*, 23/4 (1988), 609–30.

Labour's debt might be to either Anglican Christian Socialism or Nonconformity,[3] Wilson made no attempt to spell it out either in 1964 or subsequently. Nor did Morgan Phillips. A Methodist himself, who served as party secretary from 1944 to 1961, Phillips featured the supposed relationship between Methodism and Labour in a number of his speeches in the 1940s and 1950s. Phillips did not elaborate on this, nor in all probability did he feel he had to. The notion that – at least in the eighteenth century of the Methodist revival – relations with working-class social movements were, as a previous Labour Party leader, Ramsay MacDonald, put it, 'of the most intimate kind', was a popular historical convention that the contemporary works of the Methodist historian R. F. Wearmouth sought to perpetuate.[4] Nor was the relationship seen as purely historical; Labour owed a continuing debt. 'Nonconformity', MacDonald claimed, 'has trained our speakers in its pulpits and fashioned our devoted workers in its Sunday Schools'.[5] Writing in 1960, Alan Bullock could only agree. For this son of a Unitarian manse, 'the contribution of Nonconformity to the British labour movement is a commonplace: a chapel upbringing has been as characteristic of British trade union leadership, for instance, as a public school education of the leaders of the ruling class'.[6] The conventional view of Labour's debt to religion, in other words, was in terms of personnel.

Methodism and/or Marxism?

Although the intimacy of Nonconformity's relationship with trade union and labour movements in the eighteenth and nineteenth centuries has subsequently been called into question,[7] that it was widely believed to be true is not unimportant. Even if exaggerated, it marked a distinction between Labour and other European socialist

---

[3]   Nonconformity describes a disparate group of churches whose main common ground was that they were non-Anglican Protestants. The largest were the Methodists, Baptists and Congregationalists, though small denominations such as the Religious Society of Friends (Quakers) and Unitarians had political significance out of all proportion to their size. By the twentieth century, the terms Nonconformity and Free Churches were commonly used as interchangeable appellations.

[4]   J. Ramsay MacDonald, preface to A. D. Belden, *George Whitefield the Awakener: A Modern Study of the Evangelical Revival* (London: Sampson Law, 1930), p. xi; R. F. Wearmouth, *Methodism and the Working-Class Movements of England, 1800–1850* (London: Epworth Press, 1937), *Methodism and the Struggle of the Working Classes, 1850–1900* (London: Epworth Press, 1954), *The Social and Political Influence of Methodism in the Twentieth Century* (London: Epworth Press, 1957), *Methodism and the Trade Unions* (London: Epworth Press, 1959).

[5]   *British Weekly*, 10 January 1924.

[6]   A. Bullock, *The Life and Times of Ernest Bevin: Volume I, Trade Union Leader, 1881–1940* (London: Heinemann, 1960), p. 9.

[7]   See D. Hempton, *Methodism and Politics in British Society, 1750–1850* (London: Hutchinson, 1984).

movements. One of the occasions for Phillips' observation about Methodism and Marx was a speech he gave to the International Socialist conference at Copenhagen in 1950.[8] The parties of his mainly non-British audience largely shared some kind of Marxist heritage. Most Labour MPs of the early twentieth century did not. Jack Lawson was among the minority of Labour figures introduced to Marxist thinking at Ruskin College, Oxford (in his case) or through other bodies such as the Plebs League or the National Council of Labour Colleges. To Lawson, however, all this involved was mere theorizing, which paled into insignificance beside the 'visions of a people putting fresh, new values on themselves ... becoming more temperate; hungering for better homes and conditions so that they and those for whom they are responsible may be morally and materially enlarged'.[9]

These visions he had acquired as a Methodist lay preacher. There is little evidence that Marxism as opposed to the chapel had any more impact on the way Lawson's erstwhile principal at Ruskin, the Congregationalist Hastings Lees-Smith, thought about socialism. Marxism might have served as a tool for particular British socialists, including some whose Christian convictions did not waver.[10] It did not tend to become an alternative and more powerful belief system.[11] As the then Marxist Walton Newbold explained, there were particular reasons for this. Writing in the theoretical journal of the Independent Labour Party (ILP), that forerunner of Labour to which both Lawson and Lees-Smith belonged, he commented: 'The ILP is a British institution ... It has grown up in a historic environment peculiar to this country'.[12]

Britain's Distinctive Religious Heritage

As Newbold saw it, it was Britain's religious environment that made it distinctive. 'In Scotland the dominant strain in the ILP has been that of the Covenanter.[13] In England and Wales it has been that of the Nonconformist.'[14] There may have been

---

[8]   *The Times*, 3 June 1950.

[9]   J. Lawson, *A Man's Life* (London: Hodder and Stoughton, 1932), pp. 161–2 and 250. See also C. J. Simmons, *Soap Box Evangelist* (Chichester: Janay Publishing, 1972), p. 17.

[10]   P. Catterall, 'The Free Churches and the Labour Party in England and Wales, 1918–39' (unpublished PhD thesis, University of London, 1989), pp. 459f.

[11]   It will be seen that the explanation offered here for this differs somewhat from the emphasis on autodidacticism in Ross McKibbin's 'Why was there no Marxism in Great Britain?', *English Historical Review*, 99/391 (1984), 297–331.

[12]   J. T. Walton Newbold, 'The ILP: A Marxist Study', *Socialist Review*, 17 (1920), 77–86.

[13]   A reference to seventeenth-century opposition to episcopacy in Scotland.

[14]   Newbold, 'The ILP', p. 82.

established churches in both England and Scotland,[15] but neither was as dominant numerically or culturally as Continental analogues. Conflicts over education, for instance, did not pose secular against Catholic interests as in France up to 1905, but were essentially shaped by inter-church rivalries. Nonconformists, socially excluded by Erastian churches on both sides of the border, had led the struggle for the gradual concession of civil and political rights since the late seventeenth century. Liberty was indeed seen both as central to the Free Churches' historic witness and as a key principle of their faith: how can someone be morally regenerate unless they are individually responsible for their actions? Nonconformists could thereby readily portray Labour's struggle for economic rights as simply a continuation of this historic witness.[16] As the Congregationalist Labour MP Somerville Hastings put it: 'We who are Free Churchmen must never forget the debt we owe to our forefathers for the measure of political and religious liberty that is ours ... But civil and religious liberty can never be complete without economic liberty as well.'[17]

Continental Europe, in contrast, may have known Marx but was much less familiar with Methodism. There was a well-established theological exchange between Scotland and Germany, and Scottish Presbyterianism could find a number of cognate organizations on the Continent. Sister churches of English Nonconformity – and indeed, of the Church of England – were much thinner on the ground. The predominant presence in the religious landscape was, in most countries, the Roman Catholic Church. In Britain, Catholicism was certainly strong in pockets, such as around Glasgow, Lancashire and North East England, largely as a result of immigrant Irish populations. In the first two of these its presence as a large minority undoubtedly contributed to a distinctive political scene marred by sectarianism and, from the point of view of the Labour Party, the mobilization of a political Protestantism which helped to keep it out of power.[18] In parts of London's East End, there were similar conflicts between Irish Catholic and Jewish elements in the local labour movement.[19] However, in most areas, Catholicism was comparatively weak. The dynamics of the encounter between religion and socialism were therefore generally very different in the more pluralistic religious environment of the Anglophone world.

---

[15]   The Church of England was disestablished in Wales in 1921.

[16]   B. J. Snell, Chairman's address to the Congregational Union assembly in *Congregational Year Book* (1918), p. 36. Note that these views are similar and prior to T. H. Marshall's elaboration of this thesis in his *Citizenship and Social Class* (Cambridge: Cambridge University Press, 1950).

[17]   *Free Churchman*, December 1934.

[18]   See J. J. Smyth, *Labour in Glasgow, 1896–1936: Socialism, Suffrage and Sectarianism* (East Linton: Tuckwell Press, 2000); S. Davies, *Liverpool Labour: Social and Political Influences on the Development of the Labour Party in Liverpool, 1900–39* (Keele: Keele University Press, 1996).

[19]   H. Srebrnik, *London Jews and British Communism, 1935–45* (London: Vallentine Mitchell, 1995).

On the Continent, socialism often inherited or developed a distinct anti-clerical flavour in opposition to the entrenched power of the Catholic Church and its perceived role in the defence of the established order. This antagonism was not to be mitigated until after Leo XIII's encyclical *Rerum Novarum* in 1891 which, whilst still condemning socialism, was much more open than hitherto to labour organizations. Even then, MacDonald was once refused a hearing when billed to speak in Düsseldorf on the subject of 'Labour and Christianity'.[20]

In contrast, Nonconformity in Britain was itself a mild form of anti-clericalism. Political dissent, therefore, did not necessarily lead to irreligion. The role of Nonconformity in the British labour movement also helped to reduce the extent to which socialism could be popularly associated with alien, immigrant or Jewish influences. The incorporation of Nonconformity into mainstream society, completed during the Great War (1914–18), meanwhile helped to ensure that there was little dissonance between Nonconformist, socialist or British identities in the early twentieth century.[21]

Espousal of socialism for a Nonconformist could nevertheless entail rejection of, for instance, chapels where political Liberalism remained entrenched.[22] Many felt the unorthodoxy of trying to save the body as well as the soul, not least because it seemed such a departure from the simple evangelicalism of their nineteenth-century upbringing.[23] For some, undoubtedly, it offered an eschaton of a heaven on earth to rival that of Christianity, such that socialism effectively became their religion.[24] However, not least in the light of liberal theological developments in the late nineteenth century,[25] Nonconformity also offered a set of beliefs in which personal salvation could harmonize with and be seen as part of the process of converting the world to a better and more Christian social system. As Methodist lay preacher and Labour MP George Edwards put it: 'With my study of theology I soon began to realize that the social conditions of the people were not as God intended they should be.'[26] After all, the Nonconformist emphasis on the preaching of the Word had introduced Edwards to 'an inspired Book that sets up standards that touch every aspect of human life'.[27] The first female cabinet minister, Congregationalist

---

[20]   W. Ward, *Brotherhood and the Churches* (London: Oliphants, 1932), p. 99.

[21]   P. Ward, *Red Flag and Union Jack: Englishness, Patriotism and the British Left, 1881–1924* (Woodbridge: Boydell Press, 1998).

[22]   Catterall, 'Free Churches', pp. 297–300.

[23]   F. Hodges, *My Adventures as a Labour Leader* (London: George Newnes, 1925), pp. 19–20; B. Turner, *About Myself* (London: Cayme Press, 1930), pp. 176, 242–5.

[24]   See C. Pearce, 'An Interview with Wilfrid Whiteley', *Bulletin of the Society for the Study of Labour History*, 18 (1969), p. 16.

[25]   Catterall, 'Free Churches', chapter 1.

[26]   G. Edwards, *From Crow-Scaring to Westminster* (London: Labour Publishing Co, 1922), p. 36.

[27]   G. Edwards, 'Religion and Labour' (n.d., *c*.1920), broadsheet in Norfolk Record Office (Sir George Edwards Papers).

Margaret Bondfield, found from her reading of the Old Testament that: 'We could not think religion and not think of the needs of the poor.'[28] The realization of 'the sacredness of human personality and the infinite value of every individual in the sight of God', if it did not invariably lead to socialist thinking, certainly emphasized service on behalf of others.[29] Accordingly, the Quaker Alfred Salter's last message after a lifetime of service to the impoverished South London borough of Bermondsey as general practitioner, councillor and Labour MP was:

> I have tried to fulfil the task which God entrusted to me. I have loved and served the common people and have lived among them. I have worked unceasingly to bring about a new state of society where all men and women shall be free and equal, where there shall be no poverty or unemployment, where no man shall exploit or dominate his fellow men, where the cruelty and sorrows of the present system shall be swept away for ever.[30]

In addition, the distinctive presence and testimony of Nonconformity had wider effects upon the religious environment within Britain. Its challenge and competition was also a constant reminder to national churches of the need to justify their position by reaching out to serve the spiritual and social needs of the entire community, including the working classes. This, and the need to respond to the social tensions of an industrializing society led by a succession of Anglican clerics following on from Frederick Denison Maurice in 1848, helped also to ensure that socialist antagonism to the established church was muted. After all, even if their thinking only gradually developed from Maurice's reformist idealism to the more distinctively socialist political economy articulated by figures like F. L. Donaldson and Charles Gore at the end of the nineteenth century, this process of evolution was alongside and cross-fertilized with that followed by the wider labour movement, culminating with the clerical memorial at Labour's electoral success in the 1923 general election.[31]

Contrasts with the Continent

The distinctiveness of the British religious climate, and its impact upon the labour movement, was something contemporaries were well aware of. In consequence, the atheistic Arthur Ponsonby argued that militant irreligion was much less marked

---

[28]   M. Bondfield, *A Life's Work* (London: Hutchinson, 1948), pp. 352–3.

[29]   Somerville Hastings writing in *Baptist Times*, 31 January 1935.

[30]   Cited in F. Brockway, *Bermondsey Story: The Life of Alfred Salter* (London: Allen and Unwin, 1949), p. 241.

[31]   People's History Museum Manchester, Labour Party Archives [LPA], 'Memorial of the Clergy to the Labour Members of Parliament', 13 March 1923, LP/CUU/23/1. Donaldson appears to have been the inspiration behind this document.

amongst British socialists than elsewhere in Europe.[32] As Reverend F. H. Stead observed at the 1919 International Labour conference on 'Labour and Religion' held at his church, the Browning Settlement in Walworth, South London:

> On the Continent religion has been too largely the bulwark of the upper and official classes, a convenient department of state for the buttressing of the established order. In this country, thanks to the variety and vitality of the Free Churches, the official grip has been much slackened.

He, however, went on immediately to add:

> But even in this country, whatever be the numbers of the working class in attendance on this or that denomination, organised religion has been to a very great extent under middle and upper class direction. English religion has been painfully bourgeois. It has rarely or never been frankly proletarian.[33]

Notwithstanding the historical myths of the links between Nonconformity and the labour movement very much current at the time, Stead was undoubtedly correct. Nonconformity was mainly middle class in character whilst, as contemporary surveys show, notwithstanding childhood attendance at Sunday Schools, the adult working classes were largely unchurched.[34] Nevertheless, as Stead went on to point out, the distinctions he drew attention to helped to ensure that the working classes, if largely outside the churches, were not particularly hostile to them.[35] And there was still less overt hostility to the message that they preached, even from avowed materialists like the socialist journalist Robert Blatchford. Admittedly, this was particularly true when that message was attenuated to being largely concerned with brotherly love.

At the same time, the religiosity of tone that British socialism acquired reciprocally served to reduce tensions with the churches. In particular, it helped to reassure the Catholic hierarchy in Britain that, in contrast to the materialism and atheism detected in Continental socialist movements, the Labour Party was both compatible with Catholicism and a bulwark against communism.[36] With the settlement of the Irish issue after 1921 breaking up the old alliance with the Liberal Party, Labour was thus able to draw much of the Catholic working class to its

---

[32]   A. Ponsonby, *Religion in Politics* (London: National Labour Press, 1921), p. 29.

[33]   F. H. Stead, *The Proletarian Gospel of Galilee in some of its Phases* (London: Labour Publishing Co, 1922), p. viii.

[34]   Catterall, 'Free Churches', chapters 3 and 7; R. Gill, *The Myth of the Empty Church* (London: SPCK, 1993), chapter 7; D. S. Cairns, *The Army and Religion* (London: Macmillan, 1919), pp. 45–6 and 448.

[35]   Stead, *The Proletarian Gospel*, p. xi.

[36]   Knox, 'Religion and the Scottish Labour Movement', pp. 618f.; N. Riddell, 'The Catholic Church and the Labour Party, 1918–31', *Twentieth Century British History*, 8/2 (1997), 165–93.

camp. After some abortive attempts in 1919–21, small 'centre' parties nevertheless did emerge in both Liverpool and Glasgow around 1930, mainly composed of disgruntled Catholic ex-Labourites. Without support from a hierarchy fearful of alienating both the Protestant majority and its largely working-class flock, however, they could not begin to rival their equivalents in Germany.[37]

This distinction was noted there. A Leipzig thesis in 1932 was conceived explicitly to explore the distinctive contribution of religion to British socialism.[38] One consequence noted by the German socialist journalist Egon Wertheimer was the very different tone of Labour communications. There was an appeal to the emotions, to a sense of righteousness, rather than the intellect. For Wertheimer, this reflected the different constitutional, as well as religious trajectories, of the two countries. Its political exclusion under Bismarck's legislation at the end of the 1870s had led the German Social Democratic Party (SPD) instead to indulge in endless theoretical disputation. In contrast, the relatively weak Labour Party from the moment of its belated entry on the scene in 1900–6 was confronted with matters of practical parliamentary politics. British socialists, Wertheimer argued, therefore did not share a felt need for 'a constructive theoretical explanation of their movement'. Nor did they require political analysis embedded in dialectical materialism when the religious idealism derived from Nonconformity was more readily to hand.[39]

One result, Wertheimer observed, was the cultural conservatism of the British movement in matters of, for instance, sexual morality. The continuing strength of Nonconformity in the ILP in the late 1920s was reflected in an incident Wertheimer obliquely refers to: 'the avalanche of protest' that greeted C. E. M. Joad's article in the movement's journal, the *New Leader*, advocating a more relaxed approach to marital fidelity.[40] Leading the charge was the veteran socialist advocate, Katherine Bruce Glasier. Speaking of the early ILP, she argued:

> [That] the chief object of Socialist effort was to make human life sacred and not property rights. Socialists recognized that the monogamous family had long ago been proved by experience to be the best cradle of the human race. They sought, therefore, to found that family upon the firm foundations of a love marriage.[41]

The other consequence noted by Wertheimer was anti-intellectualism. This was reflected in pragmatic, un-programmatic documents like the 1918 manifesto, *Labour and the New Social Order*. As Wertheimer commented, if Marx tore apart

---

[37]   Riddell, 'The Catholic Church', pp. 167 and 170.

[38]   F. Linden, *Sozialismus und Religion: Konfessionssoziologische Untersuchung der Labour Party 1929–31* (Leipzig: Kölner anglistische Arbeiten, 1932).

[39]   E. Wertheimer, *Portrait of the Labour Party* (London: Putnam, 1929), pp. xi, 196–7.

[40]   Ibid., pp. 91–3.

[41]   *New Leader*, 27 December 1929.

the SPD's 1875 Gotha Programme, what would he do to this? In Labour, unlike its German counterpart, there was hostility, if not to intellectuals per se, then certainly to intellectualism.[42]

A Matter of Personnel?

Such a characteristic led Wertheimer to note the relative dearth of Jewish intellectuals in the British party. Jews were certainly not conspicuous in the top ranks of the party at the time, though (the non-religious) Harold Laski was elected to the party's National Executive Committee (NEC) in 1937. None appear to have served on the general council of the Trades Union Congress (TUC) during the interwar years; their scarcity within the trade union movement may well be the prime explanation of this. And, throughout the period, Jewish Labour MPs were also rare, peaking at six in 1929. They were outnumbered by their counterparts in the other parties and did not come to be well represented in the Parliamentary Labour Party (PLP) until after 1945.[43] Nevertheless, particularly in areas like the East End, Jewish voters were shifting towards Labour. Indeed, tensions with a locally Irish-dominated Labour Party and the rival attraction of communism as a means of confronting anti-Semitic fascism were to take some further to the left in the 1930s.[44]

Nonconformity, in contrast, was over represented within the PLP's ranks. Phillips' then predecessor as secretary of the Labour Party, his fellow Methodist Arthur Henderson, observed in 1929 that:

> It is a demonstrable fact that the bulk of the members of the Parliamentary Labour Party at any given time during the last twenty-five years had graduated into their wider sphere of activity via the Sunday School, the Bible Class, the temperance society or the pulpit.[45]

This has, essentially, been substantiated by careful analysis of the religious affiliations of the interwar parliamentary party. Of the English and Welsh MPs, nearly half were Nonconformist and less than 10 per cent had no religion.[46]

---

[42] Wertheimer, *Portrait of the Labour Party*, pp. 60, 228.

[43] G. Alderman, *The Jewish Community in British Politics* (Oxford: Clarendon Press, 1983), p. 174.

[44] Ibid., pp. 113–15; Srebrnik, *London Jews*, pp. 31–6 and 53f.

[45] A. Henderson, 'British Labour and Religion', in J. Davis (ed.), *Labor Speaks for Itself on Religion* (New York: Macmillan, 1929), pp. 144–5.

[46] P. Catterall, 'Morality and Politics: The Free Churches and the Labour Party between the Wars', *Historical Journal*, 36/3 (1993), 668–9. Similar figures also apply to the pre-1914 Labour Party. See D. E. Martin, '"The Instruments of the People"? The Parliamentary Labour Party in 1906', in D. E. Martin and D. Rubinstein (eds), *Ideology and the Labour Movement: Essays Presented to John Saville* (London: Croom Helm, 1979), pp. 125–46.

Religiosity was just as marked amongst Scottish MPs.[47] Studies of local councillors have found a similar relationship in places like Bolton, Bradford and Norfolk. Over half the Labour councillors elected in Norfolk in the interwar years were Nonconformist (mostly Methodist). This was grossly out of proportion to the number of Nonconformists in the county. In fact, Nonconformity was only slightly more prevalent in Norfolk than Liverpool, where Nonconformist Labour councillors were much less evident. Instead, some 43 per cent of interwar Labour councillors in Liverpool were Catholic.[48] Correspondingly, significant concentrations of Catholics were apparent in Labour municipal politics in Glasgow and North East England. And over one-third of the interwar members of the TUC general council had an identifiable religious affiliation, the bulk of them Nonconformist, whilst the proportion for the party's NEC was closer to 50 per cent (again, mostly Nonconformist).[49]

Voters, Religion and Labour

But while this substantiates Bullock's commonplace observation that the churches contributed to Labour in the form of personnel, demonstrating an electoral benefit for the party is more problematic. It is, for instance, easily supposed that predominantly working-class Catholic voters found their natural home in the Labour Party from the 1920s onwards. This seems to be borne out where the Catholic vote was highly concentrated, as along the waterfront in Liverpool. In the absence of contemporary surveys, however, we can only project back from those conducted later – such as that in Glasgow in 1974, finding 79.3 per cent of Catholics voted Labour[50] – to validate this hypothesis. Nevertheless, the Labour Party clearly identified this Catholic vote as important; and not just in those settings where the Catholic vote was so heavily concentrated.

The degree of Nonconformity evident in the Labour parties of Bolton and Bradford should not distract from their considerable efforts to court Catholic opinion. In Bolton, Catholics were selected as the running mates of Albert Law, a Wesleyan lay preacher, in this two-member constituency in the general elections of 1929, 1931 and 1935. It is, however, evident that the Catholic vote in Bolton was by no means as important as in Bradford. There the Labour Party, after the Great War, arranged a politic electoral arrangement with the city's Irish Nationalists.[51] Its candidates entered the 1919 municipal elections proclaiming Irish Nationalism to be one of the great arms of the Labour alliance.[52] The Irish were particularly

47   Knox, 'Religion and the Scottish Labour Movement', p. 612.
48   Catterall, 'Free Churches', pp. 304–25.
49   Ibid., pp. 300–305.
50   Smyth, *Labour in Glasgow*, p. 148.
51   *Bradford Trades Council Year Book* (1919), p. 9.
52   *Bradford Daily Telegraph*, 28 October 1919.

predominant in Bradford's North and West wards. Labour municipal election handbills in these wards were therefore apt to be addressed unashamedly to Catholic voters.[53] It was even alleged by some Conservative Catholics that Labour propaganda was being distributed after Mass at several churches.[54] Neither in Bradford nor elsewhere did Labour cultivate the Nonconformist vote so assiduously.

Nonconformity was less culturally distinctive than the still predominantly endogamous Catholic community. Furthermore, Nonconformist congregations were generally much smaller, spread across a number of competing denominations and often containing a greater social mix. Neither the chapel nor the established church could offer the electoral dividends that might come Labour's way from targeting Catholicism. Whilst even atheist Labour candidates could therefore be content to pander to sensibilities on issues like birth control in heavily Catholic areas,[55] Anglican or Nonconformist concerns did not receive similar favours. For instance, anxiety to avoid appearing either the prisoner of the chapels or workingmen's clubs over the still controversial drink question led an increasingly professionalized party to, by the end of the 1920s, attempt to neutralize the issue by the expedient of a Royal Commission.[56] As Joseph King pointed out to his colleagues on the Liberation Society's management committee regarding his party's attitude towards their traditionally Nonconformist cause of disestablishment: 'the Labour Party was jealous of any action from outside'.[57]

Furthermore, there was a continuing tendency derived from nineteenth-century electoral politics to associate church with Conservatism and chapel with Liberalism. This was most marked during the inter-church tensions over school building prompted by the Labour government's Education Bill in 1931. The invitations that the president of the board of education, Sir Charles Trevelyan, extended to Conservative Churchmen, Liberal Nonconformists and Labour Catholics to present the case of their various churches is an interesting comment on the perceived denominational allegiances of the various parties. Ironically, by then there were far more Nonconformists in the PLP than amongst Liberal MPs. Indeed, irritation at Trevelyan's ignoring this fact seems to have prompted C. H. Wilson to convene a committee of Free Church Labour MPs to watch over Nonconformist interests.[58] It, however, was not to survive the electoral landslide that engulfed Labour later that year. Nor does it seem to have been particularly effective in directing the behaviour of Free Church Labour MPs.

---

[53] For instance, West Yorkshire Archives, James Harrison, municipal election handbill (1927).

[54] Letters to *Yorkshire Evening Argus*, 28 November 1924.

[55] Knox, 'Religion and the Scottish Labour Movement', p. 622.

[56] *Labour and the Nation* (London: Labour Party, 1928), p. 32.

[57] London Metropolitan Archives: Liberation Society papers, A/LIB/11, Management Committee minutes, 23 February 1920.

[58] *Christian World*, 26 March 1931.

This can be illustrated by the lobby voting on the Catholic amendment to Trevelyan's 1931 Education Bill moved by a group of Labour MPs led by John Scurr. Albert Law, as a good Nonconformist, voted against this amendment, despite having given his pledges to his Catholic constituents at the previous general election.[59] Though none of Bradford's four Labour MPs were Catholic – two were indeed Nonconformists – three nevertheless voted against their government and for the amendment. Only Sir Norman Angell, who sat for the least Catholic constituency in the city, voted for the government against the amendment. William Leach, the non-churchgoer who sat for Bradford Central, seconded the amendment.

The fact that several Nonconformists who sat for Labour in other constituencies in Lancashire or Yorkshire or the East End of London, including the Congregationalist minister Gordon Lang, similarly supported the amendment, demonstrates that the virtues of Catholic support were not only appreciated in Bradford. Nowhere was this Catholic support as important as in Liverpool. It is noteworthy that the only Nonconformist Labour MP in Liverpool, Joseph Gibbins, supported Scurr's amendment, despite the deep hostility to Catholicism characteristic of many of his fellow Primitive Methodists in the port.[60] The overwhelming majority of Free Church Labour MPs joined him in supporting their Catholic colleagues on this occasion. Similar patterns of Labour sensitivity to Catholic concerns are equally apparent in Scotland.[61]

Some doubt must nevertheless remain as to whether the Catholic vote was quite as solidly pro-Labour as the party appears sometimes to have assumed. Labour made, for instance, relatively little headway in more middle-class Catholic wards like Exchange in Liverpool. Using post-war surveys can also produce ambiguous results. In general, these surveys seem to suggest that Catholics tend to be both slightly more working class and slightly more inclined to vote Labour than the overall population.[62] This suggests that Catholicism was electorally important to Labour because of its class composition, geographical concentration and cultural distinctiveness, not because of its Catholicism per se.

Indeed, that Catholicism could be a positive problem at times. A particular example was the way in which Franco's supporters played upon their defence of the Church in the Spanish Civil War. Labour's prompt issuing of publications playing up support for the Republic amongst Spanish Catholics following the war's outbreak in 1936 reflected sensitivity to where Catholic sympathies might

[59]   *Bolton Evening News*, 24 October 1931.

[60]   A. Wilkinson, *Dissent or Conform? War, Peace and the English Churches, 1900–45* (London, SCM Press, 1986), pp. 73–4.

[61]   Catterall, 'Free Churches', p. 350. Knox, 'Religion and the Scottish Labour Movement', p. 622.

[62]   See P. Catterall, 'The Party and Religion', in A. Seldon and S. Ball (eds), *Conservative Century: The Conservative Party since 1900* (Oxford: Oxford University Press, 1994), p. 654.

lie.[63] Alarm at attitudes in the Catholic press also led swiftly to a delegation of Catholic trade unionists calling upon the Archbishop of Westminster. One of their number, H. B. Morgan, recorded: 'I have seen this pleasant old gentleman almost weep over certain Press reports alleging pulpit utterances in favour of the Spanish rebels.'[64] Notwithstanding the views of the head of the hierarchy, such utterances do not seem to have been without effect. Catholic discontent over both Spain and Labour's education policy, for instance, seems to have been instrumental in a 7 per cent fall in Labour's vote in Glasgow in the November 1936 municipal elections.[65] Trevelyan's schools policy had, in 1931, already divided Labour at local level and certainly contributed to Catholic voter defections in parts of the country.[66] It also briefly revived thoughts of a Catholic trade union movement on the Continental model in Britain.[67] Meanwhile, Catholic sympathies within ward parties towards the Nationalists in Spain have been alleged for both Liverpool and the East End.[68]

Because Labour courted Catholic support, such matters – or the strife over the site of Liverpool's Catholic cathedral[69] – were always likely to prove disruptive, since they had a tendency to become problems of internal party management. Relations with the other churches were both less important and much less disruptive. Post-war surveys tend to confirm the view that Anglicans were and remained differentially Conservative in allegiance.[70] The political allegiances of the more inchoate Free Church community are more difficult to trace. In some cases, consternation at the rise of Labour after the Great War prompted expedient Liberal–Conservative municipal alliances. Lecturing on goodwill in a Yorkshire chapel in 1920, Tom Phillips was told: 'We are practising it in this municipal election. Liberals show the greatest goodwill towards the Conservatives. I am afraid neither of us love Labour.'[71] Such municipal alliances prepared the ground for a growth in Tory support in the chapels of interwar England. Conservative

---

[63]   See *Catholics and the Civil War in Spain* (London: Labour Publications Department, November 1936).

[64]   LPA, J. S. Middleton Papers, Memorandum attached to Middleton to Duffy, 22 February 1937, JSM/RC/1.

[65]   Knox, 'Religion and the Scottish Labour Movement', pp. 623–4.

[66]   Riddell, 'The Catholic Church', pp. 185–6; A. Thorpe, *The British General Election of 1931* (Oxford: Clarendon, 1991), pp. 23–4.

[67]   A. Thorpe, *A History of the British Labour Party* (Basingstoke: Palgrave, 2001, second edition), p. 83.

[68]   P. J. Waller, *Democracy and Sectarianism: A Political and Social History of Liverpool 1868–1939* (Liverpool: Liverpool University Press, 1981), p. 341; Srebrnik, *London Jews*, pp. 32–3.

[69]   Davies, *Liverpool Labour*, pp. 69–70.

[70]   Catterall, 'The Party and Religion', pp. 665–6.

[71]   *Bolton Congregationalist*, December 1920.

leader Stanley Baldwin certainly seems to have done more to court that support than his Labour counterparts.[72]

Meanwhile, the divided political allegiances of Nonconformity rapidly became a commonplace in the 1920s, even for Free Church leaders.[73] Only amongst the numerically insignificant Quakers, prompted to some extent by the anti-war stance shared with the ILP in 1914–18, does there seem to have been a general shift towards Labour. By 1926, it was estimated that half had swung behind the party[74] – though this probably reflects socialists being drawn into Quakerism as much as the other way round. This compares to oral evidence that suggests that, even amongst the supposedly more working-class denominations, such as Primitive Methodism, only one in three chapels shifted towards Labour in the interwar years.[75] Indeed, there is plenty of circumstantial evidence which suggests that Liberalism remained the dominant political creed of Nonconformity. My re-working of Michael Kinnear's table on the geographical distribution of Nonconformists in 1922 demonstrates a positive correlation between the size of the Nonconformist vote and the success of a declining Liberal Party. Labour's success, in contrast, frequently seems to have been greatest in areas where Free Churchmen were distinctly thin on the ground.[76] Their contribution to the labour movement was clearly more in terms of personnel than votes.

Historiography

Nevertheless, it is important that this contribution is not overlooked. Often religion has posed a problem all too easily ignored for many labour historians. Although predictably highlighted in a special issue of the Christian Socialist Movement's magazine,[77] most of the publications produced to mark the Labour Party's centenaries in 2000 or 2006 barely gave it more than perfunctory mention. The discipline, after all, was in its infancy in the 1960s, the decade when the thesis that modernity equals secularization was at its height. Contemplating organizations they saw as being on the advanced wing of that modernity no doubt made it easy for labour historians to conclude that 'modern working-class movements have developed an

---

[72] Contrast Baldwin's willingness to speak at Nonconformist events in the 1920s (Catterall, 'The Party and Religion', p. 648) to MacDonald's rejection of an invitation to address the Presbyterian Church of Wales conference in 1930: John Rylands Library (Manchester), Ramsay MacDonald Papers [henceforward RMD]: RMD/1/15/137f, correspondence with Rev. J. Morgan Jones.

[73] Catterall, 'The Party and Religion', p. 649.

[74] *The Friend*, 2 April 1926.

[75] C. Field, 'A Sociological Profile of English Methodism, 1900–32', *Oral History*, 4/1 (1976), 73–95.

[76] Catterall, 'Free Churches', pp. 286f. Catterall, 'Morality and Politics', p. 678.

[77] *The Common Good*, March 2006.

overwhelmingly secular, indeed often militantly anti-religious ideology'.[78] Even Bullock did not explore the commonplace about the prevalence of a religious background that he so blandly stated. A simplistic trend line accordingly developed, in which a religious environment served primarily as the late nineteenth-century chrysalis to be rejected by secular socialism some time after 1900.[79] From the late 1980s, however, a scattering of publications demonstrated the problems of this approach, if only in terms of chronology, by showing the continuing significance of religion for the Labour Party in the interwar years.[80] Meanwhile, a recrudescence of the political significance of religion globally has led to recantations of the convenient, but increasingly problematic, secularization thesis. Yet, this has found scant echo in the world of labour history. The advent of party leaders – John Smith and, to a lesser extent, Tony Blair – to whom a Christian Socialist heritage was of clear importance, stimulated some work in this area during the 1990s.[81] Obviously, faith is significant for some leading party figures. Yet, it remains seen as peripheral to the wider story of the party, compartmentally confined to the private lives and interests of a presumed minority and therefore ignored.

Modernist assumptions that the twentieth century and the rise of the Labour Party replaced nineteenth-century voting patterns around status, in which socially significant organizations like churches had leverage, with voting patterns instead located around class – in which the churches were no longer important[82] – in the past constrained interest in this subject. The working class, admittedly following the hopeful assertions early twentieth-century Labour politicians often made at the time, were reduced to a single monolithic interest group. In an interesting variant of Jesus' dictum that no man can serve two masters, it was assumed that the pull of other identities than class was much less significant.

---

[78] E. Hobsbawm, *Worlds of Labour: Further Studies in the History of Labour* (London: Weidenfeld and Nicolson, 1984), p. 33.

[79] See, for instance, R. Moore, *Pitmen, Preachers and Politics: The Effects of Methodism in a Durham Mining Community* (London: Cambridge University Press, 1974); K. O. Morgan, *Rebirth of a Nation: Wales 1880–1980* (Oxford: Clarendon, 1981); K. Middlemas, *The Clydesiders: A Left Wing Struggle for Parliamentary Power* (London: Hutchinson, 1965).

[80] See Knox, 'Religion and the Scottish Labour Movement'; Catterall, 'Morality and Politics'; Riddell, 'The Catholic Church'.

[81] C. Bryant, *Possible Dreams: A Personal History of the British Christian Socialists* (London: Hodder and Stoughton, 1996); A. Wilkinson, *Christian Socialism: Scott Holland to Tony Blair* (London: SCM Press, 1998).

[82] The classic statement of this view is: P. Clarke, 'Electoral Sociology of Modern Britain', *History*, 47 (1972), 31–55. See also K. D. Wald, *Crosses on the Ballot: Patterns of British Voter Alignment since 1885* (Princeton: Princeton University Press, 1983).

Religion and Class Consciousness

Problems with this model include the high levels of working-class Tory voters and the unconvincing nature of attempts to explain away these apparently deviant voters.[83] Class has been shown to be a crude social construct, obscuring as much as it explains patterns of voting behaviour which can be more precisely mapped onto more complex social cleavages.[84] It is also unclear how important class is as a motivating factor anyway. Except in moments of crisis, trade union branches can be as apt as churches to complain of poor attendance. Furthermore, at the exact moment when it has been argued that the electoral reform of 1918 created the opportunity for class-based voting and the Labour Party,[85] senior figures of the party were going out of their way to emphasize that Labour was not a class-based organization. Instead, as party secretary Arthur Henderson told the *Christian World*, its basis had been 'deliberately broadened ... by the adoption of the principle of individual membership. It has become a real national party'.[86] The same message was emphasized in Henderson's pamphlet *Aims of Labour* (1918) distributed widely, not least by the Free Church-linked Brotherhood Movement, in the run-up to the 1918 general election.[87] Three years later, Henderson warned that association with class conflict and 'direct action' during the industrial strife following the end of the Great War was doing great damage to Labour's electoral prospects.[88]

It was not just that class conflict alienated the churches, particularly the Catholic hierarchy.[89] Class conflict was also the weapon of Labour's enemies on the left. Furthermore, association with it undermined Labour's claim to govern the whole country in a constitutional fashion. Not everyone, however, immediately shared Henderson's apprehension of this in 1921. Robert Williams had then declared: 'Before the General Strike the general election pales into insignificance.'[90] Five years later, in his chairman's address to the TUC, he surveyed the wreckage of such delusions in that year's industrial conflagrations, concluding: 'while the

---

[83]   P. Catterall, preface to S. Ball and I. Holliday (eds), *Mass Conservatism: The Conservatives and the Public since the 1880s* (London: Frank Cass, 2002), pp. xii–xiii; Catterall, 'Free Churches', pp. 468–9.

[84]   C. Stevens, 'The Electoral Sociology of Modern Britain Reconsidered', *Contemporary British History*, 13/1 (1999), 62–94.

[85]   H. C. G. Matthew, R. McKibbin and J. A. Kay, 'The Franchise Factor in the Rise of the Labour Party', *English Historical Review*, 91 (1976), 723–52.

[86]   A. Henderson, 'Politics, Parties and People', *Christian World*, 21 March 1918.

[87]   *Brotherhood Journal*, November 1918.

[88]   LPA, NEC Minutes, May 1921.

[89]   S. Mews, 'The Churches', in M. Morris (ed.), *The General Strike* (Harmondsworth: Penguin, 1976), pp. 318–37; Catterall, 'The Free Churches', pp. 134f.; Riddell, 'The Catholic Church', p. 172.

[90]   Cited in P. S. Bagwell, 'The Triple Industrial Alliance, 1913–22', in A. Briggs and J. Saville (eds), *Essays in Labour History, 886–1923* (London: Macmillan, 1971) p. 103.

Communist Party and the Minority Movement still believed in the General Strike, the Labour Party would look forward with confidence to the General Election'.[91] Two years later, the party prepared for that election by issuing a manifesto entitled *Labour and the Nation* (1928).

This was not simply a deliberate transcending of class, or of other factional interests, for purposes of electoral rhetoric. Indeed, the rhetoric came in part in trying to portray its opponents as servants of narrow class interests, whilst Labour sought to govern in the interests of the community as a whole. Few, however, went so far as J. H. Thomas who, even in the early 1920s, admonished: 'Don't let us keep up this damnable talk of class warfare.'[92] Keir Hardie had, after all, pointed out that 'labour men [are] denounced for stirring up strife between class and class. What modern labour man ever used the same strong language towards the rich as Christ did?'.[93] Yet, he also warned that a class war mentality risked reducing socialism to the level of a faction fight.[94] Other senior party figures, such as the Anglican George Lansbury, were equally apt to portray class warfare as a reality to which Labour were merely responding in search of justice. The existing system of industrial capitalism was seen as enabling 'the few to amass huge fortunes whilst others starve!'.[95] Independent Methodist and Labour MP Wilfrid Wellock went on to argue: 'Is it beyond our dreams that society can function as a great brotherhood, can co-operate as fellow citizens instead of exploiters and exploited?'[96] The class war was fought, wrote John Scurr, to replace class hatred with fraternity.[97]

The aspirations they voiced have, historiographically, been depicted as reflecting a chapel-inspired, woolly ethical socialism which peaked before 1914.[98] This ethical socialism, it has been argued in turn, was little more than a device adopted to entice less 'advanced' brethren by those who moved through evermore radical theological positions from chapel via ILP to a position where socialism was their religion.[99] This equation between theological and political radicalism might

---

[91]   *Labour Year Book* (1927), p. 13.

[92]   Quoted in J. Scurr, 'The Class Struggle', *Socialist Review*, 14 (1924), 219.

[93]   K. Hardie, 'Christ and the Modern Movement', in C. G. Ammon (ed) *Christ and Labour* (London: Jarrold, 1912), p. 86.

[94]   Cited in E. Hunter, 'The Disease of "Leftism"', *Socialist Review*, September 1927, p. 52.

[95]   G. Lansbury, *Jesus and Labour* (London: Independent Labour Party pamphlet, 1924).

[96]   *New Leader*, 27 April 1928.

[97]   Scurr, 'The Class Struggle', p. 222.

[98]   See S. Pierson, *British Socialists: The Journey from Fantasy to Politics* (London: Harvard University Press, 1979); S. Yeo, *Religion and Voluntary Organisations in Crisis* (London: Croom Helm, 1976).

[99]   L. Smith, *Religion and the Rise of Labour: Nonconformity and the Independent Labour Movement in Lancashire and the West Riding 1880–1914* (Keele: Ryburn, 1993), p. 92.

work when applied to Quakers. It works less well when applied to Unitarians: theologically radical, but also the only Nonconformist denomination to have had more Tory than Labour MPs during the interwar years. Nor does it help to explain why an elevated concept of the Kingdom of God led so many Anglo-Catholics to socialism. A similar process was at work in Methodism, with sacramentalists like Donald Soper or R. J. Barker – who founded an organization called the Comradeship of the Common Table when ministering in Tonypandy in the 1930s – turning to Labour.

Furthermore, the extent to which even the ILP became antipathetic to religion after 1918 can, as demonstrated earlier, be exaggerated. However, the ILP had certainly changed. The advent of direct individual membership of Labour meant the ILP was no longer so important to the party. Meanwhile, Wertheimer complained, it became:

> [A] refuge for all those radical bourgeois malcontents whose war experience and disillusionment had brought them into contact with the Socialist movement, or those from the Universities who were seeking a way into the Labour movement and who sought a platform for the propagation of ideas of the most varied kinds.[100]

In the process, its centre of gravity shifted away from Nonconformist centres in Northern England. By 1931, one young Nonconformist addressing his local ILP branch on 'The Need for a Religious Basis for Social Reform' found:

> I had a terrible time. The atmosphere was hostile from the first. In discussion time I had absolutely no support. The bitterness against religion of any type, against religious bodies and people professing it has to be heard to be credited … Simply the verdict was – religion is an utter failure – socialism is good enough … If that ILP is typical the taunt of Socialist–Atheist is true.[101]

Certainly, a correspondent to the *Labour Leader* in 1922 claimed this was true of some 50 per cent of British socialists.[102] Nevertheless, Nonconformity still contributed about half the English membership of the ILP's National Administrative Council in 1926. Thereafter, however, the increasingly antipathetic position adopted by the ILP towards the wider party, culminating in its disaffiliation in 1932, was to atrophy this relationship. On the other hand, throughout the 1920s ILP publications continued to feature religious poems, stories and features, whilst Free Church ministers like Gordon Lang and Reg Sorensen served as ILP missioners.

It is true that much of this material was addressed, if indirectly, to the churches. Electioneering was only one, and probably the least important, of the purposes

100 E. Wertheimer, 'The Crisis in the ILP: An Attack', *Socialist Review*, (July 1929), 13.
101 *Christian World*, 4 June 1931.
102 A. J. Marriott, letter to *Labour Leader*, 20 April 1922.

served. A second was defensive; to rebut the charge that socialism was a materialist creed aiming simply at expropriation and overthrow of order. This was a particular concern for Catholics, and may explain why the ILP's Glasgow publication, *Forward*, was so keen to emphasize that 'atheism avowed or otherwise has no place in the ILP policy or programme'.[103] It, however, affected Nonconformists too. Conferences were organized either by sympathetic ministers like F. H. Stead at the Browning Settlement in South London, or even by Labour activists (and lay preachers) like C. G. Ammon to demonstrate the contrary. Similar events were organized by Anglican Christian Socialists at the Community of the Resurrection at Mirfield.[104] However, much more common than rebuttal was rebuke. Keir Hardie's accusation that 'modern Churchianity is not only un-Christian but anti-Christian'[105] is a fairly representative example. Party spirit, particularly amongst Nonconformist Labour politicians frustrated at the continuing Liberalism in the chapels, was undoubtedly an element in this. Considerable numbers, including presumably the 45 MPs who would only describe themselves as un-denominational in Franz Linden's survey of the 1929–31 PLP,[106] left their churches in frustration, though not all did so permanently. Many of the most vehement complaints, however, came from men of impeccable faith like Lansbury.[107] A local Labour newspaper, the *Bolton Citizen*, complained in 1933 that 'the Church has neglected its own business, has disregarded its own teachers, is ignoring its own past and is now declining its original lesson'.[108] The discarded mantle, it implied, was falling instead upon Labour. The final purpose of this rhetoric, in other words, was to emphasize the righteousness of Labour's cause.

Even contemporary comments, however, could suggest that this rhetoric lacked substance. One internal critique argued that Labour 'has sought in a vague way to achieve freedom for the worker. It has created a party bound together by a common emotion rather than by an intellectual conception'.[109] Admittedly, many early Labour MPs were inspired to work for reform by the mismatch between the rhetoric of love and brotherhood and the realities they observed on the streets. As has been seen, however, these aspirations were frequently rooted in a class-based analysis of the wrongs of the existing system which remained common down to the General Strike. What was needed, argued the Quaker Labour MP George

---

[103]   *Forward*, 30 September 1922, cited in Knox, 'Religion and the Scottish Labour Movement', 611.

[104]   Wilkinson, *Christian Socialism*, p. 137.

[105]   K. Hardie, *Can a Man be a Christian on a Pound a Week?* (London: Independent Labour Party, 1905, third edition), p. 2.

[106]   Linden, *Sozialismus und Religion*, p. 86.

[107]   See, for instance, G. Lansbury, 'Labour Thinks Little of the Church', in Davis (ed.), *Labor Speaks for Itself*, p. 160.

[108]   'Socialism in the Early Church', *Bolton Citizen*, March 1933.

[109]   Seven Members of the Labour Party, *The Labour Party's Aim: A Criticism and Restatement* (London: Allen and Unwin, 1923), p. 11.

Benson, was the replacement of the competitive waste of the present system with one based upon co-operation. 'Industry, instead of being run on a basis of haphazard anarchism, split into a thousand hostile units, would be organized for the sole purpose of rendering to the community service.'[110] Clause four of the 1918 Labour Party constitution, far from marking a caesura with pre-1914 religious socialism, was thus entirely consistent with its analysis. Nationalization, whereby class conflict under capitalism would be replaced by production for the good of the entire nation, was the means to achieve the brotherhood religious socialists aspired to.

Conclusions

Labour's emphasis on 'the nation' flowed naturally from the view that it was through collective action that the better life for all would be achieved. This was contrasted with 'the methods of Marxian Socialism, which puts such emphasis on the means, that the end to be attained is lost sight of'.[111] Quakers, as pacifists, had particular difficulties with the more extreme expressions of Marxist class conflict stimulated by the example of the Bolsheviks.[112] This incompatibility was indeed cited by Newbold as his reason for resigning from the Society of Friends in 1920, en route to becoming the first elected communist MP two years later.[113]

Instead, Christian socialists have been seen as focusing more on ends than means. Not that they were necessarily any more precise at describing these ends than Marxists, though for totally different reasons. Not for them the comforting self-righteousness of a teleology which, being inevitable, did not require description. The idea that sin exists only in the system, and therefore only the system needs to be changed, not only begs the question as to why the system should have been flawed in the first place, but also appears to rely heavily upon Pelagian notions of human perfectibility. In contrast, as Salter pointed out in 1931: 'If we are going to create a new social order wherein dwelleth righteousness, we can only create such a state through the agency of righteous men and women.'[114] Christians in the Labour Party were far from sharing the views of their Marxist counterparts that '[the] way to make people "good" is not to ask them to be good, but to give them social conditions which will enable them to be good'.[115] Changing social systems was never enough, hearts needed to be changed as well.

---

[110]   G. Benson, *Socialism and the Teaching of Jesus* (London: Independent Labour Party pamphlet, 1925), p. 8.

[111]   *Ploughshare*, June 1919.

[112]   Ibid., August 1917.

[113]   RMD/1/15/176, Newbold to MacDonald, 30 May 1937.

[114]   *Christian World*, 15 January 1931.

[115]   Dan Griffiths, letter to *New Leader*, 28 June 1929.

This is not a woolly ethicalism. In some ways, it reflected a moral order against which to measure the shortcomings of the world every bit as absolute as that of Marxism. For instance, it was to this moral order that Ben Turner appealed when introducing his 1924 Bill to nationalize natural resources with quotes from Psalm 24, Ecclesiastes and Leviticus.[116] And, as this example shows, it was entirely compatible with the increased emphasis on nationalization within the party after 1918. The Great War was not a fundamental caesura in religiosity in the party as it has sometimes been portrayed.

If there was a shift, then it might be located in the difficult decade of the 1930s. Specifically Christian insights into new technical issues such as economic planning, which very much came to the fore after the 1931 electoral disaster, are elusive. Meanwhile, the challenge of responding to the gathering international threats tended to isolate Christian pacifists like Lansbury or Wellock, whilst the narrowing of options made it more difficult to articulate distinctively Christian views on the left. This did not prevent Clement Attlee, by no means an orthodox believer, as party leader during the Second World War presenting the conflict as the defence of Christian civilization. This, however, also in the process tended to reduce Christianity into a broad normative ethicalism.

During the 1930s, as well, the generation born in the more deeply religious 1860s that led the party through its early years was by then dying off. For many, such as future Labour MP Ernest Armstrong, the Methodist chapel nevertheless remained in the 1920s a key feature of his Durham mining village and a training ground for public life.[117] Yet, not all chapels shared this vitality; at the same time, their importance to the party diminished as Labour became its own training ground. Religion accordingly seems to have been less significant to the generation who grew up in the 1920s and 1930s.[118]

The contribution of the churches to the development of the Labour Party was, however, not merely in terms of personnel. The party was also the product of the distinctive characteristics of British politics, society and culture, not the least of which was the religious environment. Defining features – such as its relative pluralism, the importance of Nonconformist churches rarely found elsewhere in Europe with their perceived relationship with the working classes, and ecclesiastical traditions of political engagement – provided a unique context for the emergence of labour politics in Britain. Results included the large presence of Christians within the party throughout its early years. The anti-clericalism of Continental counterparts was also conspicuous by its absence. Indeed, Labour's religiosity of tone helped to ensure the relatively limited appeal of Marxism in Britain. This tone did not disappear after 1918. In fact, the closeness of the relationship between Christianity and socialism seems if anything to have been

---

[116] *House of Commons Debates*, Fifth Series, vol. 174, cols. 221–5 (27 May 1924).

[117] Ernest Armstrong, written communication to the author, November 1986.

[118] P. Graves, *Labour Women: Women in British Working Class Politics 1918–39* (Cambridge: Cambridge University Press, 1994), pp. 55–6.

more emphasized during Labour's rise to governing party status in the 1920s. Socialism, accordingly, was presented not as a materialistic means to better living standards, but a moral imperative, a great crusade in which all should find fulfilment through mutual service. This was not merely woolly ethicalism. It was simply that social and individual salvation went together. The former was not sustainable without progress in the latter. As former party leader J. R. Clynes warned in 1924: 'Should Christianity ... disappear, there could be no Socialist State, for Socialist doctrines are Christianity applied to economic life.'[119]

---

[119]   *British Weekly*, 17 January 1924.

Chapter 9

Labour's Lost Soul?
Recovering the Labour Church

Jacqueline Turner

The Labour Church has a place in history synonymous with the foundation and development of the political working-class movement and the early days of the Independent Labour Party (ILP). It sits alongside the emergence of other Nonconformist and socio-religious movements such as Socialist Sunday Schools and the Salvation Army. From its inception, one of the primary challenges of the socialist movement was to communicate its message to the wider working classes. As a propaganda tool, the Labour Church undertook this role, providing a familiar social platform. As capitalism was increasingly presented as a 'sin', so people required what Keir Hardie termed 'social redemption' or 'social salvation'. The Labour Church was thus one of the means by which the socialist movement and early Labour Party came to reach those who found themselves isolated from orthodox churches and party politics.

The Unitarian Minister John Trevor founded the Manchester Labour Church in 1891, from which point it quickly carved a place in working-class society and engendered the support and respect of many luminaries within the labour movement. Trevor frequently called the Labour Church 'the soul of the labour movement'. It was established to appeal to the working class, though it promoted class unification and harmony. Its overtly political nature was established with the church's motto, which began life as 'God is our King' before being revised to 'Let Labour be the basis of civil society'. Trevor believed that a divine spirit was present in all humanity, hence the aspiration to identify the relationship of brotherhood. The Church was socialist in nature, though it became a servant of a labour movement built on ethical principles of egalitarianism and freedom of conscience, principles shared by the emerging ILP. As such, the Labour Church's theology, doctrine and social-political function made it fundamentally different from its contemporaries and predecessors

The church's political credentials were on display at the foundation conference of the ILP, held in Bradford in 1893, with *The Times* reporting that a 'social service of the Bradford Labour Church was held at which Keir Hardie spoke'.[1] Three words in *The Times* report highlight the enigma of the Church. The reference to a 'social' service indicates the confusion over the religious nature of sermons.

---

[1] *The Times*, 16 January 1893.

Services were traditional in format but focused on the socialist message and often did not include any reference to the bible or biblical scripture. The reference to the 'church' is at odds with a 'social service' and highlights the cross pollination of the two messages. Lastly, Keir Hardie 'spoke' rather than preached or gave a sermon. Hardie's language – in accord with the language of other socialist speakers – was secular but littered with religious imagery.

The Labour Church was a nationwide movement that at its height counted 100 churches with congregations of between 200 and 500.[2] Average congregations soared when speakers made guest appearances: when Hardie spoke in Dundee, the congregation spilled outside and numbered over 5,000, and a similar number reportedly accompanied Hardie at the inaugural ILP meeting.[3] The Church also spread abroad. As working-class emigration increased at the turn of the century, so congregations could be found in Australia, Canada, New Zealand and South Africa. Significantly, perhaps, the Labour Church abroad had a greater longevity than that inside the UK.

To understand the Labour Church, it must necessarily be considered within the context of the time in which it developed. The nineteenth century witnessed massive social-economic upheaval, and the application of science and technology associated with the Industrial Revolution continued to challenge accepted religious norms. The writings of Marx and others inspired socialist organizations and, after the publication *The Origin of Species* (1859), Darwin's evolutionary thesis further challenged the faith of many in the established church. The Labour Church was thus born as a response to the changes of this period, though it was not the only new church to be established. Other churches included the Ethical Church (supported by Ramsay MacDonald and establishing itself more firmly in the South of England), the Church of Humanity, the Temperance Church, and the Salvation Army established by William Booth, which had adopted a programme of social reform by 1890.[4] All of these organizations responded to the politicization of working-class congregations; they tended towards an 'ethical socialist culture' and filled the gap created by a shift away from religious orthodoxy.

John Trevor's objective in leaving his position as a Unitarian minister in the Upper Brook Street Free Church, Manchester, was similar to William Booth's reasons for leaving the Methodists: 'because he could not reach the poor people in the chapel'.[5] Both came to develop a 'deep hatred of middle-class social values' and

---

    [2] Historians differ on these figures, but see *The Clarion*, 11 January 1893, 20 September 1900 and 20 July 1906, which contain references to church numbers. The short-lived existence of some of the churches make if difficult to cite a firm number.

    [3] M. Bevir, 'Labour Churches and Ethical Socialism', *History Today*, 47/4 (1997), 50.

    [4] The Labour Church deserves greater comparison with the Salvation Army, as both Booth and Trevor shared similar backgrounds and Trevor was initially inspired by the Salvation Army. Ultimately, however, they took opposite theological routes. Booth was evangelical, whereas Trevor went on to challenge many conventional Christian doctrines.

    [5] K. S. Inglis, *Churches and the Working Class* (London: Routledge, 1963), p. 215.

the adoption and propagation of them in the Orthodox churches.[6] As the working classes began to leave the regular churches 'captured by the wealthy classes, who imposed in them both a social atmosphere in which the working man was kept an alien, and social policies which denied his aspirations for justice', so Trevor looked towards the labour movement and asked: 'is it possible, right in the heart of the Labour Movement, to build up a church upon the conception of a "sweet forbidden friendship with God" … Possible or not, this is what … I set before me as the aim of the remainder of my days.'[7]

Form and Function

It is widely recognized that the numbers attending Orthodox and Nonconformist church services decreased in the late nineteenth and early twentieth century, and that organizations, including the Labour Church, served as an alternative attraction to the dwindling churchgoers. That said, just how far this should be taken as a universal or generic comment on the functions of churches as a whole may be contended by the continued role of the church in popular culture and working-class society. The regular attendance of church was part of the social aspiration of many working-class families, 'church going' being a byword for respectability.

Unlike the evangelical Salvation Army, John Trevor and the early pioneers of the Labour Church did not set out to routinely proliferate their organization. After setting up the first church in Manchester, Trevor left the formation of new churches to local demand and activity. His main contribution to the establishment of other churches was literary, as a prolific pamphleteer and via the *Labour Prophet*. Trevor also recognized the potential conflicts in the routine establishment of congregations. 'Democratic organisation in the Labour Movement means throwing together a mass of conflicting elements, in which he must struggle to maintain a place who thinks it is his mission to serve. Moreover, I could not visit the churches systematically, such attempts as I made from time to time always failing.'[8]

As there was no formal development plan, new churches were invariably formed by people who had attended Labour Church meetings and drawn inspiration from being part of an existing congregation. As Stanley Pierson suggested, 'the chief characteristic of Labour Church expansion during its first five years was its spontaneity and the relative absence of a strong central direction'.[9] Consequently, growth was organic and somewhat haphazard; the church could be found in pockets across the country, often established in response to local

---

[6]   Ibid., p. 216.

[7]   Ibid., p. 217; *Labour Prophet*, October 1894.

[8]   J. Trevor, *My Quest for God* (London: Labour Prophet Publishing Office, 1898), p. 257.

[9]   S. Pierson, 'John Trevor and the Labour Church Movement in England 1891–1900', *Church History*, 38/2 (1960), 468.

political activity. The Bradford Church was formed as a reaction to the 1892 general election, when a local Nonconformist minister supported the local Liberal candidate against the socialist Ben Tillett. In April 1891, at the National Triennial Conference of Unitarian Churches in London, Trevor had been inspired when he heard Tillett deliver a harsh attack on the alienation of existing churches from the working man.[10] As Trevor recalled, Tillett insisted that the working classes were not irreligious, but that 'if they follow the lead of secularists and atheists, it was because these men understood and sympathized with their sorrows, and could point to a remedy beyond the knowledge of the Churches'.[11] Tillett's principles were in complete accordance with Trevor's and, in 1892, Trevor threw the support of his organization behind Tillett.[12] Fred Jowett, the strongly socialist president of the Bradford Labour Church, enthusiastically supported Tillett's candidacy and, though Tillett lost the election, predicted that the 'initial set back would not halt the march of the Bradford Labour Union'.[13]

While the first gathering of the Labour Church was in Manchester, other churches soon formed across many urban working-class areas in Britain. As churches were independently founded, the separate churches were federated by the Labour Church Union, which held annual conferences and business meetings. The most influential churches were established in Manchester, Bradford, Birmingham, Aston, Ashton-under-Lyne and London, while congregations were also prolific across the coalfields of Scotland, South Wales, the industrial North of England and the Midlands. London became the centre for Labour Church publishing, from where the *Labour Prophet* (and later the *Labour Church Record*), the *Labour Church Hymn Book*, *Labour Church Tune Book* and *Labour Tracts* were produced, and which all sold from one penny for paper covers.[14]

Despite the disparity in the geography and background of its congregations, the Labour Church held a broad appeal. Estimates of the size of a typical congregation vary massively from as few as 30 to an average of between 300 and 500 (with regularly over 500 in Dundee and Halifax). By 1895, there were probably around 50 churches at any one time in approximately 13 or 14 towns. Inglis states that 'probably there were never more than thirty churches at any one time; few of them were alive twenty years after the first one was formed'.[15] Pierson is more generous, claiming that 'up to 120 churches [existed], many of which were established and

---

[10]   R. K. Webb, 'Trevor, John (1855–1930)', *Oxford Dictionary of National Biography* (Oxford: Oxford University Press, 2004). Online, available at: www.oxforddnb.com/view/article/38078.

[11]   J. Trevor, 'Founding of the Labour Church', *Labour Prophet*, March 1893.

[12]   C. Tsuzuki, *Tom Mann 1856–1941* (Oxford: Oxford University Press, 1991), p. 93.

[13]   J. Schneer, *Ben Tillett* (Worcester: Croom Helm, 1982), p. 76.

[14]   John Trevor's working papers at Warwick; back sheet spreads of *My Quest for God* and copies of *The Labour Prophet*.

[15]   Inglis, *Churches*, p. 216.

died within months'.[16] Both the *Clarion* and the *Labour Leader* between 1891 and 1910 disclose that more than 120 churches were founded, though most were shortlived. The disparity in numbers indicates the fluid and temporary nature of some of the smaller churches.

While the Labour Church grew most rapidly in Lancashire, growth in Scotland and around the West Riding was eclectic and organic; in areas of Yorkshire, it was directly promoted by the trade unions. In places where the trade union movement was weak, and where electoral success was limited, 'it was the club life, the Labour Church or the Clarion movement which sustained the [labour] movement'.[17] The moral fibre of the trade unions was underpinned by the alternative social culture of which the Labour Church was part. Certainly, Keith Laybourn has underlined the Church's importance in much of his work, citing Philip Snowden's opinion of the Bradford Labour Church that 'the work done by the Labour Church is of the most invaluable kind. As an educational institution, its influence cannot be overstated. Sunday after Sunday it brings to the town speakers of the first rank, and in many ways helps them to keep the good work going'.[18] Bradford had a membership of more than 2,000 in 1893, and Leeds more than 1,000.

Congregations were often inspired and swelled by the appearance of guest speakers. Speakers never criticized or offered judgements on the creeds of other denominations, but they did use the opportunity to criticize other churches for excluding working-class people and to express political views and rally large crowds. Keir Hardie regularly spoke at the Labour Church and – as a Christian Socialist – became an early proponent. During the 1890s, Hardie renewed his own religious quest in the name of political change. He used it to express class-consciousness and began a 'crusade against churchianity', claiming that the rich and middle classes had annexed Jesus.[19]

Clearly, the Labour Church was candidly political and designed to attract the growing and increasingly politicized working class. At meetings of the ILP and Social Democratic Federation (SDF), often held on a Sunday, a Labour Church style of service was regularly followed and the *Labour Church Hymn Book* used. The Church was intended to give expression to the religion of the labour movement and make socialist principles more accessible to the working class by using the familiar format of a church service. While the Labour Church left theological questions to private individual conviction, it sought the realization of universal well-being through the establishment of ethical socialist principles founded in 'justice and love'. Trevor always asserted that his primary objective was to gain access to working people who appeared lost to the established churches. In the *Labour Prophet* of March 1893, Trevor stated that as a Christian and a socialist

---

[16]   Pierson, 'John Trevor', p. 478.

[17]   K. Laybourn, *Philip Snowdon, 1864–1937: A Biography* (Aldershot: Temple, 1988), p. 19.

[18]   Ibid., p. 23.

[19]   C. Benn, *Keir Hardie* (London: Metro, 1992), p. 107.

he believed that the 'improvement of social conditions and the development of personal character are both essential to emancipation from social and moral bondage' and, to that end, insisted 'upon the duty of studying the economic and moral forces of society'.[20]

Inevitably, there was opposition to the Labour Church as a radical or alternative movement. Its overtly socialist preaching concerned local middle-class employers and the tendency to almost ignore the bible in its services attracted negative comment from other denominations. Where Labour Churches were formed in response to political activity and attracted large congregations, they inevitably provided an alternative to existing Nonconformist worship and people migrated from other groups. Herbert Horner, an associate of Snowden, encapsulated these attitudes:

> In too many cases, a Nonconformist minister must preach what suits the wealthy manufacturer or those golden pillars of the Church will find means to get someone who will. They are also used to subservient acquiescence in their employees in the shop and factory and they expect the same from their spiritual employees on Sunday.[21]

Nevertheless, by 1894, both the Labour Union and the ILP considered the Labour Church vital to their propaganda, and it continued to attract the great and the good of the labour movement, including Margaret McMillan (who was a regular in Bradford, Leeds and provided guidance in London), Katherine Glasier (who spoke regularly in and around Manchester), Fred Brocklehurst (who became general secretary of the Labour Church Union), Enid Stacey and the Pankhursts.

The presence of female speakers was not unusual; yet, despite their evident popularity, the same level of female participation was not reflected on the committees and bodies that governed the church. These were male-dominated, as was characteristic of other labour organizations, though women did fare a little better in the Church if compared to religious associations. The Labour Church also paid some regard to female emancipation, disseminating the immorality of denying the female vote. That said, women were still not allowed to take the collection. Until the advent of female suffrage, politics continued to be seen as the domain of men. Though members might 'hold a solemn discussion on "how can we reach the women?", or congratulate themselves on being the only church in the country which attracted as many men as women', observers of the congregations invariably reported that they saw a majority of men.[22]

Despite all this, historians have regularly misunderstood the form and function of the Labour Church. In his sweeping account of religion in England, E. R. Norman gives the Church but a by-line; he describes it as providing 'the secular

---

[20] *Labour Prophet*, March 1893.

[21] Laybourn, *Philip Snowdon*, p. 30.

[22] Inglis, *Churches*, p. 224.

societies for working men which John Trevor inspired in 1891, and which were closely associated with emerging labour politics'.[23] Here, he references Inglis' statement that 'the need for the Labour Church was not doctrinal but social'.[24] His interpretation is characteristic of those outside the labour and socialist movements, and entirely in line with later historiography of the Labour Church as a whole. His contention that the Labour Church was purely secular misses the complexities of Trevor's thinking and the immersion of socialism into the realms of morals and its presentation as a religion in itself. Equally, Norman's claim that it was a society for working men also misunderstands one of the basic tenants of the Labour Church; while congregations were primarily working class, its doors were always open to everyone from any background.

Doctrine and Socialist Revival

The Labour Church's part in the wider Christian socialist revival of the late nineteenth century is described by Peter Jones in his seminal text on the subject, published in 1968:

> The Labour Church was a serious attempt to create or synthesize a true working-class religion: thus, its history falls under that of popular religion or British working-class culture. The doctrine of its founder, John Trevor, was closer to the Ethical Culture movement than to Christianity.[25]

Jones' view highlights both the historic debate and the enigma of the Labour Church. While Jones repeatedly insists that the Labour Church was 'barely Christian',[26] it must be accepted that John Trevor's primary aim was to reach out and attract the declining working-class congregations of other established churches and to establish a working-class religion with its own doctrine (though without the associated dogma) to create a truly egalitarian and ethical socialist-inspired church dedicated to righting social injustice. The Church's purpose was religious, social and political. However, its increasing politicization and secularization to meet political objectives ultimately contributed to its decline and was at odds with Trevor's own beliefs. Although Trevor had rejected the Bible and Christianity, he was not an atheist and strongly believed in a personal relationship with God. Secularization led to the question as to whether the Labour Church was a church

---

[23]   E. R. Norman, *Church and Society in England, 1770–1970* (Oxford: Oxford University Press, 1976), p. 179. Norman's work is typical of the work of many church historians who simply bypass the existence of the Labour Church.

[24]   Inglis, *Churches*, p. 229.

[25]   P. Jones, *The Christian Socialist Revival, 1877–1914* (Princeton: Princeton University Press, 1968), p. 29.

[26]   Ibid., p. 13.

at all. It was often used by socialist speakers to preach a secular socialist message without those speakers ever becoming a member of the church or contributing to its everyday development. Yet, without such speakers the church would have had an even more limited lifespan.

For this reason, perhaps, Jones questions the motivation of Nonconformist or ethical socialists. 'Were these reformers socialist because of their Nonconformist faith? Or were they merely socialists who happened to go to some sort of Nonconformist chapel on Sundays?'[27] Such a question is especially pertinent to the Labour Church, as its social function and its doctrine were inspired by the ethical socialist tradition. Looked at in this light, its teaching, principles and stand against any form of dogma needs to be reconsidered.

The Labour Church was based on loose principles outlined by John Trevor and published in every publication. These were:

- That the labour movement is a religious movement.
- That the religion of the labour movement is not a class religion, but unites members of all classes in working for the abolition of commercial slavery.
- That the religion of the labour movement is not sectarian or dogmatic, but free religion, leaving each man free to develop his own relations with the power that brought him into being.
- That the emancipation of labour can only be realized so far as men learn both the economic and moral laws of God, and heartily endeavour to obey them.
- That the development of personal character and the improvement of social conditions are both essential to man's emancipation from moral and social bonding.[28]

An analysis of these principles unravels the doctrine of the Labour Church.

The first two principles illustrate that Trevor always contended the labour movement to be a religious – and not purely political – movement, which he confirmed in his address to the International Socialist Congress in London in 1906: 'The attempt to bring the thought of Jesus into the life of today as a guide and standard is an anachronism, the Labour Church is not a Christian Socialist Church, but is simply based on the conception of the Labour Movement as being itself a religious movement.'[29] It is clear that Trevor wanted to found a new religion rather than reform any other branch of Christianity. Christian Socialist branches of other denominations already existed in the form of the Socialist Quaker Society, the Roman Catholic Socialist Society and the Anglican Christian Social Union. Similarly, and despite his commitment to the working class, one of Trevor's oft-

---

[27]   Jones, *The Christian Socialist Revival*, p. 390.

[28]   This is the most commonly quoted expression of the principles of the Labour Church written by John Trevor for publication in the Labour Prophet.

[29]   *Labour Prophet*, cited in Jones, *The Christian Socialist Revival*, p. 30.

repeated principles was that the church was open to everyone, regardless of class, who supported the quest for the 'abolition of commercial slavery'. There was never an attempt to appeal to the 'bourgeois instincts' of the working class, as could often be found in other religious appeals. Informality was inherent in the nature of the Labour Church and led to a concerted effort to keep its organization free of dogma and sectarianism. Individuals were free to develop their own personal relationship with God, which allowed many to maintain their spiritual links with other denominations.

The last two clauses are flagrantly socialist, though they continue to reflect Trevor's belief that the labour movement itself was a religious movement and draw together his equation of God and morality with economic and social egalitarianism. Many in the labour movement were attracted by the lack of snobbery associated with the Labour Church, as well as by the freedom it gave them to continue to worship within their own faith. The Unitarian minister Philip Wicksteed was John Trevor's mentor and a vociferous proponent of the Labour Church. He was a founder member of the London Church in 1892 and spoke at churches all over the country while maintaining his spiritual allegiance to Unitarianism. In his article 'Is the Labour Church a Class Church?', he reinforced the 'warning to all classes that they have no right to exist except so far as they serve the masses and make their life fuller and greater', an overtly socialist rather than religious statement.[30]

At the same time, all of the Church's principles are synonymous with an Immanentist belief in God. Mark Bevir's work on the Labour Church during the 1990s takes a deeper look at its theology and provides an alternative view of its religion. Bevir maintains that the Labour Church was a religious movement and contests the established view of Inglis, Pierson and Jones that it was an entirely secular, political and 'barely Christian' organization. He also contests the views of Pierson, Hobsbawm and Pelling that it was a product of 'the impact of the secularisation and class politics on non-conformism'.[31] Bevir maintains that the theology of Trevor and the early Church was entirely in line with other radical and social organizations that believed in an immanent rather than a transcendent God. Bevir describes the motives of those joining: 'People joined the Labour Church not because they were on the road to secularism but because of sincere and stable religious beliefs. Moreover their beliefs are characteristic not only of leaders of the labour movement but also of other ethical socialists.'[32]

Born out of the moral dilemmas described, ethical socialists tried to reconcile faith by adopting an Immanentist theology. They argued that God inhabited the world and revealed himself gradually 'through an evolutionary process, [and]

---

[30] P. Wicksteed, 'Is the Labour Church and Class Church?', *Labour Prophet Tracts* (1891).

[31] M. Bevir, 'The Labour Church Movement, 1891–1902', *The Journal of British Studies*, 38/2 (1999), 217–45.

[32] Bevir, 'Labour Churches', 51.

not as a transcendent figure that intervenes in our world spontaneously'.[33] God would not suddenly descend to earth on Judgement Day and consign people to heaven or hell. Thus, it was argued that Darwinism was an example of God using natural means to reveal his message. If the presence of an Immanentist God is accepted, then the Bible arguably becomes a work of history and 'represents a part of the historical unfolding of God's will as opposed to a one-off revelation'.[34] Immanentist doctrines flourished among Nonconformists; there was an increased interest in Christ the man and, therefore, a questioning of the Trinity and salvation. Ultimately, for the members of the Labour Church, God was present in the everyday life of the world; he was 'not a transcendent being who conveyed his law through dogmatic revelation'.[35] Such a belief challenged orthodox and evangelical views of what was sacred and what was secular, but supported socialism. If life on earth was a religious matter, then God's kingdom should be created within the earthly bounds of the here and now. It also suggested that God was within everyone, making everyone equal before God. Both were strong factors in support of the socialist message of equality and brotherhood, and entirely in line with the principles of John Trevor and a Labour Church that proclaimed the labour movement as an instrument for the realization of God's kingdom on earth.

Despite the differences in theology and the lack of requirement for any dogma, Trevor's preference for Labour Church service followed a traditional and familiar format: hymn, reading, prayer, music, notices and collection, hymn, address, hymn, benediction. In reality, the service was inevitably shorter and included few traditional hymns, prayers or readings. The *Labour Church Hymn Book* was mostly made up of socialist inspired songs and music, including work by such socialist luminaries as Edward Carpenter, William Morris and poetry by Charles Kingsley. Readings and addresses often had similar content to that of the visiting speakers, reference to and use of the bible declined, and addresses were increasingly taken from socialist tracts and from the same people who inspired the *Hymn Book*. Other elements were distinctly unfamiliar. There was no priest, pulpit and often no Bible; there were none of the rituals or sacraments associated with the Orthodox Church.[36] There was a chairman, though he held no centralizing or hierarchical powers, and the congregation was bound together only by mutual belief. Nevertheless, people still put on their 'Sunday best' to attend a service.

With regard the fledgling independent labour movement, Keir Hardie supported a Labour Church style of philosophy and subscribed to Trevor's view that the religion of the labour movement needed to be more conscious and individual. While it has been established that the primary social objective of the Church was education, it also provided philanthropic assistance to diverse

---

[33]   Ibid.

[34]   Ibid.; Bevir, 'The Labour Church', p. 223.

[35]   Bevir, 'Labour Churches', p. 51; Bevir, 'The Labour Church', p. 223.

[36]   Only the Leeds Church ever devised a form of baptism or acquired a marriage license. These were most often left to other churches.

projects which reflected its socialist principles (what Bevir calls the 'cultural basis for socialism'), such as shelter for the homeless, slum clearance, campaigns against lead poisoning and support for the Cinderella Club. As Bevir states, 'the emphasis on a new life of the spirit explains why Labour Churches so often provided platforms for speakers advocating new humanitarian causes, including anti-vivisection, ethical culture, theosophy, Tolstoysim and vegetarianism'.[37] Ultimately, however, the bulk of Labour Church support came from the ILP and there was a considerable overlap of membership. At the most senior level, Fred Brocklehurst was the general secretary of the Labour Church Union while also being on the ILP's National Administrative Council (NAC). Among others, Hardie, Mann, Snowden, McMillan and Tillett were all regular contributors to the *Labour Prophet* and speakers at Labour Church services. Ben Tillett typified the profile of Labour Church speakers. He remained primarily a trade unionist rather than a Christian Socialist, and although he was 'a popular preacher in the Labour Churches, he subscribed only superficially to the "religion of socialism", for he did not possess a complete alternate vision of society'.[38]

Like Tillett, speakers often used the Labour Church as a platform without thereby joining the ranks of the congregations, thus limiting its on-going influence and support. As early as 1896, Trevor spoke out against itinerant speakers who came and went without ever investing in the daily life of the Church. 'Can these prominent personages, most of whom don't belong to any Labour Church, tell us of the difficulties, trials and obstacles each church has to contend with, and the various methods adopted to make ends meet?'[39]

The marriage of radical religion and working-class politics produced an ILP–Labour Church alliance, though the gradual secularization and politicization of the Church resulted in it expressing little theology. That said, Trevor's statement at a socialist congress in August 1896 that 'the name of Christ is still a fetish in religion', reinforced the Immanentist doctrine of the Labour Church: that the fatherhood of God and the brotherhood of man formed 'the very foundations of the teaching of Jesus'.[40] Though the Labour Church was non-denominational and has been considered a political group, credence needs to be given to Bevir's assertion that it was indeed a religious movement. At the same time, dogma was anathema to the Labour Church and its status as a free church encouraged its development as it attracted both the working classes who had deserted the existing churches and those from other denominations with a political conscience. One could follow the principles of the Labour Church but still get married in the Anglican faith.

---

[37] Bevir, 'The Labour Church', p. 226.
[38] Schneer, *Ben Tillett*, p. 67.
[39] Inglis, *Churches*, p. 243.
[40] Jones, *The Christian Socialist Revival*, p. 458.

The Labour Church, Class and Socialism

As is well-known, the British labour movement proved successful in keeping on
board a myriad of working-class traditions, which the radical churches and the
Labour Church exemplified. Though the debate surrounding the popularity of
churches in general at this time remains, they were still valuable organizations
to the extent that ordinary people made judgements of what was wrong with
society through their religious commitment. According to Jones, therefore, the
inherent weakness of Christian Socialists 'was one they shared with other types of
socialist: their middle classness',[41] or what Trevor more generously termed their
'pardonable self-righteousness'.[42] Consequently, a significant factor in the success
of the Labour Church was its ability to break away from the middle-class values
of other churches, though its ability to sustain its growth without middle-class
organization, education and support proved to be limited.

In his autobiography, Trevor describes one of his key motivations for founding
the Labour Church thus: in an Orthodox Church environment, he 'could not
breathe'. Trevor frequently talked about his own experience with the church-going
working classes who found themselves increasingly alienated by the middle-class
culture of existing congregations and their social conservatism. The evangelicals
of the Anglican Church accorded responsibility for suffering to the individual, and
while it was a sin to inflict pain directly, demanding unhealthily long working hours
and savage working conditions was not deemed 'un-Christian'. Good business
was beneficial to the nation.[43] While evangelical Christians made up only a small
group, their influence was pervasive. Trevor believed that the churches saw the
slums as a sign of God's anger and working-class irreligion, while 'the working
classes who knew better left the churches'.[44] The *Labour Prophet* encouraged them
to quit the church with 'their bishops and clergy, their sects and systems ... they
must get outside the existing institutions that are so much under the power of the
capitalistic Pharaohs of this day'.[45] For A. M. Thompson, writing in *The Clarion,*
'religion had become so identified within my observation with black clothes, kid
gloves, tall silk hats and long faces that it and I appeared to have parted forever'.[46]
Indeed, the quotes above equate to two types of convert ripe to join the Labour
Church; those at odds with capitalism and those at odds with the conservatism of
the existing church. Certainly, Trevor and Wicksteed founded the Church because
they 'deplored antipathy in the churches towards ideas now filling the minds of
class-conscious working men'.[47] Wicksteed declared that it was the social attitudes

---

41   Ibid., p. 458.
42   Trevor, *My Quest for God*, p. 260.
43   Ibid., p. 353.
44   Inglis, *Churches*, p. 217.
45   Cited in ibid., p. 217.
46   Ibid.
47   Ibid., p. 218.

of the denominational churches that made a Labour Church necessary. The Orthodox Church, and even some of the larger Nonconformist denominations, was dependant on middle-class support. No other church was prepared to reorganize society in the interests of the working class; nor were any prepared to make the more radical working-class welcome. Thus, in his seminal essay *What Does the Labour Church Stand For?*, Wicksteed asked:

> [What] workman can walk into a middle-class congregation with the consciousness that the underlying assumptions, both in pew and in the pulpit, as to the proper organisation of active industrial life and the justification of social and industrial institutions, are in a militant sense his own? ... [He] cannot do that, then in asking him to join in worship you are not asking him to express and nourish the religious aspects of his own higher life, but to suppress or suspend that life in order that he may share in the devotions of others, who cheerfully accept, and in many cases would stubbornly defend, the things it is his mission to fight.[48]

As this suggests, the Labour Church provided an 'oasis' for those alienated by middle-class domination of the 'mainstream' churches. Even so, Henry Pelling, in his *The Origins of the Labour Party* (1954), describes the Labour Church as 'merely a short-lived protest against the link which the nonconformist churches had established with the middle class, and in particular against the alliance with the Liberal Party'.[49] As already described, the most significant example of Pelling's claim was in Bradford, where local Nonconformist ministers supported the Liberal candidate against Ben Tillett in 1892. Although Tillett lost, the large number of votes he won shocked the local constituency and encouraged the view that the Nonconformist churches stood opposed to the labour movement. Fred Jowett threw down the gauntlet to Nonconformist Liberals and warned that: 'If you persist in opposing the Labour Movement ... there will soon be more reason than ever to complain of the absence of working men from your chapels. We shall establish our own Labour Church.'[50]

Yet, the Labour Church was not merely a revolt against Nonconformist Liberalism. For Pierson, 'working class nonconformists accepted the Liberal ideal of self reliance and shared the view that economic life was best governed by its own natural laws'.[51] But there were many Nonconformists among the Labour Church's members and speakers. Wicksteed remained a Unitarian minister, while that Labour Church stalwart, Fred Brocklehurst, had almost taken holy orders.

---

[48]   P. Wicksteed, *What Does the Labour Church Stand For?* (London: Labour Prophet Publishing Office, 1891), pp. 7–8.

[49]   H. Pelling, *The Origins of the Labour Party* (Oxford: Oxford University Press, 1965 edition), pp. 151–2.

[50]   Inglis, *Churches*, p. 228.

[51]   Pierson, 'John Trevor', p. 463.

The Church made no specific attack on any Nonconformist denomination, and it was always at pains never to criticize their creeds. While it is possible that Labour Church members felt more bitterly let down by Nonconformism (which purported to be the friend of the common people) than by Orthodox attitudes, criticism was targeted at organized Christianity as a whole. For Hardie, writing for the *Labour Prophet* in 1892, '[the] church worships respectability and puts its ban on poverty ... I speak of no particular sect or denomination. I discern little to choose from in any of them'.[52]

Even so, the Labour Church attracted its share of criticism from Nonconformists. Its status as a church was continually brought into dispute by its Immanentist doctrine, its apparent social exclusivity, and by its secular nature. Some ministers could not conceive of a church 'which makes no recognition of His Deity, of His atoning sacrifice, of the regenerating work of the Holy Spirit; which has no place in it for the sacraments, and none for the authority of the word of God'.[53] Others considered the Labour Church a reaction to despair, a rebellion against organized churches and a warning to other denominations. In general, the Labour Church was either not supported within the Christian community or dismissed as reactionary. The Church of England saw it as a reaction to the apostasy of Anglicanism, their presentation of themselves as guardians of the sacraments but their failure in their 'duties to the poor'.[54]

Yet, the Labour Church gave the labour movement a cultural and political platform that middle-class socialism could not satisfy. Mark Bevir states that 'although British socialism owes a debt to Marxism and Fabianism, its leading characteristics derive from an ethical socialism exemplified by the Labour Churches'.[55] Indeed, the 'religion of socialism' goes a long way to explaining the attraction of the Labour Church. Socialism was presented as a substitute religion; the working-class version of socialism born out of hardship and a sense of injustice was significant in attracting members to the Labour Church.

Throughout the 1880s and 1890s, British socialists increasingly portrayed capitalism as sinful and thus requiring the 'religious conversion' of people to socialism. As Stephen Yeo suggests, socialism necessitated not only individual change, but a family or societal change as encapsulated in such social offshoots as the Clarion Cycling Club and the Labour Church.[56] It could also be seen in the quasi-religious imagery produced in socialist propaganda, pamphlets and newspapers. Even so, the strongly middle-class culture and moralism propagated

---

[52] *Labour Prophet*, November 1892.

[53] Inglis, *Churches*, p. 230.

[54] Rev. W. Henry Hunt, *Churchmanship and Labour: Sermons on Social Subjects Preached at St. Stephen's Church, Walbrook*; Sermon X, in Rev. F. Lewis Donaldson, 'The Church and the Labour Church', *Project Canterbury* at www.anglicanhistory.org.

[55] M. Bevir, 'Labour Churches', p. 50.

[56] S. Yeo, 'A New Life: the Religion of Socialism in Britain, 1883–96', *History Workshop Journal*, 4 (1977), 6–7.

by sections of the British socialist movement often struggled to find a foothold in the working-class psyche. Many followers and exponents were middle class and had a lifestyle that allowed them to follow in a continual and organized manner, which may explain the working-class preference for the Labour Church. Yeo states that, 'it would be difficult to be part of anyone's following in a continuous and organised way while remaining working class'.[57]

During the 'new unionist' era, working-class socialists concentrated upon 'knife and fork questions' and turned to the trade unions, relegating theoretical concerns to the back burner. Ultimately, political counter-attacks on the working-class movement could not be countered by socialism alone and there needed to be an organized response in parliament, albeit with a distinctly socialist foundation; supporting the view that the impact of the 'religion of socialism' during the 1880s and 1890s was so substantial that it permanently shaped the ideology of the British working class. Prominent labour leaders came to believe with religious intensity in the imminence of the socialist transformation of society. The working classes practised their leaders' theories. These were explained and their praises sung in the Labour Churches, the trade unions, and in the various socialist organizations by those who could no longer find spiritual solace in the established churches.

Conclusion

The Labour Church decreased in popularity as the labour movement grew. Despite Trevor's assertion that it was a decline in religious belief that heralded the downfall of the Church, most historians would concur that without the political element it would have declined even more quickly. The Labour Church diminished rapidly after 1900, following the establishment of the Labour Representation Committee. The quarterly *Labour Church Record* that had succeeded the monthly *Labour Prophet* ceased to be published in 1902. The Churches that enjoyed the greatest longevity were those with an established social function. The Birmingham Church was the final Church standing in 1914, acting as an independent mediator between other organizations.

As early as 1892, Trevor recognized the danger of close ties with the ILP and the temptation to use the Labour Church 'merely as a means of drawing people into the Labour Movement who would not be attracted to it by the usual methods'.[58] At a Church conference in 1898, members expressed concern about of the lack of religion in the movement and, in 1902, A. B. Forster conducted an inquest into just how much religion was left in the Church. He found '"loud and persistent" demands for economic change but little interest in the "development of the human soul"'.[59] Trevor became disillusioned and resigned in 1898 after a

---

[57]   Ibid., pp. 4–49.
[58]   Pierson, 'John Trevor', p. 472.
[59]   Inglis, *Churches*, p. 247.

long and divisive struggle with Fred Brocklehurst over the direction of the Church. Trevor and Brocklehurst clashed over the latter's ideal of 'political supremacy'. In a final attempt to secure a religious message, Trevor created a new Labour Church Ministry, an army of missionaries to spread the word, but he had no support from a Labour Church Union that was dominated by Brocklehurst and the ILP. According to Bevir, 'the decline of the Labour Church reflected the problems it had in reconciling the claims of religious purity and political effectiveness ... The conflict between religious purity and apolitical commitment to labour issues led not only to quarrels but to a sense of purposelessness'.[60] Those all-inclusive elements that made the Labour Church attractive ultimately proved to be its downfall, as the only uniting factor became political conscience.

Was, then, the Labour Church a religious movement? Yes, its Immanentist theology shows that it was, although its purpose was increasingly hijacked to meet political ends. John Trevor always maintained that the Labour Church existed to proclaim the religious nature of the labour movement rather than to bring religion and the religious to the labour movement. But such close ties made the secularization of the Church to meet political ends almost inevitable, wherein lies the contradiction between the Church and its leaders. Trevor himself recognized the dichotomy between the political and spiritual function of the Church, and was at pains to separate them. Indeed, he helped initiate an independent labour organization in Manchester in May 1892, and believed – in Inglis' words – that unless a 'distinct political organization was created alongside it, the Labour Church might occupy itself with political action at the expense of its spirituality'.[61] Fundamentally, the Labour Church aspired to realize the establishment of an egalitarian socialist society. Historians of the 1950s and 1960s asserted that it was 'un-Christian', an assumption that has been disproved by Mark Bevir's close inspection of Labour Church theology. To deny any Christianity in the movement is to undermine John Trevor's work. Trevor made many statements concerning the spirituality of the organization. His autobiography was called *My Quest for God*, not 'My Quest for Labour Politics'.

Ultimately, however, the Labour Church was never destined to survive as an independent church. Though the worship of God took many diverse forms, by 1914 it was no longer at the heart of modern industrial society; moralism was determined by secular factors rather than through religious organizations. Though the traditions of the Orthodox churches continued via marriages and baptisms, the Labour Church's attitude to faith was inherently more modern. Moralism was no longer a matter of attending church; it became a measure of the way people lived their lives and, increasingly, the way in which they cast their vote. The decline in laissez-faire economics and the slow but gradual advocation of state intervention in everyday life was evidenced by the educational and social concessions meted out by the Liberal government from 1906. As such, the Labour Church's most valuable

---

[60]   Bevir, 'Labour Churches', p. 54.

[61]   Inglis, *Churches*, p. 225.

and enduring contribution to the labour movement was its role as a propaganda tool and the establishment of a social platform for the message of the early Labour Party. Indeed, the legacy of the Church's Immanentist belief is reflected in the attitudes of many non-churchgoing Christians; the principles of right and wrong continue to apply to advances in science, technology and politics. Today, the distinction between the Labour Church and the Christian Socialist Union (of the Church of England) would be indistinct. In the 1890s, the Labour Church was different in its theology, its lack of dogma, and its very modern understanding of the relationship between Christianity and social morality. The legacy of the Labour Church is, therefore, still present within the Labour Party, and Trevor would no doubt concur with Tony Blair that 'the view that Christian faith and belief is all to do with personal morality and nothing to do with the needs of society as a whole is too partial a perspective. Similarly, the belief that through the good offices of a benign state can the good of all be achieved leaves out the sense of individual responsibility which is essential if society is to function at all'.[62]

---

[62]   T. Blair, 'Foreword', in A. Wilkinson, *Christian Socialism* (London: SCM Press, 1998).

Chapter 10
Women and Labour Politics

June Hannam

In 1923, Rose Davies, a Labour Party activist in the Rhondda, wrote in notes for a speech that:

> Woman has come into power just when all the world movements and questions concern her most vitally – and here is her opportunity. Looked at from the broad standpoint of humanity as a whole all the questions of the hour bear on women's special function, the Care of Life ... all these problems need to be penetrated and solved by her highest ideals for the good of the individual and the whole ... the greatest call of today is for Love not Hate, Life not Death, and it is to that call that the True spirit of woman always answers.[1]

In her speech, Davies points to many of the key issues that need to be considered in exploring women's activism in the Labour Party and the extent to which they helped to shape its identity and ideals. She emphasizes women's distinctive outlook and 'spirit' – their care of life and concern for humanity as a whole as well as for the individual. She also notes how the context of the time gave them both a unique opportunity and responsibility to make a difference. Most women over 30 now had the vote and their active citizenship came at a time when questions of peace, unemployment and social welfare were at the heart of the political agenda.

Women had long taken part in socialist and labour politics but in 1918, when the Labour Party changed its constitution, they could become individual members for the first time. They were able to join the mixed-sex branches and take part in all levels of ward and constituency organization.[2] At the same time, they continued to be identified as a specific group. The Women's Labour League (WLL), an organization established in 1906 to encourage women to give support to the Labour Party, was disbanded and instead women's sections were formed at

---

[1] Quoted in U. Masson, 'Davies, Florence Rose (1882–1958)', in K. Gildart, D. Howell and N. Kirk (eds), *Dictionary of Labour Biography, Vol X* (Basingstoke: Palgrave, 2003), p. 45.

[2] For a detailed discussion of membership in the branches and in the women's sections, see D. Tanner, 'Labour and its Membership', in D. Tanner, P. Thane and N. Tiratsoo (eds), *Labour's First Century* (Cambridge: Cambridge University Press, 2000); M. Worley, *Labour Inside the Gate: A History of the British Labour Party between the Wars* (London: I. B. Tauris, 2005).

a local level. Marion Phillips was appointed chief women's officer and, in 1920, when the party divided the country into nine regions, both a woman and a male organizer were appointed for each region. This raises questions about the nature of women's role as a specific group within mixed-sex politics – did they have a distinctive role to play as women in helping to build up support for the Labour Party? Or, were they simply to be seen as individual activists alongside men? If women were identified as a distinctive group, how was this to be understood? Did they have a particular outlook and field of work, such as welfare, based on their role as wives and mothers, that they could put to the service of the party; or, were they likely to highlight their specific interests as a sex? Throughout the interwar years and beyond, both the Labour Party and many of its women members were ambivalent about these issues. But this was part of a more general dilemma for women who had to work out what it meant to be an active citizen once the vote had been won. Members of feminist groups, for example, debated whether their emphasis should be on the struggle for human, rather than women's, rights, but many were concerned that this 'reinvigorated humanism' could lead them to forfeit their interests and power as women.[3]

How, then, should we understand women's engagement with Labour Party politics and the ways in which their activism informed the party's identity? This is a particularly pertinent question given the recent shift in Labour Party historiography towards a concern with the importance of political cultures and identity, as well as with socio-economic structures, in explaining the growth of Labour.[4] Interest has been shown in understanding what informs the electoral identity or political character of the Labour Party, including whether trade union cultures and traditions became those of the party, and the extent to which individual activists played a key role in constructing the party's development. Local studies, in particular, have highlighted the multiple social and political cultures within the party and, therefore, any assessment of women's distinctive contribution is not likely to be straightforward.

Labour women themselves were not an undifferentiated group. Not only did they come from a variety of social and political backgrounds, but they also engaged with their politics in very different ways. A minority of women found a space in which to pursue a high-profile role in labour politics. At a local level, they were active members of ward committees and stood for office as secretaries and treasurers, while four seats were reserved for women on the National Executive

---

[3]   K. Offen, *European Feminisms: A Political History* (Paolo Alto: Stanford University Press, 2000), pp. 370–6. For a discussion of the dilemmas central to women's struggles, in particular in mixed-sex campaigns, see P. Grimshaw, K. Holmes and M. Lake, *Women's Rights and Human Rights: International Historical Perspectives* (Basingstoke: Palgrave, 2001), Introduction.

[4]   In particular, see M. Worley (ed.), *Labour's Grass Roots: Essays on the Activities and Experiences of Local Labour Parties and Members, 1918–45* (Aldershot: Ashgate, 2005).

Committee (NEC). They took up positions within groups such as the Standing Joint Committee on Women's Industrial Organisations and stood for election to public bodies, including boards of guardians and local councils. They had varying degrees of success; in Bristol there were 11 Labour women councillors in total between the wars and in Liverpool 10, less than 10 per cent of successful Labour candidates. This can be compared to London, where almost 20 per cent of successful candidates in 1934 were women.[5] Yet, others took the opportunity to earn a living through their political work. Paid positions were available within the Labour Party itself; Marion Phillips and Mary Sutherland were employed as chief women officers in the interwar years, while other women were taken on as propagandists and regional organizers. For the first time, women were able to stand for election to parliament, although the number of candidates was only small, reaching a peak of 36 in 1931 and, during the interwar years, a total of 16 were returned.

Those who sought a career in public life tended to be well-educated women who were often unmarried. The first four Labour women MPs, for instance, were all unmarried women with experience of organizing work in trade unions and/or the suffrage movement.[6] Their experience was very different from the married women who made up the majority of women members of the Labour Party and who were not engaged in paid employment. They were active within the local women's sections that grew rapidly in the 1920s with membership reaching over a quarter of a million in 1927.[7]

Studies of women's involvement in labour politics, both at a national and at a local level, suggest that women as a group made a distinctive contribution to the party's development. They broadened the appeal of the Labour Party by tapping into the everyday experiences of local communities and, through their electioneering work and fundraising, could make a crucial difference during elections. In Sheffield, for example, when Labour registered a slight increase in control, the leader of the local council claimed that this was due to the 'wonderful band of men and women, especially the women, who have helped the cause and done exceedingly good work'.[8] Women had a particular focus on welfare questions affecting women, children and the family, and Graves suggests that they were

[5]   T. Sinnett, 'The Labour Party in Bristol, 1918–29' (unpublished PhD thesis, University of the West of England, 2006); K. Hunt, 'Making Politics in Local Communities: Labour Women in Interwar Manchester', in Worley, *Labour's Grass Roots*, pp. 83–4; S. Davies, *Liverpool Labour: Social and Political Influences on the Development of the Labour Party in Liverpool, 1900–39*, (Keele: Keele University Press, 1996), pp. 182–3.

[6]   Susan Lawrence, Dorothy Jewson, Ellen Wilkinson and Margaret Bondfield.

[7]   P. Thane, 'The Women of the British Labour Party and Feminism, 1906–45', in H. L. Smith (ed.), *British Feminism in the Twentieth Century* (London: Edward Elgar, 1990), p. 125.

[8]   S. Davies and B. Morley, 'The Reactions of Municipal Voters in Yorkshire to the Second Labour Government, 1929–32', in Worley, *Labour's Grass Roots*, p. 129. For work

the 'conscience' of the Labour Party on peace and humanitarian issues.[9] More controversially, some female activists were prepared to raise issues that highlighted gender inequalities, such as birth control and women's economic independence, thereby drawing attention to the fact that women might have different interests to men rather than simply a special field of work.[10]

It was difficult, however, for women to get their voices heard and to ensure that issues of particular interest to women as a collective group were given priority by the Labour Party. In theory, Labour was open to men and women on equal terms, but very few women were in leadership positions, either nationally or locally. Pat Thane concludes that 'by the end of 1918 women were more closely integrated into the Labour Party than before. They were no more, but also no less, influential within it than before'.[11] There were structural and ideological barriers to women's full participation in Labour Party politics.[12] Women's organizations were marginalized from the party's decision-making structures. Resolutions passed by women's conferences had no official status and the large industrial trade unions, which had few female members, controlled conference decisions. This made it more difficult to challenge the emphasis of the Labour Party on economic questions and class as the focus of political identity, and therefore areas of concern to women were seen as personal rather than as party political questions.

Pamela Graves suggests that in the 1920s there was still a space in the Labour Party for women to raise issues that could challenge male authority, in particular birth control, family allowances and the constitutional position of the women's conference. In the 1930s, however, faced with the threat of war, fascism, mass unemployment and communism, the focus of both the Labour Party and its women members was on class rather than gender. She claims that although welfare became central to the party's agenda, with both men and women supporting policies designed to help mothers and children, the arguments used were couched in the language of class and the policies suggested were far less controversial, or threatening, to male authority than issues such as birth control.[13]

---

during elections, see also P. Graves, *Labour Women: Women in British Working-Class Politics, 1918–39* (Cambridge: Cambridge University Press, 1994), chapter 5.

[9]   Graves, *Labour Women*, pp. 157–8.

[10]   C. Collins, 'Women and Labour Politics in Britain, 1893–1932' (unpublished PhD thesis, LSE, 1991), p. 261.

[11]   P. Thane, 'Women in the Labour Party and Women's Suffrage', in M. Boussahba-Bravard (ed.), *Suffrage Outside Suffragism: Women's Vote in Britain, 1880–1914*, (Basingstoke: Palgrave, 2007), p. 47.

[12]   The barriers to women's full participation in Labour politics have been explored extensively in Graves, *Labour Women*, Chapter 3; M. Francis, *Ideas and Politics under Labour, 1945–51: Building a New Britain* (Manchester: Manchester University Press, 1997), Chapter 8; A. Black and S. Brooke, 'The Labour Party, Women and the Problem of Gender', *Journal of British Studies*, 36 (1997), 419–52.

[13]   Graves, *Labour Women*, Chapter 6.

The conflicts between women activists and the male leadership of the party highlight the extent to which women engaged in mixed-sex politics had to confront difficult issues about their political identities. Historians have emphasized the 'divided loyalties' of Labour women who were torn between pursuing the interests of their sex or upholding class and party unity. It is argued that in the interwar period a 'labour' identity tended to win out over one based on gender.[14] More recent texts, however, have moved away from an approach that sets up binary oppositions – between sex and class or between women and men – to one that recognizes the complex ways in which Labour women developed and negotiated their political identities.[15] Women's priorities could change over time; they were affected by a range of issues, including the international context, economic depression and whether or not they identified primarily with the socialist agenda of the Independent Labour Party (ILP). On some questions, such as family allowances, they could join with rank-and-file men to oppose the male and female leadership of the Labour Party. Thus, Black and Brooke argue that it is crucial to 'understand the diversity, complication and, at points, pliability of Labour women's outlook and action'.[16] This chapter seeks to build on such an approach by exploring what Labour's politics meant to women themselves and how they related to that politics. In order to address issues of identity and culture it will examine not only the different ways in which the Labour Party viewed women as a specific political group, but also at the complex ways in which women themselves saw their relationship with their party.

Representing Labour Women

Although women found it difficult to reach positions of power and influence, they were clearly important to the way in which the Labour Party represented itself to the electorate. And yet, their representation was based on ambiguity and was rarely consistent. When most women over 30 gained the vote in 1918, and faced with

---

[14]   Graves, *Labour Women*; P. Graves, 'An Experiment in Women-centred Socialism: Labour Women in Britain', in H. Gruber and P. Graves (eds), *Women and Socialism, Socialism and Women: Europe between the Two Wars* (Oxford: Berghahn, 1998); H. L. Smith, 'Sex vs Class: British Feminists and the Labour Movement, 1919–29', *Historian*, 47 (1984); A. Phillips, *Divided Loyalties: Dilemmas of Sex and Class* (London: Virago, 1987). For a discussion of women's influence on Labour Party policy, see Thane, 'The Women of the British Labour Party' and 'Women in the British Labour Party and the Construction of State Welfare, 1906–39', in A. Koven and S. Michel (eds), *Mothers of a New World: Maternalist Politics and the Origins of Welfare States* (London: Routledge, 1993).

[15]   J. Hannam and K. Hunt, *Socialist Women: Britain, 1880s to 1920s* (London: Routledge, 2002); D. Howell, *MacDonald's Party: Labour Identities and Crisis, 1922–31* (Oxford: Oxford University Press), Chapters 20 and 21.

[16]   Black and Brooke, 'The Labour Party', 430.

the possibility that former suffrage activists might form a rival women's party, the Labour Party sought to present itself as the 'Real Women's Party'. It aimed to persuade female voters that it was the one party that had supported women's own issue – the suffrage – and that it stood for equal rights for both sexes, including adult suffrage and equal pay in industry.[17] This, of course, glossed over the difficulties that suffragists had encountered in persuading the Labour Party to support their cause. Throughout the interwar years, the party did little to promote equal rights in the workplace or to take up issues that challenged gender inequalities, such as birth control. Nonetheless, the view that the Labour Party had always supported women and their needs continued to be an important part of Labour's identity. In a preface to Lucy Middleton's *Women and the Labour Movement*, a celebratory account of the various ways in which women had contributed to the development of labour politics published in 1977, the prime minister, Jim Callaghan, took the opportunity to point out that 'throughout its life the Labour Party has been identified with the advancement of women's rights'.[18] He hoped that the book would inspire a new generation of women to become active in labour politics.

Broad statements about the advancement of women's rights glossed over the much more contested issue of what it meant to define women as a special category in politics and the extent to which the Labour Party simultaneously emphasized, and then denied, their specific identity and interests.[19] Martin Francis suggests that during the interwar years suffering mothers and children were at the heart of Labour Party propaganda, while David Howell notes the emphasis within the party and the trade union movement on working-class domesticity.[20] The 1918 manifesto declared women to be 'the chancellor of the exchequer of the home' and claimed that, if elected, the Labour Party would seek to implement social reforms that would be for the benefit of women and children. Nonetheless, they were not always highlighted in election manifestos nor given priority in terms of policies.

On the other hand, as noted above, the 1918 manifesto also made reference to the party's commitment to equal rights, including equal pay. These different representations of women and their needs reflected broader social and cultural expectations of the new women citizens. In the post-war context, women's social roles appeared fluid and contested. Younger women who lived in cities – often portrayed as 'flappers' – were viewed as having greater social and sexual freedoms than their pre-war counterparts. And yet, there was an increasing emphasis on the importance of women's role within the home as wives and mothers and the

---

[17]   J. Rasmussen, 'Women in Labour: The Flapper Vote and Party System Transformation in Britain', *Electoral Studies*, 3/1 (1984), 51.

[18]   L. Middleton, *Women in the Labour Movement* (London: Croom Helm, 1977), Foreword.

[19]   Collins, 'Women and Labour Politics in Britain', p. 261.

[20]   M. Francis, 'Labour and Gender', in Tanner et al., *Labour's First Century,* p. 213; Howell, *MacDonald's Party*, p. 335.

extent to which this provided the location for emotional and sexual satisfaction and well-being.[21]

The emphasis of the Labour Party's propaganda shifted as the political context changed. In the election campaign of 1929, when all women over the age of 21 were able to vote for the first time, the manifesto recognized that women played other roles than that of a mother and returned to themes of equal rights. It claimed that although there was now an equal franchise, the 'fight for women's emancipation is not yet finished'. The party recognized that the 'burden of social injustice and economic exploitation falls with special severity on women, and that women are very seriously affected by unemployment, low wages'.[22] The imagery used on the front covers of both *Labour Woman* and the ILP paper, *New Leader*, was of a young woman with 'bobbed' hair and a short dress, using the power of the vote to topple capitalism and privilege.[23] In one edition, a striking black and white image of a woman's face, depicted in a futuristic modern style, welcomed the new woman voter.[24] In the context of the political crisis of 1931, the disaffiliation of the ILP and the growing threat of war, however, women as a specific group disappeared from national election manifestos.

These ambiguities are also reflected in the very different ways in which women with a high profile represented themselves within the party. Younger women such as Ellen Wilkinson appeared as the epitome of the 'modern' woman – she shingled her hair and wore a bright green dress in parliament, which caused a sensation in the newspapers where she was referred to as the 'Green Goddess' or the 'Shingled MP'.[25] Older women, including Margaret Bondfield and Susan Lawrence, were far less flamboyant in their appearance, although Bondfield was photographed in lace collars that emphasized her femininity. But as single women with public reputations and lives devoted to a career they were very different from the wives and mothers appealed to at election times and who made up the core of the women's sections. A number of women organizers and, after 1929, seven women MPs, were married women, but their careers, social status and level of education again made them different from the 'domestic woman' who featured in Labour Party ideology.

Individual women who took an active part in Labour Party politics contributed to the ways in which the party identified itself in relation to women as a political group. Despite the difficulties they encountered, both in participating fully within the party and in ensuring that the issues they raised were given priority, they did

---

[21]   K. Holden, 'Singleness and Married Love in Interwar Britain', *Women's History Review*, 11/3 (2002), 481–503; A. Oram, 'Repressed and Thwarted, or Bearer of the New World? The Spinster in Interwar Discourses', *Women's History Review*, 1 (1992), 413–33.

[22]   Rasmussen, 'Women in Labour', p. 53.

[23]   *Labour Woman*, April 1929; *New Leader*, 18 May 1928.

[24]   *Labour Woman*, April 1928.

[25]   See, for example, *Edinburgh Evening News*, 12 December 1925; *Manchester Evening News*, 11 February 1925; *Standard*, 11 February 1925.

believe that Labour provided space for women to do 'serious political work'.[26] They made speeches, carried out organizing work, sat on representative committees and compared themselves favourably to women in the other political parties who had merely an auxiliary role. Marion Phillips saw the new organization of the Labour Party in 1918 as giving women the chance to play an active part on equal terms with men. 'They are not offered positions of responsibility as a privilege accorded to their sex but are invited to claim them as rights which belong to them as citizens, as workers and as comrades, in the great struggle for freedom, equality and security.'[27] And yet she also thought women should be appealed to as women to support the party, and that they needed encouragement and education to play their full part as citizens. Moreover, there was a danger that in assuming that women should be seen as the same as men and, therefore, not be treated as a 'privileged group', that nothing would be done to overcome the structural barriers that still stood in their way.

Pioneers and Dedicated Service

Through their writings, including autobiographies, histories of the movement and journalism, Labour women activists also contributed to the identification of women as a specific group within labour politics. They highlighted women's role in the party's development so that it would not be lost from view. In her autobiography, *A Woman's Work is Never Done* (1957), Elizabeth Andrews, women's organizer for Wales, remembered significant anniversaries and events involving women. Ursula Masson's introduction to the reprint of the book suggests that Andrews put forward a labour history in which women were at the centre and created a heritage for Labour women in South Wales.[28]

This reminds us of the importance of such accounts for influencing later generations of women activists who could feel comfortable about their place within the party. Lucy Middleton's edited collection, *Women and the Labour Movement*, sought to inform readers of how much women had contributed to the growth of the early Labour Party and to causes such as women's suffrage, internationalism, social welfare and cooperation. In her autobiography, written when the Labour Party had an overall majority for the first time and was embarking on establishing the 'New Jerusalem', Margaret Bondfield claimed that she wrote the book not to celebrate her own achievements but in the hope that her experiences 'may be of

---

[26]   N. Evans and D. Jones, 'Help Forward the Great Work of Humanity: Women in the Labour Party in Wales', in D. Tanner, C. Williams and D. Hopkins (eds), *The Labour Party in Wales, 1900–2000* (Cardiff: University of Wales Press, 2000), p. 223.

[27]   Quoted in Howell, *MacDonald's Party*, p. 338.

[28]   U. Masson, 'Introduction' in E. Andrews, *A Woman's Work is Never Done* (South Glamorgan: Honno, 1957, reprinted 2006), p. xxiv.

some service to the younger generation who would grow up in a new order of society which they can help to build'. [29]

The term pioneer was used as a device by successive generations of Labour women to ensure that women's contribution to the development of socialism, and then of the Labour Party, was recognized and not forgotten. In the 1920s and 1930s, articles in *Labour Woman* recalled earlier women propagandists such as Enid Stacy or Carolyn Martyn; obituaries of leading women such as Marion Phillips emphasized their pioneering status, while in the 1960s there was a monthly series on 'socialist women pioneers'. Such accounts highlighted the special role of such 'pioneers' in encouraging other women to become part of the movement. Lucy Middleton recalled how Marion Phillips 'encouraged the less experienced delegates' who attended Labour women's conferences and how, 'at a time when politically minded women were still hardly credible and their views of little consequence, her faith, vision and gruelingly hard work, brought a confidence and assurance to the women of the Party which will never be quenched'.[30]

Articles were often written by women who had been involved in working alongside the 'famous pioneer' in an earlier period. Writing within a narrative of progress, these accounts tend to emphasize women's contribution to building up the Labour Party and gloss over any conflicts; for example, over issues such as women's suffrage or, in the case of women MPs and organizers, between their own views and the policies of the party that they were expected to carry out.[31] And yet, there must have been difficult moments between regional organizers and head office. Marion Phillips, for instance, was known for her abrasive manner. Beatrice Webb claimed that she had a 'sharp satirical tongue' that meant that she was 'much disliked by the other leading women in the labour movement'.[32]

In writing about their own lives, the pioneers framed their stories in a narrative of dedicated service to the Labour Party. Margaret Bondfield's autobiography intertwines her own life story with that of the socialist and labour movement, with each giving meaning to the other. Describing her friendship with Julia Varley, a trade union leader, she claimed that Julia, 'like myself, believed that no matter how good one's work is, it is better if it is dedicated work'.[33] Such dedicated service was not confined to the labour movement but could encompass the wider

---

[29]   M. Bondfield, *A Life's Work* (London: Hutchinson, 1948), p. 10.

[30]   Middleton, 'We are her Memorial', *Labour Woman*, January 1969, p. 7.

[31]   For example, Masson notes that Elizabeth Andrews does not comment on her relationship with her superiors, nor with the NEC, since she writes within a narrative of progress and therefore avoids any analysis of dissension. See 'Introduction', pp. xxix–xxx. Also L. Middleton, 'We are her Memorial', p. 6, describes Phillips as 'one of the great women of her generation'.

[32]   B. Webb, *Diaries*, quoted in B. Harrion, 'Marion Phillips, 1881–1932', *Oxford Dictionary of National Biography*, (Oxford: Oxford University Press, 2004).

[33]   Bondfield, *A Life's Work*, p. 44. Elizabeth Andrews spoke of a 'lifetime of service to the labour movement', Masson, 'Introduction', p. xxvii.

community. In a review of Evelyn Sharp's autobiography in 1933, entitled 'The Story of a Pioneer', Barbara Ayrton Gould wrote that 'it appears that wherever there has been trouble, she has always been in the midst of it, seeking for truth and serving humanity'.[34]

Male labour leaders also used the concept of service to others as an acceptable discourse to explain women's role in public life. Martin Francis notes how they saw women as 'agents of family moralisation' who would bring 'motherly sympathies' to the problems of the poor. In a biography of his wife Margaret, the founder of the WLL who died young in 1911, Ramsay MacDonald claimed that 'to Margaret motherhood contained everything that was redemptive ... she believed that only by doing that work could woman fulfill her destiny and attain her maximum liberty'.[35] Women also expressed this view. Mary Macarthur, for instance, suggested that the function of the WLL was to 'bring the mother spirit into politics'.[36]

And yet, this was not the whole story. Many Labour women interpreted their motivation and their role in more complex ways and certainly did not see their 'dedicated service' as necessarily stemming from a maternal role. Generation, religion, the route taken into Labour Party politics, education and social background could all make a difference in explaining what dedicated service meant to women. For Margaret Bondfield, religion was a crucial part of her politics as she sought to bring moral change. Ann Summers suggests that political action was an extension into the practical realm of her Christian convictions and a means of realizing a set of moral principles.[37] Religion was also a key issue for Edith Picton-Turbervill, elected as an MP in 1929, who had spent many years working for the Young Women's Christian Association (YWCA); for Elizabeth Andrews, who saw socialism as 'Christianity in practice'; and for Minnie Pallister, a teacher and daughter of a Wesleyan minister, who joined the ILP during the Great War (1914–18). She claimed that in the religious press she found letters breathing 'the spirit of hatred, and she was glad to turn to the *Labour Leader* and read letters there which breathe the very spirit of Christ himself'.[38]

Time and again, Labour women activists in the interwar years refer to their desire to alleviate the suffering of working-class men, women and children, to fight injustice and poverty, and to work for peace. They saw the Labour Party as the vehicle to achieve those aims because it stood for broad ideals. Mary Sutherland, chief women's officer, wrote in an editorial in *Labour Woman* in 1931 that socialist men and women, determined 'to work to prevent unnecessary misery and suffering', and who hoped for a 'better world', knew that the only way to achieve

---

[34] B. Ayrton Gould, 'The Story of a Pioneer', *Labour Woman*, July 1933.

[35] Francis, 'Labour and Gender', p. 213.

[36] Quoted in Collins, 'Women and Labour Politics', p. 150.

[37] A. Summers, *Female Lives, Moral States: Women, Religion and Public Life in Britain, 1800–1930* (Newbury: Threshold Press, 2000).

[38] WLL, *Annual Conference Report, 1915*; E. Picton-Turbervill, *Life is Good: An Autobiography* (London: Frederick Muller, 1938).

this was to build up the Labour Party. Referring to the crisis of 1931, in which some leaders had put the country before party principle, she claimed that 'the sense that the Labour Party is more than a machine, more than a "caucus", more than an opportunity for the clever to exercise their gifts, the sense that it has grown and is sustained by a great ideal, has kept the movement solid through the past difficult year'.[39] It has been argued by Ann Summers that women were the custodians of the religious, moral and crusading aspects of party politics in the interwar years when the male political system became more secular and professionalized.[40] This tends to underestimate the extent to which men were still motivated by a vision of 'ethical socialism', particularly if they had roots in the ILP. Nonetheless, the belief that they were working to achieve a better life for humanity as a whole was at the heart of women's view of their politics and underpinned their loyalty to the Labour Party.

In seeking to keep alive a broad vision of social change, women did not necessarily look through the lens of motherly sympathy. Rather they suggested that their motivation came directly from their own experience, which could be very varied. Women who had been involved in trade union organizations often cited the conditions of women's work as a key to understanding their politics. Margaret Bondfield, for instance, claimed that it was the 'inside knowledge I obtained of the appalling conditions in the homes of women wage earners that turned me into an ardent socialist'.[41] Ruby Part, who trained as a milliner, joined the Workers' Union in 1913 at the age of 19, 'being thoroughly disgusted with workroom conditions' and was appointed as an organizer in the west of England and South Wales. She then became involved in the ILP and the Labour Party, standing as a parliamentary candidate for Wells in 1929.[42] In contrast, for Phoebe Cusden, candidate for South Oxfordshire in the same year, it was noted by *Labour Woman* that 'social services has always been the dominant motive in her public work'. At various times she had been a member of the Reading Board of Guardians, the After Care and Juvenile Employment Committee, and was active in girls' clubs and adult education. She was attracted to the Labour Party because she had always 'realised the vital need for fundamental changes in the organisation of society'.[43]

The struggle for women's emancipation or women's rights is rarely mentioned in these accounts, although we need to be careful here since many were written by women who had an official position in the Labour Party – as organizers, propagandists or MPs. They were writing long after their active involvement in the women's movement and, in particular, after the Labour victory of 1945 they were concerned to emphasize the 'onward march of labour'. Many women who did challenge the leadership of the party on gender issues, such as Dorothy

---

[39] *Labour Woman*, January 1933.
[40] Summers, *Female Lives*, p. 133.
[41] Bondfield, *A Life's Work*, p. 45.
[42] *Labour Woman*, July 1928.
[43] *Labour Woman*, September 1928.

Jewson, who lost her seat as an MP in 1924 through her stand on birth control, did not leave personal accounts or else, like Hannah Mitchell, a Labour councillor between the wars, wrote autobiographies heavily weighted towards the pre-war suffrage campaign.[44]

Most of those active in Labour Party politics between the wars could be described as the 'suffrage generation', since they had been involved in suffrage politics pre-1914. Pamela Graves argues that their political identity was influenced, even if it was not directly shaped, by the women's suffrage movement.[45] What is less clear is precisely how women's political practice in the interwar years was affected by their experience of suffrage campaigning. Some men in the party thought that women had become more demanding and Ellen Wilkinson took up this theme at the party conference of 1929 when she suggested that 'you cannot deal with the woman, the emancipated woman of 1929–30, as you could with secluded women in the days when most of these wages systems came into being. The women today regard themselves as partners in the home'.[46]

Women who challenged the Labour Party in the 1920s on birth control, family allowances and the role of the Labour women's conference usually had a suffrage background and an interest in women's rights, but many, including Dorothy Jewson and Hannah Mitchell, were also closely identified with the ILP and its attempts to shape the 'socialist agenda' of the Labour Party. They had to work out how best to achieve social change for women, and for children and men, within a mixed-sex politics that might involve compromises with a feminist agenda as the broader political and social context changed. Claire Collins has argued that even before the Great War many members of the WLL saw themselves as rivals of the women's movement and, in some areas, felt that their role in elections was being overlooked now that there was an alliance between Labour and the National Union of Women's Suffrage Societies (NUWSS).[47] Tensions arising from differences in class backgrounds and disagreements about political priorities were already apparent and affected women's allegiances and political tactics. Emma Sproson, a member of the Wolverhampton ILP, was employed as an organizer by the Women's Freedom League, but felt patronized by some colleagues. She was rarely asked to speak to audiences made up of women from 'educated' groups. Florence Harrison Bell from Newcastle, again an active member of the ILP, was

---

[44]   H. Mitchell, *The Hard Way Up: The Autobiography of Hannah Mitchell* (London: Virago, 1977).

[45]   P. Graves, '"The Doors are Open, but the Seats are Reserved for Men": Women in British Working-Class Politics, 1880–1939' (unpublished PhD thesis, University of Pittsburgh, 1989), pp. 18–79.

[46]   Howell, *MacDonald's Party*, p. 365. In 1932, Labour Party officials noted that hitherto Labour women had been dominated by suffrage activists 'who have found in the women's sections ample scope for the sex consciousness there developed'. NEC minutes quoted in Collins, 'Women and Labour Politics', p. 50.

[47]   Collins, 'Women and Labour Politics', pp. 143–75.

judged by an NUWSS organizer as a suitable speaker for 'mining villages, farming villages and industrial towns', but not for seaside towns.[48] It is hardly surprising that when she was elected as a Labour Party councilor in 1921, she waved the red flag from the town hall to express her political identity.

Political Journey

A detailed look at the political journeys of individual women can enable us to think in more complex ways about what it meant to be part of the 'suffrage generation' and a Labour woman. Elizabeth Andrews, for example, became involved in co-operative, ILP and suffrage politics simultaneously in 1910.[49] A key to her political identity was experience of class politics in the mining communities of South Wales, including the hardships suffered by miners' wives. Along with her husband, she envisaged a future in which women would be equal with men and would be valued, but she identified women primarily with a maternal role and instincts, believing that the child should be at the centre of Labour Party concerns. Her reactions to specific policy issues were therefore complicated. They were influenced by her own ideas about women's role, her concern with male unemployment and its impact on communities, and her position as a paid organizer for the Labour Party. Thus, despite claiming that married women should have the right to work, she did not support Rhondda teachers in the 1920s when they challenged the marriage bar imposed by the Labour-dominated Rhondda Urban District Council, and she failed to take up the issue of birth control.[50]

Annie Townley, organizer for the South West region throughout the interwar years, also had a complicated political journey.[51] A member of the NUWSS and the ILP before the Great War, she was employed as an organizer for the Election Fighting Fund and came to Bristol in 1913 to mobilize the local labour movement to support women's suffrage during a by-election in East Bristol. She experienced difficulties with members of the Bristol branch of the NUWSS because of their class backgrounds and Liberal sympathies, and therefore formed a new group: the East Bristol Women's Suffrage Society. Tensions were exacerbated during the war when the national NUWSS wished to stop registration work in East Bristol, partly because Walter Ayles, the Labour candidate, was a conscientious objector.

---

[48]   Quoted in Collins, 'Women and Labour Politics', p. 137.

[49]   This section relies heavily on Masson, 'Introduction'.

[50]   Ibid., p. xxiii.

[51]   For a more detailed account of her activities, see J. Hannam, '"To Make the World a Better Place": Socialist Women and Women's Suffrage in Bristol, 1910–20', in Boussahba-Bravard, *Suffrage Outside Suffragism*, pp. 164–6, 172–3.

Townley threatened that the East Bristol WSS would become autonomous and complained to Catherine Marshall that she was 'sick of the NUWSS'. [52]

During the war, Townley became more active in the Bristol WLL and, with so many men fighting or in gaol as conscientious objectors, she effectively took over the leadership of the Bristol ILP. [53] From this position, she urged the Labour Party to take more definite action to bring a speedy end to the war.[54] In the immediate post-war years, she continued to lead the ILP branch but in 1920 was recruited by the Labour Party as a regional organizer. But although she worked tirelessly to build up support among women in the region, running speakers' classes, study circles and monthly schools, there is little evidence that she subsequently challenged the party on controversial issues relating to women's rights and gender inequalities.

Ellen Wilkinson's career in parliament also illustrates the complexities of individual women's engagement in labour politics and points to the ways in which political identities had to be negotiated as the political context shifted. Born in 1891, the daughter of a cotton worker/insurance agent, she was unusual in coming from such a background and gaining a degree. She became an organizer for the NUWSS in 1913 and then, in 1915, was appointed women's organizer for the Amalgamated Union of Co-operative Employees. She was elected MP for Middlesbrough in 1924 and 1929, and in the latter government was a parliamentary private secretary to Susan Lawrence. She is usually characterized as being a strong advocate of women's rights, both in parliament and in her journalism, but she drew back from confronting the Labour leadership on birth control in the late 1920s since she feared loss of support from the electorate. In the 1930s, characterized as 'Red Ellen', she became associated with the class issue of unemployment when she led the Jarrow marchers, but she continued to raise questions about gender inequalities, in particular the right of married women to work.[55]

Although attention has been focused on the suffrage generation, there was also a war generation. Many women later cited war as the main reason why they became active in labour politics. They included Lucy Middleton (née Cox), a paid propagandist for the Labour Party and prospective parliamentary candidate in the 1930s, who was elected for Plymouth Sutton in 1945; the ILP organizer and supporter of Ramsay MacDonald, Minnie Pallister; Florence Paton (née Widdowson), daughter of a railwayman who joined the Society of Friends at the same time as the labour movement; and Mary Agnes Hamilton, a Cambridge graduate and journalist

---

[52]   Letter from Annie Townley to Catherine Marshall, 1 November 1915, quoted in Collins, 'Women and Labour Politics', p. 232.

[53]   ILP Bristol branch minutes, 22 April 1917 (Bristol University Archives). Townley became chairman of the branch in 1916.

[54]   WLL, *Annual Conference Report*, 1916.

[55]   B. Vernon, *Ellen Wilkinson* (London: Croom Helm, 1982); B. Harrison, *Prudent Revolutionaries: Portraits of British Feminists between the Wars* (Oxford: Oxford University Press, 1987), Chapter 5.

who was elected as an MP in 1929.[56] Mary Hamilton claimed that 'it was the war that brought me into active politics'. As a socialist, she believed that if the earth's resources were co-operatively organized then there would be a chance for all to have an interesting life, 'but the possibility of a war seems to me to threaten such hopes with ruin'.[57] In an interview later in her life, Lucy Middleton claimed that the hardships endured by her parents to give their children an education, and the loss of young men from her village in the war, had made her determined to enter politics 'to make the world a better place ... these were the two things that made me join the Labour Party – poverty and war'.[58] She worked as a teacher and carried out propaganda work for the ILP and Labour Party in the West Country during the early 1920s, but then moved to London to take on the paid position of secretary of the No More War Movement. When she stood as a parliamentary candidate in the 1930s, peace was also a key message in her manifestoes.

Women's engagement in labour politics, therefore, could be affected by a range of influences, including religion, family background, work, political outlook and previous experience. Tensions were common between women in the party, and not just between the sexes. Although leading women such as Marion Phillips claimed to speak for all women in Labour's ranks because of a shared class position as 'working women', this was not necessarily accepted by members in the sections who emphasized the importance of marital status. Thus, when Phillips suggested that members of committees of inquiry into maternal mortality and family limitation should be 'representatives of working women', her views were challenged by rank-and-file women who argued that they should be '*married* working women'.[59]

High-profile individuals could be ambivalent about identifying too closely with 'women's issues' in case their range of activities became restricted. Ellen Wilkinson, for example, was conscious of representing a mixed-sex constituency. She objected to being treated 'merely as a feminist' and wanted to be identified as having an interest in foreign policy and industrial questions as well as women's rights. She claimed in 1924 that 'although I'm the only woman member in the opposition and have women's interests to look after I do not want to be regarded purely as a woman's MP'.[60] Alice Arnold, for many years the only woman on the Coventry city council, also claimed the right to take an interest in financial and employment questions and refused to be confined to a role as the champion of women and children.[61]

---

[56]   Collins, 'Women and Labour Politics', p. 202; *Labour Woman*, January 1931 and July 1928.

[57]   *Labour Woman*, May 1931.

[58]   *The News*, 21 July 1978.

[59]   *Labour Woman*, June 1928, quoted in Collins, 'Women and Labour Politics', p. 346.

[60]   *Yorkshire Evening News*, 10 December 1924.

[61]   C. Hunt, 'Alice Arnold of Coventry: Trade Unionism and Municipal Politics, 1919–39' (Unpublished PhD thesis, University of Coventry, 2004).

Politics of the Emotions

If it is too simple to view women's contribution to the Labour Party and its identity through a lens of feminist versus class loyalties, or women versus men, then how can we make sense of women's loyalties to a labour politics that often marginalized them in terms of their active participation and their concerns? It is here that the question of emotional engagement in politics becomes particularly relevant. This is a dimension that is often neglected by academic observers who portray human beings as rational and instrumental in their political views and actions, and 'ignore the swirl of passions all around them in political life'.[62] Emotions could be a basis for motivating individuals to become involved in social movements and to give so much of themselves to political work. Elizabeth Andrews wrote of how she *felt* the suffering of men and women in the coalfields, while Margaret Bondfield claimed that it 'broke her heart' to go into Tonypandy.[63]

Close personal friendships were formed out of shared political work and, in turn, helped to sustain commitment to the Labour cause. Women active in labour politics referred time and again to the pleasures and enjoyment of being involved in a political movement with comrades, standing together against injustice. In a review of a book in the 1970s about two pioneering activists in the movement (the Glasiers), Lucy Middleton noted that it was a pity the 'the joy of comradeship of those early days is not as tellingly depicted as are the quarrels' and recalled her own propaganda work in the West Country in the 1920s 'as among the happiest and most rewarding years of my life'.[64] Margaret Bondfield, whose closest relationships were with the married trade union leader Mary Macarthur and a long-time companion Maud Ward, claimed to have 'no vocation for wifehood or motherhood'. Instead, she had 'an urge to serve the union' and valued 'the dear love of comrades'.[65]

In local constituencies, there was a tradition of family activism – kinship ties were important in drawing women into labour politics and in sustaining their long-term membership.[66] 'Love, passion and politics' came together in a powerful combination when husbands and wives were equally involved in the movement.[67] They formed dynamic political partnerships and it was difficult to disentangle personal from political lives. In the case of Lucy Cox and Jim Middleton, their politics was an integral part of their feelings for one another. Indeed, Jim's difficulties with his second marriage stem partly from his wife's lack of interest in

---

[62]   J. Goodwin, J. Jasper and F. Polletta, 'Introduction: Why Emotions Matter', in J. Goodwin, J. Jasper and F. Polletta (eds), *Passionate Politics: Emotions and Social Movements* (Chicago: University of Chicago Press, 2001), p. 1.

[63]   Harrison, *Prudent Revolutionaries*, p. 135.

[64]   *Labour Woman*, July 1971.

[65]   Bondfield, *A Life's Work*, p. 37.

[66]   D Weinbren, 'Social Capital: London's Labour Parties, 1918–45', in Worley, *Labour's Grass Roots*, p. 196; Tanner, 'Labour and its Membership', pp. 255–6.

[67]   G. Kinnock, 'Preface', Andrews, *A Woman's Work is Never Done*, p. xii.

politics; with Lucy, he felt he had met his 'soul mate'. He wrote in a letter to her that 'everything about us seems to chime. We have the same interests, we share and share in mind and thought openly and frankly'.[68] They used their correspondence to make sense of their relationship but found it difficult to do this outside the framework of their politics. Lucy wrote of 'the Party-reminiscences-ourselves-all inextricably woven together in the pattern of life – our life – the loveliest I've ever known'.[69] Although remaining unmarried, Ellen Wilkinson had very close relationships with three labour activists, including Herbert Morrison whom she supported for the party leadership and which was partly responsible for leading to conflicts between her and the left of the party in the late 1930s and 1940s.

Close political and emotional relationships between men and women could reinforce women's commitment to working alongside men to achieve change in the lives of both sexes. This could be particularly important at a time when the women's movement was less visible. On the other hand, working with men did not mean that women were reluctant to raise issues that highlighted gender inequalities. Men often supported the same causes as their wives, including the struggle for women's suffrage in the pre-war years and then the movement for birth control in the 1920s. Dorothy Thurtle, a councilor for Shoreditch, helped to set up a local clinic specializing in gynaecology, while in 1926 her husband Ernest, an MP, introduced a private members' bill on birth control. Similarly, the adult suffragist Jennie Baker (an ILP activist) and her husband John (an MP) were part of the birth control campaign in the 1920s.[70] There are numerous examples of how loyal support and encouragement from husbands could enable women to sustain their activism. Thomas Andrews, for example, supported Elizabeth's work as an organizer, and Jim Middleton gave emotional and practical support for Lucy in her attempt to be elected to parliament.

Women who sought a career in labour politics were torn about how to define themselves and their political identity. As noted above, almost all spoke of a life of 'dedicated service' to the Labour Party and their desire to devote themselves to creating a better world. When they spoke of the work of others, 'selflessness' was emphasized. Katherine Bruce Glasier, for example, spoke of the self-sacrifice of one of the earliest socialist propagandists, Enid Stacy: 'in those days, she never dreamed of being herself a speaker. To wait on others, to work in any way for the coming of socialism, was reward enough'.[71] This fitted well with the concepts that informed socialist politics and an interest in the well-being of the community. It provided an acceptable discourse in which to legitimize a high public profile for

---

[68]   Jim Middleton to Lucy Cox August 1935, quoted in C. E. Bloomfield, 'James Smith Middleton', Doc. 9, Middleton Papers (Ruskin College, Oxford).

[69]   Letter from Lucy Cox to Jim Middleton, July 1934, MID 34/48, Middleton papers.

[70]   J. Hannam and K. Hunt, 'Socialist Women, Birth Control and Sexual Politics in Britain in the 1920s', *ITH*, 38 (Linz: Akademische Verlagsanstalt, 2003), 183–4.

[71]   K. B. Glasier, *Enid Stacy* (London: ILP, 1924), p. 4.

women but should not be taken simply at face value, since most activists also gained personal fulfillment from working within labour politics.

Local Activism

It has already been noted that the experiences of women who had high-profile positions within the Labour Party were different from the bulk of women members of the party who worked largely from their base within the women's sections. It is here that some of the debate about the extent to which women helped to shape the policies and the identity of the Labour Party has focused. In many respects, a consensus has emerged. It is noted that women had an important but gendered role to play at a local level, where they focused on election work, fundraising, educating the next generation in the principles of the labour movement, and taking part in direct actions on peace, housing and industrial unrest.[72] This contributed to raising the profile of the party within particular communities. It is also suggested that women helped to turn Labour from a trade union based party into a more neighbourhood group, articulating specific community and occupational demands, by tapping into the everyday experiences of workers in a particular locality and convincing them that Labour's politics were about everyday life. In this way they provided an identity for the party that was not just male, working class and bureaucratic, but one that had a wider human concern.

On the other hand, women's influence varied according to the local context. In safe Labour seats controlled by strong trade union organizations, little emphasis was placed on building a mass membership and women's sections had minimal influence on the character of local politics. Areas with a diverse occupational and social base, however, were more likely to provide opportunities for women to make their presence felt.[73] The attitudes of male activists could be crucial since they predominated in the local decision-making bodies. In Manchester, for example, women found it difficult to gain selection as municipal candidates since, because of the strength of pre-war suffragism, it was feared by some men that the women's sections were breeding grounds for feminism.[74] In contrast, there is little evidence

---

[72] Graves, *Labour Women*, pp. 157–60. See also the essays in Worley, *Labour's Grass Roots*.

[73] For examples of local variations, see Evans and Jones, 'Help Forward the Great Work of Humanity', pp. 222–5; S. Ball et al., 'Elections, Leaflets and Whist Drives: Constituency Members in Britain between the Wars' and S. Berger, 'The Formation of Party Milieux: Branch Life in the British Labour Party and the German Social Democratic Party in the Interwar Period', both in Worley, *Labour's Grass Roots*, pp. 7–32 and 245–6; M Savage, *The Dynamics of Working-Class Politics: The Labour Movement in Preston, 1880–1940* (Cambridge: Cambridge University Press, 1987).

[74] Hunt, 'Making Politics in Local Communities', p. 89. Men were also reluctant to support women as candidates in York, Doncaster and Coventry – see Graves, *Labour*

of hostility in Bristol. Here the ILP rather than the trade unions had a strong influence, and the local organizer, Herbert Rogers, was keen to increase individual membership. He encouraged women to put themselves forward for election to the city council but found that their lack of experience made them nervous to take on such a public role. In the end, it was the veteran campaigner Emily Webb, chairman of the East Bristol women's section, member of the Railway Women's Guild, long-time representative on the board of guardians and a JP, who stood successfully for the council in 1929.[75] The relationship between men and women could change over time. Mike Savage, for example, argues that changing economic circumstances in Preston meant that in the mid-1920s male skilled workers felt less threatened by female labour and therefore women were able to exert greater influence on the character of the local party. With the high unemployment of 1929, men became more hostile to women and their concerns and there was a decline in women's political involvement and a shift away from welfare initiatives.[76]

To what extent were women's sections able to influence the policies of the Labour Party at a local level, in particular towards welfare? Again, the picture is not a straightforward one. In many areas, such as London and Newport, a strong women's section could make a difference in focusing the attention of the constituency party on welfare issues including health, housing and education.[77] Duncan Tanner, however, suggests that there were more complex reasons why local Labour parties put welfare on the agenda and questions the role played by women's sections. One example he uses is Swansea, where the Labour Party prioritized the introduction of improved maternity services in the 1930s, including the provision of birth control advice, and yet there was no corresponding increase in the influence of the women's section. He argues that national events – including the government's focus on maternal mortality and the Labour Party's own welfare agenda, coupled with local civic pride, encouraged men to take up these issues as well as women. They joined with key individual activists such as Elizabeth Andrews and Rose Davies who, he suggests, were effective in their campaigning because they were part of the Labour Party machinery rather than outside it.[78]

Local studies such as this also raise questions about Graves' argument that women's specific needs and interests disappeared from the agenda in the 1930s and that when welfare reforms were put forward they were discussed in terms of

---

Women, p. 160

[75]   Sinnett, 'The Labour Party in Bristol', pp. 176–7, Chapter 4.

[76]   Savage, *Dynamics of Working-Class Politics*, pp. 167–8.

[77]   Pat Thane, for example, has argued that women had an impact on welfare policies, in particular health, in London in the 1930s, when a higher number were successful in the municipal elections. See her 'Women of the British Labour Party', p. 140. Also Weinbren, 'Social Capital', pp. 202–3; Evans and Jones, 'Help Forward the Great Work of Humanity', pp. 219–20.

[78]   D Tanner, 'Gender, Civic Culture and Politics in South Wales: Explaining Labour Municipal Policy, 1918–39', in Worley, *Labour's Grass Roots*, pp. 173–9, 182.

class rather than being seen as women-centred. Campaigners for family allowances and birth control framed their arguments in the language of class as early as the mid-1920s and they emphasized the health of the working-class mother rather than her sexual autonomy. There were also local variations in the strength of the birth control campaign. In Norwich and Finchley, where Dorothy and Violet Jewson and Jennie Baker were based, there was a strong interest in the issue, whereas in Bristol, while birth control was discussed at meetings of the Women's Advisory Council, it was not pursued with any urgency within the constituency party.[79]

In many local areas, attention to women's specific interests varied *within* the first decade after the war rather than showing a simple discontinuity between the 1920s and the 1930s. In Liverpool, for example, the Labour Party, influenced by the local activist Mary Bamber, campaigned over women's working conditions and trade unionism but, from 1927, the impact of the women's section on policy declined. Davies suggests that the Labour Party nationally became more inward looking and discouraged joint action with other groups such as women's organizations while at a local level the election of a group of Catholic councillors brought religion to the centre of the agenda and led to conflicts over birth control.

In other instances, as Karen Hunt's study of Manchester shows, women continued to be involved in issues well into the 1930s, such as peace protests, housing and campaigns around maternal mortality that could form the basis for developing a gendered, rather than a class, argument and for making alliances with other political women. The Gorton women's section in particular had an 'abrasive' relationship with the executive of their local party and saw their main objective as educating women into labour politics rather than fundraising.[80] In London, too, although the national party voted against disseminating birth control information, women carried on campaigning locally until they gained a partial victory in 1930. In many areas, it was Labour Party women who ensured that clinics were active in providing the advice.[81]

As these local studies show, women's specific influence on the development and character of labour politics in the interwar years varied from place to place. The relationship with men in the party, the extent to which women raised their own interests as a sex, the issues that they took up and how they framed their arguments were all affected by local political, economic and social conditions as well as by national and international events. Individual women activists were clearly important in influencing the agenda of constituency parties and in shaping the identity of local women's sections, but in some contexts men could also make a difference by supporting women's aims and by encouraging their participation.

---

[79]   Hannam and Hunt, 'Socialist Women, Birth Control', pp. 182–5.

[80]   Hunt, 'Making Politics in Local Communities', pp. 91, 96–7.

[81]   Weinbren, 'Social Capital', p. 197; L. Hall, 'No Sex Please we are Socialists: The British Labour Party Closes its Eyes and Thinks of the Electorate', in J. Batton, T. Bouchet and T. Regin (eds), *Meetings & Alcoves: The Left and Sexuality in Europe and the United States since 1850* (Dijon: l'Institut d'histoire contemporain, 2004).

Conclusion

What this chapter has attempted to argue is that we need to exercise caution in looking at the extent to which Labour women were significant for, or helped to shape, Labour Party culture and identity. It is clearly the case that it is difficult to deal with this in isolation from the broader social ideology about appropriate roles for men and women. In a post-war period in which women could now take part in formal politics as voters, there were competing discourses about how women should be represented. This in turn was reflected in Labour Party propaganda at a national level that spoke both to the domesticated wife and mother and to the young female worker. Such images were not consistently put forward throughout the whole period, however, and women as a group with specific needs and interests were not always identified in election manifestos. In its rhetoric, the Labour Party at various times made great play of the fact that it was the party that had championed women's rights and that it provided a space for women to take an active and equal role in politics. This was then reinforced by many high profile women in their autobiographies and memoirs, in which they glossed over conflicts and difficulties. Yet, this did not mean that the party felt that it needed women to represent its public face, as can be seen in the very small numbers elected to national and local bodies.

It has been suggested here that we need to recognize the multi-layered ways in which women contributed to labour politics, which makes generalizations about their outlook, the extent to which they were feminist, and whether a distinction should be drawn between the 1920s and 1930s misleading. The few women who had a high profile in politics had a symbolic importance since they could provide a view of the Labour woman that was very different from the 'wife and mother' who predominated in the literature and also in the women's sections. Labour women sought to carve a career for themselves and to raise issues that were of interest to women in a variety of ways in this period, while at the same time trying not to be seen as confined to a specific role. They worked alongside men to achieve a better world for both sexes, but at times could conflict both with men and with other women in the party – these conflicts were not just over specific issues such as birth control, but could also relate to marital status, generation and peace questions. By drawing attention to their gender – whether as individuals or as members of a specific group of women – Labour women were bound to form part of the way in which the Labour Party identified itself and was seen by others. On the other hand, there is not one simple way to characterize that relationship and identity. What we need are more in-depth studies of key individuals and an understanding of their complex political journeys, alongside detailed research into women's engagement in local politics. Only then will we be able to get beneath the generalizations made to understand the complexities of women's relationship to labour politics in a period in which they were attempting to work out their role as active citizens in a mixed-sex movement that aimed to bring in a better world for men as well as women.

Chapter 11

The Fruits on the Tree: Labour's Constituency Parties between the Wars

Matthew Worley

I sometimes think of the Labour Party as a tree, sprung from a seed planted by a dreamer long ago; today a strong, fast-growing, fruit-bearing tree native to this little pocket of British soil, from which it draws many of its most characteristic and best qualities ... But without the trade unions our British tree would have no roots and no stability; without the constituency parties it could bear no crop of political fruit.[1]

Hugh Dalton (1937)

In 1917, Arthur Henderson began a fundamental restructuring of the British Labour Party. Where Labour had emerged from 1900 as a federation of affiliated trade unions, trades councils, socialist and co-operative societies, the party was reconstituted in 1918 as a nationwide organization with branches intended for every parliamentary constituency. A federal structure was retained but, for the first time, membership was open officially to individual men and women; local and divisional parties were formed to provide a permanent and distinctive Labour presence throughout Britain. In Henderson's words, referring to the widening franchise and the 'democratic will' facilitated by the Great War, Labour was to be transformed into a 'national popular party, rooted in the life of the democracy, and deriving its principles and its policy from the new political consciousness'.[2]

Such reorganization proved integral to Labour's subsequent growth, political development and character. The party was henceforth more able to attract and appeal beyond the already-existing organized labour and socialist movement on which it had been built; its geographical concentration began slowly to extend beyond Britain's industrial heartlands. The formation of divisional Labour parties allowed support to be cultivated across society, thereby reasserting the term 'labour' to embrace all 'whose toil enriched the community', including non-unionized workers, the middle class and the newly enfranchised working-class woman. Simultaneously, in accord with the publication of Labour's first comprehensive programme, *Labour and the New Social Order* (1918), the party began to define a

---

[1] Labour Party, *Report of the Annual Conference of the Labour Party, 1937* (London, 1937), p. 137.

[2] A. Henderson, *The Aims of Labour* (New York: B. W. Huebsch, 1919 edition), p. 18.

political ideology – a socialism – that sought to appeal to people both 'as workers and as citizens'. 'We are casting our net wide', Henderson insisted with one eye on the ramifications of the Bolshevik Revolution and the other on middle-class radicals alienated from a divided Liberal Party, because 'real political democracy cannot be organized on the basis of class interest'.[3] This chapter will explore such developments with the objective of emphasizing the importance of local party activity in building, defining and projecting Labour's social-political identity between the wars.

Re-Make/Re-Model

On the eve of the Great War (1914–18), the Labour Party was established as a permanent, significant but inconsistent feature of British politics. In terms of size, the party registered an affiliated membership of 1,612,147 in 1914. Electorally, having secured an agreement with the Liberal Party from 1903, Labour grew to occupy 42 seats in parliament following the second general election of 1910, while Labour candidates continued to make slow but steady progress in municipal politics up to the outbreak of the Great War.[4] As this suggests, however, there were clear limitations to Labour's growth and influence prior to 1914. In parliament, the Labour contingent was generally reliant on Liberal support, with an electorate that was located overwhelmingly in industrial and densely unionized localities such as in Lancashire, Yorkshire and mining constituencies in South Wales and the North East.[5] This, in turn, reflected the fact that 97.5 per cent of the party's 1914 membership was affiliated via a trade union. As such, Labour remained a marginal presence throughout much of the country, representing a minority within Britain's wider working-class population. Similarly, Labour's loose organizational framework ensured that the party appeared a rather ephemeral phenomenon in many places. While its varied components (trades councils, union affiliates and Independent Labour Party: ILP) came together as 'Labour' for electoral purposes, they continued to pursue their own distinct objectives and functions thereafter. Of course, more permanent organization was developing, such as the Manchester and Salford Labour Representation Committee and the burgeoning party in Woolwich, while the ILP persisted in flying a more overtly

---

[3]   Ibid., p. 24.

[4]   M. G. Sheppard and J. Halstead, 'Labour's Municipal Election Performance in Provincial England and Wales, 1901–13', *Bulletin of the Society for the Study of Labour History*, 39 (1979). For important qualifications with regard to such figures, see D. Tanner, 'Elections, Statistics, and the Rise of the Labour Party, 1906–31', *The Historical Journal*, 34/4 (1991), pp. 898–908.

[5]   M. Kinnear, *The British Voter: An Atlas and Survey since 1885* (London: Batsford, 1981). For a brilliant survey, see D. Tanner, *Political Change and The Labour Party, 1900–18* (Cambridge: Cambridge University Press, 1990).

socialist flag in certain parts of the country. Yet, there remained huge swathes of Britain where the Labour Party boasted little to no representation, particularly beyond the principal urban and industrial centres.[6]

The impact of the Great War helped transform Labour's position. The party's ability to contain pro- and anti-war sentiment within its ranks contrasted with the divisions that wrought the Liberal Party apart; its participation in the wartime coalition government helped legitimize its leaders and politics while also prompting the party to widen its political perspective. Equally, Labour profited from certain social-political by-products of the war, such as the state's taking control of key industries and the rising importance of trade unionism within such an economy. Labour – locally and nationally – presented itself as the defender of the people's interests, campaigning against war profiteering, rent increases and price rises. The widening of the franchise, too, appeared – ostensibly at least – to present Labour with a ready-made electorate of working-class men and women.[7] Even though Lloyd George returned to power following the 1918 general election, he did so at the head of a Tory-dominated coalition in the midst of considerable political flux, thereby allowing Labour to move into the political 'space' vacated by the still divided Liberals.[8] As such, Henderson's plans for reorganization were part of Labour's rising to the challenge and opportunity afforded by the Great War. With an expanding membership base – Labour registered 4,359,807 affiliates in 1920, 4,317,537 of whom were trade unionists – and, therefore, greater income, Labour sought to extend its apparatus and representation. Nationally, the Labour executive expanded its central apparatus, establishing a series of sub-committees to review, broaden and perfect party activity, and appointing male and female organizers to help forge party representation across nine designated regions. At the 1918 general election, 361 Labour candidates stood before the British people compared to just 56 in December 1910.[9] Locally, constituency parties were formed to establish and maintain a constant presence within their respective communities. These, moreover, were to include women's sections in recognition of the extension of the franchise to most women over 30 and the wartime increase

---

[6]   For parties emerging from such difficult conditions, see D. Matthew, *From Two Boys and a Dog to Political Power: The Labour Party in the Lowestoft Constituency, 1918–45* (Lowestoft, 1979); D. Howell-Thomas, *Socialism in West Sussex: A History of the Chichester Constituency Labour Party* (Chichester, undated).

[7]   In fact, the ramifications of the 1918 Representation of the People Act were far more complex. See D. Tanner, 'Elections, Statistics, and the Rise of the Labour Party, 1906–31', *The Historical Journal*, 34/4 (1991) and 'Class Voting and Radical Politics: The Liberal and Labour Party', in J. Lawrence and M. Taylor (eds.), *Party, State and Society: Electoral Behaviour in Britain since 1829* (Aldershot: Scolar, 1997).

[8]   For more on this, see M. Worley, *Labour Inside the Gate: A History of the British Labour Party between the Wars* (London: I. B. Tauris, 2005), pp. 30–44.

[9]   R. McKibbin, *The Evolution of the Labour Party, 1910–24* (Oxford: Oxford University Press, 1974).

in female trade unionists. Ultimately, Labour anticipated that every parliamentary division would house a Constituency Labour Party to which labour organizations and individuals would affiliate. Where divided boroughs existed, a Central or Borough Labour Party was formed to which the appropriate constituency parties affiliated. These divisional parties then established ward parties formed in accordance with municipal electoral districts, each with the same structure as the larger party organization.

The results of such reorganization were impressive. Come 1924, only three British parliamentary constituencies could not boast party representation of some form or other.[10] In the same year, Labour formed its first minority government and fought a potentially bank-breaking fourth general election in six years. True, problems and inadequacies remained across Labour's constituency apparatus, as Christopher Howard has demonstrated.[11] Many parties were run on a very limited basis, membership remained low or largely affiliated in a majority of localities, and internal wrangling could blight a party's progress. Yet, Howard – not to mention Ramsay MacDonald – must be regarded as somewhat premature in suggesting that expectations were 'born to death' by the limits of local party development in the early 1920s: the extension of Labour's constituency organization took time and suffered regular setbacks (not least with the collapse of the second Labour government in 1931), but it continued nevertheless. By the late 1930s, individual Labour members numbered nearly half-a-million, comprising 17.7 per cent of the overall membership in 1937 compared to 9.4 per cent in 1928. Linked to this, sizeable, active and vibrant divisional parties were evolving, particularly in and around the South East in places such as Twickenham, Hendon, Ilford, Lewisham and Harrow. These, moreover, often formed regional and county federations to co-ordinate their activity and offer 'mutual support' in an attempt to assert their influence both locally and within the wider Labour Party. Indeed, Labour's historic general election victory in 1945 would not have been possible without such constituency parties forging, cultivating and propagating Labour's socialist vision in the suburbs and emergent towns throughout Britain's ever-shifting economic base.

Of course, the essential foundations of the Labour Party did not change. The trade unions, from which Labour derived its bedrock support and the bulk of its finance, maintained a dominant influence on party councils and at the party conference throughout the interwar years and beyond. Thus, the reconstituted National Executive Committee (NEC) ensured a decisive trade union presence in 1918, the use of the block vote at conference guaranteed that the unions held the key to any successful resolution (not to mention the election of the executive),

---

[10]   G. D. H. Cole, *A History of the Labour Party from 1914* (London: Routledge, 1948), p. 140.

[11]   C. Howard, 'Expectations Born to Death: Local Labour Party Expansion in the 1920s', in J. Winter (ed.), *The Working Class in Modern British History: Essays in Honour of Henry Pelling* (Cambridge: Cambridge University Press, 1983).

and union-sponsored candidates continued to represent most Labour heartlands at the polls. The vast majority of the party membership remained affiliated via the trade union movement between the wars; even when individual membership reached its peak in 1937, those 447,150 members were overshadowed by 2,037,071 trade unionists. Certainly, Labour's survival and recovery following the trauma of 1931 depended on the trade unions retaining faith in the party and the Trades Union Congress (TUC) reasserting its ties with the political 'wing' of the labour movement via the National Joint Council (renamed the National Council of Labour in 1934). Nevertheless, the growth of constituency parties and individual membership had an evident impact at a local level and led later to moves to gain greater representation for divisional parties at conference and on the NEC.[12] Most obviously, perhaps, the constituency organizations gradually usurped the roles played by the trades councils and ILP within the wider Labour Party (see below). Significantly, too, aspects of the trade unions' dominance within the Labour Party were contested by such organizational change. In 1929, for example, the number of MPs sponsored by divisional parties for the first time outnumbered those sponsored by the trade unions: 128 to 115. Come the 1935 general election, 395 out of the 552 prospective Labour candidates were sponsored by their constituency organization. On the 'hustings' and in parliament, at least, Labour did not necessarily reflect a party born from the 'bowels' of the trade union movement, to use Ernest Bevin's famous phrase.

As this suggests, Labour's reorganization began to give rise to interesting variations within the party. First, the local and divisional Labour parties formed from 1918 often differed in terms of size, strength and composition. To state the obvious, a party based in a Durham or South Wales mining constituency was somewhat different to one based in, say, Canterbury, Cheltenham or East Grinstead. In the former, local Labour parties reflected the miners' union cultures and traditions; in the latter 'type', the party was often beginning from scratch, relying on individual members to build a working apparatus and adapt Labour's appeal to a sizeable middle-class or rural electorate. In Durham, Methodist miners such as Will Whiteley, Jack Swan and Joe Batey dominated the divisional party executive; in East Grinstead, Reverend H. W. Layng, Lady De La Warr and Major David Graham Pole led the way. Elsewhere, in more 'mixed' economic localities such as Norwich, Newport, Edinburgh and parts of London, various strands of the labour and socialist movement sought to combine their energies, overcome sometimes conflicting perspectives and – if possible – develop a community based party presence. In each, the approach and progress of the party was refracted through an array of determinants, ranging from local social-cultural traditions and political precedents to electoral boundary configurations and shifting social-economic developments. On a more practical level, and despite the national party's circulation of organizational guidelines, constituency parties

---

[12]   B. Pimlott, *Labour and the Left in the 1930s* (Cambridge: Cambridge University Press, 1977), pp. 111–42.

did not always conform to Labour conventions. So, in Leicester, the formation of three constituency parties as outlined in the party constitution was eschewed in favour of remaining as one borough party. Elsewhere, usually with regard to parties based on largely affiliated trade union memberships, the call to recruit individuals was ignored. Similarly, in Scotland, the ILP made little attempt to build up Labour organizations that it perceived as a rival to its own unique place within the wider party.[13]

Second, a divisional party's form, character and influence could change over time. Most obviously, for our purposes, 'suburban' parties – particularly in and around Greater London – grew in size, scope and importance over the interwar period. For example, a party such as that in Twickenham could see its membership increase from 943 to 2,082 between 1929 and 1937 (and its vote increase from 5,509 (23.7 per cent) to 22,823 (37.8 per cent) between 1923 and 1935), as the locality's social-economic composition evolved.[14] Not dissimilarly, factors such as the building of a new housing estate could impinge on a divisional party's relative import. In and around London, for example, it has been argued that the building of the St Helier housing estate contributed to Labour's growing presence in Wimbledon, Merton and Mordon over the late 1920s and 1930s; that the Hendon Labour Party appeared to benefit from the Watling estate built from 1927; and that Labour's influence in Lewisham grew in tandem with the construction of three working-class housing estates, the associational culture of which was tapped into by Labour's two constituency parties.[15] In Norwich, the divisional party made explicit reference to the fact that its ward organization and share of the vote changed in line with slum clearance and house building.[16] In similar fashion, the shifting nature of Britain's social-economic base ensured 'new' industries – and the unions in which their workers gathered – rose in prominence within divisional Labour parties between the wars. Thus, the character and composition of the Birmingham party was informed by the city's growth and economic evolution over the interwar period.[17] In Durham, Sedgefield only became a Labour seat once

---

[13]   Worley, *Labour Inside the Gate*, pp. 44–65 and pp. 82–97.

[14]   Figures taken from the Labour annual conference and F. W. S. Craig, *British Parliamentary Election Results, 1918–45* (Chichester, Parliamentary Research Services, 1983).

[15]   D. Weinbren, 'Sociable Capital: London's Labour Parties, 1918–45', in M. Worley (ed.), *Labour's Grass Roots: Essays on the Activities of Local Labour Parties and Members, 1918–45* (Aldershot: Ashgate, 2005), pp. 203–5; T. Jeffery, 'The Suburban Nation: Politics and Class in Lewisham', in D. Feldman and G. Stedman Jones (eds), *Metropolis–London: Histories and Representations since 1800* (London: Routledge, 1989), pp. 189–216.

[16]   Norwich Labour Party and Industrial Council, *Report and Balance Sheet* (Norwich, 1936 and 1937).

[17]   J. Boughton, 'Working Class Conservatism and the Rise of Labour: A Case Study of Birmingham in the 1920s', *The Historian* (Autumn, 1998); R. P. Hastings, 'The Birmingham Labour Movement, 1918–45', *Midland History*, 5 (1979–80).

a newly-built chemical works brought an influx of workers to accompany the miners in an otherwise rural constituency.[18]

Third, we should note that a large individual membership did not necessarily bring with it electoral triumph. In Wales, Newport provides a classic example of a relatively large membership party that achieved only sporadic success at the polls, both at a municipal and general election level. Elsewhere we could point to the large divisional party memberships in Ilford, Cambridgeshire and Reading, none of which ensured a Labour stronghold before the war. Ultimately, few divisional parties could claim a 'mass' membership: by 1939, just 32 parties registered more than 2,000 individual members, compared to eight in 1929.[19] Likewise, as many a trade unionist pointed out, an affiliated member was not thereby an inactive one. Indeed, the trade unions proved willing and able to mobilize their members at election time, while Labour activists acquired multiple responsibilities as Labour, trade union and co-op cardholders. That said, as Bettie Braddock noted, parties built on strong trade union foundations could sometimes appear dormant.

> Local Labour Party organisations are rather like local divisions of unions. Where a branch of industry is trouble free and the workers are well looked after, the union organisation is likely to wither, for it's extremely difficult to keep the soldiers at their peak of efficiency when there isn't any war. Conversely, if one looks at a strong Tory constituency where Labour hasn't a dog's chance of winning, one often finds that the Labour Party there is virile, well organised, and supported by strong funds. In places like [Liverpool] Exchange, or Ebbw Vale, the Labour Party hardly exists except at election times, or at times when it is part of the social life of the area.[20]

In such constituencies, Labour fused with and continued to reflect pre-existing working-class organization and cultures.

Even so, something of an incongruity underlay Labour's growth and development between the wars. While the party's organizational expansion and stability depended, in large part, on its trade union base, its progress continued at a time when trade union membership began to fall from 1920.[21] In other words, Labour came to form two (minority) governments and extended its influence into parts of Britain previously immune to socialist influence as the post-war boom gave way to recession, amidst the sluggish economic performance of the 1920s

---

[18]   M. Callcott, 'The Nature and Extent of Political Change in the Interwar Years: The Example of County Durham', *Northern History*, 16 (1980), 215–37.

[19]   Labour Party, *Report of the Annual Conference of the Labour Party*, 1929 and 1939, pp. 112–48 and 95.

[20]   J. and B. Braddock, *The Braddocks* (London: MacDonald, 1963), p. 93.

[21]   Trade union membership fell from 8,253,000 to 4,392,000 between 1920 and 1933, rising to 6,298,000 by 1939. The number of Labour affiliated trade unionists fell from 4,318,000 to 1,899,000 in the same period, rising to 2,214,000 by 1939.

and 1930s, and following a 1926 General Strike that paved the way for a Trade Disputes and Trade Union Act (1927) which restricted union power and cut into Labour's principal source of funding. In effect, the trade unions continued to provide – as Dalton acknowledged – the roots that grounded the party. But Labour needed its constituency parties to reach beyond Labour's apparently contracting base support if it was to gain a parliamentary majority. The reasons for this are not difficult to fathom. From a trade union viewpoint, a parliamentary presence was even more imperative once economic circumstances served to challenge union strength. To this end, the 'contentious alliance' between the trade unions and the Labour Party was consolidated within the social-economic context of Britain between the wars. The Edinburgh and District Trades and Labour Council put it succinctly in 1921:

> For several years, with unemployment non-existent or comparatively so, the trade unions were remarkably efficient in obtaining immediate results. With overwhelming numbers of unemployed, with capital armed with large resource funds and replete with carefully prepared machinery, the power of the strike can only be effective to an uncertain degree, and a growing realization of this fact will swell the healthy development of the Labour Party.[22]

Equally, from a political perspective, a falling trade union membership underlined the need for Labour to appeal, recruit and mobilize beyond the organized labour movement. Thus, the importance of establishing women's sections and appealing to the middle-class and non-unionized electorate took up much of the party's time over the 1920s and into the 1930s. Labour's appeal had to resonate across the community. For a number of historians, Labour's success over the interwar period (and beyond) depended on its transforming from a party based on the trade union movement to one located within the wider community or neighbourhood.[23]

Looked at broadly, Labour's network of constituency organizations is best understood as a mosaic comprised of a series of ward, divisional, borough and regional parties that each reflected values, priorities and objectives determined via a complex interaction of multiple national and local factors. They were bound together by a complementary ethos and objective, but could vary in their composition, expression and approach. While the trade unions gave Labour a solid basis, the formation of permanent constituency organizations ensured that Labour broke away from what Henderson feared was too narrow a definition of

---

[22]   Edinburgh and District Trades and Labour Council, *Annual Report for Year Ending 31 March 1921* (Edinburgh, 1921).

[23]   See, for example, M. Savage, *The Dynamics of Working-Class Politics: The Labour Movement in Preston, 1880–1940* (Cambridge: Cambridge University Press, 1987); S. Davies, *Liverpool Labour: Social and Political Influences on the Development of the Labour Party in Liverpool, 1900–39* (Keele: Keele University Press, 1996); Worley, *Labour Inside the Gate*, pp. 177–89.

its objective. 'Under the old conditions the appeal of the party was limited', he insisted. Labour was, Henderson continued, too often regarded as a class party with a programme that reflected the views of trade unionists seeking remedies for 'material grievances' such as wages, hours and conditions.[24] With its reorganization (and the publication of a comprehensive political programme), Labour could disavow such misconceptions and, in so doing, escape from the geographical confines that had previously restricted its scope for development.

Calling The People

To achieve its stated objective of political, social and economic emancipation for the people, the Labour Party had to formulate a politics that related to and sought to improve the lives of the men and women who comprised the British electorate. To vote Labour, the *Daily Herald* told its readers in 1919, was to vote for 'better education, better housing, better sanitation; in fact better everything that concerns our everyday life'.[25] It fell to the constituency organizations, therefore, to become the living expression of Labour policy and Labour values. This they endeavoured to do in two principal ways. First, from 1918, the divisional parties began to usurp many of the roles played previously by trades councils and the ILP within the Labour Party. Electoral organization, canvassing and the dissemination of propaganda became the responsibility of the divisional party. Second, the constituency parties set out both to cultivate Labour (or socialist) cultures and build an ever-growing and sustainable level of support. To this end, active constituency party members took Labour's message out of the committee rooms, off the platform and into the community, thereby contributing to the changing character of British politics over the twentieth century.[26]

Given Labour's political *modus operandi*, elections took priority. In the words of the Edinburgh party, Labour was 'not a debating society, an economic class, or a school of sociological philosophy', but a 'machine'. 'We are not schoolmasters; we are mechanics.'[27] The Norwich party, too, informed its members that 'adequate electoral machinery' was the 'main object of our party'.[28] In this, they followed Herbert Morrison's maxim that 'the silent visionary with a card index beside him

---

[24]   Henderson, *The Aims of Labour*, pp. 25–7.

[25]   Quoted in C. Wrigley, *Lloyd George and Challenge of Labour: The Post War Coalition, 1918–22* (Hemel Hempstead: Harvester, 1990), p. 248.

[26]   J. Lawrence, 'The Transformation of British Public Politics After the First World War', *Past and Present*, 190 (2006), pp. 185–215.

[27]   Quoted in J. Holford, *Reshaping Labour: Organisation, Work and Politics – Edinburgh in the Great War and After* (London: Croom Helm, 1988), p. 168.

[28]   Norwich Labour Party and Industrial Council, *Executive Report and Balance Sheet, 1934* (Norwich, 1934).

... is not less important than they who move in the limelight'.[29] The 'new school of Labour politicians is a scientific school', he suggested, which 'knows that noisy tub-thumping does not make up for careful organization'.[30] The street corner meeting and the 'star' speaker on a political platform still had their place, but Labour concentrated much of its electoral attention on distributing literature and canvassing door-to-door from the early 1920s. The *Labour Organiser* was even publishing hints on how best to address an envelope by 1923.[31] For this reason, the Loughborough party resolved in 1930 that 'no useful purpose' would be served by its holding open-air meetings. Rather, 'canvassing and getting personal contact with the electors' was deemed the best way to build Labour's influence.[32] The Newport party agent, too, urged his members to replace demonstrations with a focus on the doorstep and the holding of party socials and teas.[33] As this suggests, 'hard doorstep work' – meeting people and explaining the Labour Party's relevance to their lives – became an integral part of Labour's relationship with the electorate, and no doubt helped shape local perceptions of the party as a result.

Although difficult to quantify in terms of impact, the constituency parties retained a degree of flexibility in their dissemination of Labour policy. True, model standing orders and guidelines for party organization were issued by the national party, while the various publications produced and distributed from Eccleston Square and Transport House gave clear indication of Labour's priorities and political approach. The NEC, too, proved willing to intervene in constituency affairs on occasion. But local members, particularly during municipal elections, necessarily had to identify and cultivate issues and campaigns directly relevant to their respective jurisdiction. Similarly, it was up to local members to relate national Labour policy to the lives of their constituents. To this end, local Labour policy became focused increasingly on social-political issues, as the divisional party committees endeavoured to offer local versions of Labour socialism applicable to their constituency. So, to take just a few examples, parties could appeal in quite stark terms: 'Workers! Vote for yourselves by Voting for Witard ... The landlord wants big rents for little houses ... [and] the employer wants long hours for short wages ... The worker wants big healthy houses for low rents and higher wages for shorter hours.'[34] Or they could apply to reason and community:

---

[29]   Quoted in B. Donoughue and G. W. Jones, *Herbert Morrison: Portrait of a Politician* (London: Orion, 2001), p. 71.

[30]   Quoted in McKibbin, *The Evolution of the Labour Party*, p. 145.

[31]   *Labour Organiser*, August 1923.

[32]   Minutes of the Loughborough Borough Labour Party, 28 March 1930 (Leicestershire Record Office).

[33]   *Minutes of the Newport Labour Party*, 7 November 1924 (Wakefield: Microfilm Imaging Ltd, 1999).

[34]   *Workers! Vote for Witard* (Norwich, 1904).

Individually, we are hopeless to protect our health, to secure our life, to dispose of our dust and house refuse, to get rid of our sewage to ensure a pure and abundant water supply, or to obtain decent and proper housing. All together, acting as an organized community, utilizing the resources of all for the benefit and service of each, we can provide all these things and we can make life fuller and richer and happier for everyone ... every time you approve of these beneficent schemes you approve of socialism.[35]

Alternatively, a party could champion specifically local campaigns, be it housing issues or, as in the 1923 local elections in Gloucester, the question of vaccinations and municipal control of the smallpox epidemic.[36] Again, certain appeals were more successful than others. But Labour could not simply fall back on socialist, or progressive, platitudes in its attempt to win the working class to the socialist cause. In Leicester, ILP-initiated election campaigns outlining plans for three-bedroom houses, free education, elaborate local health schemes and a socialized municipal economy made little headway. Here as elsewhere, more piecemeal but practical policies – based on the same themes but expressed in a more realizable language – helped secure Labour a presence on the city council.[37] Taken generally, Labour sought to adapt its message to suit local circumstances. Thus, in towns such as Preston and Blackburn, 'where Labour recognized that Liberal policies alienated working-class support, Labour backed rate aid for voluntary schools, supported compensation for publicans who lost their licences, and opposed disestablishment'.[38] As this suggests, the Labour Party came to include varied traditions within its ranks, ranging from the radical, liberal and socialist to the patriotic, pragmatic and populist. In other words, Labour had to encompass and project an identity that complemented each respective constituency if it was to progress.

Bound up with the party's focus on electioneering was the need for Labour to raise funds and canvass support, tasks that bled into the constituency parties' broader objective of maintaining and recruiting members to the Labour Party. Accordingly, local, divisional and borough parties implemented and developed various schemes for dues-collecting and retaining contact with members and supporters between election times. For example, newspapers provided one obvious means of providing a regular means of communication within the wider community, although these often proved difficult to sustain. Equally, Labour clubs enabled the party to become established amongst sections of the community, providing income and a social context in which potential and actual Labour

---

[35]   *Bermondsey Labour Magazine*, January 1924.

[36]   See *Minutes of the Gloucester Trades Council and Labour Party, 1899–1951* (Wakefield: Microfilm Imaging Ltd, 1986).

[37]   D. Cox, 'The Rise of the Labour Party in Leicester', University of Leicester: MA Thesis (1959).

[38]   M. Pugh, 'The Rise of Labour and the Political Culture of Conservatism, 1890–1945', *History*, 87/288 (2002), 515–37.

members could meet. For Stephen Jones, Labour clubs became 'social adjuncts of the labour movement', and though not always centres of political activism, were 'pioneers of new kinds of commodity production and distribution, and associational forms designed to encourage participation and mutual self-help'.[39] As practicably, some divisional parties established forms of social service such as free legal advice for their constituents.[40]

More pleasurably, party socials, whist drives and raffles were organized at a local and divisional level, while Labour choirs, brass bands and theatre groups emerged to fuse such cultural pursuits with Labour's political vision. These served a duel purpose in that they provided a focus for party members between elections and, simultaneously, projected Labour values via social-cultural behaviour. Many such activities had their roots in the pre-war labour movement, with divisional parties seeking to maintain and extend pre-existing trade union and ILP initiatives between the wars. As such, galas and May Days became events to which Labour members could dress up and celebrate their political (and class) identities. In marginal constituencies, social events often proved essential to sustaining morale in unconducive circumstances. Certainly, the small but active East Grinstead Labour Party took its cultural responsibilities very seriously, presenting them as the most effective means of propagating Labour's message in so geographically dispersed a constituency after the war. To this end, its members formed an Arts League of Service in 1919, touring local towns and villages to present plays such as 'The Price of Coal'.[41]

The range of Labour's cultural activity was extensive. In Ealing, a party that numbered 3,000 by the mid-1930s offered its members dances, sports clubs, a choir, an orchestra and a burgeoning Socialist Sunday School. Party outings were also popular. Thus, the North Lambeth party toyed in 1927 between a 'circular motor coach tour' of 120 miles with tea on Saturday and Sunday, or a trip to Hampden Court followed by a boat trip to Windsor with tea and sandwiches on board. In 1937, the Halifax, Huddersfield and Colne Valley parties organized a joint excursion to North Wales; the Caerphilly party even planned trips to Europe in conjunction with the Workers' Travel Association. A number of parties organized children's outings to places such as Kew gardens, while annual picnics, Christmas bazaars and harvest festivals became typical features of local party life. Such events were usually diverse affairs, with an assortment of bands, competitions, stalls and sideshows. The Leeds party's annual gathering in 1937 included gymnastics, a

[39]　S. G. Jones, *Workers at Play: A Social and Economic History of Leisure, 1918–39* (London: Routledge, 1986), p. 147.

[40]　S. Goss, *Local Labour and Local Government: A Study of Changing Interests, Politics and Policy in Southwark from 1919 to 1982* (Edinburgh: Edinburgh University Press, 1988), pp. 9–23.

[41]　*Minutes of East Grinstead Labour Party, 1918–20* (London School of Economics).

magic show and fancy dress competition; in 1929, the Swindon party May Day festival included a balloon competition, beauty contest and firework display.[42]

Significantly, the formation of Labour women's sections was integral to much of the activity outlined above.[43] Although not as successful as the Conservative Party in attracting women to its cause, Labour was nevertheless claiming over 100,000 female cardholders by 1923 and a network of functioning women's sections.[44] These were often small but served as a means to integrate women into the party. More importantly, the women's sections – and women members more generally – began to undertake two vital responsibilities within the party.[45] First, they were generally given charge of organizing the aforementioned social events for members and constituents alike. This, of course, led to comments about women being the 'official cake makers' of the party, and activists such as Winnie Smith could complain of women being left to do the 'soppy things'.[46] Yet, as noted above, social activities became vital to the maintenance of the party between election times and related to Labour's wider objective of integrating its values and presence within a local community. While not the cut and thrust of the political struggle, such initiatives were important all the same. As one delegate informed the party conference in 1929, the bulk of the money raised by his own party had been done so by the women's section; an 'admission' that could have been echoed by many a non-trade union sponsored party.[47] 'It is noticeable', the Norwich party recorded in 1937, 'that in every effort connected with our movement, we are apt to leave the bulk of the work to our women folk'.[48]

Second, women were essential cogs in Labour's electoral 'machine'. Women, as countless memoirs and party minute books attest, were mobilized to address envelopes, post literature and canvass support, undertaking the jobs that came to dominate the political process post-1918. In Tom Johnston's words, writing (rather dramatically) about his 1922 election victory, women hustled 'the indifferent to the booths; they lent shawls and held babies: they carried the sick and dying to

---

[42]   Weinbren, 'Sociable Capital', p. 200; *Minutes of the North Lambeth Labour Party*, 13 May 1927 (London School of Economics); Colne Valley Divisional Labour Party, *Annual Report and Balance Sheet, 11 February 1939* (Wakefield: Microfilm Imaging Ltd, 1986); *Labour Organiser*, October–November 1925.

[43]   P. Graves, *Labour Women: Women in British Working Class Politics, 1918–39* (Cambridge: Cambridge University Press, 1994).

[44]   See G. E. Maguire, *Conservative Women: A History of Women and the Conservative Party, 1874–1997* (Basingstoke: Palgrave, 1998).

[45]   For more on this, see Worley, *Labour Inside the Gate*, pp. 60–5.

[46]   D. Weinbren, *Generating Socialism: Recollections of Life in the Labour Party* (Stroud: Sutton, 1997), p. 157.

[47]   Labour Party, *Report of the Annual Conference of the Labour Party, 1929*, pp. 224–5.

[48]   Norwich Labour Party and Industrial Council, *Executive Report and Balance Sheet, 1937* (Norwich, 1937).

the polls on mattresses – and they won'.[49] Ultimately, the influx of women into the Labour Party from 1918 allowed and facilitated the broadening of Labour's perspective. Issues relevant to working-class women were henceforth put before the party, while an 'appeal to women' became a staple of Labour election material. True, this often appeared as mere 'tokenism' and women continued – with much justification – to feel sidelined by their male comrades. Nationally, few Labour women entered or were proposed to stand for parliament between the wars, and women were in the minority on party committees throughout its apparatus. But the activities to which Labour women applied their energies were increasingly those which brought the party into the public sphere and made tangible Labour's presence within the neighbourhood. Over time, moreover, the different male and female 'spheres' of interest and activity that characterized British politics and society in the early twentieth century became blurred, as social policy – housing, health and welfare – made its way to the top of many local parties' agenda.

Overall, the divisional parties sought to transform Labour from a party based in and appealing to the organized male working class, to a 'people's party' located within the community. Appeals to middle-class voters, women, the non-union worker and the rural population were duly made, if sometimes to limited effect. Certainly, the rural voter tended to remain aloof from the Labour Party, while it often took time for local parties to attract significant numbers of women and middle-class members to its ranks. Even so, the party's share of the vote steadily increased across the interwar period, bar 1931, and diversified in terms of its geographical distribution. Most notably, the party's vote grew in areas where 'new' industries and divisional parties lay the foundations for a Labour presence. With regard to the latter, Labour was by 1935 able to pick up votes in areas where it had barely made an impression in the early 1920s. Thus, the Labour vote in Ilford – where a large individual membership developed over the 1930s – rose from 5,414 (17.1 per cent) in 1922, to 25,241 (36. 9 per cent) in 1935, and there were similar increases in places such as West Lewisham, Chelmsford, Luton and Bedford. Labour still fell short of winning some of these seats of course, but such constituencies appeared far more attainable in 1935 than at any time previously.

The cultural value of the divisional Labour parties is harder to measure. For those involved, such activity was a cherished and valuable component of their Labour membership. Indeed, the accounts of Labour culture given in Dan Weinbren's *Generating Socialism* (1997) are testament to the lively social-cultural context created by party members and to which the party more generally lent its support.[50] Even so, Labour culture could not claim to rival the development and

---

[49]   Quoted in I. S. Wood, 'Hope Deferred: Labour in Scotland in the 1920s', in I. Donnachie, C. Harvie and I. S. Wood (eds), *Forward! Labour Politics in Scotland, 1888–1988* (Edinburgh: Polygon, 1989), pp. 30–1. See also Margaret Lloyd's comments in Weinbren, *Generating Socialism*, p. 184; *Minutes of the Peterborough Divisional Labour Party*, 8 February 1925 (Wakefield: Microfilm Imaging Ltd, 1986).

[50]   Weinbren, *Generating Socialism*, pp. 57–77.

popularity of professional or non-associated sports and leisure cultures during the interwar period, most obviously association football, the pub and the cinema. By the 1920s, commercialized leisure had become well established in Britain, and Labour succeeded mainly in supplementing, imitating or building on already existing working-class organizations and interests. Arguably, too, the party's progress ensured that its objectives appeared better served via the implementation of municipal policies – extending funding to libraries, education, health and sports facilities – than by setting up party equivalents. Ultimately, the constituency parties' importance lay in their providing Labour with the mechanism to effectively contest elections and thereby acquire the power to legislate in the interests of the wider community. Although results varied across Britain, it was only by the cultivation of such an effective political 'machine' that Labour was able to win and sustain the support necessary to unsettle the time-honoured configuration of British politics in the early twentieth century.

Individual Members and Collective Identities

The creation of permanent constituency organizations was essential to Labour's becoming an effective national political party. Nevertheless, it also gave expression to certain tensions existent within the labour and socialist movement. As Arthur Henderson was all too aware, Labour could not transform itself overnight from a party dependent on the trade unions to a free standing political organization based solely on individual membership. 'Conference', the party secretary presumed, 'would give short shrift to such a proposition'.[51] He was not wrong. 'Had any party', A. G. Walkden of the Railway Clerks asked in objection to the 'contemptuous manner' that the trade union rank-and-file was sometimes talked about during the debate of 1918, 'got a better foundation than the 2,500,000 subscribers of the [Labour] Party'?[52] For this reason, the constituency organizations were 'grafted' onto the wider party, leaving the trade unions dominant within the Labour's federated structure.

Such a decision was not just practical. Given Labour's origins and development, it also reflected certain deep-seated concerns and convictions within the wider labour movement, particularly the trade unions. Put bluntly, some Labour members retained a suspicion of what they regarded as middle-class socialists and feared dilution of Labour's working-class basis should the constituency organizations exert too great an influence within the party. This, of course, had long characterized trade union attitudes towards the ILP and 'intellectuals' not rooted in the working class or workplace. In George Milligan's words, speaking in 1918, he 'did not

---

[51]   Labour Party, *Report of the Annual Conference of the Labour Party*, January–February 1918 (London, 1918), p. 99.

[52]   Ibid., p. 103.

want middle-class or higher-class leaders to come and tell them what to do'.[53] His fellow dockworker James Sexton similarly warned of 'cranks' coming into the party, while W. J. Davis of the Brassfounders insisted that 'brains' did not need importing into the Labour Party 'because we have commonsense and intelligence of our own, and brains sufficient to work out our own salvation'.[54] Most trade unionists were less brusque; and most trade unions recognized the need for the party to reform its constitution in 1918. But the underlying substance of such apprehension was entrenched. Speaking sometime later, in 1935 with regard to Sir Stafford Cripps' Socialist League, Ernest Bevin commented that: 'I saw [Sir Oswald] Mosley come into the labour movement ... and I see no difference between the tactics of Mosley and Cripps', the implication being that those who came to Labour from beyond the working class or organized labour movement were less than reliable and therefore likely to split and divide the Labour ranks.[55] From such a perspective, Marquand's 'progressive dilemma' can be inverted to become the trade unionist's dilemma: how was a 'Labour' party – a workers' party built on the organized working-class and designed to give working people representation in the running of the everyday lives – to pursue its objectives without being pushed down utopian cul-de-sacs under the patronage of intellectuals, be they liberal or socialist. 'The difference between intellectuals and the trade unions', Bevin wrote in 1935, was that the intellectual had 'no responsibility of leadership. We, however, must be consistent and we have a great amount of responsibility. We cannot wake up in the morning and get a brain wave, when father says "turn" and half a million people turn automatically. That does not work.'[56] This, furthermore, explains the unions' qualified response to calls from the constituency parties for greater representation in the 1930s, especially as the main spokesman for such reform was Ben Greene, an Oxford-educated factory manager with a sympathy for German National Socialism.

Although class-prejudiced, such anxieties did have some legitimacy. As Kevin Morgan has demonstrated, Labour reorganization served to make the party reliant on 'more traditional sources of finance and cultural capital'.[57] To compete nationally, and in places where neither trade unionism nor the ILP had self-sufficient standing, Labour began increasingly to rely on rich benefactors to contest these constituencies, so reneging its former opposition to people 'buying' their candidatures. As a result, the number of middle-to-upper-class Labour candidates increased, meaning that evermore Holford Knights, Picton-Turbervills and Ponsonbys came to sit next to

---

[53]   Quoted in Tanner, *Political Change*, p. 399.

[54]   *Labour Party Annual Report*, 1918, p. 102; *Report of Proceedings of the Fiftieth Annual Trades Union Congress TUC*, September 1918 (London, 1918), p. 252.

[55]   Labour Party, *Report of the Annual Conference of the Labour Party*, 1935, p. 180.

[56]   Letter from E. Bevin to G. D. H. Cole, 31 December 1935, quoted in A. Bullock, *Ernest Bevin: A Biography* (London: Politico, 2002 edition), p. 188.

[57]   K. Morgan, *Labour Legends and Russian Gold* (London: Lawrence and Wishart, 2006), p. 131.

the Jones, Lawsons and Thornes in the House of Commons over the 1920s and 1930s. The party became 'professionalized' as well as centralized from 1918, thereby precipitating a shift away from what Morgan calls the apostles of socialism and experienced trade unionism towards the politicians of a modernized political machine. By the 1930s, the constituency party became the standard route into the Labour Party for the ambitious politician, particularly once the ILP disaffiliated in 1932. Simultaneously, the expansion of the PLP was due in large part to the growing presence of non-union candidates and MPs.[58]

As such, constituency parties helped facilitate a shift in Labour's composition that was necessary, but which brought with it certain social, cultural and political tensions. These, moreover, were given expression throughout the party. Within the PLP, a trade union 'group' of MPs was established in 1926, partly in response to the changing character of the parliamentary party. On the NEC, Susan Lawrence would complain of the 'drunkards and nitwits' that she sat with, while conference continued to bristle with reference to class background amidst discussions on executive representation, constituency party influence and Sir Stafford Cripps' 'rich pals' in the Socialist League.[59] At a local level, meanwhile, class tensions occasionally soured relations between party members and their (prospective) parliamentary representative. Hugh Dalton famously fell foul of his Peckham constituency in the 1920s, where his attempts to 'advise' his local comrades rubbed against the social grain.[60] In Birmingham, where Sir Oswald Mosley had for some time held an effective but contentious influence within the party, the borough president pointed to both Mosley's ambition and his class background as explanation for the aristocrat's leaving Labour in early 1931. 'The fact that his schemes were turned down not only by the cabinet but by the Parliamentary Labour Party which is composed of men from the mines and railways, men from the workshops and factories, created a position that was utterly unacceptable to a man used to having his own way in everything he touched.'[61]

Of course, it would be misleading to suggest that intra-party squabbles could be neatly divided along such class lines, or even between affiliated and individual members. Labour's federated structure ensured an array of overlapping traditions, memberships and political perspectives. Within the new constituency parties, problems could arise just as easily as a result of competing trade union priorities, while a divisional party too reliant on or informed by trade unionism could alienate as well as attract members and voters to Labour, even in industrial and working-class areas.[62] To take two examples, the Nottingham labour movement was hampered

---

[58] Ibid., pp. 131–42.

[59] Quoted in B. Pimlott, *Hugh Dalton* (London: Harper Collins, 1995), p. 221; Labour Party, *Report of the Annual Conference of the Labour Party*, 1937, pp. 156–64.

[60] Pimlott, *Hugh Dalton*, pp. 164–70.

[61] J. Johnson, 'Birmingham Labour and the New Party', *Labour Magazine* (April 1931), 534–6.

[62] Worley, *Labour Inside the Gate*, pp. 88–9.

in the 1920s by disagreements between the skilled Lace Workers' Society and the Workers' Union, leading to internal disputes over policy and strategy that impinged on Labour's standing in the city.[63] In Preston, as Mike Savage has shown, Labour's breakthrough in the 1920s was informed by its reaching beyond the predominant weavers' union towards neighbourhood organization and related social-political issues; its difficulties in the early 1930s stemmed, in part, from the reassertion of the textile unions' influence over the party agenda.[64]

Equally, the trade unions were not alone in having qualms about divisional parties built on individual membership: the ILP, too, was affected by the formation of permanent Labour constituency organization. Prior to 1918, the ILP had seen itself as providing the socialist soul of the Labour Party, dedicating itself to propagating socialism and transforming Labour into an overtly socialist party. The new divisional parties encroached on such territory, providing an alternative way into the party for non-unionized socialists, intellectuals, women and professionals (not to mention aspiring candidates), while clause four had ostensibly committed Labour to socialism via the common ownership of the means of production. Although the ILP briefly flourished in the immediate post-war period, as it took advantage of Labour's broader electoral challenge and reinvented itself as a socialist 'think tank' within the larger party, it eventually succumbed to tensions emanating from within the new party structure. Most importantly, differences over policy and with regard to the ILP's formal relationship to the Labour Party paved the way for a decline in membership and influence that, by 1932, led to a painful disaffiliation.[65]

More generally, the creation of divisional parties formed part of Labour's broader process of centralization, which in turn provoked frictions and changes of emphasis within the party. Thus, greater central direction and authority necessarily meant that certain limits were imposed on the scope, character and approach of the party's constituency organizations. Although the NEC intervened decisively in local affairs only on occasion – usually to ensure that communists were suppressed or to settle intra-party disputes – the divisional apparatus was made more uniform from 1918 and clear lines of procedure introduced. As noted above, and for all Labour's inherited tradition of 'making socialists' and aspiring to a Labour culture, the reorganization of 1918 came with a clear emphasis on electioneering. Consequently, educational initiatives (though benefiting the few) were often neglected throughout the party, while social-cultural activity tended to appear as an adjunct to Labour's priority of filling the ballot box. In the words of Syd Bidwell, a Labour recruit from

---

[63]   P. Wyncoll, *The Nottingham Labour Movement, 1880–1939* (London: Lawrence and Wishart, 1985), p. 183.

[64]   Savage, *The Dynamics of Working-Class Politics*, pp. 188–200.

[65]   D. Howell, *MacDonald's Party: Labour Identities and Crisis, 1922–31* (Oxford: Oxford University Press, 2002); G. Cohen, 'The Independent Labour Party, Disaffiliation, Revolution and Standing Orders', *History*, 86/282 (2001); Worley, *Labour Inside the Gate*, pp. 98–103 and 142–4.

1930s Southall, the Labour Party spent 'a lot of time on explaining how to run elections', but it 'never [took] political education seriously'.[66] Linked to this, there was a clear unwillingness to tolerate too overt a challenge to central authority from the party's smaller affiliates, as the ILP, Socialist League and, less decisively, the Labour League of Youth each discovered. Given this, the divisional organizations were expected to carry out Labour policy and promote Labour values, but not to set the party's agenda or question its approach. This became even more apparent once Labour progressed to government, as national solutions to the underlying ills of society replaced local initiative and nationalization eclipsed earlier Labour plans for 'municipal socialism'.

None of the above should be overstated: Labour retained a relatively loose framework and local parties retained a significant degree of flexibility in terms of their activities and the propagation of party policy. As suggested, the extension of Labour's apparatus and political appeal actually brought about diversification in the composition of the party. For Henderson, after all, such reorganization was designed to acknowledge the importance of the individual voter rather than the vested (union or class) interest.[67] Ultimately, however, the divisional parties were formed and expected to carry out a principal function: that is to ensure the election of a Labour government. In so doing, the social and ethical origins of the party gave way – notably but never totally – to political expediency. Simultaneously, the party's appeal to the 'individual voter' jarred with the collective ethos that underpinned both its socialist and trade union identity.

Conclusion

The constituency parties formed from 1918 became yet another important component of the foundations underpinning the Labour Party. They were never as dominant or powerful as the trade unions; nor would they forge as recognizable a tradition within the party as the ILP. Taken generally, the divisional (and local) parties encapsulated the diversities that could exist beneath the Labour banner whilst simultaneously providing the means by which Labour could develop a nationwide party machine capable of winning a general election. As such, they were a necessary part of Labour's growth from a pressure group – or party of protest and reform – to a national political organization based on a distinct political programme with its sights on governmental power. In so becoming, the constituency organizations overrode certain Labour traditions, simultaneously eclipsing the trades councils and the ILP within the wider party apparatus and compromising the distinctive character of early Labour politics. Arguably, however, their positive influence outweighed the negative.

---

[66] Weinbren, *Generating Socialism*, p. 12.
[67] Henderson, *The Aims of Labour*, p. 25.

So, what did the constituency parties bring to the Labour Party? First, they enabled Labour to compete with both the Liberals and the Conservatives on a national basis, providing the party with a nationwide apparatus to forge a sustainable electoral challenge. Second, and linked to this, the provided the mechanism by which Labour could function within a shifting social-economic and political context. Their permanency and open membership allowed Labour to reflect – in principle at least – all sections of the community, and offered a means by which the party could establish links with the people on whose vote its success depended. Their initiation ensured that Labour did not remain tied to specific geographical or industrial localities. Third, therefore, the constituency organizations widened access to, and thus the composition of, the Labour Party. This was crucial with regard to attracting women to the Labour cause, but was also important in terms of allowing entry to non-socialists and non-trade unionists. Fourth, the constituency organizations enabled Labour to carve out a social-political 'space' within local communities throughout the country. This was given expression via the various cultural initiatives undertaken by Labour members, as well as by the establishment of door-to-door dues collecting and leafleting, and the provision of services – especially once in control of a municipal authority – beneficial to the wider community. The extent to which this proved effective varied across Britain, just as levels of Labour support and the political temper of Labour members could vary from place to place.

Overall, Labour was presented in 1918 with an opportunity to transform British politics and, by extension, British society. To this end, the party was broadly successful in that it replaced the Liberals as the principal alternative to the Conservative Party and rose to government within six years of the war's end. The formation of constituency Labour parties was integral to this and Labour's continued growth to majority government in 1945, even if the political fruit referred to by Dalton could sometimes prove a little rich for many a Labour palette.

Chapter 12

'A Union of Forces Marching in the Same Direction'? The Relationship between the Co-operative and Labour Parties, 1918–39

Nicole Robertson

The concept of political neutrality was of central importance to the co-operative movement. A commitment to this principle was laid down in the original rules of the Rochdale Pioneers in 1844.[1] G. D. H. Cole has emphasized that 'political neutrality' originally meant abstention from 'faction fights' between the rival groups that were appealing for working-class support. As conditions changed, the term 'political neutrality' was used in a broader sense, and came to be understood as neutrality between the Liberal and Conservative parties and their competition for control of the government.[2] At the Co-operative congress of 1917, however, this principle was abandoned; a motion calling for *direct* representation of the co-operative movement in parliament 'as the only way of effectively voicing its demands and safeguarding its interests' was passed by a majority of 1,979 to 201.[3] The passing of this resolution marked the co-operative movement's formal entrance into the political scene. In 1918, ten candidates sponsored by the co-operative movement stood in a general election for the first time.

Writing in 1925, Alfred Barnes (Co-operative Party chairman) stated that the Co-operative Party and the Labour Party were 'organically related' and 'complementary to one another'.[4] Others supported a close relationship between the two parties as representing 'a union of forces marching in the same direction'.[5] Yet, relations between the two parties did not always run smoothly. This chapter will examine the relationship between the national executives of the Labour and

---

[1]   Original Rules of the Rochdale Pioneers (1844), cited in J. Bailey, *The British Co-operative Movement* (London: Hutchinson University Library, 1960 revised edition), pp. 19–20.

[2]   G. D. H. Cole, *A Century of Co-operation* (Manchester: Co-operative Union, 1944), pp. 78–9.

[3]   *Co-operative Congress Report*, 1917, p. 549 and p. 567.

[4]   A. Barnes, *Co-operative Aims in Politics* (Manchester: Co-operative Union, 1925), p. 5.

[5]   *Co-operative Congress Report*, 1927, p. 427.

Co-operative parties, while focusing simultaneously on relations between the individual parties at a local level.

Surprisingly, perhaps, such a subject has received relatively little academic attention. Ivor Bulmer-Thomas, in his account of the growth of the British party system, only briefly mentions that the two national parties drew up working arrangements regarding candidates and elections.[6] Older histories of the Labour Party tend not to discuss Co-operative–Labour relations in any detail.[7] Likewise, Thomas Carbery's history of the Co-operative Party does not explore the relationship between the two parties in any depth.[8] Work that does deal with the subject, most notably G. Rhodes' *Co-operative–Labour Relations* (1962),[9] tends to provide a chronological insight at a national level rather than exploring developments within the localities. In recent years, there have been some interesting unpublished local studies of the Co-operative Party in the north-west and south-west of England.[10] Despite the fact that the first MP to be sponsored by the co-operative movement was from Kettering (A. E. Waterson in 1918), and the Midlands returned a number of Co-operative MPs during the period 1918–39, little has yet been written about relations between individual Co-operative and Labour parties in this area of the country. The chapter therefore uses examples from four areas within the Midlands: Birmingham, Kettering, Leicester and Nottingham. These four areas provide variety in terms of the size of their population and local co-operative societies, and in the political orientation of their parliamentary representatives.[11] Although geographically located within the same region of the country, they illustrate the ways in which the relationship between the two parties could differ between, and within, individual areas. Whether a Co-operative–Labour candidate stood in a particular district was not in itself an indicator that their relationship was always harmonious.

In discussing relations between the two parties, four main issues will be addressed. The first is the nature of the relationships established between individual

---

[6]   I. Bulmer-Thomas, *The Growth of the British Party System: Volume One, 1640–1923* (London: John Baker, 1965), pp. 244–5; and *Vol. 2, 1924–65*, pp. 32–3.

[7]   G. D. H Cole, *A History of the Labour Party from 1914* (London: Routledge & Kegan Paul, 1951, revised edition); H. Pelling, *A Short History of the Labour Party* (London: Macmillan, 1965).

[8]   T. F. Carbery, *Consumers in Politics* (Manchester: Manchester University Press, 1969).

[9]   G. W. Rhodes, *Co-operative–Labour Relations* (Loughborough: Co-operative Union, 1962).

[10]   J. Southern, 'The Co-operative Movement in the North West of England 1919–39: Images and Realities' (University of Lancaster PhD, 1996); M. Hilson, 'Working-Class Politics in Plymouth 1890–1920' (University of Exeter PhD, 1998).

[11]   N. Robertson, '"A Good Deal … and a Good Deal More": The Impact of the Co-operative Movement on Communities in the Midlands, 1914–60' (University of Nottingham PhD, 2006).

Co-operative and Labour parties. The second is the subsequent problems with, and breakdowns in, these agreements. It is important not to see these parties as simply electoral machines, but also to consider the social activities they organized. Third, therefore, such activity is explored along with the extent to which they made politics accessible. The political programme forms the fourth issue for examination. Did the Labour and Co-operative parties share a similar political outlook? To what extent did they diverge, and what consequences did this have?

The 'Unification of the Forces of Democracy'?

In May 1917, the Co-operative congress resolved that the time had arrived when co-operators should secure direct representation in parliament.[12] The 'Scheme for Co-operative Parliamentary Representation', adopted at the National Emergency Congress of 1917, stated that affiliation with any political party was beyond their present scope, but the necessity and desirability of friendly relations with such of the party organizations as would best promote the co-operative movement's interests was fully recognized.[13] Arthur Henderson reiterated this desire for a close working relationship and, in 1917, even suggested that 'he would be prepared that the Labour Party as now known should cease, if by doing so they could combine the whole of the democracy into a great people's party'.[14]

The co-operative movement, however, had a history of distancing itself from labour politics. In 1900, it was invited, alongside representatives of the trade unions, Fabians, Independent Labour Party (ILP) and Social Democratic Federation (SDF), to take part in the drafting of a scheme for labour representation in parliament. Yet, the movement declined to be represented.[15] Throughout the period which saw the birth of the Labour Party, the co-operative movement remained opposed to direct political action. There were those who believed that, as a business organization, the movement ought to remain non-political, and others who expressed concerns about the financial implications of political action. But there were also fears that affiliation with Labour would alienate co-operative members who were Liberal and Conservative in political support.[16] Although Sidney Pollard states that, during the period before the Great War (1914–18), the 'natural groundswell which drove the co-operative movement into the arms of the Labour Party seemed to be irresistible',[17] Tony Adams argues that there was no clear line of evolution towards

---

12   *Co-operative Congress Report*, 1917, p. 549.

13   Ibid., pp. 549–50; Cole, *A Century of Co-operation*, p. 316.

14   C. Wrigley, *Arthur Henderson* (Cardiff: GPC Books, 1990), p. 142.

15   A. Bonner, *British Co-operation* (Manchester: Co-operative Union, 1970 revised edition), p. 95.

16   Rhodes, *Co-operative–Labour Relations*, p. 9.

17   S. Pollard, 'The Foundation of the Co-operative Party', in A. Briggs and J. Saville (eds), *Essays*

Labour, emphasizing instead the 'long and hard road of persuasion, debate and political struggle'.[18]

During the interwar period, the form that relations between the two parties should take continued to be the cause of much controversy within the co-operative movement, with the movement's political wing retaining a certain degree of independence from the Labour Party.[19] In her work on the north-west of England, Jayne Southern emphasizes how the relationship between the co-operative movement and the Labour Party formed a source of contention at a regional level. The proposed Labour–Co-operative Party alliance caused a major rift between northern co-operators and the Co-operative Union, as the Northern Section opposed closer links with Labour, fearing 'disunity and the eclipse of the distinctive co-operative principles'.[20] Similarly, the relationship between the Co-operative and Labour parties was the subject of debate among the individual political organizations examined in this chapter. The support for an alliance between the two parties could vary considerably between different cities and towns within the same region. This can be seen when examining the different attitudes that existed in Nottingham compared with those in Kettering and Birmingham.

Although the Nottingham Co-operative Society decided to affiliate to the local Labour Party, there were reservations among co-operators concerning the potential consequences of this alliance, especially the financial implications. Co-operators feared that the affiliation fee paid to the Nottingham Central Labour Party would be 'increased until the members became so dissatisfied that they declined to trade or leave their savings with the society'.[21] Concerns also centred upon the danger this alliance might pose to the unity and strength of the society in the future, since its position had been built up by 'good members of all shades of religion and social thought'.[22]

A comparison with Kettering emphasizes how much the support for Co-operative–Labour relations could vary. The Kettering Co-operative Society thought that the scheme outlined for the political representation of co-operators

---

in *Labour History, 1886–1923* (London: Macmillan, 1971), p. 194.

[18] T. Adams, 'The Formation of the Co-operative Party Re-Considered', *International Review of Social History*, 32/1 (1987), 52.

[19] For example, the Co-operative Party remained responsible to the decisions of the Co-operative Congress. In the words of the National Co-operative Authority, whilst they were 'willing and desirous of having means for consultation with the Labour Party on all matters affecting Co-operative trade', they deemed it unnecessary for the movement to affiliate to the National Council of Labour 'as many of the matters considered by that Council are outside the interest of the Co-operative Movement'. See meeting on 5 September 1935 of the National Co-operative Authority, cited in Rhodes, *Co-operative–Labour Relations*, p. 43.

[20] Southern, 'The Co-operative Movement', pp. 89–90.

[21] *The Wheatsheaf* (Nottingham edition), February 1921, p. ii.

[22] Ibid. This bears similarities to the TUC and politics in the 1890s, when great hostility to the notion of 'independent labour politics' was present among the older generation.

'did not go far enough', so it authorized the district committee to meet delegates of trade unions and Labour associations to 'draft negotiations with a view to joint activity, believing such action [would] result in the common benefit of the worker'.[23] Relations were formalized by the establishment of the Mid-Northants Co-operative and Labour Council. The *Kettering Co-operative Magazine* noted the good working relationship that existed between the various bodies of the labour movement in the town, emphasizing the 'cordial and loyal assistance rendered by the allied organisations'.[24]

Similarly, in Birmingham, a general desire for close relations between the Co-operative and Labour parties existed. In 1920, the Birmingham Co-operative Party offered to 'render all the help possible' when asked by the Rotton Park Ward Labour Party to assist with the municipal elections.[25] As the Birmingham Co-operative Party developed and devised new political schemes and propaganda, it emphasized that the 'trade union branches, ILP and the Labour Party were heartily joining in'.[26]

It was not until 1927, with the Cheltenham Agreement, that the parties at national level formalized their relationship. Under this agreement, the co-operative movement retained its own political machinery. It did not affiliate to Labour; nor did its constituent co-operative societies, except for a very few (notably the Royal Arsenal Co-operative Society), affiliate to the national Labour Party.[27] When the significance of the 1927 agreement is considered, it becomes apparent that this was the cause of much greater concern within the co-operative movement than within the Labour Party. Thomas Carbery emphasizes that 'to the Labour Party it was a mere tidying up process'.[28] This seems to be supported by the report of the 1927 Labour conference, where the issue was quickly dealt with. Arthur Henderson succinctly described how:

> there was a desire expressed on the part of the Co-operative Party that the existing practice should be put into the form of an Agreement. They were merely asking conference to accept that Agreement which, they held, was simply regulating what had been the practice where Co-operative and Labour candidates had been endorsed during the past year.[29]

---

[23]   *Co-operative Congress Report*, 1918, 'Midland Section', p. 393.

[24]   Ibid., May 1920, p. 70.

[25]   Birmingham and District Co-operative Representation Council Minutes, 21 July 1920.

[26]   Birmingham and District Co-operative Party, 'Annual Report', 1919.

[27]   R. Rhodes, *An Arsenal for Labour: The Royal Arsenal Co-operative Society and Politics, 1886–1996* (Manchester: Holyoake Books, 1998), pp. 90–1.

[28]   Carbery, *Consumers in Politics*, p. 32.

[29]   Labour Party, *Report of the Labour Party Conference,* 1927 (London, 1927), p. 173.

There was very little discussion beyond this.

In contrast, the issue caused far more controversy within the ranks of the co-operative movement, and highlighted that 'the Movement still had serious political divisions as far as working with the Labour Party was concerned'.[30] Some co-operators viewed this arrangement as 'an endorsement of the better aspects of the existing practice and an agreement between equals'.[31] For others, however, it represented 'a step on the way to absorption' by the Labour Party.[32] After much discussion and debate, the agreement was eventually passed with a narrow majority (just 3 per cent of the vote).[33]

The Cheltenham Agreement made provisions for a joint sub-committee to be established and ruled that local Co-operative parties were to be eligible for affiliation to the divisional Labour parties, but stated explicitly that this was not intended to interfere with existing arrangements where such had already been established.[34] The annual report of the Labour Party also stressed the point that this agreement was not arbitrary and was intended to operate only where it was mutually acceptable. Thus, '[the] object of the Agreement is simply to facilitate joint working where the two Parties are willing to enter into local agreement and to provide means of national consultation and mutual support where such are deemed desirable'.[35]

That being so, relations between the two parties continued to vary considerably within individual localities. The establishment of a Kettering Co-operative and Labour Council in 1919, for example, can be contrasted with the situation in Leicester. Here, relations between the Leicester Labour Party and the Leicester Co-operative Political Council developed at a much slower pace. The Leicester Co-operative Political Council was established in 1917 and, thereafter, the Leicester Labour Party made several attempts to persuade it to affiliate.[36] However, as the Cheltenham Agreement ruled that, at a local level, Co-operative parties or councils were *eligible* for affiliation to divisional Labour parties but that this was to be *optional*, the Leicester Co-operative Political Council was able to dismiss the Labour Party's proposals and continued to do so until after the Second World War.[37]

---

[30]   Rhodes, *Co-operative–Labour Relations*, p. 31.

[31]   Carbery, *Consumers in Politics*, p. 33.

[32]   *Co-operative Congress Report*, 1927, p. 426.

[33]   Ibid., p. 433.

[34]   *Co-operative Congress Report*, 1927, pp. 95–6.

[35]   Labour Party, *Report of the Labour Party Conference,* 1927, p. 8.

[36]   The Leicester Co-operative Political Council was approached by the Leicester Labour Party in 1917, 1918, 1919 and 1935. See Leicester Co-operative Society (LCS) Board Minutes.

[37]   In 1946, however, it was the Leicester Labour Party that was not prepared to accept co-operative affiliation, as it feared 'communist tendencies were prevalent in the co-operative political party'. A bitter dispute ensued, with the Leicester Labour Party accusing one of the members of the Council, Mr R. V. Walton, of being 'embroiled in communism',

Conflict Rather Than Co-operation

Of course, even when the constituency Co-operative and Labour parties reached agreement, this did not necessarily mean that their relationship was always amicable. Co-operative parties were keen to ensure that they influenced the constituency Labour parties in the selection of candidates for both municipal and general elections, and this was the root cause of much disagreement. In Nottingham, for example, an agreement was reached whereby all candidates put forward by the Nottingham Co-operative Society for public positions under the auspices of the Labour Party were duly nominated and selected by a properly convened meeting of members of the Co-operative Society. Along with any other candidate running under Labour Party auspices, and after receiving the endorsement of the director of the society, such candidates had the right to use the title, stores or other property of the society subject to being fully paid-up shareholders of a co-operative body in the city.[38] Co-operators firmly defended such a position, and this was evident when the St Ann's Ward Labour Association appealed to the Nottingham Co-operative Society for financial assistance for the board of guardians' election. It was declined, and its policy that 'we only support candidates directly nominated by us' was reiterated.[39]

The influence that constituency Co-operative parties exercised over Labour parties must not be exaggerated, however. As events in Birmingham between 1923 and 1925 highlight, there were instances where Co-operative electoral progress in local elections were hampered by their relationship with Labour. In 1921, the Birmingham and District Co-operative Party had reached an agreement with the Birmingham Borough Labour Party to establish a joint advisory committee that would 'correlate and co-ordinate the forces and activities of the Labour and Co-operative movements in respect to representation in parliament and on all local administrative bodies'.[40] Through this body they conferred in the selection of candidates and the organization of both parties was utilized during the electoral campaign. In 1923, however, the Birmingham Central Labour Party repudiated the existing agreement in favour of expanding its own organization. Endeavours to obtain a settlement before the general election failed, thereby hampering the Co-operative Party campaign of 1923. As the dispute continued, the preparation for the municipal election in 1924 was affected and the results were disappointing. In the Deritend division, the approval of the Co-operative candidate – Fred

---

and stating that the Labour Party was 'not prepared to allow any communists to get in by the back door'. See LCS Board Minutes, 20 June 1946. Affiliation of the Leicester Co-operative Political Council to the Leicester Labour Party finally took place in 1948.

[38] *The Wheatsheaf* (Nottingham edition), August 1919, p. i.

[39] Nottingham Co-operative Society (NCS) Directors' Quarterly Meetings Minute Book, 23 April 1928.

[40] Birmingham and District Co-operative Party Agreement with the Labour Party, 1921.

Longden – 'was only forthcoming from the Labour Party at the last moment, and we [the Co-operative Party] ... have every cause to think that if some permanent arrangement can be carried out in regard to this constituency, success will be ours'.[41] An arrangement was eventually reached in March 1925.

During the 1930s, the reports of the Co-operative Party given at the Co-operative congress create a mixed impression of the relationship between itself and the Labour Party. Some co-operators expressed that '[our] Party, the Labour Party and the Trade Union Movement should come together to form one solid block against Reaction'.[42] Yet others proclaimed that '[the] Co-operative Party has got to say: "We are the Party standing on our own legs". We ought not to keep hanging on the coat tails of the Labour Party'.[43] Differences of opinion at congress were reflected within the localities. Although it was reported that an increasing number of agreements reached between Co-operative and Labour parties were being sent forward for registration by the National Joint Committee,[44] disagreements continued throughout the interwar period.

In Leicester, relations between the two parties remained strained. Here, as noted above, the Co-operative Party declined Labour approaches to affiliate. There were also occasions where the constituency Labour Party refused to support Co-operative candidates in local elections. In 1937, for example, the Leicester Co-operative Political Council wrote to the Leicester Labour Party asking for its support for a Co-operative candidate against a Conservative in the Evington ward of the city. The Labour Party declined.[45] Even in areas where the two parties had set up joint committees, problems continued to arise throughout the 1930s. In Nottingham, the Co-operative and Labour Party (central division) Joint Committee met less frequently, and there were periods where the committee ceased meeting altogether.[46]

G. W. Rhodes concludes that, during the 1930s, friction between the two parties was caused by the Labour Party's assumption that the Cheltenham Agreement was only a temporary measure (pending affiliation) and by its desire for the Co-operative Party to surrender its finances and autonomy to Labour's policy and organization. The Co-operative Party, however, insisted that it retained a large degree of control over candidates in receipt of any grant from the national funds of the co-operative movement.[47]

---

[41] Birmingham and District Co-operative Party, 'Annual Report', 1924.

[42] *Co-operative Congress Report*, 1936, p. 495.

[43] Ibid., p. 497.

[44] *Co-operative Congress Report*, 1933, p. 111.

[45] LCS Board Minutes, 22 September and 29 September 1937.

[46] In Nottingham, it was announced that 'the general feeling of the Political Council was that the Co-operative Party should discontinue the joint arrangement'. See Nottingham Co-operative and Labour Party Central Division Minutes, 22 June 1937. No further explanation was provided for this decision.

[47] Rhodes, *Co-operative–Labour Relations*, p. 39.

Problems concerning issues of finance and control were the subject of much local and national disagreement. Most notably, these issues were clearly visible in Birmingham. By 1932, the Birmingham Co-operative Party felt that it had been forced to develop tighter procedures over its candidates. It devised a scheme whereby the names of the prospective candidates had to be put forward to the Co-operative Party executive for approval before they could be placed on Labour Party nomination lists. The Co-op's funding for a candidate's electoral expenses (the 'political grant') would be withheld if a candidate was nominated without seeking this approval. This was done not only to maintain closer control over the party's political agenda, but also to guard its financial position. It was a measure both to prevent the Labour Party forcing it to foot the bill for 'no hope' elections and to prohibit it from nominating a candidate who would then join the Co-operative Party and attempt to claim the political grant.[48] Despite these careful measures, the Birmingham Co-operative Party was frequently required to help the Birmingham Borough Labour Party out of severe financial difficulties during the course of the 1930s.

Rhodes argues that during this period the National Co-operative Authority believed that the Labour Party was trying to 'hamper and confine' the political activities of the co-operative movement.[49] Yet, in Kettering, the Labour Party felt that the co-operative movement was confining *its* activities. In 1936, the local newspaper reported how 'the Kettering Labour Party, which ceased activity soon after the formation of the Mid-Northants Co-operative and Labour Council, was reformed'. It stated that this course of action was deemed necessary because of concerns that 'individual Labour membership had dropped away or had become absorbed into the co-operative movement'.[50] Thus, there was a 'desire for the expression of political opinion through a distinctly Labour channel'.[51] It was quick to emphasize that this would not be in opposition to existing organizations, such as the trades council or the co-operative movement. By November of the same year, however, the two parties seemed to be 'proceeding with the same cordial relationship that [had] hitherto operated in the division'.[52]

---

[48] Minutes of the Council and Executive Committee of the Birmingham and District Co-operative Party, 1931; C. Shelly, 'Birmingham Co-operative Party in the 1930s: Co-operative and Labour Movement Politics' (University of Warwick, MA Dissertation, 1987), pp. 36–7.

[49] Rhodes, *Co-operative–Labour Relations*, p. 53.

[50] *Kettering Leader and Guardian*, 21 February 1936, p. 1.

[51] Ibid.

[52] Ibid., 28 October 1938, p. 6. There were further tensions in the 1940s.

The Politics of Entertainment

Of course, the relationship between the two parties was not limited to selecting and financing candidates. Their joint activities went beyond the immediate political sphere. After the Great War, leaders of the Labour Party encouraged constituency parties to mix politics with the social life of working people.[53] From early on, the importance of providing recreational facilities and social functions was recognized by individual Labour and Co-operative parties as a means of bringing together their members and supporters.

Activities in Nottingham and Kettering provide interesting examples of how Co-operative and Labour politics could be successfully combined with a programme of entertainment. This, certainly, seems to have been a sphere in which Co-operative and Labour parties worked well together. In Nottingham, the two parties saw entertainment as an important element of their election campaign. The speeches of the prospective Labour–Co-operative candidate for the Nottingham central division (Mrs Barton) and the Labour candidate for West Nottingham (Arthur Hayday), for example, were interspersed with the community singing of labour songs. Likewise, in 1931, the promotion of the candidature of A. E. Waterson included a combined reception, whist drive and dance to which 500 people were invited.[54] Furthermore, the Co-operative and Labour Party Joint Committee held whist drives on a weekly basis.

These events could be interpreted as a means of developing relations between the two parties by giving their supporters the opportunity to socialize together, and as an informal means of highlighting the unity between the parties. They also served as fundraising occasions. These whist drives seem to have become popular events in their own right. Even when it was resolved that the Co-operative and Labour Party Joint Committee be suspended, it was determined also that the whist drives continue.[55]

The social activities of the Co-operative and Labour parties in Kettering provide one of the most striking examples of how social activities were used in an attempt to make politics more accessible. By 1924, the Co-operative Political Council realized that 'allotments and outdoor games are the strongest attraction to the majority of citizens, to such an extent that it is quite impossible for outdoor meetings to surpass them in rivalry'.[56] Therefore, the Mid-Northants Co-operative

---

[53]   C. Howard, '"Expectations Born to Death": Local Labour Party Expansion in the 1920s', in J. Winter (ed.), *The Working Class in Modern British History: Essays in Honour of Henry Pelling* (Cambridge: Cambridge University Press, 1983), pp. 76–7.

[54]   P. Wyncoll, *The Nottingham Labour Movement, 1880–1939* (London: Lawrence and Wishart, 1985), p. 229; Nottingham Co-operative and Labour Party Central Division Minutes, 9 December 1930.

[55]   Nottingham Co-operative and Labour Party Central Division Minutes, 12 May 1936.

[56]   *The Kettering Co-operative Magazine*, August 1924, p. 98.

and Labour Council embarked upon several new ventures. In 1925, it held its first flower, fruit and vegetable show, which became an annual event. In 1926, the Co-operative and Labour Institute (in which the headquarters of the Co-operative and Labour Council was based) opened in the town centre. The institute provided a place where 'workers and supporters could meet and mould their forces into a great united body' within a social environment.[57]

In addition to rallying members in Kettering itself, social activities provided an important means of mobilizing political support in the surrounding villages, and this seems to go some way in accounting for the Co-operative–Labour candidates' electoral success in this constituency. The Mid-Northants constituency was widely scattered, being composed of four urban districts and 86 villages. Thus, the Co-operative and Labour Council devised a system in the villages involving 'sub-agents' and 'key-men' who helped 'keep in touch with residents by means of concerts and socials'.[58] In this way, social events could play an important part in rallying political support in rural areas that were geographically removed from the urban centres in which the headquarters of the parties were based.

Ideals and Political Programme

Those who supported an alliance between the Co-operative and Labour parties were keen to emphasize that this was a logical step as, in terms of political outlook, they shared common ground. They emphasized that Tory and Liberal parties represented the 'profit-making interests in land, capital, and finance', and that there would be a continual 'fight between the wage-earner interests and the profit-making interests as represented by the Tory Party and the Liberal Party'.[59] As Mrs Palmer (representative of the Southampton Co-operative Society at the Co-operative congress) stated:

> I ask you, is it not a fair proposition that we have more in common with the interests of the Labour Party in the House of Commons than we have with the landed interests or the profit-making interests in finance and commerce? I say unquestionably it is so.[60]

In terms of personnel, the two parties often shared common ground. As Ross McKibbin has highlighted, politically active co-operators were also usually active members of the Labour Party. He cites the example of the King's Norton Co-operative Political Council (in Birmingham). The secretary of this body was one of the founder members of the divisional Labour Party, and Labour supporters

---

[57]   *Kettering Leader and Guardian*, 30 July 1926, p. 13.

[58]   *Co-operative News*, 20 April 1929, p. 2.

[59]   *Co-operative Congress Report*, 1927, p. 428.

[60]   Ibid., p. 428.

dominated the political council.[61] There are numerous other examples of Co-operative activists who were also active in constituency Labour parties and vice versa. In Birmingham, E. Reynolds (candidate for the Acocks Green ward at the municipal election of 1930) and G. A. Charles (candidate for the Yardley ward at the municipal election of 1933) were both prominent co-operators and members of the Labour Party. It appears that Waterson's previous experience and affiliations to labour organizations helped to make a successful working relationship between the different facets of the labour movement possible. Waterson stood as a Co-operative candidate in 1918 for Kettering, and as a Co-operative–Labour candidate for Central Nottingham in 1931. He was the former secretary of the Midland District Council of the National Union of Railwaymen, and had been chairman of the Derby Labour Party. The *Co-operative News* reported how 'nearly every trade union with a branch in the district, and nearly every co-operative society and democratic organisation, [was] represented in the signatures to the nomination papers handed in on behalf of Waterson'.[62]

Those who supported an alliance between the Co-operative and Labour parties were keen to emphasize that, in terms of political objectives, the two were 'fundamentally in agreement' and were, therefore, in a position to 'build their political programmes from a common foundation'.[63] It was argued that, although Liberalism and Conservatism differed on many political issues, they were agreed that 'land, capital, machines, plants, railways, and finance [should] be privately owned'.[64] By contrast, Co-operation promoted:

> [The] common ownership of things essential to life; and when it is a question of these things being used for the aggrandisement of the few at the expense of the many, Co-operation must come down on the side of common ownership. The Labour Party is the only party in Parliament that stands for that.[65]

The political doctrines of the Co-operative and Labour parties certainly had more in common with one another than they did with either the Conservative or Liberal parties. But although their ideals were broadly similar, they were not identical. Where the Labour Party advocated nationalization, municipal or other public ownership, co-operators advocated a co-operative system under consumers' control.[66] These

---

[61]   R. McKibbin, *The Evolution of the Labour Party, 1910–24* (London: Oxford University Press, 1974), p. 189.

[62]   *Co-operative News*, 7 December 1918, p. 786.

[63]   A. Barnes, 'The Co-operator in Politics', in L. Woolf (ed.), *Fabian Essays on Co-operation* (London: Fabian Society, 1923), p. 20.

[64]   *Co-operative Congress Report*, 1927, p. 423.

[65]   Ibid., p. 423.

[66]   G. D. H. Cole, *The British Co-operative Movement in a Socialist Society* (London: George Allen & Unwin, 1951), p. 100.

differences were highlighted by those who opposed the Cheltenham Agreement. As Mr B. H. Fletcher (of the Macclesfield Co-operative Society) argued:

> Co-operators believe in voluntary association. The Labour Party advocates collectivism. Co-operators believe in voluntary effort, that is, the organisation of production and distribution by voluntary association. The Labour Party desire State ownership and State control, and they are not agreed as to either municipal milk or coal supplies and other matters.[67]

Labour and the Nation (1928) declared the co-operative movement to be 'an indispensable element in the Socialist Commonwealth' and pledged to work in the fullest alliance with it.[68] However, there is evidence to suggest that the Labour Party did not always take co-operative ideology and ambition seriously. The co-operative movement, for example, objected to Labour's policy on the subject of agricultural marketing boards, which it viewed as 'inconsistent with the consumers' claims to final control'.[69] Peter Gurney's research highlights how these differences became more apparent during the period of Labour government after the Second World War. He argues that a lack of sympathy with, and consideration of, the co-operative cause was symbolized by the Labour government's nationalization of the co-operative colliery along with all the other privately owned collieries.[70] The Labour Party's plans for the permanent nationalization of the wholesale trade in meat, as formulated in its 1949 manifesto *Labour Believes in Britain*, also failed to take account of the co-operative system of consumers' control.[71]

Promoting the interests of workers as producers rather than consumers was another area in which the two parties had a different focus. Co-operators, who advocated an independent Co-operative Party and opposed affiliation to the Labour Party, stated that the industrial interests of the trade unions dominated Labour. Whereas the Labour Party was representative of the working class in the sphere of production, the Co-operative Party represented the working class chiefly as consumers, and 'the interests of the producers and consumers are not always one and the same'.[72] There was concern that if the Co-operative Party embarked on a close working relationship with Labour, Co-ops would become mere pawns 'in the game of producers' aims and objects, to the subjection of

---

[67] *Co-operative Congress Report*, 1927, p. 426.

[68] The Labour Party, *Labour and the Nation* (London: Labour Party, 1928), p. 24.

[69] Cole, *A History of the Labour Party*, p. 337.

[70] F. W. Leeman, *Co-operation in Nottingham* (Nottingham: Nottingham Co-operative Society Ltd, *c.*1963), p. 162, cited in P. Gurney, *Co-operative Culture and the Politics of Consumption in England, 1870–1930* (Manchester: Manchester University Press, 1996), p. 317.

[71] Cole, *A History of the Labour Party*, pp. 100–1.

[72] A. Temple, *Co-operative and Labour Party Politics* (London: published by the author, 1938), p. 5.

anything for which Co-operative Societies, as representing the consumers, aim at'.[73] Some co-operators feared that, as a result of their relations with Labour, the Co-operative Party would compromise its own sense of political identity and its distinct message would be lost.[74]

T. W. Mercer expressed concern that the Co-operative Party lacked a philosophical basis and had no distinct programme, adding that 'many co-operators unconsciously confuse the aims of the co-operative movement in politics with those of the political Labour Party'.[75] When discussing the Co-operative Party, historians have also criticized the 'dreadful lack of clarity as to the political philosophy of the Party'.[76] Certainly, its programme – incorporating demands for a more equal education system, adequate housing provision for the people and improved maternity care – was very similar to the manifesto issued by the Labour Party. Leaders of the Co-operative Party, however, emphasized that the party represented a distinct economic interest in parliament that had previously been neglected: that of the consumer. Alfred Barnes argued that the Co-operative Party was the only party to represent the consumer in politics and was the 'first consumers' party to makes its appearance on the floor of the House of Commons'.[77]

At a local level, a commitment to the consumer formed a key aspect of the political programme of candidates approved by the Co-operative Party. In the Sparkbrook division of Birmingham, F. Spires' election address in the 1918 general election stated that, if he were elected, his efforts would be directed towards ensuring the consumer was charged lower prices for food, milk, coal and clothing.[78] Similarly, in 1931, standing in the municipal election for Central Nottingham, A. E. Waterson's campaign slogan and promise was to 'hold up the flag of the consumers'. The *Co-operative News* reported how 'Mr. Waterson stands four-square for the straight principles of free trade and fair play for the consumer'. His electoral address emphasized co-operative values and drew attention to the difference between the 'co-operative way' of providing the consumer with value for the money they spent, and the capitalist system where 'there are too many middlemen living on the backs of the people. The greater differences between the

---

[73]   Ibid., p.13.

[74]   *Co-operative Congress Report*, 1927, p. 426.

[75]   T. W. Mercer, 'Co-operative Politics and Co-operative Progress', in Co-operative Wholesale Society, *People's Year Book* (Manchester, 1921), p. 85. Mercer was a prominent figure in the co-operative movement. He had contested the Moss Side division in a parliamentary election as a Co-operative candidate. He was a former education secretary to the Plymouth Society and was the first editor of the *Co-operative Review*.

[76]   Carbery, *Consumers in Politics*, p. 35.

[77]   A. Barnes, *Consumer Politics in Peace and War: The Case for Political Action by Co-operators* (Manchester: Co-operative Union, c.1940s), p. 3.

[78]   *Co-operative News*, 7 December 1918, p. 786.

prices of commodities at the source of production and the price the consumer pays demands not merely serious examination, but legislation'.[79]

It can be argued that the effectiveness of the co-operative movement in representing and defending the interests of consumers in parliament was, at times, hindered by its relationship with the Labour Party. For example, A. V. Alexander (a prominent Co-op MP) campaigned to establish a Consumers' Council. It was intended that such a council would inquire into the operations of trading associations alleged to be operating against the interests of the public. In doing so, it was hoped that such a council would form a valuable 'weapon in the hands of consumers'.[80] But although the 1930 Consumers' Bill passed its initial reading in the Commons, in 1931 – when Labour suffered one of the most catastrophic defeats in its history – the bill disappeared.[81]

Despite this, it is important to recognize that the Co-operative Party benefited from its association with the Labour Party. The co-operative movement needed a 'voice' in parliament because neither the Liberals (who supported the private traders, often to the detriment of co-operative organizations) nor the Tories (who were allied with the shopkeepers) took notice of co-operative grievances and concerns. Thus, although the Co-operative Party's association with Labour made the Liberals and Tories more hostile to it, the relationship with the Labour Party ensured that issues raised by the co-operators were given a stronger voice. For example, during the 1924 Labour government, co-operators were consulted on consumer issues and obtained direct representation on all important committees (such as the Royal Commission on Food Prices) to the extent that Alexander declared 'Co-operation has been recognised as it never was before'.[82] Furthermore, it was extremely unlikely that the Co-operative Party would have got anywhere running candidates against Labour. Co-operators were reminded that independent representation on local councils and in general elections would involve '[taking] on all comers, including the Labour candidates … That would be political folly'.[83]

---

[79]   Ibid., 24 May 1930, front page.

[80]   F. Hayward, *The Co-operative Boycott and its Political Implications* (Manchester: Co-operative Union, 1930), p. 13.

[81]   Carbery, *Consumers in Politics*, p. 189.

[82]   Alexander, *The Business Value of Political Action to the Co-operative Movement* (Manchester: Co-operative Union, 1928), p. 8.

[83]   J. Bailey, *Facing the Future – Together* (Manchester: Co-operative Union, *c.*1946), pp. 3–4.

Conclusion

Henry Pelling's assertion that 'the 'Co-operative Party became closely integrated with the Labour Party'[84] masks the complex nature of the relationship between the two parties. Indeed, there were those within the Co-operative Party who promoted a close relationship between the two parties and saw this as representing the 'unification of the forces of democracy'.[85] Likewise, there were those within the Labour Party who recalled how 'Co-operative and Labour Party members work together as a team, and are, in effect, indistinguishable'.[86] However, there was also opposition to such an alliance. This was mainly from co-operators who felt that 'Labour Party people' viewed the Co-operative Party 'as a mere appendage of the Labour Party', and as a source of money.[87]

Although the national executives of the Co-operative and Labour parties accepted the Cheltenham Agreement, relations did not always run smoothly. Moreover, this agreement specifically stated that it was not intended to interfere with relationships that had already been established within the constituencies. Thus, the relationships that developed between the Co-operative and Labour parties at the constituency level played a central role in shaping the labour movement within the localities. As can be seen with the examples of Birmingham, Kettering, Leicester and Nottingham, even within cities and towns in the same area of the country, the nature of the relationship between the two parties varied, in some respects considerably. Most notably, in Leicester, unlike the other three areas, the Co-operative Political Council did not affiliate to the local Labour Party until after the Second World War. Disagreements between the parties often centred on the method of selecting candidates and the financial assistance that each party should provide. Indeed, one of the incentives behind the 'new' agreement of 1946 between the national executives of both parties was the 'growing and continual conflict between the Co-operative ... and Labour Parties in the constituencies'.[88]

In areas where the two parties were able to form a close working relationship, they could develop a wide variety of activities in an attempt to extend their influence. These parties used traditional methods of political propaganda and 'educational schemes' to increase support, but were also aware that there were considerable benefits to be gained by engaging in wider social-political activities. The social activities and recreational facilities provided by the Co-operative and Labour parties were an essential method of mobilizing support and potential voters. They were also an informal means of highlighting the unity between the two parties.

---

[84] Pelling, *A Short History of the Labour Party*, p. 47.

[85] Barnes, 'The Co-operator in Politics', p. 26.

[86] C. R. Attlee, *The Labour Party in Perspective – and Twelve Years Later* (London: Victor Gollancz Ltd, 1949), p. 67.

[87] Temple, *Co-operative and Labour Party Politics*, p. 1.

[88] Cited in Carbery, *Consumers in Politics*, p. 111.

The personal experience of individual activists could enhance relations between the two parties. Individuals could be involved in the various facets of the local labour movement, becoming important figures in the constituency Labour and Co-operative parties and trade unions. Such experience could help bind together the different factions of the labour movement and contribute to a successful working relationship. This was certainly true of A. E. Waterson. Such 'sharing' of personnel, however, was deemed by some to be a disadvantage. In private correspondence between Eleanor Barton (Co-operative–Labour candidate for Nottingham and one of the founder members of the Sheffield Co-operative Party) and Alderman A. Ballard (secretary of the Sheffield Co-operative Party), Ballard stated that he found himself 'very busy these days trying to keep an active Co-operative membership'. He added that the development of the Labour Party in the Hillsborough division made this especially challenging, as 'our people so often tend to forsake the Co-op in favour of the Labour Party, at least the more active and useful members of our organisation'.[89]

McKibbin has argued that it is unlikely that Labour gained many votes from its alliance with the Co-operative Party that it would not have got anyway. However, good working relations between the two organizations made available 'ancillary benefits'; for example, finance for the Labour Party and for trade union activities.[90] It is also important to recognize that the Co-operative Party benefited from its association with Labour. As Cole argued, there was no possible room for a second entirely independent working-class party operating side by side with the Labour Party.[91] The co-operative movement needed a 'voice' in parliament, and its relationship with the Labour Party ensured that, once Labour gained power, its representatives were given positions in office.[92] Members of the Co-operative Party also obtained direct representation on governmental and departmental committees 'to an extent hitherto inexperienced'.[93] To some co-operators, this was evidence that 'in the Labour Government we [the Co-operative Party] have a friend. They have expressed their friendship in every possible way during the time they have been in office'.[94] Certain individuals within the Labour Party recognized that the Co-op had an important role to play within society. For example, although

---

[89]   Private correspondence from Alderman A. Ballard to Mrs Eleanor Barton, 23 June 1950 (Sheffield Archives, 'Eleanor Barton, CPR 38').

[90]   McKibbin, *The Evolution of the Labour Party*, p. 189.

[91]   Cole, *A Century of Co-operation*, p. 317.

[92]   *Co-operative Congress Report*, 1925, p. 93; J. Shepherd and K. Laybourn, *Britain's First Labour Government* (Hampshire: Palgrave, 2006), p. 65. Thus, in 1924, A. V. Alexander was appointed parliamentary secretary of the board of trade; R. Morrison became private secretary to the ministry of transport; A. Barnes was private secretary to the financial secretary to the treasury; and S. F. Perry was appointed parliamentary private secretary to the minister of health.

[93]   *Co-operative Congress Report*, 1925, p. 94.

[94]   *Co-operative Congress Report*, 1924, p. 410.

promoting municipal trading, some Labour members acknowledged that the values of co-operation could be infused with this. As Clement Attlee stated:

> [Broadly] speaking, the line of demarcation would seem to be that, where the commodity is in universal demand, and is of undifferentiated quality, it is generally better that it should be supplied by a State or municipal agency, but, where the element of choice enters in, the Co-operative Society gives the consumer greater freedom.[95]

It is quite possible, however, that in a few places, such as Birmingham in 1923–5, potential Co-operative Party electoral progress was stunted as the higher profile Labour Party overshadowed it. Problems of this nature were not limited to individual constituencies. The national executive of the Co-operative Party felt that there were occasions when the Labour Party failed to enter into consultation with its representatives and was often dismissive of its policies.

In 1937, when commenting on relations between the Co-operative and Labour parties, Clement Attlee argued that 'the strength of the Labour Movement will be enhanced by a frank recognition of the different functions of its various organisations, and by a ready spirit of mutual understanding'.[96] However, just as during the interwar years, attempts to improve relations between the two parties after the Second World War would continue to be marked by disagreements concerning organization, finance and policy.

[95] Attlee, *The Labour Party in Perspective*, p. 68.
[96] Ibid., p. 71.

Chapter 13

Counter-Toryism: Labour's Response to Anti-Socialist Propaganda, 1918–39

Laura Beers

The choice before the country is between Conservatism and a Labour Ministry ... The public views with the utmost alarm the programme of the Labour Party. The main planks in the Labour platform are Nationalisation and the Capital Levy, both of which involve *terrific taxation and probable disaster to the national industries.*

Daily Mail, 14 November 1923

While the Liberal Party continued to play an important role in British politics throughout the 1920s,[1] by 1923 the Conservatives had come to view Labour as their principal political adversary, and both Conservative Central Office and the conservative press trained the bulk of their fire on the 427 Labour candidates during the 1923 election campaign.[2] The violence of Conservative propaganda and press attacks on Labour in this period is difficult to appreciate, especially in light of the two parties' respectful relationship within parliament. While quotes such as the above, from the conservative *Daily Mail*, actually made reference to the substance of Labour policy, much anti-Labour propaganda in the 1920s simply dealt in stereotypes and scare-mongering. Conservative Party propaganda, including the 1924 election poster 'It's Your Money He Wants', unsubtly insinuated that British socialism was a front for rapacious Soviet greed, and statements from Conservative politicians such as the die-hard Lord Birkenhead played on fears

---

[1] Even Maurice Cowling, who argues persuasively for the polarization of British politics between 1918 and 1924, admits that the Liberal decline was a 'more contingent matter than the statistics suggest' and that the period between 1926 and 1931 was one of 'acute' uncertainty in which numerous alternative outcomes were within the realm of the possible. See M. Cowling, *The Impact of Labour, 1920–1924* (Cambridge: Cambridge University Press, 1971).

[2] Beatrice Webb recorded in her diary that: 'To read the capitalist press, whether Tory or Liberal, the Labour Party barely exists as a political party: it is a mere group of disorderly extremists without brains or money – of course they don't say this in so many words, they only imply it by refusing steadfastly to report anything about the Labour Party' (London School of Economics Library, Beatrice Webb diary, 19 November 1923). But her observation leaves one wondering how often she actually read the 'capitalist press', as – by 1923 – the conservative press, like the Conservative Party, had clearly focused its attention on Labour as its principal target.

that MacDonald and Clynes were Britain's 'Kerenskys' – seemingly 'moderate men' who were nonetheless merely fronts for the 'avowed extremists' from which the labour movement 'derives its vitality and driving power'.[3] Such attacks were meant to undermine Labour's efforts to present itself as a responsible, progressive second party of the state, and a viable alternative to Conservative rule. Bolshevik scare-mongering was most notable during the 1924 'red scare' election. Yet, such rhetoric remained a staple of Conservative strategy throughout the decade, with the formation of the National government in many respects marking the culmination of the Conservatives' decade-long effort to restructure the terms of party-political debate as 'Labour versus the Public'.[4]

Ross McKibbin has described the Conservative Party's predominance in the 1920s as based 'not on economic self-interest but on ideologically determined class-stereotypes and conventional wisdoms'. Britain's 'constitutional classes', he contended, rallied around Conservatism, despite the averse impact on many of its supporters of the deflationary economic policies which the party advocated, because they saw Labour as the party of the manual working classes and held deep-rooted prejudices against manual labourers as 'sectional, collectivist, and masculine', 'greedy' and 'full of malevolence'.[5] Over the past two decades, McKibbin's argument, or at least his conclusion that interwar voters came to identify Conservatism with the 'public' or 'national' interest, has become a kind of conventional wisdom of its own. However, his explanations of *why* and *how* this process took place have come under increasing pressure from historians of the Conservative Party.

Recent scholarship has shown that, rather than being the passive beneficiaries of existent anti-Labour stereotypes and conventional wisdoms, the Conservatives actively sought to craft a 'national' political rhetoric which would help the party to hold onto power in the era of mass democracy. David Jarvis, in particular, has emphasized the constructive aspects of Conservative propaganda in the 1920s, arguing that Tory fears that the 1918 Representation of the People Act would lead to the rise of Labour 'played a critical role in shaping the reorientation of post-war Conservatism'.[6] Others have argued that the success of the 'New Conservatism' owed much to Baldwin's self-fashioning as a traditional 'English' leader, who could unite the country and heal the wounds created by war, industrial strife

---

    [3]   *Daily Mail,* 15 October 1924.

    [4]   R. McKibbin, 'Class and Conventional Wisdom: The Conservative Party and the "Public" in Interwar Britain', in his *Ideologies of Class: Social Relations in Britain, 1880– 1950,* (Oxford: Oxford University Press, 1990), pp. 259–93.

    [5]   Ibid., pp. 285, 282 and 272.

    [6]   D. Jarvis, 'British Conservatism and Class Politics and the 1920s', *English Historical Review,* 11/440 (1996), 59–84. See also D. Jarvis, 'Mrs. Maggs and Betty: The Conservative Appeal to Women Voters in the 1920s', *Twentieth Century British History,* 5/2 (1994), 129–52.

and unemployment.[7] But the party's reincarnation was as much about policy as presentation. Whereas Edwardian politics – and the 1923 election campaign – centred around protectionism and free trade, the New Conservatism recast the political struggle as between a Tory party which represented 'sound finance, low taxation, economic stability, Christian duty, and national unity' and the 'socialist' Labour Party 'as an economically irresponsible tax-and-spend party, concerned only with the sectional interests of trade unions, and also atheistic'.[8] The scholarship on interwar Conservatism has successfully illuminated the content and style of anti-Labour politics in the 1920s, but has tended to neglect Labour responses to such Conservative strategies.[9] Labour responded to Conservative propaganda by adjusting both its policies and its presentation in order to neutralize anxieties about the potential consequences of Labour government, and to make Labour appealing to voters outside of the party's traditional male industrial base.

The following chapter considers Labour's policy and propaganda in the interwar period in light of the political struggle between Labour and Conservatism. It argues that the hysterical representation of socialist politics by Labour's opponents helped to reinforce pre-existing tendencies towards gradualism, parliamentarianism and financial orthodoxy within the movement, as party and trade union leaders shied away from policies and actions which could be presented as reckless or unconstitutional. The chapter begins with an overview of the Conservative Party and the conservative press's characterizations of Labour in the 1920s, and then goes on to consider the effect of anti-Labour propaganda on the content and emphases of Labour's political programme. The following section, in turn, looks at Labour Party propaganda between the wars and argues that, rather than allow their opponents to set the terms of the political debate, Labour sought to construct an alternative framework for explaining the industrial and societal problems of the 1920s and the role of politics in ameliorating those problems. Without suggesting that Labour policy and discourse was simply reactive, the chapter emphasizes the links between Conservative characterizations of Labour and Labour's self-fashioning as a sober and responsible party of progressive reform. Specifically, it argues that the party's increased emphasis on gradualism and incremental localized reforms reflected as much Labour's desire to be perceived as 'legitimate'

---

[7]   J. Ramsden, *The Age of Balfour and Baldwin* (New York: Longman, 1978); S. Nicholas, 'The Construction of a National Identity: Stanley Baldwin, "Englishness" and the Mass Media', in M. Francis and I. Zweiniger-Bargielowska (eds), *Conservatives and British Society* (Cardiff: University of Wales Press, 1996), pp. 127–46; P. Williamson, *Stanley Baldwin: Conservative Leadership and National Values* (Cambridge: Cambridge University Press, 1999).

[8]   E. H. H. Green, 'Conservatism, Anti-Socialism and the End of the Lloyd George Coalition', in his *Ideologies of Conservatism: Conservative Ideas in the Twentieth Century* (Oxford: Oxford University Press, 2002), p. 132.

[9]   For a notable exception to this, see M. Pugh, 'The Rise of Labour and the Political Culture of Conservatism, 1890–1945', *History*, 87/288 (2002), 514–37.

as it did the natural sympathies of Philip Snowden or Ramsay MacDonald with the financial orthodoxies of the period.

The chapter focuses primarily on the 1920s, during the period in which Labour was concerned to establish and cement its position as the second party of the state, and 'the only alternative to ... Tory Government'.[10] However, Conservative characterizations of Labour as dangerously revolutionary and unfit to govern did not disappear with the solidification of Labour's role as the principal party of the left in the late-1920s, as the hysteria of the National government's 1931 election propaganda attests.[11] The chapter concludes with a survey of Labour's responses to such propaganda in the 1930s, and argues that many of the same tactics which were employed by MacDonald's party in the 1920s remained central to Labour strategy after 1931. Indeed, the 1930s labour movement proved remarkably successful in (re)establishing its position as a respectable party of opposition and a potential party of government. While evidence shows that the majority of voters remained unwilling to vote Labour in 1940,[12] arguably few continued to believe that Labour remained outside the constitutional pale.

Conservative Representations of Labour after the Great War

Conservative attacks on Labour in the decade after the Great War (1914–18) centred on the dual assertions that the Labour Party was sectional, foreign-influenced and dangerously revolutionary, and that industrial labour was violently anarchical and unconstitutional. Arguments in favour of Conservative government were normally structured against the threat of 'socialism', as the Conservative Party and the conservative press invariably referred to Labour in the 1920s. The language is significant. Labour's opponents recognized the propaganda potential of a party which claimed to represent 'labour' in a country where roughly three-quarters of the population were manual workers.[13] During the 1923 election campaign, Asquith defensively derided the party's name as 'a misnomer, an ambiguity, indeed an

---

[10]   1929 Labour Party manifesto. Available at: www.labour-party.org.uk/manifestos/1929.

[11]   For National government representations of Labour during the election campaign, see Andrew Thorpe, *The British General Election of 1931* (Oxford: Oxford University Press, 1991), chapter 9.

[12]   Gallup poll and Mass-Observation data suggest that the swing to Labour took place in the spring of 1942. See discussion in P. Addison, *The Road to 1945* (London: Jonathan Cape, 1975), pp. 15 and 162–3.

[13]   McKibbin cites the percentage of the British population classified as working class in 1921 as 78.29 per cent; in 1931 as 78.07 per cent; and in 1951 as 72.19 per cent. See R. McKibbin, *Classes and Cultures: England 1918–51* (Oxford: Oxford University Press, 1998), p. 106.

equivocation'.[14] The previous year, *The Times* had made Conservative reservations about the party's name explicit, asserting that: 'Exception … might justly be taken to the name "Labour" since the Labour Party has by no means a monopoly on the wage earning vote, and many of its tenets are frankly socialist. Indeed, the name "Socialist" might be more adequate than the name "Labour".'[15] Although the Labour Party declined to indulge its opponents by officially adopting this 'more adequate' moniker, the *Daily Mail* first started referring to the 'Socialist Party' (or, initially, the 'Labour-Socialists') in November 1922; the *Daily Express* followed suit a few months later; and, by 1924, the terms 'Labour Party' and 'Socialist Party' were being used interchangeably in the conservative press. Conservative literature similarly rejected Labour's rhetorical claim to represent manual workers. The party journal *Gleanings and Memoranda* consistently referred to the 'Labour' Party in inverted commas, and the journal's monthly digest of Labour Party news was printed under the heading 'Socialist Politics', a catch-all category which also contained reports of the activities of the Communist Party of Great Britain (CPGB), or the 'British Bolsheviks', and ongoing news of atrocities in Soviet Russia.

By calling the party 'socialist', the Conservatives sought to evoke a set of analogies and stereotypes associated with the socialist-dominated coalition governments in Germany and (from 1924) in France, with all of their connotations of economic instability and large-scale labour unrest.[16] Notably, the Catholic Cardinal Bourne, who had little sympathy for Labour, 'publicly deprecated its being called socialist' on the grounds that the label conveyed an 'anti-Catholic connotation' which the party's principles did not embody.[17] This attempt to depict Labour as foreign-influenced went beyond the use of the title 'socialist'. Two weeks before polling day in 1923, the *Daily Mail* launched a creative smear campaign which played up the Labour Party's membership of the Second International, which the paper consistently referred to as the '*Sozialistische Arbeiter Internationale*', and suggested that a Labour government would merely be a front for 'DICTATION FROM SOCIALISTS OF GERMANY AND RUSSIA'.[18] The unpatriotic character of the Labour leadership was underscored in a 1924 Conservative publication, *A Handbook for Anti-Socialists*, which contained a series of sketches of Labour leaders under the heading 'A Dictionary of anti-National Biography'; trade unionists such as Robert Smillie, George Hicks and Alf Purcell were characterized by Conservative Central Office as 'in the main extremists and

---

[14]   Asquith, speaking at Perth, 11 October 1923, quoted in *Gleanings and Memoranda*, November 1923, p. 504.

[15]   *The Times*, 2 November 1922.

[16]   For a contemporary analysis of the use of stereotypes by the press, see W. Lippmann, *Public Opinion* (New York: Dover, 2004 edition), pp. 192–3.

[17]   *Daily Express*, 24 May 1929.

[18]   *Daily Mail,* 20 November 1923.

Bolshevik sympathizers'.[19] Conservative speeches and party literature made a practice of quoting avowedly left-wing politicians as representative of the 'true' Labour agenda in an effort to undermine the sober and pacific propaganda of their opponents. The *Daily Express* foreshadowed the rhetoric of the 1920s during the 1918 general election campaign when it argued that 'a large proportion of the rank-and-file of the trade unions will certainly not vote for the Socialist Falstaff, the pacifist Bardolph, or the anarchist Pistol'.[20]

In the three elections between 1922 and 1924, the 'Labour-Bolshevists'[21] were also presented as a threat to law and order, an attack which could be expected to resonate in particular with the new female electorate.[22] On 24 October, the day before the publication of the 'Zinoviev letter', the *Mail* ran an article on 'Angry Socialist Hooligans', reporting that: 'Candidates, as well as women supporters, have been attacked or threatened. There is no mean trick to which the Socialist mobs have not stooped. ... There does not seem to be much doubt that Bolsheviks with Bolshevik money are at work stirring up riots and attacks on all opponents of Socialism.' The same day, the *Express* warned readers that campaign violence, carried out on behalf of the socialists by rowdies who were 'often of alien origin', 'goes far beyond the limits of legitimate excitement. It is a familiar form of terrorism, and marks a well-defined stage on the road to the strangulation of liberty ... London is a day's march closer to Moscow and the people of this country are moving towards a supine enslavement'.[23] The following day, the *Mail* ended its leader on the implications of the Zinoviev letter by suggesting that 'the organized violence at the elections is part of the Bolshevik plan' of 'armed insurrection' outlined in the letter.[24] As with other attacks on Labour in conservative newspapers, in emphasizing alleged Labour rowdyism, the press was following the lead set by Conservative Central Office.[25]

Finally, the alleged relationship between the Labour Party and Bolshevism was deployed not only to suggest that the party was a threat to the public constitutional order, but also to the private social order. *Gleanings and Memoranda* included a monthly index of items 'Of Interest to Women' which party propagandists could use to persuade women voters of the merits of Conservatism. The October 1924

---

[19]   *A Handbook for Anti-Socialists* (London: Boswell, undated [1924?]); *Gleanings and Memoranda*, October 1924, p. 474.

[20]   *Daily Express*, 15 November 1918.

[21]   *Daily Express,* 2 November 1922.

[22]   Jarvis, 'Mrs. Maggs', p. 144; J. Lawrence, 'The Transformation of British Public Politics after the First World War', *Past & Present*, 190 (2006), 207–8.

[23]   *Daily Express*, 24 October 1924.

[24]   *Daily Mail*, 25 October 1924. On the association of election rowdyism with Bolshevik brutality, see J. Lawrence, 'The Transformation of Public Politics in Britain, 1900–30', unpublished manuscript, Harvard University (2003), p. 17.

[25]   Lawrence, 'The Transformation', *Past and Present*, p. 199; Jarvis, 'Mrs. Maggs', pp. 144–5.

issue, for example, drew attention to a National Minority Movement conference resolution to infuse state education with a 'recognition of the class struggle' as well as emphasizing the appalling housing conditions in Soviet Russia and the Bolshevik 'war on religion'.[26] The link between Labour, Bolshevism and atheism was particularly stressed during the 1924 election campaign in headlines in the conservative press such as 'Torturers of Christians: Bolshevik Comrades of Mr. MacDonald', and 'Cabinet's Moscow Friends', which outlined the 'horrors a "loan" would support', including a 'malignant war on the church'. Labour's Russian cronies were also said to support the 'torture of women' in a country where 'Marriage is easier than the purchase of a broadcasting license, and can be dissolved by a "husband" taking his "wife" before a local official and there discarding her, as a buyer returns damaged goods to a shop.'[27] Over the previous two decades, the Conservative Party had developed a political language which emphasized the defence of the family, and made conscious appeals to 'the sanctity of "hearth and home" and the "domestic idyll"'.[28] In 1924, this discourse of family was yoked to the campaign against socialism to a greater degree than in any previous election.

In addition to playing on voters', and particularly female voters', fears of Bolshevik brutalization, the Conservatives also depicted Labour as dangerously fiscally unorthodox, and the strike weapon as nationally divisive, economically ruinous and, at its extreme, unconstitutional. Conservative Central Office and the Tory-owned press made much of the 'capital levy', which remained a part of the Labour Party programme from 1918 through 1923. The proposed levy amounted to a one-time charge on incomes over £5,000 intended to pay off the war debt; however, in Conservative representations, it became the first step on the road towards the Bolshevist abolition of private property. Headlines in the Tory press such as 'Savings Levy: Even The Threat Upsetting Swiss Trade', and 'The Capital Levy Bubble: How It Burst In Czechoslovakia' were intended to remind middle-class voters of the destructive effects of continental socialism.[29] Jarvis has noted how Conservative politicians consistently sought to understate the lower limit of incomes that would be affected by Labour's proposed capital levy, insinuating to working-class voters that a Labour government would threaten their pianos or their friendly society accounts.[30] In 1922, the *Daily Mail* characterized the proposal as a 'Programme of Plunder' to 'seize the people's savings' through a policy which '*threaten[ed] every man's house and furniture, and every woman's clothes and*

---

[26]   *Gleanings and Memoranda*, October 1924, p. 398. See also 'Bolshevism: Soviet War on Religion' in the July 1923 edition, pp. 100–102. The National Minority Movement was set up by the CPGB in the early 1920s to promote left-wing policy inside the Trades Union Congress and its affiliated unions.

[27]   *Daily Mail*, 9 October 1924; 11 October 1924; 13 October 1924; 15 October 1924.

[28]   J. Lawrence, 'Class and Gender in the Making of Urban Toryism, 1880–1914', *English Historical Review*, 108/428 (1993), 649; Jarvis, 'Mrs. Maggs', pp. 145, 149–51.

[29]   *Daily Mail*, 2 November 1922; 24 November 1923.

[30]   Jarvis, 'British Conservatism', p. 81.

jewellery, as was done in Russia'.[31] The reference to clothes and jewellery suggests that the intended audience for such discourse included women as well as men. As with appeals to the 'domestic chancellor of the exchequer' in Conservative propaganda and the conservative press, such language was intended to speak to the supposed materialism and fiscal conservatism of female voters.[32]

Conservatism also sought to de-legitimize and, in 1927, to partially de-legalize, large-scale strike action, claiming that national strikes in vital industries were not a legitimate response to industrial grievances but an assault on the constitution. This rhetoric of unconstitutionality in fact predated the Great War. The series of strikes in vital industries which took place in 1911 were characterized by one contemporary critic as 'part of a huge political scheme'.[33] In August 1911, Asquith had threatened to 'employ all the forces of the Crown'[34] against the striking railwaymen, a boast that elicited the (admittedly unhelpful) response from Keir Hardie that if the prime minister were to call in the troops to break up the strike, next time 'the colliers and ironworkers would [also] be called out, and then they would see what the soldiers could do. The men were bound to win, and God help the Liberal Party when they did'.[35] But while industry-wide strikes were already perceived as dangerously destabilizing in the Edwardian era, the constitutional threat of organized labour took on a new and more menacing aspect after the formation of the Triple Alliance. The Lloyd George coalition government based much of its supposed legitimacy on the need to mediate between the unions and the public and head off the 'anarchist' threat of 'unconstitutional' strike action, such as the nine-day railwaymen's strike in 1919.[36] Four months before the strike, a war office circular had been leaked to the press suggesting that the government would be justified in using soldiers to combat national strike action 'in the interests of the general public.'[37]

This rhetoric of public interest, or 'Labour versus the public', was effectively deployed by the government during the General Strike in May 1926. During the nine days of the conflict, the government consistently presented the strike as a

---

[31]   *Daily Mail,* 1 November 1922 (emphasis in the original).

[32]   Jarvis, 'Mrs. Maggs', p. 143. On the use of the rhetoric of the 'domestic chancellor' in the conservative press, see A. Bingham, *Gender, Modernity and the Popular Press in interwar Britain* (Oxford: Oxford University Press, 2004), pp. 127–32.

[33]   Winston Churchill on the transport workers' strike, quoted in *Gleanings and Memoranda,* September 1911, p. 229.

[34]   R. Jenkins, *Asquith* (London: Collins, 1978), p. 234.

[35]   Quoted in *The Times,* 21 August 1911.

[36]   For Lloyd George's characterization of the strike as an 'anarchist conspiracy', see P. Bagwell, *The Railwaymen: A History of the National Union of Railwaymen* (London: Allen & Unwin, 1963), p. 393. For a discussion of the post-war coalition as a 'deliberately counter-revolutionary force', see J. Turner, *British Politics and the Great War* (New Haven: Yale University Press, 1992), p. 387, *passim.*

[37]   *Manchester Guardian,* 30 May 1919.

struggle by all patriotic Britons to defend the constitution against the threat of revolutionary trade unionism. In a show of national political unity, the Liberal politician and lawyer Lord Simon was called in to give his official judgement that the strike was illegal, a verdict which confirmed the BBC director-general Lord Reith's determination to support the government in the conflict.[38] The government-sponsored newspaper, the *British Gazette*, characterized the strike as a 'HOLD-UP OF THE NATION' and presented the struggle as between 'The Constitution or a Soviet'.[39] Even Baldwin, who usually played the 'good cop' to the 'bad cops' at Conservative Central Office, used uncharacteristically inflammatory language in condemning the strike as an attack on 'the safety and security of the British constitution'.[40] Baldwin's success in recasting the conflict in these terms was devastating to the trade unionists. As Philip Williamson has noted: 'Once Baldwin translated the General Strike from an industrial dispute into a supposed threat to the "basis of ordered government" and a "challenge to Parliament and the road to anarchy and ruin", the Trades Union Congress (TUC) leaders themselves grasped that defeat was inevitable.'[41] Observers who only had access to the conservative press, conservative radio broadcasts, or Conservative Party propaganda could be excused for believing that, to quote a speech by Winston Churchill to the tellingly named Anti-Socialist and Anti-Communist Union in February 1929, a second Labour government would be 'bound to bring back the Russian Bolsheviks, who will immediately get busy in the mines and factories, as well as among the armed forces, planning another general strike.'[42]

'Allaying the Apprehensions of the Bourgeoisie': Labour Party Policy in the 1920s

Of course, no potential voter, even one living in a cottage in Tunbridge Wells or the most benighted slums of urban Birmingham, was only exposed to Conservative propaganda. Tory voices were not the only ones articulating a new language of party politics in the decades after the Great War, and the Labour Party offered its own interpretation of the political struggle which differed markedly in both tone

---

[38]   Simon's speeches on the illegality of the strike were subsequently published in book form, accompanied by a narrative of the strike as a sort of anti-strike souvenir. Lord Simon, *Three Speeches on the General Strike* (London: Macmillan, 1926). BBC Written Archive Centre, Reading, CO/34, Reith, 'Report to the Board of Directors', 18 May 1926.

[39]   *British Gazette*, 5 May 1926.

[40]   Stanley Baldwin, BBC broadcast, 8 May 1926, reported in R. Page Arnot, *The General Strike, May 1926: Its Origins and History* (London: LRD, 1926), pp. 194–5.

[41]   Philip Williamson, *Stanley Baldwin* (Cambridge: Cambridge University Press 1999), p. 241.

[42]   Quoted in M. Gilbert, *Winston S. Churchill*, vol. 5 (London: Heinemann, 1976), p. 313. The speech was reprinted in pamphlet form as *Ringing the Alarm*.

and substance from that of the Conservatives. Nonetheless, Labour politicians and industrial leaders were aware of the potential impact of Conservative propaganda on public opinion, and much of the avowed constitutionalism and conservatism of the 1920s labour movement can arguably be attributed to a desire to distance themselves from Conservative calumny. This is particularly evident in the party's increasingly attenuated relationship to 'socialism' and to British and foreign communism in the 1920s, and in its retreat towards a determined fiscal orthodoxy in the aftermath of the Great War.

In 1924, the party jettisoned the capital levy from its election manifesto after three years of the Conservatives using the proposal as a sword with which to skewer their opponents. In previous elections, certain Labour candidates, including Ben Tillett, had reportedly attempted to disassociate themselves from the policy;[43] and Labour MPs were not eager to face the electoral consequences of continuing to champion a policy which so clearly antagonized the electorate, in particular female voters.[44] Nationalization was similarly played down as a policy issue in the 1920s. While Labour remained committed to 'the common ownership of the means of production, distribution, and exchange', party propagandists recognized that the issue would not be popular with the electorate.[45] During the 1922 election, Hugh Dalton, then candidate for Maidstone, expressed his support for workers' control in an election speech – only to find any references to his comments 'kept out of the press by Hunt, our voluntary agent, who is indeed a "realist"!'[46]

In March 1923, Philip Snowden tabled a resolution in the House of Commons arguing that:

> [In] view of the failure of the capitalist system … and believing that the cause of this failure lies in the private ownership and control of the means of production and distribution, this House declares that legislative effort should be directed to the gradual supersession of the capitalist system by an industrial and social order based on the public ownership and democratic control of the instruments of production and distribution.[47]

---

[43]   *The Times*, 28 June 1923.

[44]   On 2 November 1922, the *Daily Mail* published an article on the women's vote written by a female activist for a 'Wee Free' constituency in London who professed herself to be 'sympathetic to Labour and would probably be working for it if there were a Labour candidate in my constituency' noted that '*the very foolish manifesto on the Capital Levy has done Labour incalculable harm in this election*' (emphasis in the original).

[45]   A. Thorpe, *A History of the British Labour Party* (London: Macmillan, 1997), pp. 49 and 53.

[46]   H. Dalton, *The Political Diary of Hugh Dalton* (London: Cape, 1986), entry for 22 May 1922.

[47]   Hansard, *Parliamentary Debates*, vol. 161, 20 March 1923, c. 2472.

The ensuing debate is the first and last instance in which the question of the total nationalization of large-scale industry was raised by Labour in the Commons before 1945. During the first Labour government, MacDonald attempted to diffuse attacks on the party's alleged hypocrisy on the question of nationalization, by stating that while he felt 'perfectly convinced' that:

> [When] public opinion considers the question … it will make large changes in the nature of our social system, he had no intention of allowing the Labour government to [sit] here producing half-a-dozen, twenty or one hundred Bills in a month or two and saying, 'Before we came in we had one state of society and after we came in we find another state of society'. The thing is absolutely absurd and that sort of error underlies nine-tenths of the attacks that are being made upon us now.[48]

It could be argued that such a statement reflected the party's ultimate confidence in the 'gradual supersession' of capitalism. Yet, Labour's shift to a rhetoric of the 'inevitability of gradualness' also indicated, as its opponents sneeringly pointed out, the 'fact that the Socialists know they cannot win … without the aid of middle-class votes. Hence the idea of "gradualness" is to be given publicity, and prospect of an immediate millennium is postponed in order to allay the apprehensions of the *bourgeoisie*.'[49]

This new emphasis on gradualness was accompanied by a rhetorical shift within party literature. Early Labour publications made frequent reference to socialism – MacDonald himself was the author of *Socialism and Society* (1905), *Socialism* (1907), *Socialism and Government* (1909) and *Socialism after the War* (1918), among others. Yet, as Matthew Worley has pointed out, the post-war party actively 'refrained from using the "S" word … Indeed, the term was not used in any of Labour's general election manifestos between 1918 and 1923, and was used just once in 1924 (in the final paragraph) and twice in 1929 (including a negative reference to Tory "misrepresentations" of the word).'[50] References to nationalization also became less frequent. The 1929 manifesto contains only one use of the word – in connection with the mining industry. While pledges to undertake 'electrification' and the 'reorganization of railways and transport' suggested plans for national monopolies over vital industries, the party's eschewal of the term itself is noteworthy. The muted articulation of Labour's transformative social agenda in the 1920s arguably reflects what one historian has characterized recently as 'a conception of the Labour Party's purpose … in which Labour sought first to achieve acceptance as an estate with its distinctive and legitimate claims

---

[48]   Hansard, *Parliamentary Debates*, vol. 174, May 1924, c. 648.

[49]   *Gleanings and Memoranda*, August 1923, p. 122.

[50]   M. Worley, *Labour Inside the Gate: A History of the British Labour Party between the Wars* (London: I. B. Tauris, 2005), p. 150.

and interests, to be treated on equal terms within the existing governing order, and only secondarily the transformation of that order'.[51]

A similar recognition of the realities of electoral politics was evident in the party's treatment of women's issues, notably birth control. Despite the sympathy of many members of the party for a more adequate provision of information about birth control to working-class women, the party leadership repeatedly deflected pressure from women activists to make the amendment of the ministry of health's existing practice in providing information about and access to birth control into a party-political issue, on the grounds that such a policy would be electorally unpopular.[52] After considerable debate, the movement did agree to continue to run birth control advertisements in the TUC-owned *Daily Herald*,[53] and the second Labour government did discretely allow local clinics to provide information on birth control.[54] Nonetheless, the leadership's reticence about the issue reflects the anxieties of a party which was coming under fire for its alleged association with Bolshevik hostility towards religion and the family, and was particularly anxious about its perception among female and Catholic voters.[55]

Finally, the emphasis of Conservative propaganda on Labour's alleged association with, and even infiltration by, Soviet communism had reverberations on the party and trade unions' relationship with the CPGB. David Howell has emphasized the protracted process of excluding communists, particularly communist trade unionists from the party in the 1920s, and attributed the party's unwillingness to completely ban communist membership before 1928 to the strength of trade union autonomy within the party organization.[56] While Kevin Morgan has recently argued that Labour in the 1920s was more tolerant of communist participation than previous scholarship has suggested,[57] the perennial efforts of the National Executive Committee (NEC) to delimit the participation of avowed communists

---

[51]   N. Owen, '"MacDonald's Parties": The Labour Party and the "Aristocratic Embrace", 1922–31', *Twentieth Century British History*, 18/1 (2007), 11.

[52]   D. Howell, *MacDonald's Party: Labour Identities and Crisis, 1922–31* (Oxford: Oxford University Press, 2002), pp. 351 and 355.

[53]   Labour Party Archive (LPA), Manchester, LP/DH 'Reports of *Daily Herald* Editor and the Circulation and Advertising Managers', 21 May 1928, and the decision of the Board of the Victoria House Printing Company, 18 September 1928.

[54]   Howell, *MacDonald's Party*, p. 355.

[55]   Pamela Graves, *Labour Women: Women in British Working-Class Politics, 1918-1939* (Cambridge: Cambridge University Press, 1994), pp. 91–3. On the broader issue of Labour sensitivity to the Catholic vote, particularly in relation to education, see N. Riddell, *Labour in Crisis: The Second Labour Government, 1929–31* (Manchester: Manchester University Press, 1999), pp. 110–114 and 157–9.

[56]   Howell, *MacDonald's Party*, chapter 22.

[57]   K. Morgan, *Labour Legends and Russian Gold* (London: Lawrence & Wishart, 2006), p. 13.

within the party indicated many Labour leaders' recognition that 'the failure to separate Labour and Communist would make Labour electorally vulnerable'.[58]

Of course, Labour policy in the 1920s was not shaped exclusively in reaction to Conservative propaganda. The first Labour government made the Russian Treaty a legislative priority, despite accusations from its opponents that the treaty was a 'monstrous document' through which the 'British taxpayers ... were to provide the money by the sweat of their brows' for a loan whose benefits would never reach the British people, but would instead lead to unemployment and 'crushing taxation.'[59] Labour's commitment to reopening lines of communication with Russia was again evident five years later, as Arthur Henderson re-established diplomatic relations in 1929, and restarted trade between the two countries with the Temporary Commercial Agreement of April 1930.

Labour's continued support for renewed commercial relations with Russia reflects the ambiguities of the movement's relationship with the Bolshevik state. The leadership's desire to expel British communists from the party and trade union leadership reflected both the political danger of seeming association with Bolshevism and the sincere revulsion against Soviet barbarism and authoritarianism of many leaders of political and industrial Labour.[60] Yet, many Labourites believed that the best way to curb Soviet excesses was through cooperation and engagement, and, furthermore, Labour remained committed to the principles of free trade and to the belief that the revival of the international trading system was the surest solution to the problems of the British economy. These dual views dictated the party's continued support for renewed relations with Russia, a logic which MacDonald's secretary spelled out in 1929: 'to pretend that Russia does not exist ... [is] only throwing it into the hands of its most dangerous extremists, creating tremendous world problems (especially in the East), and depriving British workmen and capital of sources of income which, in the national interest, should be open to them.'[61] While anxieties about electoral perceptions played a role in shaping Labour's attitude towards domestic and international communism in the 1920s, they were not the only factor influencing party policy.

The same can be said for Labour's increasingly conservative approach to economic questions. While MacDonald was able to buttress his opposition to the ILP's *Living Wage* programme in 1926 by stating that 'the politics that have

---

[58]   Howell, *MacDonald's Party*, p. 386.

[59]   Robert Horne, 18 September 1924, quoted in *Gleanings and Memoranda*, October 1924, p. 409; 'Motor Show Marvels', cartoon, *Daily Mail*, 18 October 1924.

[60]   The 1922 party conference passed a motion condemning the death sentences passed on 47 Socialist Revolutionaries by the Bolshevik state. See discussion in J. Callaghan, *Socialism in Britain since 1884* (London: Basil Blackwell, 1990), pp. 100–101.

[61]   Rose Rosenberg (MacDonald's personal secretary) to A. Ash, 16 April 1929. Quoted in A. Williams, *Labour and Russia: The Attitude of Labour to the USSR, 1924–34* (Manchester: Manchester University Press, 1989), p. 82.

become associated with it are really deplorable',[62] his objections to the imposition of a national minimum wage stemmed partially from a belief in orthodox financial doctrines which argued that higher wages would lead to higher production costs, lower sales margins and corporate bankruptcy.[63] Susan Pedersen has argued that Labour's move away from fiscal radicalism in the 1920s was part of a broader acceptance by both the Conservative and Labour leaderships that the corporatist, inflationary and fiscally unorthodox policies of the coalition should not be allowed to continue after the immediate shock of demobilization had subsided.[64] Arguably, the main impact of Conservative propaganda was to reinforce a move away from socialist economics which already had significant support within the party leadership.[65]

Before moving on to discuss Labour's attempts to create an alternative political rhetoric in the 1920s, it is worth noting that the party's efforts to damp down the impact of anti-socialist hysteria were aided by the reality that any half-aware interwar voter would be hard pressed to accept that the Conservatives actually believed their own propaganda. As John Ramsden has noted, the Conservatives were attempting to 'have it both ways' in the 1920s: they accepted, and arguably facilitated, the emergence of Labour as the second party of the state, in the belief that the party would not subvert the existing constitutional order, but then sought to gain political mileage out of 'denouncing the same men as irresponsible and dangerous'.[66] Labour was able to trot out Conservative praise of Labour's accomplishments – as when Snowden quoted his successor Winston Churchill's claim that the 1925 budget surplus 'may be justly laid to the credit of the careful and scrupulous finance by which Mr. Snowden's administration of the Treasury was distinguished'[67] – which seemed to confirm Labour allegations that Conservative propaganda

---

[62]   Quoted in Howell, *MacDonald's Party*, p. 270.

[63]   MacDonald wrote of the *Living Wage* proposals in the 27 March 1926 issue of *Forward* that: 'Socialism is not going to come by the legal declaration of a minimum nominal wage and consequential nationalization of bankrupt industries'. Quoted in Howell, *MacDonald's Party*, p. 269.

[64]   S. Pedersen, 'From National Crisis to "National Crisis": British Politics, 1914–31', *Journal of British Studies*, 33/3 (1994), 331–5.

[65]   For an in-depth discussion of the acceptance of financial orthodoxies by the Labour leadership, see P. Williamson, *National Crisis and National Government* (Cambridge: Cambridge University Press, 1992), esp. chapters 6 and 8.

[66]   Ramsden, *Balfour and Baldwin*, p. 199. For the argument that the Conservative Party connived in Labour's displacement of the Liberal Party in the early 1920s, see Cowling, *The Impact of Labour*..

[67]   Philip Snowden, Party Election Broadcast, 3 May 1929, reprinted in *The Listener*, 8 May 1929.

was a cynical 'bogey' designed to frighten the electorate.[68] Nonetheless, the party recognized that it was not enough to point out the inconsistencies in Tory propaganda. Labour policy and publicity in the 1920s – and, in a different respect, in the 1930s – focused on discrediting the 'old bogey' of Labour's alleged irresponsibility through a positive appeal to the middle classes and to female voters which both engaged with and subverted the anti-Labour propaganda of the Conservative Party and the conservative press.

Labour's Appeal to 'The Nation' between the Wars

Despite the party's origins, the leaders of the interwar Labour movement no longer perceived their remit as solely the representation of the manual working classes. The party saw itself not merely as a pressure group, but as the only political alternative to Conservatism, and 'presumed an identity between [its] own higher interests and those of the nation'.[69] As such, they believed that it should be possible – if only the public could be made to understand Labour's aims – to convert a broad majority to the Labour camp. As Herbert Morrison proclaimed in 1923, 'by careful propaganda, by talking to them in language which they understand rather than in some of our classic phrases which may be unintelligible or repugnant to them', Labour should be able, 'in due course', to secure 'a considerable number of supporters from among the middle classes' and those who are 'workers on their own account'.[70] The same belief was held about the new female electorate, and Labour propaganda in the 1920s and 1930s made a conscious appeal to both of these constituencies.

While the Conservatives depicted Labour as a threat to family values, Labour deployed an alternative language of family in which the party, through its social policies and its defence of 'free food', was the defender of the working-class family against disease and poverty, and the guardian of childhood education. Margaret Bondfield made the party's determination to challenge Conservative discourses on the relationship between politics and the family explicit in her 1929 party election broadcast, which was targeted specifically at newly enfranchised female voters.[71] She directly attacked the Conservative propaganda of the 1920s which sought to elide Labour policy with the atheism and alleged anti-family ethos of the Russian Bolsheviks, denouncing such tactics as a 'scandalous violation of

---

[68]   The party's 1929 election manifesto includes a section on the 'old bogey' of Labour's alleged crypto-Bolshevism.

[69]   Williamson, *National Crisis*, p. 17.

[70]   H. Morrison, 'Can Labour Win London without the Middles Classes?', *Labour Organiser*, October 1923, p. 19 (reprinted from the *London Labour Chronicle*).

[71]   Each party was allowed one 15-minute broadcast to the newly enfranchised 'flapper' voters. The Duchess of Atholl broadcast for the Tories, and Megan Lloyd George and Mrs Wintringham jointly broadcast for the Liberals.

decent electioneering'. Instead, she argued, Labour was an advocate for mothers and children. In a campaign pledge that prefigured the New Labour slogans of 80 years later, she promised that, if elected, 'Labour will build a broad highway for all children from the nursery school to the university.'[72]

The concept of the domestic chancellor of the exchequer has usually been viewed in terms of Conservative efforts to persuade female voters of the necessity for economic retrenchment in the interwar period.[73] However, the Tories did not hold the monopoly on such discourse.[74] Labour's 1918 manifesto argued that 'Woman is the Chancellor of the Exchequer of the home. Labour stands with the Co-operative Movement in its insistence on reasonable food prices and fair distribution, and in its resistance to unfair taxation.' In his 1935 election broadcast, Clement Attlee denounced the National government's policy of cutting wages and restricting production in an attempt to raise prices by declaring: 'It sounds quite mad, doesn't it? If you had too much food in the house, you would not put the children on half rations and destroy the food.'[75] While Conservative rhetoric appealed to women in their role as miniature budget balancers, Labour discourse spoke to women's commonsense as household consumers.

The party similarly struck back against Conservative attempts to alienate the middle classes from the labour movement. Strikes were presented not as the defence of a section at the expense of the wider 'public', but as the attempt by one sector of the population to protect not only its own standard of living but that of all of the nation's producers. During the 1919 railway strike, the National Union Railwaymen (NUR) produced posters, newspaper advertisements and cinema propaganda which argued that the strike was not an 'anarchist conspiracy', or even a 'battle between the community and a section of it', but an attempt by the railwaymen to defend the status of all workers.[76] The most striking poster was dominated by a drawing by Will Dyson, the celebrated *Daily Herald* cartoonist, of a railwayman and his family. The quiet dignity of the man and his wife, and the wretched appearance of their four children and elderly dependent grandmother are heartrending. The caption explains to the viewer that the man only wants a living wage to keep himself and his family, and that if the government deprives him of that wage 'it will be your turn next' (see Figure 13.1). J. H. Thomas's press release to the newsreel companies reiterated this theme: 'Railwaymen are not fighting the country. ... We are fighting for the lowest paid wage-earners against a conspiracy to lower wages. If the wages of

---

[72]   Bondfield's broadcast was reported in *The Listener*, 22 May 1929.

[73]   Jarvis, 'Mrs. Maggs', pp. 144–5 and 149–51; Bingham, *Gender, Modernity*, pp. 127–32.

[74]   For references to the domestic chancellor within the Labour press in this period, see Bingham, *Gender, Modernity*, pp. 132–4.

[75]   Clement Attlee, Party Election Broadcast, reprinted in *The Listener*, 6 November 1935.

[76]   *The Times*, 27 September 1919.

railwaymen are reduced other trades will follow … We fought to free England. Railwaymen played their part in the struggle. We were promised an England worthy of our sacrifices.'[77]

Figure 13.1   NUR poster, 1919

---

[77]   *Railway Review*, 10 October 1919.

This depiction of organized Labour as representative of the nation, and Conservatism (and Liberalism) as representative only of vested interests was reiterated during the General Strike seven years later. As we have seen, the government presented the strike as an assault on the constitution. Again, Labour argued against such an interpretation. The TUC's publicity and communications sub-committee during the strike identified its task as '[trying] to show that the action of the Trade Unions was not directed against the public',[78] and the TUC's strike paper, the *British Worker*, emphasized that the strike was 'No Attack On The Constitution', and that insinuations that the strikers were 'violating law and order' were 'quite unjustifiable'.[79] And while the high instance of volunteerism during the strike suggests the limits of public sympathy for the strikers' cause, there is also little evidence that the 'public' truly believed government claims that the strike was the first step towards violent revolution[80] – although this may have been due less to Labour propaganda than to the reality that, as Kingsley Martin noted at the time, 'even the suburban housewife (probably the lowest type of intelligence in England) has spoken to a busman or underground conductor and will feel doubtful of his murderous intentions.'[81]

After conflicts over industrial policy, the principal policy disputes between Labour and the Conservatives in the 1920s concerned Labour's proposed loan to and commercial treaty with Russia, and the broader issue of fiscal policy, particularly the balance between direct and indirect taxation and the imposition of imperial preference. Given the divided attitudes of the Conservatives on tariff reform, the party, as noted above, focused the bulk of their propaganda on Labour's relationship with Russia. Labour, in turn, emphasized the evils of Tory taxation and social policy. The party was aided in its efforts in this respect by being out of office for most of the period, and hence being able to criticize the concrete failings of the Conservative governments without committing themselves to specific remedies.

In place of the Conservatives' narrative of an existential struggle between the nation and a motley crew led by the 'Socialist Falstaff' et al., Labour depicted post-war politics as a struggle between 'the small minority (less than 10 per cent of the population) who own the great part of the land, the plant and the equipment without access to which their fellow-countrymen can neither work nor live', and 'all who work, whether by hand or brain' – including the middle-classes and agricultural labourers.[82]

---

[78]   TUC Archive, Modern Records Centre, Warwick University, Mss 292/252.62/12, 'Publicity and Communications sub-committee minutes', 1 May 1926, 5:30pm.

[79]   *British Worker*, 6 May 1926.

[80]   On the general complacency of the public during the strike, see A. Perkins, *A Very British Strike* (London: Macmillan, 2006).

[81]   K. Martin, *British Public Opinion and the General Strike* (London: Leonard Woolf, 1926), p. 89.

[82]   Labour Party, *Labour and the Nation* (London, 1928); *Labour and the New Social Order* (London, 1918).

Such an emphasis can be seen as early as 1918, when the party presented itself as the only party 'genuinely determined to introduce a fair system of taxation and to relieve the burden on the middle and working classes',[83] and was in particular evidence during the 1929 general election.

While the election campaign focused on the question of unemployment, Labour also gave considerable publicity to the standard of living of those lucky enough to be employed.[84] Party propaganda paid particular attention to the government's de-rating scheme, which sought to spur job creation in industry by reducing the rates paid by industrial enterprises. Labour presented de-rating, which Churchill's colleague Neville Chamberlain had dismissed as 'half-baked' and likely to reduce the accountability of local government,[85] not as a failure on its merits, but as another example of Tory special interest politics – a theme summed up in an election leaflet headlined 'Tories hand out gifts to the wealthy and penalize householders and shopkeepers!'[86] The Labour-owned *Daily Herald* ran an open letter to shopkeepers in 1929, reminding them of the iniquities of the de-rating scheme.[87] In his campaign speeches, MacDonald promised 'justice to retail tradesmen' if Labour were elected with a working majority.[88] What exactly such 'justice' would entail was left purposefully vague, a fact which did not stop the party from attacking the current scheme.

Labour's emphasis on the government's mistreatment of ratepayers was part of a broader appeal to middle-class voters, which focused primarily on local government. The London Labour Party leader Herbert Morrison had long been concerned about the importance of the middle-class vote in London. In September 1923, he published a survey in the *London Labour Chronicle* on 'The Census and the Middle-Class Vote', which argued that Labour could not win London without winning over a significant proportion of the middle classes.[89] The middle classes were presumed – however stereotypically – to be particularly enamoured of economy and efficiency, and the party's appeal to these voters in both local and national elections throughout the interwar period focused primarily on its record in local government administration.

---

[83]   *Daily Mail*, 6 December 1918.

[84]   Unemployment was not only fore-grounded by the Liberals and by the Labour Party and *Daily Herald*, but announced to be the 'supreme issue' of the election by the *Daily Express* (19 April, 10 and 21 May 1929), and 'the most urgent [question] confronting the nation today' and the 'central issue at this election' by the *Daily Mail* (17 and 13 May 1929), and emphasized by each of the party leaders in their election broadcasts (see *The Listener*, 17 April–22 May 1929).

[85]   Quoted in G. Stewart, *Burying Caesar: The Churchill–Chamberlain Rivalry* (London: Weidenfeld & Nicholson, 1999), pp. 41–4.

[86]   Labour Party leaflet no. 29/95.

[87]   *Daily Herald*, 13 May 1929.

[88]   *Daily Herald*, 6 May 1929.

[89]   H. Morrison, 'Can Labour Win', p. 19.

On one level, Labour's emphasis on its effectiveness in local government was an attempt to exorcise the ghost of 'Poplarism', which the Municipal Reform Party continued to trot out at local elections throughout the period. Party literature such as *A Burden on the Rates*, and articles in the Labour press such as 'Labour Lowers Rates by 12s. 7d.: In Walthamstow East, where Labour has controlled municipal affairs for 14 years, electors are proof against Tory scare',[90] sought to break the association between the party and municipal profligacy. But party propaganda also championed Labour's accomplishments in local government and suggested that, given the opportunity, these local successes could be replicated on the national level. Thus, during the 1929 general election campaign, the *Daily Herald* devoted the top half of its picture page to photographs of achievements in Labour-controlled boroughs, such as house building, slum clearance, provision of health and dental care, and swimming pools. The caption below a photograph of a row of council houses published on 15 May read: 'Labour Houses to Let – Not "for Sale" at High Prices. Here are some built under the 1924 Wheatley Act'. The party's proposals on social policy combined local and national initiatives, as in the *Daily Herald's* 'little letter' to 'a young mother', which promised that Labour would not only extend the school leaving age and provide maintenance grants to allow families to keep children in school but also build better schools in the localities.[91] As with the 'domestic chancellor', Labour sought to appropriate the Conservative rhetoric of 'Safety First' in 1929, arguing that 'Real "Safety First"' meant not stability and more of the same, but a social policy which would provide for the 'health of the people by decent housing'.[92]

Conclusion

Duncan Tanner has argued that the party's successful self-presentation as a 'practical, responsible and effective party of reform' played an important role in its 1929 electoral breakthrough.[93] The 1931 crisis temporarily threw into doubt Labour's claims for its responsibility and competence to govern; however, the effects of the crisis were ultimately short-lived. By 1935, the party had regained the ground lost in 1931, though the decline in the number of three-cornered contests meant that they returned barely more than half as many MPs as in 1929. This relatively quick recovery was partially due to the leadership's refusal to take the lesson from 1931 that the party should abandon its national strategy and revert

---

90   Labour Party leaflet no. 27/8; *Daily Herald*, 17 October 1935.

91   *Daily Herald*, 17 May 1929.

92   MacDonald, quoted in *Daily Herald*, 22 May 1929.

93   D. Tanner, 'Class Voting and Radical Politics: The Liberal and Labour Parties, 1910–31', in J. Lawrence and M Taylor (eds), *Party, State and Society: Electoral Behaviour in Britain since 1820* (Aldershot: Scolar, 1997), p. 122.

to a dependence on its unionized industrial base.[94] The 1930s Labour party, like its MacDonaldite predecessor, remained focused on competing with the Conservatives in the national arena. Labour propaganda in the decade before the Second World War similarly sought both to negate and deflect Conservative attacks and to put forward an alternative vision for Britain which would appeal to a broad national electorate. In terms of political rhetoric and strategy, at least, 1931 was not the major turning point in Labour policy.

In the aftermath of the 1931 electoral disaster, Attlee wrote to Christopher Addison emphasizing the importance of '[laying] plans for the future'. It was imperative, he argued, that the party 'work out a constructive policy complete in every detail and ready for use'.[95] As Philip Williamson has written of the task facing the post-1931 party: 'The expectation remained that socialism could be secured through the existing political system, if the party went about it in the right way. A great propaganda effort would be needed to give the next Labour government a real socialist mandate ... There must be "no more MacDonaldite slush & general phrases": socialism had to be, and be seen to be, practical.'[96] The result was a flurry of socialist planning, much of which would be used in laying the groundwork for the post-1945 welfare state.[97] Labour's constructive proposals for a socialist Britain were publicized in a series of pamphlets, policy papers and public events such as the 'Socialist Crusade Week' in September 1937. The word 'socialism', which had been largely absent from Labour rhetoric in the 1920s, resurfaced with a vengeance after 1931, proclaiming the party's recovery of its ideological roots in publications such as *The Socialist Goal* and *Socialism or Smash!*[98] But while the party's rediscovery of 'socialism' indicated a disenchantment with the 'illusions of reformism' championed by MacDonald,[99] the Labour leadership remained aware of the political realities of 1930s Britain, and unwilling to champion policies which could be seen as 'over-ambitious, impractical, and likely to frighten the electorate'.[100]

---

[94]   For this view, see H. Pelling, *A Short History of the Labour Party* (London, 1961), chapter 5; D. Marquand, *The Progressive Dilemma* (London, 1991), pp. 46–7. Ralph Miliband is still the most prominent advocate of the argument that Labour policy did not change dramatically after 1931, and that the party remained dedicated to a gradualist parliamentary socialism. See his *Parliamentary Socialism* (London: Allen & Unwin, 1961).

[95]   Quoted in Howell, *MacDonald's Party*, p. 410.

[96]   Williamson, *National Crisis*, p. 461.

[97]   R. Toye, *The Labour Party and the Planned Economy, 193–51* (London: Royal Historical Society, 2003).

[98]   Labour Party pamphlets, nos. 32/06 and 32/29.

[99]   Quoted in B. Donohue and G. W. Jones, *Herbert Morrison* (London: Phoenix Press, 2001 edition), p. 182.

[100]   LPA, NEC minutes, 16 June 1932, in reference to the Society for Socialist Inquiry and Propaganda's *Labour Programme for Action*.

Thus, the NEC refused to endorse the *Programme for Action* produced by the Society for Socialist Inquiry and Propaganda in 1932. Two years later, the party conference defeated the Socialist League's resolutions calling for the immediate nationalization of all industries without compensation on the grounds that, to quote Morrison, the party had to 'consider what we can persuade the country to accept', and not even the 'workers', who were themselves deeply 'concerned about their little investments' could be persuaded to accept a policy of 'confiscation'.[101] The party's unwillingness to provide fodder for the Conservative press and propaganda mill was particularly evident in the NEC's response to Stafford Cripps' November 1934 statement that he 'regarded a financial crisis as inevitable' if Labour were to come to power, and its implication that such a crisis would be a necessary step on the road to socialism. The day after Cripps' statement, the NEC took the extraordinary step of issuing a press release which directly repudiated responsibility for the barrister's remarks.[102]

During the 1935 election campaign, Labour broadcasters specifically rebutted National government insinuations that a Labour government would lead to financial collapse and Soviet-style immiseration. Where Conservative leaders sought to elide Labour with Bolshevism, the party's broadcasters drew parallels with the socialist government in Sweden.[103] Where Conservative leaders depicted Labour as hysterical pacifists, Labour's speakers emphasized the coincidence of their position with that called for in the Peace Ballot.[104] Instead of championing the 'romantic nonsense'[105] advocated by left-wingers such as Cripps and Douglas Cole, the national party leaned heavily on its track record in implementing limited municipal socialism to substantiate its claims still to be a responsible governing party. Morrison notably concluded his 1935 party election broadcast by stating:

> The choice you have to make is quite clear. Just as last year London had to choose between a Conservative County Council which could not make up its mind about anything, and a Labour Council that knew what to do and how to do it, so the nation must now decide between Tory negation and the positive and constructive policy of the modern Labour Party.[106]

Two years later, the NEC produced a 16-page pictorial presentation of *Labour's Immediate Programme* (1937) in colour and photogravure, titled *Your Britain*, as propaganda for its 'Socialist Crusade Week'. While the magazine's pages

---

[101]   Quoted in Donoughue and Jones, *Herbert Morrison*, p. 187.

[102]   NEC press release, 28 November 1934 (filed in NEC minutes).

[103]   Greenwood election broadcast, reported in *The Listener,* 13 November 1935; Morrison election broadcast, reported in the same edition.

[104]   Clynes election broadcast, reported in *The Listener,* 6 November 1935; Greenwood election broadcast.

[105]   Morrison, quoted in Donoughue and Jones, *Herbert Morrison*, p. 187.

[106]   Morrison election broadcast.

contained summaries of Labour policy on international affairs, agriculture, public ownership, the party's proposals for a national health service, expanded national pension schemes and raising the school leaving age, the publication's cover underscored the party's emphasis on municipal reforms: the cover photo showed a father returning home to his garden suburb to be greeted by his happy wife and healthy baby, and the caption read: 'A Labour Council has built this pleasant estate of happy homes for the people'.[107] The NEC successfully sold over 600,000 copies of the publication to local party organizations – well above the sale of any previous party publication during a non-election year – and its success inspired several successive editions. The popularity of the document inspired *The Times* to suggest that the Conservatives '[study] the tactics and methods of the opposing party', whose propaganda effectively appealed to voters through 'reference to the politics of the locality and the home'.[108]

Labour's limited electoral recovery after 1931 should not disguise the extent of the party's achievement in the 1930s. In October 1931, one of the party's founders and former leaders had dismissed its programme as 'Bolshevism run mad'.[109] Its bid for power was hampered by the reality that 'its past action was inglorious, its future plans implausible, and its credibility drastically weakened'.[110] As Arthur Henderson himself admitted in his post-mortem on the 1931 election: 'It is little short of a miracle that Labour should have polled almost one-third of the total votes cast.'[111]

Post-1931, the labour movement, as it had in the 1920s, sought to 'build afresh'.[112] In so doing, it was influenced not only by internal party policy-makers, but by an awareness of external political realities. Just as party activists in the 1920s had worked to dispel perceptions of the party as foreign-influenced and dangerously revolutionary, any campaign to return Labour to power in the 1930s would have to begin by tackling perceptions (encouraged by the National government) that Labour was incompetent and irresponsible. While studies of party policy in the 1920s and 1930s have consistently emphasized the substantial ideological differences between the various wings of the labour movement, they have been less quick to identify how and why certain party leaders embraced the positions they did.[113] An examination of Conservative rhetoric about Labour and Labour's responses to that rhetoric sheds light on the many pressures facing

---

[107] Labour Party pamphlet no. 38/86.

[108] 'Lessons of the Election', *The Times*, 6 November 1937.

[109] Philip Snowden election broadcast, reprinted in *The Listener*, 21 October 1931.

[110] Pedersen, 'From National Crisis', p. 327.

[111] Henderson, 'Report on the General Election', 10 November 1931 (Filed in NEC minutes).

[112] Ibid.

[113] B. Pimlott, *Labour and the Left in the 1930s* (Cambridge: Cambridge University Press, 1977); Williamson, *National Crisis*; Howell, *MacDonald's Party;* Toye, *Politics of Planning.* Riddell (*Labour in Crisis*) is exceptionally strong on the relationship between

Labour policy-makers between the wars. While Labour policy would never simply be reactive,[114] party leaders were ever aware of the harsh realities of party politics. Ultimately, electoral competition reinforced tendencies towards conservatism and constitutionalism, as advocates of moderation repeatedly emphasized the risks of seeming to fulfil Conservative stereotypes about socialist rule.

---

pragmatic electoral considerations and policy choices, as is Howell in his discussion of women's issues (*MacDonald's Party*, chapters 22 and 23).

[114] Despite the rise of opinion polling in party politics from the late-1950s onwards, Labour policy-makers remained resistant to 'government by public opinion'. In 1956, the party refused to adjust its policy on education, despite evidence of public disapproval. See L. Beers, 'Whose Opinion?: Changing Attitudes Towards Opinion Polling in British Politics, 1937–64', *Twentieth Century British History*, 17/2 (2006), 202.

Index